ACTS
for
EVERYONE

PART 1
CHAPTERS 1–12

D0369990

ACTS
for
EVERYONE

PART 1
CHAPTERS 1–12

N. T.
WRIGHT

Westminster John Knox Press

First published in 2008 in Great Britain by
Society for Promoting Christian Knowledge
36 Causton Street
London SW1P 4ST

and in the United States of America by
Westminster John Knox Press
100 Witherspoon Street
Louisville, KY 40202

08 09 10 11 12 13 14 15 16 17 — 10 9 8 7 6 5 4 3 2 1

British Library Cataloguing-in-Publication Data
A catalogue record for this book is available from the British Library.

ISBN: 978-0-281-05308-7 (U.K. edition)

United States Library of Congress Cataloging-in-Publication Data is
on file at the Library of Congress, Washington, D.C.

ISBN: 978-0-664-22795-1 (U.S. edition)

Maps by Pantek Arts Ltd, Maidstone, Kent, UK.

Typeset by Graphicraft Ltd, Hong Kong
Printed in Great Britain at
Ashford Colour Press

CONTENTS

INTRODUCTION

On the very first occasion when someone stood up in public to tell people about Jesus, he made it very clear: this message is for *everyone*.

It was a great day – sometimes called the birthday of the church. The great wind of God's spirit had swept through Jesus' followers and filled them with a new joy and a sense of God's presence and power. Their leader, Peter, who only a few weeks before had been crying like a baby because he'd lied and cursed and denied even knowing Jesus, found himself on his feet explaining to a huge crowd that something had happened which had changed the world for ever. What God had done for him, Peter, he was beginning to do for the whole world: new life, forgiveness, new hope and power were opening up like spring flowers after a long winter. A new age had begun in which the living God was going to do new things in the world – beginning then and there with the individuals who were listening to him. 'This promise is for *you*', he said, 'and for your children, and for everyone who is far away' (Acts 2.39). It wasn't just for the person standing next to you. It was for everyone.

Within a remarkably short time this came true to such an extent that the young movement spread throughout much of the known world. And one way in which the *everyone* promise worked out was through the writings of the early Christian leaders. These short works – mostly letters and stories about Jesus – were widely circulated and eagerly read. They were never intended for either a religious or intellectual elite. From the very beginning they were meant for everyone.

That is as true today as it was then. Of course, it matters that some people give time and care to the historical evidence, the meaning of the original words (the early Christians wrote in Greek), and the exact and particular force of what different

writers were saying about God, Jesus, the world and themselves. This series is based quite closely on that sort of work.
But the point of it all is that the message can get out to everyone, especially to people who wouldn't normally read a book
with footnotes and Greek words in it. That's the sort of person
for whom these books are written. And that's why there's a
glossary, in the back, of the key words that you can't really get
along without, with a simple description of what they mean.
Whenever you see a word in **bold type** in the text, you can go
to the back and remind yourself what's going on.

There are of course many translations of the New Testament
available today. The one I offer here is designed for the same
kind of reader: one who mightn't necessarily understand the
more formal, sometimes even ponderous, tones of some of
the standard ones. I have of course tried to keep as close to the
original as I can. But my main aim has been to be sure that the
words can speak not just to some people, but to everyone.

The book of Acts, which I quoted a moment ago, is full of
the energy and excitement of the early Christians as they
found God doing new things all over the place and learned to
take the good news of Jesus around the world. It's also full of
the puzzles and problems that churches faced then and face
today – crises over leadership, money, ethnic divisions, theology and ethics, not to mention serious clashes with political
and religious authorities. It's comforting to know that 'normal
church life', even in the time of the first apostles, was neither
trouble-free nor plain sailing, just as it's encouraging to know
that even in the midst of all their difficulties the early church
was able to take the gospel forward in such dynamic ways.
Actually, 'plain sailing' reminds us that this is the book where
more journeys take place, including several across the sea, than
anywhere else in the Bible – with the last journey, in particular, including a terrific storm and a dramatic shipwreck. There
isn't a dull page in Acts. But, equally importantly, the whole
book reminds us that whatever 'journey' we are making, in our
own lives, our spirituality, our following of Jesus, and our work
for his kingdom, his spirit will guide us too, and make us fruit-
ful in his service. So here it is: Acts for everyone!

To
John Pritchard and Mark Bryant
Fellow workers for the kingdom of God

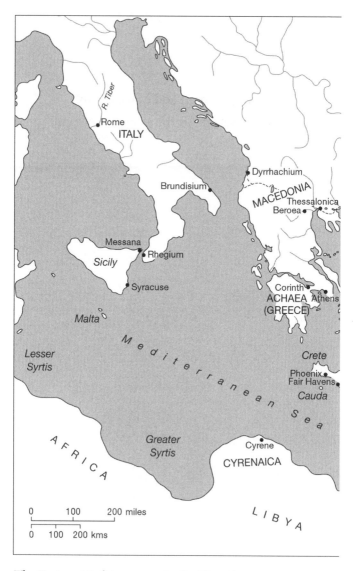

The Eastern Mediterranean in the First Century AD

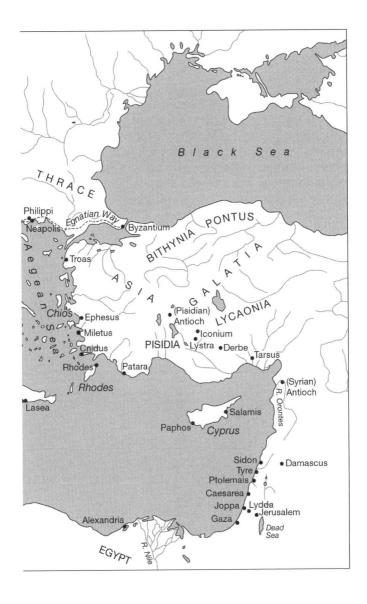

ACTS 1.1–5

Here Comes the Sequel!

[1] Dear Theophilus,

The previous book which I wrote had to do with everything Jesus began to do and teach. [2] I took the story as far as the day when he was taken up, once he had given instructions through the holy spirit to his chosen apostles.

[3] He showed himself to them alive, after his suffering, by many proofs. He was seen by them for forty days, during which he spoke about God's kingdom. [4] As they were having a meal together, he told them not to go away from Jerusalem, but to wait, as he put it, 'for the Father's promise, which I was telling you about earlier. [5] John baptized with water, you see; but in a few days from now you will be baptized with the holy spirit.'

The English playwright Alan Bennett wrote a famous play about the equally famous madness of a well-known king. In the eighteenth and nineteenth centuries, England had four kings in succession all called 'George', and the third of them – George III, in other words – suffered for a fair amount of his reign from some kind of mental illness, probably porphyria. So Bennett called his play *The Madness of George III*.

But when they came to make a movie of the play, the moviemakers faced a problem. Moviegoers were used to sequels: *Spiderman II*, *Superman III*, and so on. A title like that meant that there had been an earlier film of the same name. So they were worried that if people saw a title like *The Madness of George III* they would assume they had missed the first two films in the sequence – and perhaps they wouldn't go to see what they took to be the third. So the filmmakers just called the movie *The Madness of King George*.

The opening paragraph of the book we are now going to read declares, clearly and solidly, that, unlike Bennett's play and film, it is indeed a sequel. There has been a previous book, and this one continues the story. In fact, it even suggests a kind of title: *The Deeds and Teaching of King Jesus II* – not *Jesus the Second*, of course, because there is only one King Jesus, but the second book about what the one and only Jesus did and taught.

At first sight, this is a strange title, since Jesus himself only appears on stage, as it were, during the first nine verses of this first chapter. But Luke, whose first volume we know as the **gospel** which bears his name, is telling us with his opening sentence one of the most important things about the whole book which is now beginning. *It is all about what Jesus is continuing to do and to teach.* The mysterious presence of Jesus haunts the whole story. He is announced as King and Lord, not as an increasingly distant memory but as a living and powerful reality, a person who can be known and loved, obeyed and followed, a person who continues to act within the real world. That, Luke is telling us, is what this book is going to be all about. We call it 'The Acts of the Apostles', but in truth we should really think of it as 'The Acts of Jesus (II)'.

Luke is already warning us, then, that this is an unusual type of book. At one level, it shares a good deal with some of the literature of the day. It has quite a lot in common, for instance, with the work of the great first-century Jewish historian Josephus. Some of the New Testament writers are cheerfully innocent of any pretensions to literary style, but Luke knows what he's doing with his language, with the structure of the book, and with his entire presentation in his pair of volumes. He is not, like Mark, aiming for the first-century equivalent of the airport bookstall. He is aiming for what today we call 'the intelligent reader'. One would expect to see a review of this book, not necessarily in the tabloid newspapers, but in *The Times Literary Supplement* or *The New York Review of Books*. Not that Luke is snooty or highfalutin'. He doesn't talk down to his readers; his book is such a page-turner that anyone who enjoys a good story will be drawn along with excitement the whole way – even if he then leaves them with something of a puzzle at the end, which corresponds as we shall see to the puzzle we've just encountered at the beginning . . .

But the unusual nature of the book is that we are supposed (so Luke is telling us) to read it on at least two levels. At one level, it is of course the story of the early church – told very selectively, of course, like all history (if you wrote down every single thing that happened in a single day you would already fill a library), and told with an eye, as we shall see, to particular concerns and interests. But Luke wants us to read it, all the way through, as a book about Jesus, a book indeed with Jesus as the principal actor, rather like some of the plays by another great playwright of recent years, Samuel Becket, where the action on stage sometimes crucially depends on a person whom the audience never actually sees.

If this is so, one of the results is that there is a third level as well on which Luke wants us to read his work. *This is a play in which we are invited to become actors ourselves.* The stage opens up and we discover we're in the middle of the action. That is part of the point of the 'ending' which isn't really an ending: the story continues, and we are part of it! What we are reading, from this moment on, is the opening scene, or set of scenes, in a play whose action we ourselves are called to continue. As they say, it ain't over yet. We need to refresh our minds as to how the opening scenes worked so that we can play our parts properly, 'in character', in line with the inner nature of the unfolding drama.

As we do so, Luke is keen that we latch on to two things which are fundamental to his whole book and indeed his whole view of the world. First, it is all based on the **resurrection** of Jesus. In the last chapter of his gospel, Luke described some of the scenes in which Jesus met his followers after being raised from the dead: it really was him, he really was alive, richly alive, in a transformed body that could eat and drink as well as walk and talk, but which seemed to have . . . some different properties. His body could, for instance, appear and disappear, and come and go through locked doors.

To us, that sounds as if he was a ghost, someone less than properly embodied. What Luke and the other writers who describe the risen body of Jesus are saying, rather, is that Jesus is *more* than ordinarily embodied, not less. His transformed body is now the beginning of God's new creation; and in God's new creation, as we know from passages like Revelation 21 and Ephesians 1, **heaven** and earth will come together in a new way. Jesus' risen body is the beginning of that, the beginning of a heavenly reality which is fully at home on, and in, this

3

physical world ('earth'), and the beginning of a transformed physical world which is fully at home in God's sphere ('heaven'). This, indeed, will help us in the next scene. But the point of the resurrection itself is that without it there is no gospel, no *Deeds and Teachings of King Jesus II*. There would only be the sad and glorious memory of a great, but failed, teacher and would-be **Messiah**. The resurrection of the Jesus who died under the weight of the world's evil is the foundation of the new world, God's new world, whose opening scenes Luke is describing.

The second thing he wants us to latch onto, indeed is so eager to get to that he puts it here, right up front, is the presence and power of the **holy spirit**. He will have much more to say about this in due course, but already here he insists that the **spirit** is present when Jesus is teaching his followers about what is to come and, above all, that they are about to discover the spirit as a new and powerful reality in their own lives. Jesus, Luke says, pointed them back to the beginning of his own **kingdom**-work, the time when **John the Baptist** summoned all Israel to a **baptism** of **repentance** and renewal. It's going to be like that, he said, only much more so. Instead of being plunged into water, you'll be plunged into the holy spirit. Instead of a renewal which would form them as the re-stored Israel, waiting for God to become their king as so many Jews of the day had hoped, they would experience a renewal which would form them as the restored humanity, celebrating the fact that God was becoming king of the whole world, *and knowing that as a reality inside their own selves*. That is the very heart of the spirituality, and indeed the theology, of 'The Acts of the Apostles'. God is at work to do a new thing in the whole world. And it catches up, within its powerful movement, every child, woman and man who comes within its orbit.

Jesus told his followers to wait for this to happen before they tried to do anything too much. That is important advice. Far too often, to this day, people blunder ahead, assuming that if they know a little about Jesus, and about God's kingdom, they can just go off and put things into action in whatever way occurs to them. Luke would tell us to wait: to pray for the presence and power of the holy spirit, and to find our calling and our energy from that source. If this is a play in which we are all called to take different parts, it is a play in which the only true acting is what happens when the spirit of the playwright himself takes charge.

ACTS 1.6–8

When, What and How?

⁶So when the apostles came together, they put this question to Jesus.

'Master,' they said, 'is this the time when you are going to restore the kingdom to Israel?'

⁷'It's not your business to know about times and dates,' he replied. 'The Father has placed all that under his own direct authority. ⁸What will happen, though, is that you will receive power when the holy spirit comes upon you. Then you will be my witnesses in Jerusalem, in all Judaea and Samaria, and to the very ends of the earth.'

'Are we nearly there yet?'

Any parent who has been on a car journey with small children will know the question – and the tone of voice in which it's usually asked. Sometimes the child is so eager (or so bored), so quickly, that the question gets asked before you have even left your own street.

And of course it all depends what you mean by 'nearly'. If I drive from my home in the north of England all the way to London, I could reasonably say that I was 'nearly' there when we had got to within an hour of the capital. But if I am driving from my home to the town where my parents live, which takes about an hour, I would only say I was 'nearly' there when I was a few minutes away. It's all relative.

Jesus must have had similar reflections when faced with the question the **apostles** were eager to ask him. 'Apostle', by the way, is one of the words Luke regularly uses to describe the **Twelve** – or, as they now were, the Eleven, following Judas' death – whom Jesus had chosen as special witnesses. The reason why there were twelve of them is obvious to anyone

5

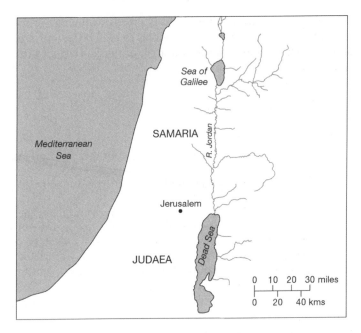

Acts 1.6–8

who understands Jewish culture and history. There had been twelve tribes of Israel, and Jesus was signalling, in his choice of twelve close followers to be around him, that God had called him to renew and restore the people of Israel. So it isn't surprising that they of all people were keen to ask the question, 'Are we nearly there yet? Is this the time? Is it going to happen at last?'

They must, after all, have been very puzzled. Nothing that had happened in the previous few weeks had corresponded at all to their game plan. As far as they were concerned, when Jesus called them and taught them in Galilee during the previous three years or so, they were signing on for some kind of Jewish renewal movement. They believed that God had appointed Jesus to be the true King of Israel, even though most of their contemporaries were still (to say the least) suspicious of him. They had seen Jesus rather like King David in the Old Testament, who for several years was a kind of king-in-waiting, standing in the wings with a ragtag group of followers wondering when their turn would come. Jesus' motley band of followers had imagined that he would be king in some quite ordinary sense, which was why some of them had asked if they could have the top jobs in his government. Jesus, with his extraordinary healing power and visionary teaching, would rule in Jerusalem, and would restore God's people Israel.

The result of this, as many Jews of the time believed, was that, when God restored Israel, the whole world would be turned around at last. Israel would be the top nation, ruling over the rest of the world. That's what had been promised, more or less, in the Psalms (look at Psalm 72, or Psalm 89) and the prophets (read Isaiah 40—55). Of course, the nations of the world would then be judged for their wickedness. But there might also be the possibility that the blessing God gave to Israel would come at last upon the whole creation.

All of this could be summed up in the phrase: 'restore the kingdom to Israel'. That's what they were hoping for, and the question was natural: 'Are we nearly there yet?' They hadn't been expecting that Jesus would die a violent death. His crucifixion made it look as though they were wrong: he wasn't the **Messiah**, they weren't heading for the top jobs, Israel wasn't being renewed, and the world was carrying on in its wicked way, with the rich and powerful oppressing the poor and needy. Business as usual. And then he had risen from the dead, again confounding their own and everyone else's expectations. What did it mean? Did it mean that their dreams of 'restoring the kingdom to Israel' were now back on track?

Well, it did and it didn't. Like everything else, the dream of the **kingdom** had been transformed through Jesus' death and **resurrection**. Just as Jesus had told them they would have to lose their lives to save them, so now he had to explain that they had to lose their kingdom-dreams – of an earthly kingdom with ordinary administrative and governmental power, in charge of subject states – in order to gain them. But at this point many people, reading Acts, have gone badly wrong.

7

It would be easy to imagine that what Jesus (and Luke) meant at this point was something like this: 'No, no, you're dreaming of an earthly kingdom, but I'm telling you about a heavenly one. You think what matters is reorganizing this world, but I'm preparing you for the next one. What counts is not what happens in this world of space and time, but where you're going to spend eternity. I'm going off to **heaven**, and you must tell people how they can follow me there.' From that point of view, the answer to 'Are we nearly there yet?' is 'No, we're not going there at all, actually.'

That certainly isn't what Luke means. But, like the children in the car, we ourselves are going to have to wait, as his book unfolds, to see just what he does mean. We know enough from his first volume, though, to see where it's all going. God's kingdom is coming in and through the work of Jesus, not by taking people away from this world but by transforming things within this world, bringing the sphere of earth into the presence, and under the rule, of heaven itself. So when is this all happening? Again, many people, reading this passage, have assumed that Jesus' basic answer is 'No': No, this isn't the time, all of those things will happen a long way off in the future. No, we're not nearly there yet; you have a lot of things to do, tasks to perform, and only when you're finished all of them will I 'restore the kingdom to Israel'. And, actually, there is a sense in which all that is indeed true. There is a 'still-future' dimension to everything that happens in this book, as we shall see. But wait a minute. Is that really what Jesus' answer means?

I don't think it is. Jesus does indeed warn them that they won't be given a timetable. In terms of the children in the car, he is telling them that they simply aren't going to have a sense of where they are on the calendar of God's unfolding purposes. But what he goes on to say hints at something different. 'You will receive power . . . and you will be my witnesses, from here in Jerusalem to the ends of the earth.'

'My witnesses'? What does that mean? Quite simply this: in the resurrection (and the **ascension**, which is about to happen), Jesus is indeed being enthroned as Israel's Messiah and therefore king of the whole world. He is the one at whose name

8

every knee shall bow, as Paul puts it in Philippians 2.10. In the world of the first century, when someone was enthroned as king, that new authority would take effect through heralds going off throughout the territory in question with the news, 'We have a king!' That was always proclaimed as good news, because everyone in the ancient world (unlike many in the modern world) knew that anarchy is always worse than authorized government. Governments may be bad, but chaos is worse. So the heralds, the messengers, would go off to the far reaches of the kingdom (imagine, for instance, a new Roman emperor coming to the throne, and heralds going off as far as Spain to the west, Britain to the north, and Egypt to the southeast), to announce that Claudius, or Nero, or whoever, was now the rightful king, and to demand glad allegiance from supposedly grateful subjects.

And that is what Jesus is telling them they must now do. You're asking about the kingdom? You're asking when it will come about, when Israel will be exalted as the top nation, with the nations of the world being subject to God through his vindicated people? Well, in one sense it has already happened, Jesus is saying, because in my own death and resurrection I have already been exalted as Israel's representative. In another sense it is yet to happen, because we still await the time when the whole world is visibly and clearly living under God's just and healing rule. But we are now living in between those two points, *and you must be my witnesses from here to the ends of the world.* The apostles are to go out as heralds, not of someone who may become king at some point in the future, but of the one who has *already* been appointed and enthroned.

Notice the subtle difference, in verses 7 and 8, between the words 'authority' and 'power'. God has all authority, and it is through him and from him that all 'authorized' rule in the world must flow. We don't have that ultimate authority; no human, in whatever task or role, ever does. It all comes from God. But what God's people are promised is *power*; the word used here is *dynamis*, from which we get 'dynamite'. We need that power, just as Jesus' first followers did, if we or they are to be his witnesses, to find ways of announcing to the world that

9

he is already its rightful king and lord. And in the next chapters of Acts we see what that witness, and that power, are going to mean.

But for the moment we notice one thing in particular, which will help us as we read into the rest of the book. Jesus gives the apostles an agenda: Jerusalem first, then Judaea (the surrounding countryside), then Samaria (the hated semi-foreigners living right next door) and to the ends of the earth. Sit back and watch, Luke says. That's exactly the journey we're about to take. And, like the child who stops asking the question because suddenly the journey itself has become so interesting, we find there's so much to see that we won't worry so much about the 'when'. Jesus is already appointed and enthroned as the world's true king. One day that kingdom will come, fully and finally. In the meantime, we have a job to do.

ACTS 1.9–14

Ascension!

⁹As Jesus said this, he was lifted up while they were watching, and a cloud took him out of their sight. ¹⁰They were gazing into heaven as he disappeared. Then, lo and behold, two men appeared, dressed in white, standing beside them.

¹¹'Galileans,' they said, 'why are you standing here staring into heaven? This Jesus, who has been taken from you into heaven, will come back in the same way you saw him go into heaven.'

¹²Then they went back to Jerusalem from the hill called the Mount of Olives, which is close to Jerusalem, about the distance you could travel on a sabbath. ¹³They then ('they' here means Peter, John, James, Andrew, Philip, Thomas, Bartholomew, Matthew, James the son of Alphaeus, Simon the zealot, and Judas the son of James) entered the city and went to the upstairs room where they were staying. ¹⁴They all gave themselves single-heartedly to prayer, with the women, including Mary, Jesus' mother, and his brothers.

We were having supper with some friends who had recently moved to western Canada.

'So,' my wife began, 'does Vancouver feel like home?'

'It's not home,' replied the wife energetically. 'It's **heaven**!'

'Well, my dear,' commented her husband, a theologian, reproachfully and perhaps over-piously, 'if you knew your business, you would know that heaven is your true home.'

'No,' she replied. 'Home is where there's hard work, and hassle, and all kinds of difficulties. Here I'm free from all that. This is heaven!'

I have often pondered that conversation, and I want to take issue with the theologian-husband. Though many hymns and prayers (mostly from the nineteenth and early twentieth century) speak of heaven as our home, that isn't how the Bible normally puts it. In the Bible, heaven and earth are the two halves of God's created world. They aren't so much like the two halves of an orange, more or less identical but occupying different space. They are more like the weight of an object and the stuff it's made of, or perhaps the meaning of a flag and the cloth or paper it's made of: two (related) ways of looking at the same thing, two different and interlocking dimensions, the one perhaps explaining the other. Talking about 'heaven and earth' is a way, in the Bible, of talking about the fact, as many people and many cultures have perceived it to be, that everything in our world (call it 'earth' for the sake of argument, though that can be confusing because that is also the name we give to our particular planet within our particular solar system, whereas 'earth' in the Bible really means the entire cosmos of space, time and matter) has another dimension, another sort of reality, that goes with it as well.

You could call this other reality, this other dimension, the 'inner' reality, if you like, thinking perhaps of a golf ball which has an outer reality (the hard, mottled surface) and an inner reality (the tightly packed, springy interior). But you could just as easily think of earth as the 'inner' reality, the dense material of the world where we live at the moment, and 'heaven' as the outer reality, the 'side' of our reality that is open to all kinds of other things, to meanings and possibilities which our 'inner' reality, our busy little world of space, time and matter sometimes seems to exclude.

If these illustrations don't help, leave them to one side and concentrate on the reality. The reality is this: 'heaven' in the Bible is God's space, and 'earth' is our space. 'Heaven' isn't just 'the happy place where God's people go when they die', and it certainly isn't our 'home' if by that you mean (as some Christians, sadly, have meant) that our eventual destiny is to leave 'earth' altogether and go to 'heaven' instead. God's plan, as we see again and again in the Bible, is for 'new heavens and new earth', and for them to be joined together in that renewal once and for all. 'Heaven' may well be our *temporary* home, after this present life; but the whole new world, united and transformed, is our eventual destination.

Part of the point about Jesus' **resurrection** is that it was the beginning of precisely that astonishing and world-shattering renewal. It wasn't just that he happened to be alive again, as though by some quirk of previously unsuspected 'nature', or by some extraordinary '**miracle**' in which God did the impossible just to show how powerful he was, death suddenly worked backwards in his particular case. It was, rather, that because on the cross he had indeed dealt with the main force of evil, decay and death itself, the creative power of God, no longer thwarted as it had been by human rebellion, could at last burst forth and produce the beginning, the pilot project, of that joined-up heaven-and-earth reality which is God's plan for the whole world. This is part at least of the explanation of the sheer strangeness of Jesus' risen body, which hits us in all the Easter stories. At the very point where they're explaining that it really is him, that he isn't a ghost, that he can eat and drink, just at that moment he appears and disappears at will. It seems as though the first **disciples** really didn't know what to make of it either, and were simply doing their best to tell it like they had seen it.

But once we grasp that 'heaven and earth' mean what they mean in the Bible, and that 'heaven' is not, repeat *not*, a location within our own cosmos of space, time and matter, situated somewhere up in the sky ('up' from whose point of view? Europe? Brazil? Australia?), then we are ready, or as ready as we are likely to be, to understand the **ascension**, described here quite simply and briefly by Luke. Neither Luke nor the other early Christians thought Jesus had suddenly become a primitive spaceman, heading off into orbit or beyond, so that if you searched throughout the far reaches of what we call 'space' you would eventually find him. They believed that 'heaven' and 'earth' are the two interlocking spheres of God's reality, and that the risen body of Jesus is the first (and so far the only) object which is fully at home in both and hence in either, anticipating the time when everything will be renewed and joined together. And so, since as T. S. Eliot said, 'humankind cannot bear very much reality', the new, overwhelming reality of a heaven-and-earth creature will not just yet live in both dimensions together, but will make itself – himself – at home within the 'heavenly' dimension for the moment, until the time comes for heaven and earth to be finally renewed and united. At that point, of course, this renewed Jesus himself will be the central figure.

That is the point of the event, and its explanation, as we find them in verses 9–11. Jesus is 'lifted up', indicating to the disciples not that he was heading out somewhere beyond the moon, beyond Mars, or wherever, but that he was going into 'God's space', God's dimension. The cloud, as so often in the Bible, is the sign of God's presence (think of the pillar of cloud and fire as the children of Israel wandered through the desert, or the cloud and smoke that filled the **Temple** when God became suddenly present in a new way). Jesus has gone into God's dimension of reality; but he'll be back on the day when that dimension and our present one are brought together once and for all. That promise hangs in the air over the whole of Christian history from that day to this. That is what we mean by the '**second coming**'.

There are two other things which are, as we say, 'going on' in this passage. Some first-century readers would have picked up one of these, some the other, some perhaps both. First, one of the central Old Testament promises for the early Christians was in Daniel 7, where 'one like a **son of man**' is brought up, on the clouds of heaven, to the 'Ancient of Days', and is presented before him and given kingly power over the nations, and particularly over the 'beasts', the monsters representing the forces of evil and chaos. For someone who had long pondered that passage – and there are plenty of signs that the early Christians did just that – the story of Jesus' ascension would indicate that Daniel 7 had been fulfilled in a dramatic and unexpected way, with the human figure who had suffered at the hands of the evil powers of the world now being exalted into the very presence of God himself, there to receive kingly power. This fits so well with the previous passage (verses 6–8) that it is hard to suppose that Luke did not intend it.

Second, many of Luke's readers would know that when a Roman emperor died, it had become customary to declare that someone had seen his soul escaping from his body and going up to heaven. If you go to the top end of the Forum in Rome, stand under the Arch of Titus, and look up, you will see a carving of the soul of Titus, who was emperor in the 80s of the first century, ascending to heaven. The message of this was clear: the emperor was becoming a god (thus enabling his son and heir to style himself 'son of god', which is a useful title if you want to run the world). The parallel is not so close this time, since Luke is clear that it was not Jesus' soul that ascended into heaven, leaving his body behind somewhere, but his whole, renewed, bodily, complete self. But there is then a sense that Jesus is *upstaging* anything the Roman emperors might imagine for themselves. He is the reality, and they are the parody – a theme we will notice more than once as Luke's story unfolds. And when, at the end of Luke's book, the good news of Jesus is being preached in Rome itself, openly and unhindered, we have a sense of 'Of course! That's how it had to be.' He is the world's true and rightful king, sharing the very throne, and somehow even, so it seems, the identity, of the one true God.

The first and most important response to this extraordinary, unprecedented and still hard-to-describe event is of course worship. Luke often tells us about the early Christians devoting themselves to prayer. As we go back with them on this occasion from the Mount of Olives to the house where they were staying, and look round the room and see these puzzled but excited men and women – including Jesus' own mother –

giving themselves to prayer, we ought to feel a strong identification with them. All those who name the name of Jesus, who worship him, who study his **word**, are called to be people of worship and prayer. Why?

Well, it's obvious, isn't it? It is precisely in worship and prayer that we, while still on 'earth' in the sense I've explored already, find ourselves sharing in the life of 'heaven', which is where Jesus is. The constant references to prayer in Acts are a sign that this is how these very ordinary, frequently muddled, deeply human beings, the **apostles** and the others with them, found that their story was being bound up with the story of 'what Jesus was continuing to do and to teach'. From the ascension onwards, the story of Jesus' followers takes place in both dimensions. That, by the way, is why there was an inevitable head-on clash with the Temple, because the Temple was thought to be the key spot where heaven and earth overlapped. The resurrection and ascension of Jesus are launching a claim to the contrary, and Jesus' followers had to work out what that would mean. As we in our own day not only read Acts but try to follow Jesus and witness to his lordship over the world, it is through prayer and worship that we, too, can know, enjoy and be energized by the life of heaven, right here on earth, and work out what that will mean in terms of other claims, other lords, other ways of **life**.

ACTS 1.15–26

Restoring the Twelve

[15]Around that time Peter stood up in the middle of the gathering, which by this stage numbered about a hundred and twenty.

[16]'My dear family,' he said, 'the holy spirit spoke long ago, through the mouth of David, about Judas, who became a guide to the people who arrested Jesus. There it is in the Bible, and it had to come true. [17]He was counted along with us, and he had his own share in the work we've been given.'

([18]Judas, you see, had bought a field with the money his wickedness had brought him, where he fell headlong and burst open, with his innards all gushing out. [19]This became known to everyone who lived in Jerusalem, so that the field was called, in their local language, 'Akeldamach', which means 'Blood-place'.)

[20]'For this is what it says in the book of the Psalms:

Let his home become desolate
and let nobody live in it.

and again

Let someone else receive his overseeing task.

[21]'So this is what has to be done. There are plenty of people who have gone about with us all the time that our Master Jesus was coming and going among us, [22]starting from John's baptism until the day he was taken from us. Let one of them be chosen to be alongside us as a special witness of his resurrection.'

[23]So they chose two: Joseph who was called Barsabbas, with the surname Justus, and Matthias.

[24]'Lord,' they prayed, 'you know the hearts of all people. Show us which one of these two you have chosen [25]to receive this particular place of service and apostleship, from which Judas went away to go to his own place.'

[26]So they cast lots for them. The lot fell on Matthias, and he was enrolled along with the eleven apostles.

The older I get, the more I dislike trying to follow the complicated instructions that come with new technology. I'm not what they call technophobic. On the desk where I am working there is a computer. It is linked to a cell phone which includes addresses, diary details and so on. Beside me there is an iPod containing hundreds of hours of music. On another desk there is a microphone connecting me to radio stations, and a broadcast-quality pocket-sized voice recorder. I've had to learn how to use all of them, and I get there eventually. But there is always the awful moment when the new toy comes out of its box, and I stare at it in horror, realizing that I have to learn a whole new language, to figure out which complex buttons and switches do what, how to plug different cables into their proper sockets, and so on. At times like that the written instructions had better be good. I'm in uncharted territory and I need someone to hold my hand.

That must have been exactly how the **apostles** felt in the very early days. What are we supposed to *do*? You might suppose that they would want to rush out and tell everyone about Jesus right away, but they didn't do that. (Perhaps, along with their enormous excitement at his **resurrection**, and now his **ascension**, there may have been a realistic awareness that those who brought about Jesus' death would have no compunction about attacking them as well. Perhaps, too, they were careful to remember Jesus' instructions about waiting for God's power to come on them before going off to do what had to be done.) Was there a set of instructions and, if so, how could they get access to it?

They faced a particular problem right at the start, rather like the sort of problem I had the other day when one of the cables I'd been sent for a new piece of equipment simply didn't fit the socket it was supposed to. There they were, the spearhead of Jesus' plan to renew and restore God's people – and there were supposed to be twelve of them. Only eleven were left. How could they model, and symbolize, God's plan for Israel (and therefore for the world) if they were, so to speak, one patriarch short of a true Israel? Did they just have to stay like that, and if not what should they do about it?

As with everything else that happened in the early church – and Luke is probably already hinting at this in the present passage – they went to two sources for instructions: to the **word** of God, and to prayer. By 'the word of God' I mean, as they seemed to have meant, something more than scripture but not less. For them, the Jewish Bible (what we call the Old Testament) was not just a record of what God had said to his people of old. It was a huge and vital story, the story of the earlier part of God's purposes, full of signposts pointing forward to the time when, further forward within the same story, the plans God was nurturing would come to fruition. Prophets and kings had listened to what the **spirit** had been saying to them, and had written things which, like seeds sown in the dark earth and long watered, would eventually emerge as plants and would bear fruit.

So it was that, from within the life of constant prayer to which Jesus' followers had given themselves after his ascension, they pondered the Psalms which spoke, as several Psalms speak, of a time when God's people, and God's true king, would be opposed by a traitor from within their midst, betrayed by one who had been counted a close friend and colleague. Here they found, not indeed a road map for exactly where they were – scripture seldom supplies exactly that – but the hints and clues to enable them to see how to feel their way forward in this new and unprecedented dilemma. The Psalms made it quite clear: it is not only all right for someone else to take the place of the one who has gone, it is the proper thing to do. It doesn't mean, in other words, that God's plan, or their obedience to it, has gone worryingly wrong. The tragedy of Judas is held within the strange, dark, overarching purpose of God.

We had better get used to this theme of God's plan, overruling complex and problematic circumstances; because for Luke, as for his near-contemporary Josephus, the idea of God's providence, still at work even though things may seem sad and dark, is extremely important. And the defection of Judas must have seemed like that in a high degree to the apostles. Judas had been their friend. Until a few short weeks before, he had been one of them in every possible sense. They had known him intimately, and he them. The tragic story of his untimely death is told in quite a different form here from what we find in Matthew 27.3–10, and since nobody in the early church attempted to tidy things up we probably shouldn't try either. One way or another – whether it was actual suicide, as Matthew says, or whether it was the sudden and violent onset of a fatal disease, as Luke suggests – Judas was no longer among them. Insofar as they could make any sense of this, it was a scriptural sense. Insofar as they could see what to do as a result, it was a scripturally rooted sense of direction. That is the main point Luke wants us to grasp here.

And so they chose Matthias. Or rather, they would say, God chose Matthias. They used the well-known method of drawing lots (having already chosen a very brief short list of candidates!). Some have seen this as rather arbitrary, and have suggested that, had the choice been delayed until after the **day of Pentecost** and the arrival of the **holy spirit** in power, they might have done it differently. Luke doesn't seem to think so, since part of his point is precisely to show how, from the beginning, the apostles did what they did in the light of the scriptures and in the context of prayer. Part of his point, too, is to insist that what the apostles go on to do really is, in the proper sense, 'the restoration of the kingdom to Israel', even though it didn't look like they, or anyone else at the time, would have thought such an event would look like. And for that they needed the powerful symbol of the **Twelve** to be restored.

Nor does Luke imagine that the choice of people for particular offices (as in this case) and tasks (as in many others to come) is always plain or straightforward. There is at least one tragic story later in the book where serious disagreement over the choice of someone for a particular job leads to a major row. What concerns Luke most, in the present case, is the fact that God 'knows the hearts' (verse 24), and that it is therefore up to God who gets chosen for a role, and a task, in which the particular disposition of the particular heart matters very much indeed. And the role itself, and task itself, are important as well. The person to take Judas' place must be someone who had gone about with them all since the time of John's **baptism** right through, and who was, along with the Eleven, a witness to Jesus' resurrection.

This 'person specification' in verses 21 and 22 is extremely interesting. It shows that from the beginning the early Christians saw themselves as being the continuation (just as Luke indicates in the first verse of the book) of the **kingdom**-work of Jesus which had begun with John's baptism. And it shows that those roots were important for how they understood themselves. Because of that, in fact, one possible candidate who was not considered was James the brother of the Lord, who quickly became a prominent leader even though he wasn't one of the Twelve. He had not, it seems, been a believer until the Lord appeared to him personally (John 7.5; 1 Corinthians 15.7). And it shows that the primary apostolic task was to bear witness to the resurrection of Jesus himself. As we shall see, if you take that away from Acts you are left with nothing. The resurrection defines the church, from that day to this. The church is either the movement which announces God's new creation, or it is just another irrelevant religious sect.

I always feel both sorry for, and curious about, Joseph called Barsabbas, also known as Justus, who was the candidate not chosen. There is no suggestion that his heart was not right with God, or that he was otherwise unsuited for the task. He was, after all, one of the 'last two' in the consideration of the Eleven. They would have trusted him. We have no idea what happened to him after this, just as we have no idea, for that matter, what happened to Matthias himself. Part of Christian obedience, right from the beginning, was the call to play (apparently) great parts without pride and (apparently) small parts without shame. There are, of course, no passengers in the kingdom of God, and actually no 'great' and 'small' parts either. The different tasks and roles to which God assigns us are his business, not ours.

ACTS 2.1–4

Here Comes the Power

> [1]When the day of Pentecost had finally arrived, they were all together in the same place. [2]Suddenly there came from heaven a noise like the sound of a strong, blowing wind, and it filled the whole house where they were sitting. [3]Then tongues, apparently made of fire, appeared to them, moving apart and coming to rest on each one of them. [4]They were all filled with the holy spirit, and began to speak in other languages, as the spirit gave them the words to say.

Sometimes a name, belonging to one particular person, becomes so attached to a particular object or product that we forget where it originally came from. The obvious example is 'Hoover': in England at least we speak of 'the Hoover' when we mean 'the vacuum cleaner', happily ignoring the fact that quite a lot of vacuum cleaners are made by other companies which owe nothing to the original Mr Hoover. It is as though Henry Ford had been so successful in car production that people said 'the Ford' when they meant 'the car', even if in fact it was a Volvo.

Something similar has happened with the word 'Pentecost'. If 'Pentecost' means anything at all to most people today, it is probably something to do with 'Pentecostalism'. And that – again, if it means anything to people at all – probably signifies a somewhat wild form of Christian religious experience and practice, outside the main stream of church life, involving a lot of noise and waving of arms, and (of course) **speaking in tongues**. We often forget that all Christians, not only those who call themselves 'Pentecostalists', derive their meaning from the first Pentecost. We often forget, too, perhaps equally importantly, just what 'Pentecost' itself originally was and meant.

For a first-century Jew, Pentecost was the fiftieth day after Passover. It was an agricultural festival. It was the day when farmers brought the first sheaf of wheat from the crop, and offered it to God, partly as a sign of gratitude and partly as a prayer that all the rest of the crop, too, would be safely gathered in. But, for the Jew, neither Passover nor Pentecost were simply agricultural festivals. These festivals awakened echoes of the great story which dominated the long memories of the Jewish people, the story of the **Exodus** from Egypt, when God fulfilled his promises to Abraham by rescuing his people. Passover was the time when the lambs were **sacrificed**, and the Israelites were saved from the avenging angel who slew the firstborn of the Egyptians. Off went the Israelites that very night, and passed through the Red Sea into the Sinai desert. Then, 50 days after Passover, they came to Mount Sinai, where Moses received the **law**. Pentecost, the fiftieth day, isn't (in other words) just about the 'first fruits', the sheaf which says the harvest has begun. It's about God giving to his redeemed people the way of life by which they must now carry out his purposes.

All of that, and more besides, keeps peeping out from behind what the New Testament says about the **spirit**, and about Pentecost in particular. For Luke there is a kind of easy assumption that people would know about the first fruits. He

21

can more or less take it for granted that readers will see this story, of the **apostles** being filled with the spirit and then going on to bear powerful witness to Jesus and his **resurrection** and to win converts from the very first day, as a sign that this is like the sheaf which is offered to God as the sign of the great harvest to come. And, when we look closely at the way some Jews told the story of the giving of the law on Mount Sinai, we can see some parallels there, too. When the Israelites arrived at Mount Sinai, Moses went up the mountain, and then came down again with the law. Here, Jesus has gone up into **heaven** in the **ascension**, and – so Luke wants us to understand – he is now coming down again, not with a written law carved on tablets of stone, but with the dynamic energy of the law, designed to be written on human hearts.

'Pentecost', then, is a word with very particular meaning, which Luke is keen that we should grasp. But of course the first **day of Pentecost**, and the experience of God's spirit from that day to this, can no more be reduced to theological formulae and interesting Old Testament echoes than you can reduce a hurricane to a list of diagrams on a meteorologist's chart. It's important that someone somewhere is tracking the hurricane and telling us what it's doing, but when it comes to Pentecost it's far more important that you're out there in the wind, letting it sweep through your life, your heart, your imagination, your powers of speech, and transform you from a listless or lifeless believer into someone whose heart is on fire with the love of God. Those images of wind and fire are of course what Luke says it was like on the first day. Many Christians in many traditions have used similar images to describe what it is sometimes like when the spirit comes to do new things in the lives of individuals and communities.

It is most significant, in the light of what we said before about the ascension, that the wind came 'from heaven' (verse 2). The whole point is that, through the spirit, some of the creative power of God himself comes from heaven to earth and does its work there. The aim is not to give people a 'spirituality' which will make the things of earth irrelevant. The point is to transform earth with the power of heaven, starting with those parts of 'earth' which consist of the bodies, minds, hearts and lives of the followers of Jesus – as a community: notice that, in verse 1, Luke stresses the fact that they were all together in one place; the spirit comes, not to divide, but to unite. The coming of the spirit at Pentecost, in other words, is the complementary fact to the ascension of Jesus into heaven. The risen Jesus in heaven is the presence, in God's sphere, of the first part of 'earth' to be transformed into 'new creation' in which heaven and earth are joined; the pouring out of the spirit on earth is the presence, in our sphere, of the sheer energy of heaven itself. The gift of the spirit is thus the direct result of the ascension of Jesus. Because he is the Lord of all, his energy, the power to be and do something quite new, is available through the spirit to all who call on him, all who follow him, all who trust him.

The wind and the fire are wild, untameable forces, and the experience of the wind rushing through the house with a great roar, and the fire coming to rest on each person present, must have been both terrifying and exhilarating. Of course, there are many times later in this book, as there are many times in the life of the church, when the spirit works softly and secretly, quietly transforming people's lives and situations without any big noise or fuss. People sometimes suppose that this is the norm, and that the noise, the force and the fire are the exception – just as some have supposed, within 'Pentecostal' and similar circles, that without the noise and the fire, and particularly the speaking in tongues, something is seriously lacking or deficient. We should beware of drawing either conclusion. Luke clearly intends to describe something new, something that launched a great movement, as a fleet of ships is launched by the strong wind that drives them out to sea or a forest fire is started by a few small flames. He intends to explain how it was that a small group of frightened, puzzled and largely uneducated men and women could so quickly become, as they undoubtedly did, a force to be reckoned with right across the known world.

In particular, Luke highlights this strange phenomenon of 'speaking in tongues'. This has been a prominent feature of some parts of church life in the last century or so, though for many previous generations and in many parts of church history it has been virtually unknown. It occurs, it seems, in other religions, as Paul was aware (1 Corinthians 12.2–3). Some people try to sweep 'tongues' aside as if it was a peculiar thing which happened early on and which, fortunately, doesn't need to happen any more. Sometimes this is combined with a sense of the need to control the emotions, both one's own and other people's. But 'speaking in tongues' and similar phenomena are, very often, a way of getting in touch with deeply buried emotions and bringing them to the surface in praise, celebration, grief or sorrow, or urgent desire turned into prayer. It is hard, seeing the importance of 'tongues' in the New Testament, and their manifest usefulness in these and other ways, to go along with the idea that they should be ruled out for today's church.

In particular, it is precisely part of being a genuine human being, made and renewed in God's image, that people should do that most characteristic thing, using words and language, in quite a new way. We are called to be people of God's **word**, and God's word can never be controlled by rationalistic schemes, or contained within the tight little frameworks that we invent to keep everything tidy and under control.

People sometimes feel guilty if they think they haven't had such wonderful experiences as the **apostles** had on the first Pentecost. Or they feel jealous of those who seem to have had things like this happen to them. About this there are two things to say. First, as we saw in the first chapter, God moves mysteriously among his people, dealing with each individual in a different way. Some people are allowed remarkable experiences, perhaps (we can't always tell) because they are going to have to go into difficult situations and need to know very directly just how dramatically powerful and life-transforming God can be. Other people have to work in quiet and patient ways and not rely on a sudden burst of extra power to fix all the problems which in fact need a much more steady, and perhaps much deeper, work. There is no room for pride or jealousy in a well-ordered **fellowship**, where everybody is as delighted with the gifts given to others as with those given to themselves.

Second, it is clear from words of Jesus himself (Luke 11.13) that God longs to give the holy spirit to people, and that all we have to do is ask. What the spirit will do when he comes is anybody's guess. Be prepared for wind and fire, for some fairly drastic spring-cleaning of the dusty and cold rooms of one's life. But we should not doubt that God will give his spirit to all who seek him, and that the form and direction that any particular spirit-led life will take will be (ultimately, and assuming obedience and **faith**) the one that will enable that person, uniquely, to bring glory to God.

ACTS 2.5–13

New Words for New News

[5]There were devout Jews from every nation under heaven living in Jerusalem at that time. [6]When they heard this noise they came together in a crowd. They were deeply puzzled, because every single one of them could hear them speaking in his or her own native language. [7]They were astonished and amazed.

'These men are all Galileans, aren't they?' they said. [8]'So how is it that each of us can hear them in our own mother tongues? [9]There are Parthians here, and Medians, Elamites, people from Mesopotamia, Judaea, Cappadocia, Pontus, Asia, [10]Phrygia and Pamphylia, Egypt and the parts of Libya that belong to Cyrene; there are people from Rome, [11]proselytes as well as Jews; there are Cretans and Arabs. We can hear them telling us about the powerful things God has done – *in our own languages!*'

[12]Everyone was astonished and perplexed.

'What does it all mean?' they were asking each other.

[13]But some sneered.

'They're full of new wine!' they said.

I once went to an international conference for Christian students, where I had to give some lectures – on Luke, as it happens. There were students there from all over Eastern Europe: Poles, Russians, Romanians, Hungarians, as well as people from the Czech Republic, Germany, France and elsewhere. I was excited by what I was going to say, and I set off talking at a good pace. Meanwhile, behind soundproof screens,

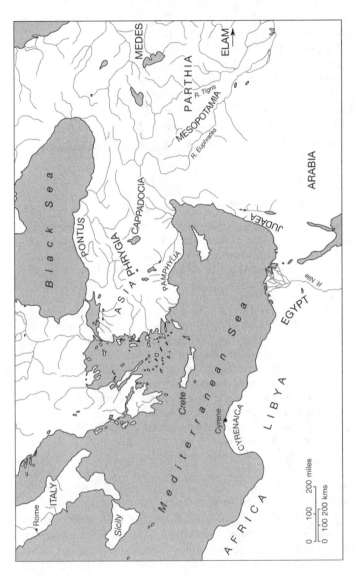

Acts 2.5–13

the translators worked to keep up and to put my words into the languages of the various students who were listening through headphones.

When it came to coffee time, the young woman from Hungary who had been doing her best with my enthusiastic lecture came up. She was almost in tears.

'Dr Wright,' she said, 'you are going to have to go much, much slower. You see, the average word in Hungarian is two or three times as long as its equivalent in English. Even if your English was easy to translate all the time, it is physically impossible to speak the Hungarian words at the same pace as the English ones. There are just too many syllables.'

I learnt my lesson, and spent the week talking (for me) very, very slowly, keeping my eye on the glass screens and watching for signs of distress among the hard-working translators. But my mind kept jumping across – not least because I was talking about Luke's theology – to this scene at the start of Acts. Somehow, on the **day of Pentecost**, they didn't need translators. Everybody understood in their own language.

What language would they have been expecting? At that time, all around the Mediterranean world, everybody's second language was Greek. Ever since the conquests of Alexander the Great, 400 years earlier, Greek had been to much of that world what English is for many people in the world today. People who travelled, as the people in this story seem to have done, would pretty certainly be able to get by in Greek, while probably speaking at least one other language, if not two or three. Jews in Palestine would know, and usually speak, Aramaic, but some might well know some classical Hebrew as well. Many people would know at least some Latin, as the Roman Empire gradually imposed itself on many of the countries originally conquered by Greece.

But on the day of Pentecost they didn't need to switch languages, or to worry about translation. It was all done for them. People are often surprised by this, because many have seen 'the gift of tongues' not as the gift of being able to speak other specific languages, but rather as the gift of a kind of heavenly babble, a succession of syllables and sounds which, though they may sound like a language, do not appear to be so in fact, either to the speaker or to any listeners. For many devout Christians who '**speak in tongues**' as part of their regular life of prayer, either in public or private or both, there is no expectation that anyone will 'understand' in the same way as, if I suddenly spoke Arabic in a crowded bus in Jerusalem, many people would understand what I was saying.

But there are well-attested instances, in modern as well as ancient times, of people 'speaking in tongues' suddenly, at the **spirit**'s bidding, in particular situations where they have no idea that someone from a particular language and culture is present, and indeed without themselves knowing a single word of that language in the ordinary sense – and discovering that someone present can understand them. I have met people to whom this has happened, and I have no reason to think they were deceiving either themselves or me. I have no explanation for this other than that God can do whatever God wants to do, and that it isn't up to us to set bounds to the ways in which God can and does reach out, either when the **gospel** needs to make an impact on someone, or some group, that is otherwise peculiarly difficult to penetrate, or when someone is present in special need or distress. Or whatever.

But this phenomenon, strange though it is to most of us, highlights something else that is going on in the narrative at this point, and to which Luke wants to draw our attention. The whole question of Acts 1, you remember, was of how God would fulfil the promise to extend his **kingdom**, his saving, sovereign rule, not only in Israel but *through* Israel, to reach the rest of the world. In other words, the question had to do with the challenge to see how God was going to fulfil what he had said to Abraham in Genesis 12.3: 'In you, and in your family, all the families of the earth will be blessed.' And this promise to Abraham comes directly after the dramatic and comic chapter in which the people of Babel are building a tower, thinking arrogantly to make a name for themselves. God's response, as always, to human pride and arrogance is to overturn the project and ridicule the people, which he accomplishes by confusing their languages so that they cannot understand one another and cannot therefore work together on creating a human society which would have no need of the creator God.

Now, Luke is implying, with the day of Pentecost this curse is itself overturned; in other words, God is dramatically signalling that his promises to Abraham are being fulfilled, and the whole human race is going to be addressed with the **good news** of what has happened in and through Jesus. (The summary of the message in verse 11 is that it concerned 'God's powerful deeds'; in other words, the dramatic and extraordinary things God had done in and through Jesus, as in 10.38–43.) Granted, all the people present were Jewish or at least proselytes (**Gentiles** who had converted to Judaism), since the reason they were in Jerusalem was to attend the Jewish festival. But they had come from all over, from countries each of which would have its own native language and local dialects. Luke gives the list of where they came from in a great sprawling sweep, covering tens of thousands of square miles, from Parthia and Mesopotamia in the north and east to Rome in the west and Egypt and Arabia in the south, together with the island of Crete. The point is not to give an exact list of precisely where everyone came from in the crowded city of Jerusalem that day, but to splash across the page the sense of a great polyglot company all hearing words spoken in their own language.

Hardly surprisingly, to some it sounded simply like the slurred and babbling speech of people who have had too much to drink. Again and again in Acts we find opposition, incredulity, scoffing and sneering at what the **apostles** say and do, at the same time as great success and conviction. And again and again in the work of the church, to this day, there are always plenty who declare that we are wasting our time and talking incomprehensible nonsense. Equally, some Christians have been so concerned to keep up safe appearances and to make sure they are looking like ordinary, normal people that they would never, under any circumstances, have been accused of being drunk, at nine o'clock in the morning or any other time. Part of the challenge of this passage is the question: have our churches today got enough energy, enough spirit-driven new life, to make onlookers pass any comment at all? Has anything happened which might make people think we were drunk? If not, is it because the spirit is simply at work in other ways, or because we have so successfully quenched the spirit that there is actually nothing happening at all?

ACTS 2.14–21

It's All Coming True at Last!

¹⁴Then Peter got up, with the eleven. He spoke to them in a loud voice.

'People of Judaea!' he began. 'All of you who live in Jerusalem! There's something you have to know! Listen to what I'm saying! ¹⁵These people aren't drunk, as you imagine. It's only nine o'clock in the morning! ¹⁶No, this is what the prophet Joel was talking about, when he said,

¹⁷In the last days, declares God, I will pour out my spirit on all people.
Your sons and your daughters will prophesy;
Your young men will see visions, your old men will dream dreams;
¹⁸Yes, even on slaves, men and women alike, will I pour out my spirit in those days, and they shall prophesy.
¹⁹And I will give signs in the heavens above, and portents on earth beneath,
blood and fire and clouds of smoke.
²⁰The sun will be turned into darkness, and the moon into blood,
before the day of the Lord comes, the great and glorious day.
²¹And then everyone who calls on the name of the Lord will be saved.'

We don't always plan our holidays very carefully, but on this occasion we had. We had read the brochures. We had worked through the alternative places to stay. We had looked at the special things we could do when we got there. And, in particular, we had planned the travel.

Or so we thought. Of course, once you set off on a journey involving trains and planes and buses and cars, there are many hidden snags. We got to the airport all right, but the flight was delayed, and we spent half a day playing cards in the airport lounge. Then we had to get a different train at the other end, going a different route. It was dark by the time we reached . . . but was this our destination? Was it the right town, the right station? How would we know? It didn't look like we'd thought it would.

Then, a sigh of relief. There, just as we had been told weeks before, was the man with the sign, collecting us tired stragglers and putting us on the bus to the hotel. We had arrived. It was the end of the journey; the promises had come true; now the holiday could really begin.

Project the journey on to a larger timescale, 2,000 years long. And, instead of a holiday, imagine a moment, long promised, dreamed of, planned for, mulled over, prayed for, ached for, agonized over: a moment when things would work out right at last, when hopes would be realized and good times would begin. A moment when a huge sigh of relief would give way to a huge sense of new possibilities: now, at last, things could really start!

That is how the Jews of the first century read their scriptures. They saw themselves as the generation for whom it should all come true. In the book of Daniel, one of the Old Testament books people studied most carefully in the first century, there was a prophecy of an exile that would last for 490 years, starting with the Babylonian **exile**. And the Babylonian exile had taken place . . . well, somewhere between 400 and 500 years before, depending on how you calculated it (and plenty of people did it different ways). That was, if you like, the travel brochure that kept them moving forwards: if only they kept going long enough, they would surely, eventually, arrive at the destination! But at the same time they studied, memorized, prayed over and puzzled over many other old texts, texts which spoke of terrible things that would happen but of a time when it would all be reversed, when God would bring them to a new place and do quite new things with them. And some of the texts spoke of the signs that they would see when they arrived at that new moment, the signals that would say, 'You're here! This is where you were going!'

It's only by imagining that world, a world where people were puzzling and praying over ancient texts to try to find urgently needed meanings in times of great stress and sorrow, that we can understand how Peter could even think of launching in to a great long quotation from the prophet Joel in order to explain the apparently confused babbling and shouting that was going on. If I was asked by a crowd to explain why my friends and I appeared to be behaving in a drunken fashion I don't somehow think I would at once start quoting chunks of the Bible, even the New Testament. But Jerusalem was full of people who were eager for signs that maybe the people of Israel had at last arrived at their destination, even if it didn't look like they thought it was going to do. Yes, says Peter. We've got to the point where all that the brochures said is starting to come true. These are indeed 'the **last days**'.

What did that mean, 'the last days'? It was a general term for the time to come, the time when promises would be fulfilled. The story would arrive at its climax, the journey would reach its destination, and so all sorts of new things would start to happen. So what Peter was offering wasn't simply an explanation for strange behaviour, even for strange religious phenomena (always a dangerous thing in a crowded city at the time of a big religious and national festival). It was a challenge: we've arrived! The journey's over! Here are the signs of the destination! Time to have a fresh look around and see where we are!

But, though Peter declares that these are indeed 'the last days' which the prophet Joel had spoken of, they are not 'the last day' itself. There remains another 'day' (not necessarily a period of 24 hours, but 'a moment', 'a coming time') which the prophets referred to as 'the day of the Lord'. (We remind ourselves that 'the Lord' is the way they would speak to avoid saying the name of Israel's covenant God, YHWH.) The early Christians, breathtakingly, took that idea of 'the day of the Lord', and went on using it – only now with 'the Lord' referring to Jesus. They seem to have made this transition apparently without effort or problem, as we can see frequently in Paul and elsewhere. The early Christians believed, in other words, that they were living in a period of time between the moment when 'the last days' had been launched and the moment when even those 'last days' would come to an end on 'the day of the Lord', the moment when, with Jesus' final reappearance (already promised in Acts 1.11), **heaven** and earth would be joined together in the great coming renewal of all things (see 3.21).

In the light of this hope, we shouldn't be surprised that among the signs of things coming true there would be 'signs in heaven and earth'. But nor should we imagine that people in the first century would necessarily have taken these, as we say, 'literally'. Mention of 'blood, and fire, and clouds of smoke', and of 'the sun being turned into darkness and the moon into blood' could refer to a great eclipse or other natural phenomena. But those who were used to the language of biblical prophecy knew well enough that these were regular ways of referring to what we would call 'earth-shattering' events, things in society and global politics that would shake to the foundations what we call 'the fabric of society'. Terrifying times, in other words; times of great instability and uncertainty.

But the prophet didn't just warn of times of fear and trembling. Part of the point of 'the last days' was that they were the time of new creation – and the new creation would start with God's own people! This is where the quotation from Joel functions as a direct explanation of the otherwise bizarre behaviour of the **apostles**, shouting out in several different languages the powerful things that God had done. Peter connects it directly with the promise of Joel that God would pour out his **spirit** in a new way. Up to this moment, God has acted by his spirit among his people, but it's always been by inspiring one person here, one or two there – kings and prophets and **priests** and righteous men and women. Now, in a sudden burst of fresh divine energy released through the death and **resurrection** of Jesus, God's spirit has been poured out upon a lot of people all at once. There is no discrimination between slaves and free, male and female, young and old. They are all marked out, side by side, as the nucleus of God's true people.

This itself is striking, when you think about it. If the prophecies of Joel are coming true, the spirit is available for all God's people . . . so why is the spirit not being poured out on the chief priests, on the official religious leaders and teachers? The answer, as politically uncomfortable in the first century as anywhere else, is that the spirit seems to be indicating that the work of new creation is beginning here, in this upper room, where Jesus' friends and family have gathered: not in the Temple, not in the rabbinic schools, not in the back rooms where the revolutionaries plot violence, but here, where those who had been with Jesus, and had seen him alive again after his resurrection, find themselves overwhelmed with the fresh wind of the spirit and unable to stop speaking about what they have seen and heard.

This work of God is wonderfully inclusive, because there is no category of people which is left out: both genders, all ages, all social classes. But it is wonderfully focused, because it happens to all 'who call on the name of the Lord' (verse 21). Here, once more, 'the Lord', which in Joel meant Israel's God, YHWH, now seems to mean Jesus himself. And with this Luke introduces a vital and complex theme in his work: '**salvation**'. All who call on the Lord's name will be *saved*.

'Being saved' doesn't just mean, as it does for many today, 'going to heaven when they die'. It means 'knowing God's rescuing power, the power revealed in Jesus, which anticipates, in the present, God's final great act of deliverance'. Peter will now go on to encourage his hearers to 'call on the Lord's name', and so to know that 'salvation', that rescue, as a present reality as well as a future hope. If these really are 'the last days', then 'salvation' has already begun. Anyone who knows they need rescuing, whatever from, can 'call on the Lord' and discover how it can happen.

ACTS 2.22–36

David Speaks of Jesus' Resurrection

[22]'You people of Israel,' Peter continued, 'listen to this. Jesus of Nazareth was a man marked out for you by God through the mighty works, signs and portents which God performed through him right here among you, as you all know. [23]He was handed over in accordance with God's determined purpose and foreknowledge – and you used people outside the law to nail him up and kill him.

[24]'But God raised him from the dead! Death had its painful grip on him; but God released him from it, because it wasn't possible for him to be mastered by it. [25]This, you see, is how David speaks of him:

'I set the Lord before me always;
Because he is at my right hand, I won't be shaken.
[26]So my heart was happy, and my tongue rejoiced,
And my flesh, too, will rest in hope.
[27]For you did not leave my soul in Hades,
Nor did you allow your Holy One to see corruption.
[28]You showed me the path of life,
You filled me with gladness in your presence.

[29]'My dear family, I can surely speak freely to you about the patriarch David. He died and was buried, and his tomb is here with us to this day. [30]He was of course a prophet, and he knew that God had sworn an oath to him to set one of his own physical offspring on his throne. [31]He foresaw the Messiah's resurrection, and spoke about him 'not being left in Hades', and about his flesh 'not seeing corruption'. [32]This is the Jesus we're talking about! God raised him from the dead, and all of us here are witnesses to the fact! [33]Now he's been exalted to God's right hand; and what you see and hear is the result of the fact that he is pouring out the holy spirit, which had been promised, and which he has received from the Father.

[34]'David, after all, did not ascend into the heavens. This is what he says:

'The Lord said to my Lord,
Sit at my right hand,

³⁵Until I place your enemies
Underneath your feet.

³⁶'So the whole house of Israel must know this for a fact:
God has made him Lord and Messiah – this Jesus, the one you
crucified.'

I watched the Press Gallery during the speech. For most of the
time, the journalists looked bored. One was sharpening his
pencil; another was varnishing her nails. Then, quite suddenly,
all that changed. Notebooks were seized, shorthand phrases
flew onto the paper. One began sending text messages back to
base. The speech which, up to that point, had been important
but not that important, had instantly turned into something
that would make tomorrow's headlines. The speaker had suddenly given a broad hint that he wasn't just commenting about
important issues that were happening that day. He was launching his campaign to be leader of his party, which meant he
hoped to be Prime Minister within the next year or two.

That is the impression we get from the move which Peter
makes at this point in his speech. Up to now, he has been
showing that the extraordinary phenomenon of the wind, the
fire and the babbling tongues are best explained by claiming
that the '**last days**' have arrived, the time which the prophet
Joel had spoken of. But now he changes tack. The reason the
'last days' are here is because of the **resurrection** of Jesus, nothing more nor less. But the resurrection of Jesus demands to be
explained, not as an odd, isolated '**miracle**', as though God suddenly thought of doing something totally bizarre to show how
powerful he is. The resurrection of Jesus is best explained as
the fulfilment of specific promises made by God through King
David. And they show that the one who has been raised from
the dead is the true son and heir of David. He, in other words,
is *the rightful king of Israel*. This is the point where the journalists go scurrying off to file their reports: revolution is in the
air!

Note how Luke insists that, for him as for all the early Christians, 'resurrection' wasn't about a disembodied spirit going off

to **heaven**, leaving a body behind in a tomb. That is precisely what the word 'resurrection' did *not* mean. 'Resurrection' was and is about a physical body being very thoroughly dead, but then being very thoroughly alive again, so that the normal corruption and decay which follows death wouldn't even begin. This point is made graphically through Peter's quoting from Psalm 16 in verses 25–28, and returning to it again in verse 31. The Psalm – which both Luke and Peter take as having been written by David himself – speaks of a 'way of life' in which one who dies will not be abandoned, and will not suffer the usual fate of the dissolution of the flesh. Instead, because of God's utter and faithful reliability, the person in question will somehow come through death and out the other side.

Now, says Peter to rub the point in (verses 29 and 30): we know that David cannot have been referring to himself when he wrote this. After all, he died and was buried, and his flesh decayed and corrupted in the normal way. The only sense we can make of the Psalm is to read it prophetically; that is, to see it as expressing a deep 'Davidic' truth which would remain mysterious until, one day, a **son of David** would appear to whom it would actually happen. Then we would know that he was the one in whom the strange, dark prophecies had come true. Then we would know that 'the last days' had indeed arrived. *And then we would know that he was indeed the rightful king.* Peter has worked back, from the babbling of tongues being a sign of 'the last days' and the outpouring of God's **spirit**, to the resurrection of Jesus as the sure and certain sign that he is the **Messiah**, the one Israel had been waiting for.

He ties the two points together in verse 33. Jesus has now been exalted at God's right hand (as in Daniel 7, and as in Psalm 110, which he is about to quote). That is why he has been able to pour out the holy spirit with such dramatic effect. The extraordinary phenomena of Pentecost were the signpost. But Easter was the reality to which they pointed. And the meaning of Easter is: 'God has made this Jesus, whom you crucified, both Lord and Messiah.'

What does the word 'Lord' add to 'Messiah'? It seems to refer to Psalm 110, quoted in verses 34 and 35: 'The Lord said to my

Lord, sit at my right hand, until I place your enemies under-neath your feet.' Here, as in several 'messianic' Psalms, we find that Israel's true king is the world's true Lord; that's how the logic of messiahship, if we can put it like that, works out. Israel is God's chosen people for the sake of the world; so Israel's true and final king, when he arrives, will be the world's rightful sovereign. The early Christians, following Jesus him-self (see Luke 20.41–44), went back to Psalm 110 again and again to make this point. They saw it tying together Jesus' Davidic ancestry with God's fresh action in raising and exalt-ing him, and thus declaring him to be the true Messiah. And they saw in this Psalm, too, the massive sense, looming up behind even the exalted title of Messiah, that in Jesus they had been looking at the human face of God himself.

It is only in the light of this that we can begin to understand verse 27, which summarizes, in a sharp and difficult way, the point of view of the whole New Testament. On the one hand, Jesus' shameful and horrible death was the act of wicked, unscrupulous, lawless people. The leaders of the Jewish people had handed Jesus over to the pagans, in full knowledge of the brutally effective torture and death they would inflict on him. At every stage of the process – Judas' betrayal, Peter's denial, the trumped-up charge, the kangaroo court, the cynicism of the Jewish leaders, Pilate's vacillation, cowardice and indiffer-ence to justice, the crowd baying for blood, the mocking of the soldiers and one at least of those crucified alongside him – Jesus' path to his death had been marked by all kinds of evil, doing its worst to him. But the early Christians quickly came to see, in the light of the resurrection and the gift of the spirit, that even this, all this, was what Israel's God, the creator God, had determined must take place.

God's plan of salvation, Peter is saying, was always intended to reach its climax with Israel's Messiah undertaking his ultim-ate rescuing task. The anointed king would come to the place where evil was reaching its height, where the greatest human systems would reveal their greatest corruption (Rome, with its much-vaunted system of justice revealing itself rotten at the core; Israel, with its celebrated Temple and hierarchy, revealing itself hollow at its heart), and where this accumulated evil would blow itself out in one great act of unwarranted violence against the person who, of all, had done nothing to deserve it. That, the early Christians believed, was what God had always intended.

Acts does not, at this point, offer a developed 'theology of the cross' such as we find in Paul, Hebrews and other writers later on. What it does is simply to say: (a) God intended Jesus to die as the climax of his rescue operation; (b) the intentions and actions that sent Jesus to his death were desperately wicked. This doesn't for a moment justify the wickedness. Rather, it declares that God, knowing how powerful that wickedness was, had long planned to nullify its power by taking its full force *upon himself, in the person of his Messiah, the man in whom God himself would be embodied.*

There is much, much more to be said about the meaning of the cross than this. Acts will introduce it step by step. But this is a powerful point to begin with. Peter has launched the early Christians on a double collision course with the authorities. Jesus is the true King, which means that his followers need no longer regard the current authorities as absolute. What is more, the authorities themselves were responsible, along with the pagans, for Jesus' death. Their power was called into question: all they could do now would be to repent.

That is, of course, the call to all who have bought into, and perpetrated, systems of evil. The **good news**, the great news, of Jesus is that with his resurrection it becomes clear not only that he is Messiah and Lord, but that in his death he has dealt evil itself a blow from which, though it still retains some real power, it will never recover.

ACTS 2.37–41

God's Rescue Plan

[37]When they heard this, the crowd were cut to the heart.

'Brothers,' they said to Peter and the other apostles, 'what shall we do?'

> [38]'Turn back!' replied Peter. 'Be baptized – every single one of you – in the name of Jesus the Messiah, so that your sins can be forgiven, and you will receive the gift of the holy spirit. [39]The promise is for you and for your children, and for everyone who is far away, as many as the Lord our God will call.'
>
> [40]He carried on explaining things to them with many other words.
>
> 'Let God rescue you', he was urging them, 'from this wicked generation!'
>
> [41]They welcomed his word and were baptized. About three thousand people were added to the community that day.

It's one thing to discover you are driving along the wrong road. It may be frustrating, and even embarrassing if you have people in the car who thought you knew where you were going. But you can at least admit the mistake, turn round and set off again, this time in the right direction.

But it's quite another thing if you are sliding down a steep slope – say, on a toboggan, or on skis, or (as we sometimes used to do) on tin trays over grass – and suddenly realize you are heading for a sheer drop. You seem to be accelerating towards it, and the slope is too steep for you to check your speed, let alone to stop, turn round, and go back up again out of danger. What are you going to do?

The answer may well be that there's nothing you can do. You need to be rescued.

You need, in fact, someone to stand in the way: someone who has managed to get a fixed foothold on the slope, and who will catch you, stop you, and help you to safety. And if you were lucky enough to see someone offering to do that, you'd have to steer towards them and be ready for the shock of a sudden stop. Better that than plunging over a cliff.

The key thing to realize, in reading the early chapters of Acts, is that Jesus himself had warned his fellow Jews that they were precisely in danger of accelerating towards a cliff. If you read Luke's **gospel** straight through, you will notice how the warnings which Jesus gave seem to increase in quantity and volume all the way to chapters 19, 20 and 21, where he solemnly declares that if the nation as a whole, and the city of

40

Jerusalem in particular, don't stop their headlong flight into ruin, their enemies will come and destroy them. The warnings are very specific. Israel (so Jesus declares) has bought into a way of life which is directly opposite to what God wants: a way which ignores the plight of the poor, which embraces violence, which denies God's call to his people to become the light of the world. Again and again Jesus warns, 'If you don't turn back, you're heading for disaster' (Luke 13.5). When he arrives in Jerusalem he bursts into tears as he describes, in a prophetic vision, a great military force laying siege to the city and leaving no stone on top of another. This will happen, he says, 'because you didn't know the way of peace', and 'because you didn't realize that God was visiting you' (Luke 19.41–44).

But then we watch in amazement – horror, even – at a new twist in the plot. Jesus has announced God's judgment on the nation that has gone its own way, the way of violence. But then we realize that Jesus himself has, again and again, taken Israel's identity upon himself. He is the representative Israelite, the **Messiah** who sums up his people in himself. And we realize that he believes it's his calling to go to the place where the judgment is about to fall on rebellious Israel, and to take that judgment – the one he himself had announced – onto himself. He speaks of himself as the 'green tree', the one you wouldn't expect to see thrown onto the fire, while all around him are the dry twigs ready for burning (Luke 23.31). He warns that, though he is bearing Israel's judgment, dying on a charge of which he was innocent but thousands around him were guilty (Luke 23.2–5, 18–25), those who nevertheless persisted in their headlong rush towards the sheer drop of violence would reap the consequences.

And, of course, when the crowds, the chief **priests** and the other leaders rejected Jesus at that Passover, Jesus himself saw that as the culmination of their rejection of his way of peace, his **kingdom**-way, the way he had been urging them to follow all along. It wasn't that their sending of Jesus to his death was an isolated act of folly or sin. It was the symptom of their rejection of God's way. It was the sign of what Jesus had said many times: this generation is wicked and corrupt, heading for disaster.

41

But now, with Jesus' **resurrection**, Peter and the others can unpack the meaning of the crucifixion for the benefit of the crowds. This is, perhaps, the first beginning, the first small glimpse, of the church's developing understanding of the purpose of the cross. That understanding doesn't begin as an abstract theory about 'sin' or 'judgment'. It begins as the very concrete and specific awareness: 'this corrupt generation' is heading for disaster, but Jesus stands in the way and can stop them from falling over the cliff. The message is then clear: 'Be rescued' – in other words, let God rescue you, let Jesus rescue you – from the ruin that will come upon the city and the nation, not as a specific punishment for rejecting Jesus, but as the necessary consequence of that entire way of life of which rejecting Jesus was a key, telltale sign.

But how do you steer towards Jesus? How does he catch you, stop you, and rescue you? Peter and the others are quite clear – and the message of the Christian gospel fans out from this point to all people and all times. You need to turn back. But the way to do that is to become part of the kingdom-movement that is identified with Jesus, part of the people who claim his life, death and resurrection as the centre and foundation of their own. You need, in other words, to be baptized, to join the company marked out with the sign of the 'new **exodus**', coming through the water to leave behind slavery and sin and to find the way to freedom and **life**. You need to allow Jesus himself to grasp hold of you, to save you from the consequences of the way you were going ('**forgiveness** of sins') and to give you new energy to go in the right way instead ('the gift of the **holy spirit**'). To do all that is to 'turn back' from the way you were going, and to go in the other direction instead. That is what is meant by the word 'repent'.

All this was very concrete and specific for the crowd in Jerusalem on that first Pentecost. Join this movement, allow the death and resurrection of Jesus to become the badge you wear, the sign of your identity, with you and your children (verse 39) sharing in the new life of the baptized community, the life which has the stamp of Jesus upon it, the life which is defined in terms of turning away from the course you were on and embracing Jesus' way instead. And, though circumstances change, we can see how the same **message** translates without difficulty to everyone in every society and at every moment in time. 'The promise is for you, and for your children, *and for everyone who is far away, as many as the Lord our God will call.*' That means all the rest of us.

What we are witnessing, in this passage, is the beginning of the Christian theme called '**salvation**'. It isn't simply about 'going to **heaven**', though of course it includes the promise, not only of heaven after death but, beyond that, of resurrection into God's new creation. 'Salvation' is therefore pointing towards a very concrete and particular reality in the future. If God's ultimate intention was to 'save' only disembodied '**souls**', that wouldn't be *rescue from* death. It would simply allow the death of the body to have the last word. 'Salvation' regularly refers constantly, not least in Luke and Acts, to specific acts of 'rescue' within the present life: being 'saved' from *this* potential disaster, here and now.

That, of course, is something Luke stresses throughout his work. What God has promised for the ultimate future has come forward to meet us in Jesus Christ. We should expect signs of that future to appear in the present. And, whenever we are in a mess, of whatever sort and for whatever reason, we should remember this: we are 'turn-back-and-be-rescued' people. We are 'repent-and-be-baptized' people. We have the right, the birthright, to cash in that promise at any place and any time.

No wonder 3,000 people signed up that very day.

ACTS 2.42–47

The New Family

[42]They all gave full attention to the teaching of the apostles and to the common life, to the breaking of bread and the prayers. [43]Great awe fell on everyone, and many remarkable deeds and signs were performed by the apostles.

[44]All of those who believed came together, and held everything in common. [45]They sold their possessions and belongings and divided them up to everyone who was in need. [46]Day by

day they were all together attending the Temple. They broke bread in their various houses, and ate their food with glad and sincere hearts, 47praising God and standing in favour with all the people. And every day the Lord added to their number those who were being rescued.

A couple of years ago I took part in a charity walk. It was a sunny day, there were thousands of people taking part, and we went through some breathtaking scenery. We were put in several groups, with a few hundred setting off every few minutes. I was in the first group, and it was enormously exciting; though it wasn't a race, there was a sense of trailblazing, of leading the way for thousands to follow. We went off at a cracking pace, too fast perhaps but thoroughly enjoying ourselves.

It was only after a couple of miles that those of us in the leading pack paused for breath. We knew we were more or less on the right track, but it was as well to be sure. Yes, there were the landmarks: the river, the hill, the wood behind the village. And there, up ahead, was a tiny flag fluttering in the breeze. A moment's pause, admiring the view, allowing some others to catch up, and then off we went again.

That is the mood Luke creates at the end of chapter 2. His book has got off to a flying start, with the extraordinary conversation between the risen Jesus and the **apostles**, and then the spectacular events of the **day of Pentecost**. Peter's address to the puzzled crowds, the first public statement of the **good news** about Jesus and his **resurrection** and about God's rescue operation through him, now in full swing, is dramatic, full of energy and possibility and hope. And now, at the end of that first Pentecost, we pause for breath, look around, and see where we've got to.

Luke is careful to point out the landmarks. In fact, Acts 2.42 is often regarded as laying down 'the four marks of the church'. The apostles' teaching; the common life of those who believed; the breaking of bread; and the prayers. These four go together. You can't separate them, or leave one out, without damage to the whole thing. Where no attention is given to teaching, and to constant, lifelong Christian learning, people quickly revert to the worldview or mindset of the surrounding culture, and end up with their minds shaped by whichever social pressures are most persuasive, with Jesus somewhere around as a pale influence or memory. Where people ignore the common life of the Christian family (the technical term often used is '**fellowship**', which is more than friendship but not less), they become isolated, and often find it difficult to sustain a living **faith**. Where people no longer share regularly in 'the breaking of bread' (the early Christian term for the simple meal that took them back to the Upper Room 'in remembrance of Jesus'), they are failing to raise the flag which says 'Jesus' death and resurrection are the centre of everything' (see 1 Corinthians 11.26). And whenever people do all these things but neglect prayer, they are quite simply forgetting that Christians are supposed to be **heaven**-and-earth people. Prayer makes no sense whatever – unless heaven and earth are designed to be joined together, and we can share in that already.

Those of us who grew up in Christian families, with 'going to church' as a habit of life from our earliest days, may sometimes think of all this as quite humdrum and ordinary. In some churches, of course, it does feel that way. But imagine a world without this astonishing teaching! Imagine a society where there was no 'common life' built around a shared belief in Jesus! Imagine a world without 'the bread-breaking', or a world without prayer! Life would be bleak indeed – as it often is for many people, not least those who embrace a relentlessly secularist lifestyle, shutting the door on any of these possibilities. And if you lived in such a world, and then suddenly found yourself swept up in this pattern of teaching, fellowship, bread-breaking and prayer, you would know that new dimensions had opened up before you, and new vistas of how the world might be had suddenly become visible. You would be awestruck. That, says Luke, is how it was at the beginning (verse 43). And that awe was only increased as the power of the **spirit** was at work through the apostles, as it had been with Jesus, power to heal and transform people's lives.

This shared life quickly developed in one particular direction, which is both fascinating and controversial. The earliest

45

Christians lived *as a single family*. When you live together as a family under one roof, you don't see *this* chair, *this* table, *this* bottle of milk, *this* loaf of bread, as 'mine' rather than 'yours'. The breadwinners in the household don't see the money they bring in as 'theirs' rather than belonging to the whole household. That's part of what it means to be a family. In the ancient world this was often highlighted by members of a family all working in the same trade or business together, so that you might have three generations, including cousins, working alongside one another, trusting each other, sharing a common purse out of which everyone got what they needed.

The early Christian impulse was to see things exactly like that. We are 'family'! We are brothers and sisters! Our **baptism**, our shared faith, our fellowship at 'the bread-breaking', all point in this direction. When the **Twelve** (with their larger company of friends and followers, as in Luke 8.1–3) were going about with Jesus, they had a common purse; various people contributed to it out of their resources; they behaved as a single family. How do you continue with that when, quite suddenly, several thousand join the movement?

With difficulty, it seems. But they were determined to do it. Not to do it would be to deny something basic about who they were. (They didn't, at this stage, seem to have a word for 'who they were'; that developed gradually, as we shall see; but they were, at least, 'the people who had been with Jesus' (4.13), 'the people who bore witness to his resurrection', 'the people who were filled with the holy spirit', 'those who believed' (verse 44), 'those who were being rescued' (verse 47).) They seem not to have sold the houses in which they lived, since they went on meeting in individual houses (verse 46). Rather, they sold extra property they possessed – a highly significant thing for a people for whom land was not just an economic asset but part of their ancestral heritage, part of God's promised inheritance.

And they had a word for this way of ordering their life, a word which we have often taken to refer to feelings inside you but which, for them, was primarily about what you do with your possessions when you're part of this big, extended family. The word is 'love', *agapē* in Greek. When Paul tells the

Thessalonians that, since they already love one another, they must do so more and more, he doesn't primarily mean that since they already have warm feelings for one another, they must have even warmer ones. He means that, since they already care practically for one another, they must work at making that more and more of a reality (1 Thessalonians 4.9–12). The challenge remains for every generation in the church, especially now that Jesus' followers number several million all around the world. Many Christians and agencies give themselves tirelessly to the work of making this practical sharing of resources a reality in all the complexities of our contemporary world.

When Jesus' followers behave like this, they sometimes find, to their surprise, that they have a new spring in their step. There is an attractiveness, an energy about a life in which we stop clinging on to everything we can get and start sharing it, giving it away, celebrating God's generosity by being generous ourselves. And that attractiveness is one of the things that draws other people in. They were praising God, says Luke (verse 47), and stood in favour with the people; and day by day the Lord was adding to their number those who were being rescued. Of course they were, and of course he did. That's how it works. Where the church today finds itself stagnant, unattractive, humdrum and shrinking – and, sadly, there are many churches, in the Western world at least, of which that has to be admitted – it's time to read Acts 2.42–47 again, get down on our knees, and ask what isn't happening that should be happening. The **gospel** hasn't changed. God's power hasn't diminished. People still need rescuing. What are we doing about it?

ACTS 3.1–10

More than He Bargained for

¹One day, Peter and John were going up to the Temple around three o'clock in the afternoon. ²There was a man being carried in who had been lame since birth. People used to bring him every day to the Temple gate called 'Beautiful', so that he could ask for alms from folk on their way in to the Temple. ³When he

saw Peter and John going in to the Temple, he asked them to give him some money. [4]Peter, with John, looked hard at him.

'Look at us,' he said.

[5]The man stared at them, expecting to get something from them.

[6]'I haven't got any silver or gold', Peter said, 'but I'll give you what I have got. In the name of the Messiah, Jesus of Nazareth, get up and walk!'

[7]He grabbed the man by his right hand and lifted him up. At once his feet and ankles became strong, [8]and he leaped to his feet and began to walk. He went in with them into the Temple, walking and jumping up and down and praising God. [9]All the people saw him walking and praising God, [10]and they knew that he was the man who had been sitting begging for alms by the Beautiful Gate of the Temple. They were filled with amazement and astonishment at what had happened to him.

There was once a young man who sneaked into church hoping nobody would notice him. The only reason he'd come was because he was keen on a girl who sang in the choir, and he hoped that if he was in the service he'd be able to see her at the end of the service and ask her out. He wasn't quite sure what to do, but he saw people going in and sitting down, so he did the same. Just as the service was beginning, an usher came up to him.

'Excuse me,' he said. 'The person who's supposed to do the reading hasn't turned up. Could you possibly do it?'

The young man was horrified for a moment, but then thought quickly. The girl he had his eye on was there, in the choir. She would be most impressed if she heard him reading in the service.

'All right,' he said. He took the Bible and looked through the reading the usher had showed him.

It came to the moment. He went up, opened the Bible, and began to read. It was from John's **gospel** and he vaguely recognized it.

'Anyone who doesn't enter the sheepfold by the gate,' he heard his own voice say, 'but climbs in by another way, is a thief and a bandit.'

He was thunderstruck. This was what he'd done! He was standing here, pretending to be a regular Bible-reader, when in fact he'd only come in to meet a girl. He forced himself to go on, aware of his heart beating loudly. If he was a bandit, coming in under false pretences, what was the alternative?

'I am the gate for the sheep,' said Jesus. 'The bandit only comes to steal, kill and destroy. I came that they might have life, and have it full to overflowing.'

Suddenly, something happened inside the young man. He stopped thinking about himself. He stopped thinking about the girl, about the congregation, about the fact that he'd just done a ridiculous and hypocritical thing. He thought about Jesus. Unaware of the shock he was causing, he swung round to the clergyman leading the service.

'Is it true?' he asked. 'Did he really come so that we could have real life, full life like that?'

The clergyman smiled.

'Of course it is,' he replied, quite unfazed by this non-liturgical outburst. 'That's why we're all here. Come and join in this next song and see what happens if you really mean it.'

And the young man found himself swept off his feet by the presence and the love of Jesus, filling him, changing him, calling him to follow, like a grateful sheep, after the shepherd who can be trusted to lead the way to good pasture by day and safe rest at night. He got more, much more, than he bargained for.

Something like that happened to the man who was sitting by the Beautiful Gate of the Temple in Jerusalem. You can see similar sights in many parts of the world today, not least in the Middle East. People often sit or stand in the same place each day, begging from passers-by. If you go that way, you get to know them. In the Fall of 1999 I taught at Harvard, and walked most days through Harvard Square past two or three beggars who each had their own regular pitch. Sometimes I gave them money. About five years later I went back for a short visit, and walked down the same street. They were still there; I suppose I shouldn't have been surprised.

Certainly the people who went into the Temple by that gate day after day and week after week wouldn't have been surprised to see the cripple. His friends brought him there every day. He would beg what he could, and at night they would take him back home.

So his request to Peter and John was what he asked everybody, every hour of every day. 'Have pity on me! Have pity on me!' – in other words, 'Give me some money!'

And of course he got far more than he bargained for. Peter's response is all the more interesting in view of what we heard at the end of the previous chapter about the believers sharing their property. Money had stopped being the most important thing for them. There was a new power, a new kind of life, which they had discovered. So what Peter said was the natural response. He didn't have any money, but he had something much better, something of a different order entirely. He didn't even ask the lame man if he would like to be healed. He just went ahead and healed him in the name of Jesus.

This story is the first occurrence in Acts of two interesting phenomena. First, Luke emphasizes that Peter and John looked hard at the man. They stared intently at him. What were they looking for? A sincere spirit, ready to receive more than he'd asked for? A heart full of pain and sorrow, ready to be touched by God's healing love? Somehow there is something important about that deep, face-to-face contact: not only did Peter and John stare at him, but they told him to look hard at them, too. No good turning your face away in embarrassment, as often happens with beggars who are ashamed to catch your eye, and of passers-by who are equally ashamed to look at beggars. What is about to happen is something that involves a deep human contact as well as a deep work of God.

Second, what Peter says will resonate through the next chapters and on into the wider story which Luke is telling. He doesn't just say, 'Stand up and walk', as Jesus himself would probably have done. He makes it quite clear where the healing power resides.

'In the name of the **Messiah**, Jesus of Nazareth,' he says, 'get up and walk!'

It is the power of the name of Jesus that counts, here and everywhere. The idea of names having power is strange to those of us who live in the modern Western world (though we sometimes catch a dim echo of it when some important person, a civic or business leader, or perhaps a senior politician, says, 'Just mention my name and they'll let you in'). But most people in the first-century world, and many people in non-Western countries today, know exactly what's going on here. Of course names carry power: the power of magic, the invocation of hidden forces, the summoning up of new possibilities beyond normal human ability. And the point which resonates through the narrative from now on is this: the name 'Jesus' now carries that power. Mention his name, and new things will happen. This is as true now as ever it was. In this story, it turned a cripple who sat outside the Temple into a worshipper who went all the way in. There's something to ponder.

This points us to something else that's going on here. Up to now, in Acts, the whole story has taken place in Jerusalem, but

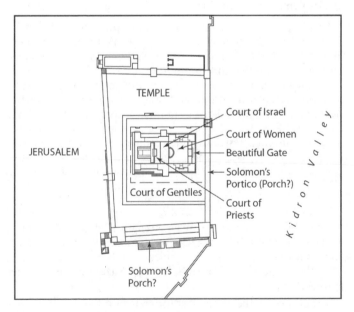

Acts 3.1–10, 11–16

not in or around the Temple. Now we find that the believers were regularly going to worship in the Temple, even though (as we saw at the end of the previous chapter) the most important things they did (their teaching, **fellowship**, bread-breaking and prayer) happened elsewhere. But the demonstration of the power of Jesus' name took place, not in the Temple, but outside the gate. God is on the move, not confined within the institution, breaking out into new worlds, leaving behind the shrine which had become a place of worldly power and resistance to his purposes. This theme will come to a head four chapters from now. Whereas Luke's **gospel** began and ended in the Temple, what he is telling us now is that the good news of Jesus, though beginning in Jerusalem, is starting to reach outside to anyone and everyone who needs it.

ACTS 3.11–16

An Explanation is Called for

[11]All the people ran together in astonishment towards Peter and John, and the man who was clinging onto them. They were in the part of the Temple known as 'Solomon's Porch'. [12]Peter saw them all and began to speak.

'Fellow Israelites', he said, 'why are you amazed at this? Why are you staring at us as though it was our own power or piety that made this man walk? [13]"The God of Abraham, the God of Isaac, the God of Jacob – the God of our ancestors" – he has glorified his child Jesus, the one you handed over and denied in the presence of Pilate, although he had decided to let him go. [14]But you denied the Holy One, the Just One, and requested instead to have a murderer given to you; [15]and so you killed the Prince of Life. But God raised him from the dead, and we are witnesses to the fact. [16]And it is his name, working through faith in his name, that has given strength to this man, whom you see and know. It is faith which comes through him that has given him this new complete wholeness in front of all of you.'

'How did you do that?'

I stood beside the car as it spluttered into life. I had fiddled and jiggled with everything I could, and hadn't been able to make it start. (This, I should say, was a long time ago, in the days when you could poke around in car engines more easily than you can today.) My next-door neighbour, who was coming by, had offered to lend a hand. He had leant over the engine, done something I couldn't see, and suddenly the car had come back to life.

'Oh,' he said, 'don't thank me. It's a trick I learned from Jim down at the garage. He got fed up with me asking him what was wrong with my car and he showed me one of the most common faults and the easy way to sort it out.'

Now of course a crippled man isn't the same as a lifeless car engine. And the healing power of the name of Jesus isn't the same as a trick you learned in a garage. But the underlying point is still valid: it isn't that Peter or John were anyone special, just as it wasn't that my friend was a trained or clever mechanic. He simply trusted someone who knew how, who did have the power to make things happen. Peter and John, surrounded by an amazed crowd, were able to say the same.

'It wasn't us; it was Jesus!'

Or rather, it was the God who was at work in and through Jesus and is at work through him still. Peter, launching into an impromptu address, and eager perhaps to deflect attention from himself in such a prominent place as the **Temple** (where Jesus himself had taught great crowds only a few weeks before), takes care to refer to God in rather a dramatic, almost formal way: 'The God of Abraham, of Isaac, and of Jacob – the God of our ancestors.' Why does he do it like that?

This way of referring to God is actually a quotation. It comes from the book of Exodus (3.6). It's a famous passage, and Peter and his hearers would know it and would understand the point of the reference. Jesus himself had quoted it when debating with the **Sadducees** in the Temple a few weeks earlier (Luke 20.37), and he certainly intended that people should pick up the whole context of the passage. The point is this: Exodus 3 is the moment when God calls Moses, at the burning bush, and tells him to go back from the desert into Egypt and to lead his people out from slavery into freedom. God assures Moses that this isn't just some odd experience he's having; this really is Israel's God speaking, Abraham's God, the God who made promises to the ancestors of the presently enslaved Israelites and is now about to make those promises come true. Peter, quoting this passage, is saying, 'It's happening again!'

Peter, in other words, is doing what all the early Christians did all the time. Faced with a question to which the answer is something to do with Jesus, he goes back in his mind to the **Exodus**. That was when God acted spectacularly to fulfil his promises and rescue his people. That was when they **sacrificed** the Passover lamb, when they came through the water, when they were given the **law**, when they went off in search of their inheritance. All these themes jostle together in the New Testament, clustering around the question of who Jesus is and how it is that God acts through him. And, again and again, we get the sense: when we look at Jesus, and see what happens through his name, it is as though, like Moses, we are standing by the burning bush, seeing something spectacular, which ought to say to us that the creator God, the God of Abraham, is living and active and keeping his promises once again.

In particular, this sets Peter up to say some extraordinary things about Jesus, things which again will be picked up by Luke as the story moves forwards.

First, Jesus was the innocent 'servant'. The word 'servant' in verse 13 could equally be translated 'child', but 'servant' was a regular meaning of the word. In the Greek translation of Genesis 24, Abraham sends his servant to find a wife for Isaac, and the word used for 'servant' is the same as the word here, even though the servant in question wasn't Abraham's own child and certainly wasn't young. So the meaning 'servant' is probably uppermost. As we shall see more fully in due course, the idea of an 'innocent servant' should send our minds back to Isaiah 53, one of the all-time central passages in early Christian understanding of who Jesus was and why he died.

This points on to another theme. Just as in his account of Jesus' trial and death, Luke emphasizes that Jesus was innocent of the crimes of which he was charged – and that people who were released instead, like Barabbas (Luke 23.25), were guilty. That, as we saw earlier, is central to Luke's interpretation of the cross: Jesus dies on a charge of which he was innocent but plenty of other people were guilty. It is a matter of literal historic truth, as well as of theological interpretation, that 'the one bore the sins of the many' (Isaiah 53.12).

Second, Jesus was the 'Holy One, the Just One'. Jesus is referred to like this again in Acts (4.27, 30; 7.52; 22.14), and it's worth reflecting on these titles. Of course, the main point is that Jesus *was* 'holy'. His closest followers and friends had had ample opportunity to see his life close up at first hand, and they continued to be astonished at the sheer God-centredness, the utter integrity and total love which Jesus always displayed. And certainly, in terms of Pilate's initial, and official, verdict (verse 13), Jesus was 'innocent' or 'just' in contrast to Barabbas, the murderer released in his place. But both words, 'holy' and 'just', carry echoes once more of Isaiah. They serve to strengthen the impression that Peter is insisting that if his hearers want to know why and how the cripple has been healed, they should think first of the Exodus (God freeing those who had been enslaved), second of Isaiah (God's servant bearing the sins and infirmities of his people), and finally of Jesus in the middle of both those stories, making them come true in a new way.

That is why, third, Jesus is also 'the prince of life'. The word 'prince' here can also mean 'the one who initiates something': he is not so much the ruler *over* 'life', as the sovereign one who brings **life**, who *initiates* new life, who pioneers the way through death, decay and corruption and out the other side into a kind of 'life' that nobody had imagined before. And the point is that Jesus was already doing this during his public career. Wherever he went, he brought new life, the life which indicated that God was now in charge. This makes it all the more ridiculous, paradoxical even, that his own people rejected him and sent him to his death: they *killed* the prince of *life*! But, of course, God raised him up – the **resurrection** continues to be at the heart of the proclamation of the church and the explanation of why new life is now happening – so that his work of bringing new life continues unchecked.

With all this, it's not surprising that Peter goes on to insist on the central explanation for how the cripple was healed. He adds just one new note, which is enormously important in early Christianity. It is the name of Jesus, *through faith in his name*, which has done this. He repeats the point to rub it in. Using the name of Jesus isn't a matter of a new kind of magic, mumbling a secret word, a kind of abracadabra, which will make things happen automatically. There has to be faith, faith in the one who speaks the name, faith in the one who hears it. Other names, used in magic, keep people enslaved to the power of the name itself and the one who invokes it. The name of Jesus makes people grow up, become whole people, rinsed out and renewed, standing on their own feet literally (as the cripple now was), morally, spiritually and personally. That's what we find in verse 16, where Luke uses an unusual word to mean 'complete wholeness'. That's what is on offer through the **gospel** message which announces the powerful name of Jesus. Believing in him and in the power of his name is the way to wholeness, in the twenty-first century just as in the first.

ACTS 3.17–26

Restoration and Refreshment

[17]'Now, my dear family,' Peter continued, 'I know that you acted in ignorance, just as our rulers did. [18]But this is how God has fulfilled what he promised through the mouth of all the prophets, that his Messiah would suffer. [19]So now repent, and turn back, so that your sins may be blotted out, [20]so that times of refreshment may come from the Lord, and so that he will send you Jesus, the one he chose and appointed to be his Messiah. [21]He must be received in heaven, you see, until the time which God spoke about through the mouth of his holy prophets from ancient days, the time when God will restore all things. [22]Moses said, 'The Lord your God will raise up for you a prophet like me, one from among your own brothers; whatever he says to you, you will listen to him. [23]And everyone who does not listen to that prophet will be cut off from the people.' [24]All the prophets who have spoken, from Samuel and his successors, spoke about these days too. [25]You are the children of

the prophets, the children of the covenant which God established with your ancestors when he said to Abraham, 'In your seed shall all the families of the earth be blessed.' [26]When God raised up his servant he sent him to you first, to bless you by turning each of you away from your wicked deeds.'

I remember a hot, hot walk in the Scottish highlands. (It's true: there are times, even at altitudes of 4,000 feet, when you can be just as hot in Scotland as anywhere in Europe.) We climbed Braeriach and Cairn Toul, the third and fourth highest mountains in the British Isles, on a cloudless and windless day, and walking at a good pace, too.

For the last few miles back down the path we fantasized about how it would be when we got back to camp. There would be water to wash in, a stream where we could cool down our feet after we'd taken our boots off; there would be tea and food . . . but most of all we wanted something cold to drink. (We'd long since gone through the water we'd brought with us.) Only a few more miles . . . and then, what was this? A Land-Rover was coming up the track towards us. It was one of the camp staff.

'I reckoned you'd be hotter than you thought you were going to be,' he said. 'So I put a couple of crates of this and that in the car and brought it up.'

We stared in amazement, and then, gratefully, got stuck in to the various soft drinks he'd brought. It tasted good, good as it only tastes when you are tired and dry. It was still good to get back to the camp, but the refreshment had come to meet us before we even finished the walk.

That is the image we need to have in mind in reading this passage. Like some other bits of the New Testament, even good stories like the ones in Acts can get a little dense, and we can miss the big things that are going on. The point to watch for here is verse 21. There is coming a time *when God will restore all things*. And, though that final day will be truly wonderful, *it can be anticipated with 'times of refreshment' in the present*.

This is one way of putting a central truth for which the early Christians had a wide variety of expressions. God would 'sum up all things in Christ' (Ephesians 1.10); through Christ, he would 'reconcile all things to himself, making peace by his blood, shed on the cross' (Colossians 1.20); he will make 'new heavens and new earth, in which justice will dwell' (Revelation 21.1 and 2 Peter 3.13); he will overcome every power which destroys and corrupts his good creation, so that eventually God will be 'all in all' (1 Corinthians 15.28); the whole creation will be 'set free from its slavery to decay, to share the liberty of the glory of God's children' (Romans 8.21). Like so much early Christian belief, this is basically a Jewish belief about the future, based on the solid rock of belief in God as both creator and judge, but rethought now around the events to do with Jesus. In this present passage we can actually watch this process going on.

The ultimate promise of verse 21, that there will be a final restoration of all things, is firmly rooted in the Jewish prophets. What has changed now is that the final restoration has already happened to Jesus himself: what God is going to do to the whole of creation, he has done for Jesus in raising him from the dead. That is why Jesus now remains 'in **heaven**', in other words (as we have already seen) in God's sphere. Heaven is the place where God's purposes for the future are stored up, like pieces of a stage set waiting in the wings until they are needed for the final great act of the play. When Jesus finally reappears, heaven and earth will come together as one. That will be the great renewal of all things.

But we don't have to wait, so to speak, until we get back to camp. When people turn away from the life they have led, and the wicked things they may have done, and turn back to God – the technical term for all that is the solid old word 'repent' – then 'times of refreshment' can come from the very presence of the Lord himself, a kind of advance anticipation of the full and final 'refreshment' that we can expect when God completes the work at last. This notion of 'refreshment', though itself unusual in the New Testament, is by no means unusual in Christian experience, as again and again, in worship and sacrament, in reading the scriptures, in Christian **fellowship** and prayer, we taste in advance just a little bit of the coming together of heaven and earth, the sense that this is what we were made for, the new world which we shall finally enjoy. It is there, available, ready for all who seriously seek it.

In case anyone should suppose he was just making all this up, or just tossing out empty promises, Peter again insists, in more detail this time, that all this has happened in direct fulfil-ment of what the prophets had said. He goes for the big names: not just Isaiah, whom he referred to earlier, but Moses himself, the greatest prophet of them all; Samuel, who anointed the first kings of Israel; and Abraham too, who though not nor-mally thought of as a prophet is on one occasion designated as such (Genesis 20.7). It was Abraham who received the first and perhaps the greatest promise of all, which dominates the very structure of biblical thought: in you, and in your family, all earth's families are to be blessed (verse 25, quoting Genesis 12.3 – and compare Genesis 18.18; 22.18; 26.4; 28.14).

Peter, you see, is claiming much more than simply a few random proof-texts which, if you shut one eye and concentrate hard, can be made to sound a bit like things that had happened to Jesus. He is understanding the Old Testament as a single great story which was constantly pointing forwards to some-thing that God was going to do through Abraham and his family, something that Moses, Samuel, Isaiah and the rest were pointing on towards as well. This great Something was the restoration of all things, the time when everything would be put right at last. And now, he says, it's happened! It's happened in Jesus! *And you can be part of it.*

This is the point of the appeal at the start and the finish of this passage. When the **good news** of Jesus is announced, it is, of course, about God the creator setting everything right. But part of the point of saying that this final restoration can come forward into the present is that God longs to see it happen to individual men, women and children, right now, in anticipa-tion. Because of Jesus' death and **resurrection**, anyone who turns away from the life they've been leading and turns to God instead – anyone, including the crowds who bayed for Jesus' blood and the Jewish rulers who sent him off to Pilate to be crucified – anyone at all can know in advance the joy of being forgiven, of being refreshed by the love and mercy of God, of discovering new **life** and purpose in following Jesus.

The description of **forgiveness** here is particularly striking. In another echo of Isaiah (43.25), Peter speaks of sins being 'blotted out' as one might wipe a blackboard clean of chalk marks. Something that was written up as an accusation against us is simply wiped out when we turn away – when we not only say 'sorry', but actually, in mind and action, turn round in the opposite direction. And all this happens because of Jesus.

Already, with the quotation of the promise to Abraham in verse 25, Peter is hinting at something quite new which is yet to appear, but which will become a major theme in Acts, namely, the time when non-Jews will discover that the Jewish promise fulfilled in Jesus is available equally to them. But Peter explains (and Luke, writing up the speech, stresses) that what is going on at the present moment is the main chance for those Jewish people who had opposed Jesus, rejected him and sent him to his death, to say 'sorry' and to discover God's forgiveness. Tragically, Christians have sometimes taken passages like this and suggested that they meant that the Jewish people were somehow always to be blamed for what had happened. The reverse is the case. Not only is there no sense, in Acts or elsewhere, that the Jewish people somehow bear guilt or blame beyond the initial people who rejected Jesus himself. There is, on the contrary, the extended invitation, rooted in God's covenant faithfulness, for them to receive forgiveness and refreshment as much as anyone else. The promise of the restoration of all things is, after all, a deeply Jewish promise. None of the first Christians, who were of course all themselves Jewish, would have imagined that God would turn his back on the very people who had carried that promise through so many generations.

ACTS 4.1–12

Resurrection Plus the Name of Jesus Equals Trouble

[1]As they were speaking to the people, along came the priests, the chief of the Temple police, and the Sadducees. [2]They were thoroughly annoyed that they were teaching the people and proclaiming that 'the resurrection of the dead' had begun to happen through Jesus. [3]They seized them and put them under guard until the next day, since it was already evening. [4]But a large number of the people who had heard the message – about five thousand of them – believed it.

[5]On the next day their rulers, the elders and the scribes gathered in Jerusalem, [6]along with Annas the high priest, Caiaphas, John, Alexander and all the members of the high-priestly family. [7]They stood them in the midst.

'How did you do this?' they asked them. 'What power did you use? What name did you invoke?'

[8]Peter was filled with the holy spirit. 'Rulers of the people and elders,' he said, [9]'if the question we're being asked today is about a good deed done for a sick man, and whose power it was that rescued him, [10]let it be known to all of you, and to all the people of Israel, that this man stands before you fit and well because of the name of the Messiah, Jesus of Nazareth, whom you crucified, but whom God raised from the dead. [11]He is the stone which you builders rejected, but which has become the head cornerstone. [12]Rescue won't come from anybody else! There is no other name given under heaven and among humans by which we must be rescued.'

I cherish the remark attributed to a bishop who complained that he didn't seem to be having the same impact as the first **apostles**.

'Everywhere St Paul went,' he said, 'there was a riot. Everywhere I go they serve tea.'

Well, it wasn't just St Paul, either. We shall indeed watch in the later chapters of Acts as Paul goes from place to place and all kinds of trouble gets stirred up. But the message about Jesus as **Messiah** and rescuer meant trouble long before Paul started preaching it; indeed, as we shall see before too long, Paul was himself one of the leaders in making trouble for the people

61

who were calling on the name of Jesus and declaring that God had raised him from the dead. So what was it about this early **message** which got the authorities, and others too, so alarmed and angry? Wouldn't it be simply great news to know that God was alive and well and was providing a wonderful rescue operation through his chosen Messiah?

Answer: not if you were already in power. Not if you were one of the people who had rejected and condemned that Messiah. And not, particularly, if you were in charge of the central institution that administered God's **law**, God's justice and the life of God's people, and if you strongly suspected that this new movement was trying to upstage you, to diminish or overturn that power and prestige and take it for itself. To understand all this – and opposition to the Christian message, which begins here in Acts, continues as a major theme all through from this point – we need to get inside what these people believed on the one hand and what the news of Jesus' **resurrection** actually meant on the other.

It is significant that it was the leaders of the **Temple** hierarchy, not least the **Sadducees**, who were so angry with Peter and John. As we know from other passages, the Sadducees were Jewish aristocrats, including the **high priest** and his family, who for some years had wielded great power in Jerusalem and among the Jewish people generally. They guarded the central shrine, the most holy place in Judaism, the place where for a thousand years the one true God had promised to meet with his people. They oversaw the sacrificial system by which this God had promised to maintain and restore **fellowship** with his people. And – just as a spin-off, of course! – they exercised great power economically, socially and politically. It was with the **high priest** and his entourage that the Roman governor would normally do business. They had the troops and the Temple police, and they had the whip-hand over the people. They could get things done, or stop things being done.

And that is why they strongly disapproved of the idea of 'resurrection'. This comes as a surprise to many people today. For at least the last 200 years in the Western world people have laughed at 'resurrection', whether that of Jesus or that of anyone else. Those who have stuck out against this mockery, and declared that they do believe in resurrection anyway, have been thought of as 'conservatives' rather than the modern 'liberals'. But resurrection always was a radical, dangerous doctrine, an attack on the status quo and a threat to existing power structures. Resurrection, you see, is the belief which declares that the living God is going to put everything right once and for all, is going (as we saw in the previous chapter) to 'restore all things', to turn the world the right way up at last.

And those who are in power, within the world the way it is, are quite right to suspect that, if God suddenly does such a drastic thing, they (to put it mildly) cannot guarantee that they will end up in power in the new world that God is going to make. What's more, people who believe in resurrection – as did the **Pharisees**, a radical populist group at the time – tend to be more ready than others to cause trouble for the authorities in the present. They believe, after all, that the God who will eventually put the world the right way up is likely to bring about some advance signs of that final judgment. They believe, too, that if they themselves try to produce such advance signs, but die in the process, God will raise them from the dead at the end anyway. Resurrection, whichever way you looked at it, was not what the authorities wanted to hear about.

So what made them angry wasn't just Peter's announcement that God had raised Jesus from the dead. It was, as Luke puts it, a much larger thing: that Peter *was preaching the resurrection of the dead*, and announcing this revolutionary doctrine 'in Jesus'. In other words, Peter was saying not only that Jesus himself had been raised, but that this was the start and the sign of God's eventual restoration of everything (3.21). That was bound to be bad news for the chief priests and the Sadducees, however much it was exactly what plenty of others wanted to hear (Luke notes a further 5,000 coming to faith on the spot).

But the really sinister thing about this section is the further question the authorities ask. 'What name did you use to do this?' Our minds go back to the accusations that were hurled at Jesus himself: was he, after all, in league with Beelzebul? Was he using some kind of black magic? (See Luke 11.14–23.)

Was Jesus – and were the **disciples**, now – the kind of people Deuteronomy 13 had warned about, people who were leading Israel astray to worship false gods?

Just as Jesus answered that question by reference to the **holy spirit**, at work in and through him to launch God's **kingdom**-project, so Peter, himself filled with the holy spirit, announces boldly that the 'name' in question is that of 'Jesus, the Messiah, from Nazareth'. He continues, in words that would hardly endear him to the authorities: 'You crucified him' (not that they did, as Luke knows; it was the Romans who did so; but the chief priests had precipitated it by handing him over on a capital charge and by pressing Pilate for a verdict of condemnation). The name of Jesus, in other words, isn't just the name through which healing power can flow into people. It is a name which is already a sign of contradiction.

In particular, Jesus is the place where God is building . . . the new Temple! This is a new level of subversion, which will burst out dramatically in Stephen's speech in Acts 7. As Jesus himself had hinted, he is the one prophesied in Psalm 118, which speaks of a stone that has been rejected by the builders but has become the head cornerstone of the whole building. When builders are searching around for ordinary stones to put up a wall or a house, they reject the one with the odd shape, because it won't fit. But they may then find, when they get to the top of the building, that the one with the strange angles is the very one they want. This passage in Psalm 118 already came to the early Christians full of hints about the Temple itself. God will build a new Temple, thus declaring the present one redundant.

For first-century Jews who were part of regular discussions about who the Messiah might be and what he might do, the 'stone' in this text would carry echoes of other passages as well. In particular, there is Daniel 2, which speaks of the 'stone' cut out of a mountain, which would smash to pieces the blasphemous statue of pagan empire and would itself become a kingdom filling the whole world. The implication is clear. God is indeed turning the world the right way up. He is doing so through the powerful name of Jesus. And, since this will involve the replacement of the present Temple with a new organization based on Jesus himself, the chief priests (who have the present Temple as their power base) hold no terrors for those who follow this Jesus.

Actually, Psalm 118 is full of meaning which would be directly relevant to what Peter and John were saying. It's a Psalm of the Temple, of people going up to it to celebrate God's new day and to claim his **salvation** (verses 21, 24, 25). It's a Psalm about God's life-giving power (verses 15–18), including in particular the way in which God brings his people through trouble and rescues them from danger. And it's a Psalm which, relying on God's mercy (verse 4), celebrates God's victory over all the powers of the world (verses 10, 14). 'It is better to trust in the Lord', sings the Psalm (verses 8–9), 'than to put any confidence in mortals, or in princes.' In other words, this was exactly the Psalm the apostles needed as they stood before the authorities.

All this gives us reason to ask, rather carefully, just why it is that Acts 4.12 has been so unpopular within the politically correct climate of the last few generations in the Western world. 'No other name'? People say this is arrogant, or exclusive, or triumphalist. So, indeed, it can be, if Christians use the name of Jesus to further their own power or prestige. But for many years now, in the Western world at least, the boot has been on the other foot. It is the secularists and the relativists who have acted the part of the chief priests, protecting their cherished temple of modernist thought, within which there can be no mention of resurrection, no naming of a name like that of Jesus. And the apostles, in any case, would answer: Well, who else is there that can rescue people in this fashion?

ACTS 4.13–22

The Clash of Loyalties

[13]When they saw how boldly Peter and John were speaking, and realized that they were untrained, ordinary men, they were astonished, and they recognized them as people who had been with Jesus. [14]And when they saw the man who had been healed standing with them, they had nothing to say in reply. [15]They

ordered them to be put out of the assembly while they conferred among themselves.

¹⁶'What can we do to these men?' they said. 'This is a spectacular sign that has happened through them. All Jerusalem knows it, and we can't deny it! ¹⁷But we certainly don't want it to spread any further among the people. So let's threaten them with awful consequences if they speak any more in this name to anybody.'

¹⁸So they called them in and gave them orders not to speak at all, or to teach, in the name of Jesus.

¹⁹But Peter and John gave them this reply.

'You judge', they said, 'whether it's right before God to listen to you rather than to God! ²⁰As far as we're concerned, we can't stop speaking about what we have seen and heard.'

²¹Then they threatened them some more, and let them go. They couldn't find any way to punish them, because of the people, since everyone was glorifying God for what had happened. ²²After all, the man to whom this sign of healing had happened was over forty years old.

Jennifer was teaching some basic geography to a class of eight-year-olds. They were studying Australia. They had just drawn a rough map together, and had worked out where the main cities were. Then Jennifer asked the class if anyone could say what sort of things most people in Australia did.

'Swimming!' shouted several voices.

'Yes,' replied Jennifer, 'but most people don't make a living by swimming.'

'Barbecuing!' said several more.

'Yes, they do a lot of that,' said Jennifer, 'but that's just how people cook their food. First they have to buy it, and for that they need money. What do they do to earn the money in the first place?'

'Well,' said a little girl at the back, 'a long time ago, nearly all Australians worked on farms. They looked after sheep and cattle and they grew all sorts of crops. Nowadays people in the big cities do all sorts of other things too, of course, like business and making cars and building houses and all the other things people get up to. But still a large number of Australians are farmers, and the further you go inland the more likely you are to find them running farms.'

The whole class stared at the little girl who had spoken so confidently.

'How did you learn all that?' asked Jennifer. 'We've only just started studying Australia today! Did you read a book about it?'

'No,' said the girl, tossing her head with a mixture of pride and embarrassment. 'It's just that we used to live there. My dad used to run a cattle farm with several thousand cows. I knew all about it from as soon as I could talk.'

There are, in other words, more ways of learning things than studying them in books. Book-learning, in fact, is often a poor substitute for first-hand experience if you want really to get inside a subject or have it inside you. And that was what was so striking about Peter and John.

The authorities were no doubt used to rounding up trouble-makers and teaching them a lesson. Normally such people, rabble-rousers of one sort or another, wouldn't have been able to string together more than a few sentences once they were put on the spot and received a direct challenge. But with Peter and John it was different. Clearly they hadn't been to rabbinical school to study the scriptures. In the small society of ancient Judaism people would know who the up-and-coming bright young students were; these men certainly weren't that type. They were 'untrained, ordinary men'. What's more, they had come out with a shrewd use of a Psalm, such as you might expect to get only if someone had sat in class and learned about various types of biblical interpretation. But they hadn't. What on earth was going on?

Like the little girl who used to live in Australia, Peter and John had a secret – a secret that enabled them to run rings round the book-learning of the authorities. They had been with Jesus. They had been with him night and day. They had seen and heard him pray. They knew how he read the scriptures, in his fresh, creative way, drawing out their inner message and finding his own vocation in the middle of it. Now that he had died and had then been astonishingly raised, and had then been exalted into the heavenly realm, all Peter and John had to do to explain what they were about was to develop the lines of thought they had heard him use over and over again. This didn't just give them 'boldness' in the sense of courage to stand up and say what they thought. Sometimes people can be bold even when they're muddled. It gave them something more: a clarity, a sharp edge, a definite point at which to stand. And the authorities knew it.

They were therefore at a loss. They couldn't deny that the crippled man had been healed. But nor could they simply shrug their shoulders and say nothing, as though it was of no concern to them that people were going around saying that **resurrection** had begun to happen, that Jesus of Nazareth was the **Messiah,** and that his name was so powerful that invoking it would cure chronically sick people. As we shall see in later chapters, they would soon find plenty of ways of punishing Jesus' followers, but for the moment they were stuck. And so, in what must have been an embarrassing climb-down, all they could do was to tell Peter and John not to speak any more in the name of Jesus.

They must have known, in issuing this order, that they were trying to shut a door when a howling gale was already blowing through it. After all, anyone who has found any word, any name, that will enable sick people to be healed is very unlikely to stop using it just because the authorities forbid it. But Peter's answer to them is more than merely pragmatic. It is theological, and forms the basis of all Christian resistance to the powers of this world from that day to this. We could paraphrase it like this: 'You're the judges around here? Very well, give me your legal judgment on this one! If we're standing here in God's presence, should we obey God, or should we obey you?'

Peter answers his own question. They can actually answer it how they like, but he and his friends are not going to stop speaking in the name of Jesus, and about all the things which God has done through him.

Now of course it is always possible for anyone to claim the name of Jesus, and the right to speak in his name, and to use this as justification for any sort of rebellion against authority that they choose. Such claims have a right to be heard, though they must then be judged on their merits. But the point about this one, which distinguishes it from many claims that might be made which simply borrow the name of Jesus as an excuse for running with an agenda someone has reached on quite different grounds, is that the people making the claim have already shown that they are living by it, and that it has power, **kingdom**-power, healing power. It makes the lame walk, just like Jesus did. Paul put it crisply: the kingdom of God is not about talk, but about power (1 Corinthians 4.20). Where God's power is at work to bring real change, real healing, real new life, there the people who are naming the name of Jesus to bring it about can stand up before judges, whether political or religious, and say with integrity that they are speaking for God. It will be costly; that's part of the deal. But it will be true.

ACTS 4.23–31

Look upon Their Threats

[23]When they had been released, they went back to their own people, and told them everything that the chief priests and the elders had said. [24]When they heard it, they all together lifted up their voices to God.

'Sovereign Master,' they said, 'you made heaven and earth, and the sea, and everything in them. [25]And you said through the holy spirit, by the mouth of our ancestor David, your servant,

'Why did the nations fly into a rage,
And why did the peoples think empty thoughts?
[26]The kings of the earth arose
And the rulers gathered themselves together
Against the Lord and against his anointed Messiah.

[27]'It's true: Herod and Pontius Pilate, together with the nations and the peoples of Israel, gathered themselves together in this very city against your holy child Jesus, the one you anointed, [28]to do whatever your hand and your plan had foreordained to

69

take place. ²⁹So now, Master, look on their threats; and grant that we, your servants, may speak your word with all boldness, ³⁰while you stretch out your hand for healing, so that signs and wonders may come about through the name of your holy child Jesus.'

³¹When they had prayed, the place where they were gathered was shaken. They were all filled with the holy spirit, and they boldly spoke the word of God.

In the early summer of 1989, I went to Jerusalem to teach, and to work on a couple of books, one of which was about Jesus himself. One day, sitting in my borrowed room at St George's Cathedral, I was struggling with a few pages I was trying to write, concerning the battles Jesus had over his exorcisms – the battles, that is, both with the **demons** themselves and with the people who were accusing him of being, himself, in league with the devil. I was conscious, as I was struggling with this material, that it was not only difficult to say what had to be said historically, but that it was difficult to get it straight theologically, and that in attempting both tasks I was myself straying into a field of forces which I would have preferred to avoid.

Suddenly, just as I had got down onto the computer a few paragraphs in which I had at last said what I wanted to say, there was a loud bang. All the electric systems in the building went dead. A workman downstairs, trying to fix something else, had put a nail straight through a main cable. He was lucky to be alive. And I had lost my morning's work.

It was such a shock, after my hours of silent struggle with the text, the history and the meanings, that I almost burst into tears. I went next door, sat down at the piano, and played for a few minutes to calm myself down and clear my head. Then I came back into my room and knelt down at the prayer desk. For some reason (perhaps I had heard them in the cathedral earlier that day, or that week) the words of Acts 4.29 came straight into my head.

'Now, Lord,' I prayed, 'look upon their threats; and grant to your servant to speak your word with all boldness, while you stretch out your hand to heal, and signs and wonders are performed in the name of your holy child Jesus.' I went back to the desk and reconstructed the morning's work.

I have prayed that prayer many times, not usually in such dramatic circumstances, but often with a sense that today, just as much as in the **apostles**' time, there is a battle going on. Sometimes it is with actual, official authorities, as in Acts 4. Sometimes it is with the spirit of the age, with the implied mood of an organization, a family or a club, where certain things are done and said and certain other things are emphatically 'not done' or 'not said' – including, it may be, a definite statement of Christian truth, which bursts upon a room in such circumstances like someone saying a rude word. Sometimes the battle is internal, where things I badly want to do, say or think conflict with what the text really is saying, and I have to recognize my own bias, repent and allow the text to re-form my outlook and behaviour. Whatever, the battle is real. I do not say it is always necessarily with actual dark powers, though I would never rule that out. I just know that when you come to speak or write about Jesus, about his cross, about his **resurrection**, about the new **life** which can break chains and set people free, there seem to be powers around the place which do their best to oppose what you are doing.

The previous passage included a reference to Psalm 118, and we saw just how important that Psalm was for the early church faced with opposition from the authorities. Now we find the apostles at prayer, returning to their friends after a trip to the **Temple** which, against expectations, had gone on from one afternoon to the next morning. And this time the Psalm they focus on is Psalm 2. Another spectacular poem, full of meaning relevant for exactly this situation.

Psalm 2 begins by questioning, before God, why the nations are in such an uproar, and the rulers scheming and plotting. This question stands within a long Jewish tradition in which God places his chosen people amidst the warring and violent nations of the earth, as a sign of his coming **kingdom**, the sovereign rule by which he will eventually bring peace and justice to the world. And on this occasion the means by which God will do this is through his anointed King, the one who will be hailed as '**son of God**'. To this 'son of God', declares the Psalm, God will give not just the promised land as his inheritance, but all the nations of the world. The promises to Abraham have been extended, rather as in Psalm 72 or Psalm 89, and now they embrace the whole world.

So when the apostles quote Psalm 2 in their confident, exhilarated prayer in verses 25 and 26 they are not just finding a vague proof-text to help them anchor a general sense that all the world is against them. They are calling up a very specific text which speaks graphically and powerfully of the **Messiah** as the son of God, destined to rule the whole world. Woven deep into the heart of early Christian belief was exactly this note, as we find in a passage in Paul. In Romans 1.3–5, where he may be drawing on an early Christian confession of **faith**, he declares that in the resurrection God demonstrated that Jesus really was his son, the Messiah from the seed of David, and that this Jesus was therefore the Lord of the whole world, claiming allegiance from all people.

Praying like this is confident praying, not because people necessarily feel more devout than at other times, but because they are rooting themselves firmly in the ancient tradition of scripture. They start their prayer by invoking God as the creator of heaven, earth, the sea and everything else – the God, in other words, of the Old Testament, the God who can be appealed to for all that takes place within his domains. Then follows the quote from the Psalm. Then the present situation is placed firmly on the map of the scriptural story which has already been celebrated. As a result, the prayer can acknowledge, as Acts already has, the strong theological point that even the apparently disastrous things that took place as Jesus went to the cross were not outside God's will (verse 28). The wickedness of rulers is held in check by, and contained within, the overall purpose of God, who makes even human wrath turn to his praise.

With the ground thus prepared, the main triple thrust of the prayer is quite straightforward. Not 'Lord, please cause them to die horribly' or 'Please stop them being so unpleasant.' Not 'Lord, let this persecution stop,' or even 'Please convert the authorities, so that your work can go forward.' Rather, quite simply, 'Now, Lord, look on their threats; let us go on speaking boldly; and will you please continue to work powerfully.' The opposition are there, and God knows about them. We are here, and we need to be faithful, to continue to speak of Jesus boldly and confidently. And here is the power of God, which is not in our possession but which, because of Jesus, will continue to be at work to set up signposts pointing people to the new thing which is happening through him.

The church needs to learn, in every generation, what it means to pray with confidence like this. We do not go looking for persecution. But when it comes, in whatever form, it certainly concentrates the mind, sends us back to the scriptures, and casts us on God's mercy and power. The church needs, again and again, that sense of God's powerful presence, shaking us up, blowing away the cobwebs, filling us with the **spirit**, and giving us that same boldness.

ACTS 4.32–37

Signs of the New Covenant

[32]The company of those who believed had one heart and soul. Nobody said that they owned their property; instead, they had everything in common. [33]The apostles gave their testimony to the resurrection of the Lord Jesus with great power, and great grace was upon all of them. [34]For there was no needy person among them, since any who possessed lands or houses sold them, brought the money from the sale, [35]and placed it at the feet of the apostles, who then gave to each according to their need.

[36]Joseph, a Levite from Cyprus, to whom the apostles gave the surname 'Barnabas' (which means 'son of encouragement'), [37]sold some land which belonged to him, brought the money, and laid it at the apostles' feet.

Some politicians' phrases pass into folk legend. I am old enough (just) to remember Harold Macmillan saying, 'You've never had it so good.' Some Americans can remember Roosevelt talking about the 'New Deal'. And generations to come will still talk about Margaret Thatcher as the 'Iron Lady'.

Other phrases from other sources stick in people's minds. People speak of 'killing the fatted calf' when they mean 'laying on a great party', even though most of them probably couldn't tell you that it came from Jesus' **parable** of the prodigal son in Luke 15. Many people will quote 'conscience doth make cowards of us all' and speak of 'slings and arrows of outrageous fortune' without knowing that they come from Shakespeare's *Hamlet*. And so on.

We are blessed, of course, with an abundance of literary sources to quote from, even though these days people often prefer electronic entertainment to reading. But it's not so long ago that in many homes the only real, solid book would be the Bible. In fact, the weekend I am writing this, a newspaper article is bemoaning the fact that new translations of the Bible have now deprived many devout people of that sense of familiar resonance you get when you hear a phrase and instinctively know that it's part of your world.

We have to remind ourselves of this whenever we try to track how the New Testament uses the Old. As we have seen in the last few passages in relation to the Psalms, frequently a short quotation will carry with it an entire passage, maybe even an entire world and an entire worldview, from the larger context from which it comes. And many careful readers have pointed out that something similar is going on here, in verse 34 in particular. Luke has already told us that the first Christians, living in Jerusalem, sold property and distributed it to those who were in need. Why does he repeat the point here? What is he adding?

The early Christians were by no means the first Jews of their day to try their hand at communal living. The best-known other example is in the **Dead Sea Scrolls**, where we find a description of the '**covenant** community' that formed itself around a character called 'the Teacher of Righteousness', who probably lived in the first century BC or a little earlier. This Teacher claimed (or his followers claimed on his behalf) that through his work God had established the 'new covenant' spoken of by the prophets, especially Jeremiah and Ezekiel. He, the Teacher, had been opposed by the priestly hierarchy of the day, based in the Temple. Indeed, the Teacher may himself have been a priest, perhaps a rival claimant for the title of high priest. Scholars discuss all this at great length. But the point here is this: in making the claims they did, the group who wrote and studied the Scrolls (which include large chunks of the Old Testament and several books of commentary upon it) saw themselves as the community in which the ancient ideal of Israel as God's covenant people was coming true. So *they shared their possessions.* First they gave them in trust to the community; then, when they were clear they wanted to join irrevocably, they signed them away for good.

It looks as though the early Christians did something very similar, and for a very similar reason. They believed that God had established the 'new covenant', not through the Teacher of Righteousness, but through Jesus of Nazareth. They therefore saw themselves as the 'covenant community' in whom God's promises were coming true. And among these promises we find Deuteronomy, which speaks of what life will be like when God finally establishes his people. And in Deuteronomy we find chapter 15, which gives commands for how, every seven years, there must be a remission of debts: everyone who is owed money must remit the claim. However, the passage goes on (verse 4), 'there will be no needy person among you, because the Lord is sure to bless you in the land that the Lord your God is giving you.'

And now at last we see what Luke is up to.

He is making the striking, controversial claim that the early Christian movement was, in effect, the true covenant community that God had always intended to set up. It had been achieved by the massive and total forgiveness of sins and debts accomplished by Jesus in his death; Jesus had, after all, announced as his agenda (in Luke 4) the programme of 'jubilee' set out in Isaiah 61, and had gone around talking about forgiveness both of sins and of debts. Now his followers were, in the most practical way possible, making real the implied promise of covenant renewal. Not only would they forgive debts every seven years; they would not keep their own private property to themselves, but would share it in common. As we noticed before, this didn't mean that they sold the roofs over their own heads, because then they would have had nowhere to meet or indeed to live. And later on, when Paul is going around the world talking about Jesus, it is assumed that people still have houses to live and eat in (1 Corinthians 11.22), even though Paul makes it quite clear that the gift of love given by God in Christ must be matched by the sharing of money, not just within the believing community in a single city, but across large distances and cultural barriers (Romans 15.25–29; 2 Corinthians 8—9). So strong is this principle in the churches Paul founded that within a very short time he has to write to the Thessalonians warning against the danger of people sponging off the community when they are quite capable of earning their own living. That danger would only have emerged in a community where the sharing of property was a foundation principle.

Luke has used this repeated description of the church to round off the two chapters which describe the healing of the crippled man, the hearing of Peter and John before the authorities, and the powerful prayer which followed. This has given him a chance to introduce several themes which will be important as the book progresses. Now he emphasizes the way in which the early church was living as the true people of God – not least, we may suspect, in order to highlight an emerging paradox. The Temple authorities thought *they* were the guardians of the official traditions of Israel; but, in the very same city, there was a community which was practising the life of the true covenant people of God, and thereby quietly upstaging all that went on in the Temple. What you do with money and possessions declares loudly what sort of a community you are, and the statement made by the early church's practice was clear and definite. No wonder they were able to give such powerful testimony to the **resurrection** of Jesus. They were demonstrating that it was a reality in ways that many Christians today, who often sadly balk at even giving a tithe of their income to the church, can only dream of.

In particular, this paragraph shows us what is meant when, in various early Christian writings (e.g. Philippians 2.1–4; Ephesians 4.1–4), people talk about being of one heart and mind. No doubt there is always a call to try to think alike with one another, to reach a deep, heart-level agreement on all key matters. But the early Christians, being Jewish, did not make as sharp a distinction as we do between heart and mind on the one hand and practical life on the other. 'Being of one heart and **soul**' in this passage seems to mean not just 'agreeing on all disputed matters' but also 'ready to regard each other's needs as one's own'. Here again there is an important Old Testament echo, and again in a covenantal context: 'I will give them', promises God to Jeremiah, 'one heart and one way' (Jeremiah 32.39; similarly, Ezekiel 11.19). Yes, says Luke; and it's happened through Jesus. This is the 'new covenant' community, right here, where all this is going on. And this establishes the claim of Jesus' people to be the true assembly of God's people, while those who run the Temple are just a sham. This in turn increases the tension that is starting to build between Jesus' followers and the Temple authorities, a tension which comes to the boil in just a few chapters' time.

Meanwhile, Luke uses this note about property-sharing in the community to introduce us to a character who will be important as the book progresses. A man named Joseph was given the nickname, by the **apostles**, of 'Barnabas', which means 'son of encouragement'. He was a 'Levite', that is, a member of the Israelite tribe of Levi, which provided the minor officials who worked in the Temple. (The priests themselves were the descendants of Aaron, one family within the tribe of Levi.) Barnabas provides a concrete example for Luke of someone who sold property and brought the proceeds to the apostles.

It may be that the property in question was on the island of Cyprus, where he came from, and where, with Paul, he would go as part of the first overseas missionary journey (Acts 13). But Barnabas, as we shall see, lived up to his nickname, not only in the matter of his own property but also when it came to taking risks to help people in a difficult spot (9.27;

11.22–26). As in his **gospel**, so here in Acts, Luke keeps popping people like this into his story, not only making it more vivid but helping us to get a sense of what following Jesus looks like in practice.

ACTS 5.1–11

Disaster

[1]There was, however, a man named Ananias, married to a woman called Sapphira. He sold some property, [2]and, with his wife's knowledge, kept back part of the price. He brought the rest and laid it at the apostles' feet.

[3]'Ananias!' said Peter. 'Why did Satan fill your heart, to make you tell a lie to the holy spirit and to keep back part of the price of the land? [4]While it was still yours, it belonged to you, didn't it? And, when you sold it, it was still in your power! Why did you get such an idea in your heart? It isn't humans that you've lied to: it's God!'

[5]When Ananias heard these words, he fell down and died. Everyone who heard about it was scared out of their wits. [6]The young men got up, took him away, and buried him.

[7]After an interval of about three hours, his wife came in, not knowing what had happened.

[8]Peter spoke to her.

'Tell me', he said, 'did you sell the land for this much?'

'Yes', she replied, 'that was the price.'

[9]'So why,' Peter answered, 'did you agree together to put the holy spirit to the test? Look: the feet of those who have buried your husband are at the door – and they will carry you out too!'

[10]At once she fell down at his feet and died. The young men were just coming in, and they found her dead, so they took her out and buried her beside her husband. [11]Great fear came upon the whole gathering, and on all who heard about these things.

Charles Haddon Spurgeon, the great Victorian Baptist preacher, recounted the story of how, on one occasion, he was preaching as usual when he found himself denouncing someone in the congregation whom he didn't know. Words came into his mouth describing how this man was cheating his employer, stealing from him, and apparently getting away with it. But, he found himself saying, this man should repent at once, or he would be found out.

At the time Spurgeon was surprised and somewhat anxious: where had this come from? Who was he talking about? Why had it happened? But, after the service, a young man came up to him in great consternation. 'Please,' he said, 'don't tell my master. I'll give it all back.' The man repented, made full restitution, and the situation was saved. And Spurgeon was left pondering the strange reality that, without asking for it or seeking it, he had been given a 'word of knowledge' about someone he didn't know.

Stories like that, which crop up relatively frequently in contemporary accounts of great preaching movements and other similar revivals, help to set the context for grappling with Acts 5, but they hardly make it much easier for us today. Let's face it: most of us would have been relieved if Ananias and Sapphira had been confronted with their cheating, had confessed and repented, and had either gone back to the beginning and decided what they really wanted to do or had simply given the rest of the money over, as they said they already had. Instead, swift judgment falls on them, judgment of a sort which (despite popular impressions to the contrary) is highly unusual in the Bible. Mostly, nations and individuals who do wrong seem to get away with it for a long time, and even if judgment comes eventually it's not always in the form people expect. What is different here? What is Luke trying to tell us in and through it all?

Part of what he is trying to tell us, whether we like it or not (and many of course don't), is that the early Christian community, without even trying, was functioning somewhat like the **Temple** itself. It was a place of holiness, a holiness so dramatic and acute that every blemish was magnified. Remember how, when the Ark of the **Covenant** was brought to Jerusalem in the first place, carried on an ox-cart, one of its guardians put out his hand to steady it when it wobbled and was at once struck dead, much to King David's annoyance (2 Samuel 6.6–9). The Temple itself contained warnings against anyone approaching who was unfit to do so. **Gentiles** were kept well out of it (see Acts 21.28–29); Jewish women could only go in as far as a certain point; only the **priests** could go into the inner court; and only the **high priest** himself could go into the central shrine, the 'holy of holies', and then only once a year, taking all kinds of precautions.

This sense of dangerous holiness emanates from some of Israel's ancient traditions, not just about the Temple but about the behaviour of the whole community. Leviticus 10 tells of two sons of Aaron who infringed the holiness of the sanctuary and suffered the consequences. Joshua 7 carries a story which is, in its way, not unlike our story of Ananias and Sapphira: following the destruction of Jericho, a man named Achan takes some of the things that should have been devoted to the Lord, and when trouble comes on the community as a result he is found out, and swift and supernatural judgment is visited on him. Similarly, 2 Chronicles 26 tells of King Uzziah infringing the sanctuary and being struck down with leprosy.

We don't like those stories, of course, any more than we like Acts 5, but we can't have it both ways. If we watch with excited fascination as the early church does wonderful healings, stands up to the bullying authorities, makes converts to right and left, and lives a life of astonishing property-sharing, we may have to face the fact that if you want to be a community which seems to be taking the place of the Temple of the living God you mustn't be surprised if the living God takes you seriously, seriously enough to make it clear that there is no such thing as cheap grace. If you invoke the power of the holy one, the one who will eventually right all wrongs and sort out all cheating and lying, he may just decide to do some of that work already, in advance. God is not mocked, as Paul puts it (Galatians 6.7). Though we sincerely hope he will not normally act with such sudden and swift judgment, leaving no room for the possibility of **repentance** and restoration (and we note that this sort of thing never seems to happen again in the early church, with the possible exception of 1 Corinthians 11.30, and the warning of 1 Corinthians 5.1–5), we either choose to live in the presence of the God who made the world, and who longs passionately for it to be set right, or we lapse back into some variety or other of easy-going paganism, even if it has a Christian veneer to it. Holiness, in other words, is not an optional extra. How God chooses to make that point is in the last analysis up to him, since he is the only one who knows the human heart. But the earliest Christians were quite clear. To name the name of Jesus, and to invoke the **holy spirit**, is to claim to be the Temple of the living God, and that is bound to have consequences.

In particular, this passage puts down a very clear marker about lying. Some of the greatest theologians have agonized over this question (is it right, for instance, to tell a murderer the truth about where his intended victim is hiding?) and have come up with various answers. But however we address the hard cases, our culture, which today is notoriously full of spin and smear, of people who hardly even bother any more to disguise the fact that they are telling half-truths to force their point across, and of politicians and other famous people who lie massively, publicly and dramatically – our culture is due a sharp dose of the warning which a story like this can provide. Ananias didn't have to lie. He could, had he wished, have sold the property, kept back part of the money, and said, 'I choose to give this part.' Had he been embarrassed to do that, he could simply have refrained from selling the property in the first place. Peter implies in verse 4 that there was no actual compulsion about doing what was described at the end of the previous chapter, and Barnabas is held up there not as an example of what everybody was doing but as a striking and special occurrence. The key thing was the lie.

The real, deep-level problem about lying is that it misuses, or abuses, the highest faculty we possess: the gift of expressing in clear speech the reality of who we are, what we think, and how we feel. It is, as it were, the opposite of the gift of tongues. Instead of allowing God's spirit to have free rein through our faculties, so that we praise God in words or sounds which enable us to stand (however briefly) at the intersection of **heaven** and earth, when we tell lies we not only hold heaven and earth apart; we twist earth itself, so that it serves our own interests. Lying is, ultimately, a way of declaring that we don't like the world the way it is and we will pretend that it is somehow more the way we want it to be. At that level, it is a way of saying that we don't trust God the creator to look after his world and sort it out in his own time and way. And it is precisely the claim of the early church that God the creator has acted in Jesus Christ to sort the world out and set it right. Those who make that claim, and live by that claim, must expect to be judged by that claim. This is a terrifying prospect. But if we took the underlying message of Acts 5 more seriously, we might perhaps expect to see more of the other bits of Acts, the bits we all prefer, coming true in our communities as well. Like the next section, for instance.

ACTS 5.12–16

Healed by Peter's Shadow

[12]Many signs and wonders were performed by the apostles among the people. They were all together in Solomon's Porch, [13]while none of the others dared to join them, though the people spoke highly of them. [14]But more people, a crowd both of men and women, believed in the Lord, and were added to their number. [15]They used to bring the sick into the streets, and place them on beds and mats so that at least Peter's shadow might fall on them as he went by. [16]Crowds gathered from the towns around Jerusalem, bringing people who were sick, or infested with unclean spirits. All of them were cured.

Imagine you are the manager of a great concert hall or opera house – the Metropolitan in New York, say, or the Albert Hall in London. For generations now this has been the place to which concert-goers have flocked in their thousands, week after week, year after year. All the glittering international stars have played and sung here. Every performance is reported in the national press. A grateful public subscribes for whole seasons of concerts all at once.

And then, quite suddenly, in the middle of your busy season, a small informal group begins to perform, day after day and night after night, right outside the main door of the concert hall. It's a motley collection of musicians, and they're playing a strange mixture of ancient classical music and rowdy new songs, sometimes putting them together in an unprecedented fashion.

Well, you think, people come and people go, strange things happen, there's probably no harm in it. But then you realize that a lot of the people who ought to be coming into the concert hall are coming to see and hear this little ragtag group of musicians. Crowds gather, and stay outside listening to the new music rather than coming inside to hear the advertised programme. And soon the leaders of the new band become well known. People are talking about *them*, and writing newspaper articles about them, rather than paying attention to the 'proper' stars. Now, as manager, you become seriously worried. Perhaps it's time to call the police and have them moved on, or even arrested for disturbing the peace . . .

And now we see why it was that things began to escalate in Jerusalem in the days and weeks after Pentecost. It might not have mattered so much if Peter, John and the rest had met, and drawn crowds, far away – in Galilee, say, or out in one of the villages. When Jesus had done that, he caught people's attention all right, but he was able to establish a large following without the Jerusalem authorities worrying particularly about it. (The **Pharisees**, who did keep checking up on Jesus in Galilee, were not the 'official' authorities; they were a self-appointed pressure group.)

But Peter and the others were continuing to meet in one of the great porches of the **Temple**. To understand this, you need to remember that the Temple in Jerusalem was not a single building, like a great church or cathedral. It was more like an entire area of the city, covering dozens of acres, walled off and with several gates and porches. There were trees and shrubs and various buildings, houses where the **priests** on duty would lodge during their days of service and, in the middle, the Temple proper, with its sequence of courts leading in towards the holy of holies. So the **apostles** had taken up the habit of worshipping in the Temple and then staying around beside one of the porches where there would be plenty of room for crowds to gather around them. The crowds were coming, as they came to Jesus, for healing, but of course for teaching as well. And we would be right to assume that the teaching continued down the lines of Peter's opening address in Acts 2, drawing together the ancient scriptures, not least the Psalms and the prophets, and the extraordinary new events concerning Jesus.

This was, as we say, 'in your face' as far as the authorities were concerned. And this explains what happened next. It also explains why Luke says that 'none of the others dared to join them', except of course for those who actually became believers themselves. It was a bold gesture, and was bound to draw comment and resentment from the authorities.

But this is where part of the point of the healings comes in. As with Jesus' ministry, so with his followers. The healings were not simply a matter of providing urgent medical care for people who needed it, though that was of course enfolded within the larger purpose. It was a matter of God's power going out and doing new things: a work of new creation, in deep continuity with the original creation, and indeed mending bodies and lives within that original creation, but demonstrating by its power and character that something new was afoot, something in the light of which believing in Jesus' **resurrection** didn't seem such a strange thing after all. (I well remember a conversation with a leading biblical scholar, much older than myself, who told me that for most of his career he had accepted the view that 'the resurrection' was, basically, an event that happened within the minds and hearts of the **disciples** rather than something that happened to the body of Jesus – until, in his own family and his own body, he had experienced remarkable healing as an answer to the prayers of the church. Suddenly it dawned on him that maybe God really was not only *interested in* restoring creation but actually *capable of doing it*. That is sometimes how it works.) And where new power is at work, even if its results are a matter for celebration – who could resent people being healed, we may ask? – then those who currently hold power are bound to be alarmed. Consider the reaction of the mainstream medical profession to the rise, in our day, of 'alternative' therapies; and imagine how a great modern hospital would react if a clinic offering a quite different style of treatment opened up right outside its front door.

One of the peculiar things about both Jesus' healings and those of the apostles is the way in which, at certain times and places, things seem to happen which don't happen anywhere else. I have no idea why it might be that in Jerusalem, at that time, Peter's shadow falling on people might cause them to be healed, and why we don't hear any more about that kind of thing; just as I have no idea why it should be that in Ephesus, later in the story (19.12), handkerchiefs were taken from Paul's body and laid on the sick to make them well, which again doesn't seem to have happened anywhere else. There is always a strange unknown quality about God's healing. In our 'democratic' age we tend to suppose that if God is going to do anything at all it would only be fair that he would do it all the same for everybody, but things just don't seem to work like that. I have no idea (if it comes to that) why, in a few chapters' time, James is killed and Peter escapes.

All of that is part of the mystery of living at the overlap between the **present age**, with its griefs and sorrows and decay and death, and the **age to come**, with its new **life** and energy and restorative power. I don't think it has anything much to do with the devotion or holiness of those involved. In the apostolic age they seem simply to have accepted that God can do whatever he pleases and that, when people pray and trust him, he will often do much more than we dare to imagine – while accepting also that frequently things don't work out as we would like, that people still get sick and die (nobody imagined that the healing offered by Peter, any more than that offered by Jesus, made people immortal!), and that many sad and tragic things continue to happen for which we have no particular explanation.

Thus the fact of so many people coming to Jerusalem and being cured was not simply a matter of a sudden burst of healing energy. It was about (and everyone there knew it was about) the establishment of a new reality in a dangerous place: the power of the living God becoming concrete, definite, undeniable, not simply a matter of a few people telling a very strange story and behaving from time to time as if they were drunk. It is when the church, through prayer and wisdom and often in the teeth of opposition, acts with decisive power in the real world – to build and run a successful school, or medical clinic; to free slaves or remit debts; to establish a housing project for those who can't afford local rents, or a credit union for those ashamed to go into a bank; to enable drug users and pushers to kick the habit and the lifestyle; to see hardened and violent criminals transformed by God's love – that people will take the message of Jesus seriously. Of course there will then be opposition, because we shall be invading territory that is currently under alternative occupation. But God's power will be at work, and people will know it.

ACTS 5.17–26

The Words of This Life

[17]Then the high priest got up, and all who were with him, namely the group called the 'Sadducees'. They were filled with righteous indignation, [18]and seized the apostles and put them in the public jail. [19]But an angel of the Lord came in the night, opened the prison doors, and brought them out.

[20]'Go and take your stand in the Temple', he said, 'and speak all the words of this Life to the people.'

[21]When they heard this, they went in at early morning and began to teach.

When the high priest arrived with his entourage, they called the official Assembly and all the elders of the children of Israel, and they sent to the prison to have the apostles brought in. [22]But when the attendants went, they didn't find them in the prison. So they came and reported back.

[23]'We found the jail shut up with maximum security', they said, 'and the guards were standing in front of the doors. But when we opened up we found nobody inside.'

[24]When they heard these words, the commander of the Temple police and the chief priests were at a loss about them,

with no idea what had happened. [25]But then someone came with a message for them.

'Look!' he said. 'The men you put in prison are standing in the Temple and teaching the people!'

[26]Then the commander went with his attendants and brought them. They didn't use force, though, because they were afraid that the people might stone them.

When our second child was born, we had decided on names. If it was a boy, it would be Oliver; if it was a girl, it would be Emily. Well, it was a girl (we got our Oliver later); but when we looked at her, we both knew she wasn't Emily. Who was she? Puzzled, we racked our brains.

'What's she called?' asked the nurse as we went back to the ward.

'We don't know!' we replied. 'We'll tell you in a while.'

We sat there with this little scrap in her cot, and went right back through our long list, alphabetically. When we arrived at the Rs, we knew who she was. It didn't feel as though we were making something up; it was more as if we were discovering something that was already true. Rosamund. A beautiful name for a beautiful young lady.

Sometimes, when people want to give a name to a new building, or a new business company, or even a new town, they have a competition. People sit round and think it out and come up with bright ideas.

One of the fascinating things about Acts is that nobody knew what to call the new movement. Even the angels seem to have had trouble with it. It wasn't called 'Christianity' for quite some time; indeed, it's only in chapter 11, when the movement has reached some non-Jews up north in Syria, that anyone calls the followers of Jesus 'Christians', that is, '**Messiah**-people'. Even so, there is still a bewildering variety of names and descriptions given not just to the **apostles** and their larger company but to the movement itself, to the fact that something new was happening. Later on we find it referred to as 'the Way'. Here, for the only time, but significantly, it is referred to as 'this **Life**'. 'Go and stand in the **Temple**,' said the angel, 'and speak to the people *all the words of this Life.*'

It's a strange way to put it but we can see what was meant. What the apostles were doing was quite simply to *live* in a wholly new way. Nobody had lived like this before; that, indeed, was one of the extraordinary challenges which impinged on people as the **gospel** set off around the wider world. This was 'a way of life', as we say, that people hadn't ever tried. In fact, nobody had ever imagined it.

But of course it wasn't just 'a way of life' in the sense of 'a way of conducting your personal day-to-day living', though it was that – a way which involved living as 'family' with all those who shared your belief in Jesus, a way which involved a radically new attitude to property and particularly to the sacred symbol of the holy land, a way which meant that, though you would still worship in the Temple, the centre of your life before God came when you broke bread in individual houses, in remembrance and invocation of Jesus. It was all of that, but it was much more. It was 'a way of Life' in the sense that Life itself had come to life in quite a new way; a force of Life had broken through the normally absolute barrier of death, and had burst into the present world of decay and corruption as a new principle, a new possibility, a new power. And it was this Life, of course, which was carrying the apostles along with it, like a strong wind driving sailing boats out across a wild sea.

And this Life had to be spoken as well as lived. 'Go and speak to all the people *the words* of this Life.' Of course the words had to be rooted in the reality of the way the apostles were living, and the work of healing they were doing. But wordless symbols, however powerful, remain open to a variety of explanation. From the very beginning, the apostolic **faith** has been something that demands to be explained, that needs to be taught. There is much to say, because people fill their heads with all kinds of half-truths or downright untruths. Things need to be spelled out carefully step by step: who Jesus was and is, what God did through him, how it all drew to its head the long scriptural story of God's people, what it all meant in terms of the long-awaited '**kingdom of God**'. As we shall see in the next chapter, it was one of the two primary tasks to which the apostles were called (the other of course being prayer). People sometimes scoff at the wordiness of Christianity, and it is of course all too possible for people to go on and on about not very much. But without the words to guide it, faith wanders in the dark and can easily fall over a cliff. The angel didn't just get the apostles out of prison; they were given specific instructions for an urgent continuing task. 'Go and speak to the people all the words of this Life.' We don't even know, yet, what to call it, but you've got to get on and speak it.

And this was of course even more 'in your face' as far as the authorities were concerned. We shouldn't be surprised, granted what had happened so far (and the provocative fact that the apostles were meeting, in increasing numbers, literally on the doorstep of the Temple), that the **high priest** and his aristocratic family and colleagues would regard the movement as a direct threat to their status, power and importance. (They would of course have said it differently; they would have said that it was a direct threat to the honour of God and the proper reverence for God's House, the Temple.) Luke uses a particular word to describe how they felt, a word which we need to unpack a bit.

They were, he says, filled with 'righteous indignation'. The word I have translated that way is often simply expressed as 'zeal'; but 'zeal' to a first-century Jew didn't just mean what it means to us. With us, it means a fervent, enthusiastic approach to whatever is going on: a baseball coach makes a 'zealous attempt' to enthuse the team, a politician becomes 'very zealous' for a particular reform she is championing, and so on. But with first-century Jews 'zeal' had a very specific meaning. It was 'zeal for the honour of God'. When you cashed this out, it often meant 'zeal for the purity of the Temple and the land'. And, particularly in the case of the **Pharisees** (as we shall see with Saul of Tarsus), it meant 'zeal for the **law**'. In other words, they were all aware that their God was a holy God, who had called Israel to be his special people, a people gathered around the symbols of Temple, land, law and family identity. Anything that challenged those symbols was a challenge to God, and had to be resisted 'zealously'. Only if we grasp that will we understand what is going on at this moment and in several later moments.

The present challenge was all about the power of the **Sadducees** and the chief **priests**. They had this power because they were the guardians of the central shrine, the holiest spot on earth. They could not simply allow the apostles to carry on the way they were doing. God's honour would be compromised; Israel would be led astray; disaster might strike. These people had to be stopped. And so the authorities did their best. They had efficient police and secure jails. But one of the things we find in Acts is that there are no locked doors in the kingdom of God.

This, too, is sometimes a real puzzle. Why does Paul languish in jail for two whole years (Acts 24.27), when he ought to be on his way to Rome, and when God is capable of sending an angel and letting people free? This is the kind of mystery we have to get used to. It's no use pretending that, because that's what 'ought to have happened', maybe nothing at all happened, no angel, no release, no puzzlement of guards (another echo there, this time of Jesus' own **resurrection**). That kind of dog-in-the-manger theology won't get us anywhere, and reduces Acts and indeed the whole New Testament to a pile of irrelevant old mumblings. The apostles were teaching 'the words of this Life'; the authorities were increasingly worried that they were undermining the very fabric of Judaism as they had known it, and so were desperate to prevent them taking things any further. But, as the next passage reveals, they were in danger of fighting, not against a human movement, but against God himself.

ACTS 5.27–42

Human Inventions and Divine Instructions

[27]So they brought them and stood them in the Assembly. The high priest questioned them.

[28]'We gave you strict orders, didn't we?' he demanded. 'We told you not to teach in this Name, and look what you're doing!

You have filled Jerusalem with your teaching, and you're trying to bring this man's blood on us!'

[29]'We must obey God, not humans!' responded Peter and the apostles. [30]'The God of our ancestors raised Jesus, after you had laid violent hands on him and hanged him on a tree. [31]God exalted him to his right hand as Leader and Saviour, to give repentance to Israel and forgiveness of sins. [32]We are witnesses of these things, and so is the holy spirit, which God gave to those who obey him.'

[33]When they heard this, they were infuriated, and wanted to kill them. [34]But then a Pharisee by the name of Gamaliel stood up in the Assembly. He was a law-teacher, highly respected by all the people. He ordered the men to be put outside for a short while.

[35]'Men of Israel,' he said to the gathering, 'take good care what you intend to do to these men. [36]Before these times Theudas rose up, claiming to be someone special, and about four hundred men went off to join him. But he was killed, and all the people who had trusted him were dispersed. The movement came to nothing. [37]After that, Judas the Galilean arose, in the days of the Census, and drew a crowd after himself. But he was killed, and all those who trusted him were scattered. [38]So my advice to you now is this. Leave off from these men; let them be. You see, if this plan or this work is of merely human origin, it will come to ruin. [39]But if it's from God – well, you won't be able to stop them. You might even be found to be fighting against God!'

They were persuaded by him, [40]and they called the apostles back in. They beat them and told them not to speak in the name of Jesus. Then they let them go. [41]They, however, went out from the presence of the Assembly celebrating, because they had been reckoned worthy to suffer disgrace for the Name. [42]And all day, in the Temple and from house to house, they did not stop teaching and proclaiming Jesus as the Messiah.

We stared at the parcel as it lay on the floor inside the front door. Nobody had heard the delivery man. Nobody knew why it had arrived at this time of the day. The parcel was bulky, somewhat misshapen, with various semi-legible scrawlings on various labels. It looked as if it had been wrongly delivered somewhere else and then, through different addresses crossed out and replaced, had found its way to us.

'The key thing is,' said one of the children, 'where has it come *from*?'

It was just at the time when the newspapers were full of terrorist threats, of parcel bombs being delivered to unlikely places, of warnings about suspicious packages. There was no particular reason why anyone should target *us*, of all people, but you never know, and conspiracy theories are always more attractive than boring or obvious answers.

We poked and prodded it. Eventually someone spotted a small scribble round the back. It was the name of a place we had visited some months before. At once light dawned. It wasn't a bomb, or anything else suspicious. It was the winter clothes we had had for a particular foreign visit. We hadn't needed them on the rest of the trip, so we'd left them to be parcelled up and sent back to us by slow freight.

The key thing is, where has this come *from*? That was the question which the Jerusalem leaders were faced with as they thought, angrily and resentfully, about this new call-it-what-you-will movement ('this **Life**', 'the Way', or whatever). This, interestingly, was a question Jesus himself had faced, not about his own ministry (though that was implied as well), but about **John the Baptist**: where had all that come from? Was it from God, or was it a purely human invention (Luke 20.1–7)? Had John the Baptist had a genuine call from God, or did he just wake up one day and think, of his own initiative, that it might be a good idea to splash water over people and say that God's **kingdom** was on the way? And the question, naturally, had direct practical implications. If God wasn't in the movement, then it was leading people astray and ought to be stopped. But if God was working through it, *then it meant that God's kingdom really was on the way, and in a surprising and disturbing manner*. There was no third option.

The chief **priests**, of course, were quite clear that God simply couldn't be in 'this Life', this subversive new gang who were going around talking about Jesus and getting everybody excited. For a start, they weren't operating through the proper channels. Everybody knew that God lived in the **Temple** and worked through it to bring **forgiveness** and **salvation** to his people. For another thing, the **apostles** were going on telling people that Jesus had been crucified because they, the crowds and their leaders, had sent him to his death, and were insisting that people should repent of that as a kind of basic sin; in other words, the chief priests, instead of being the people who told everyone else how to behave, were being labelled as the chief sinners! Clearly they couldn't let this sort of thing go on. So they brought the apostles back from the Temple and questioned them again.

Peter's answer only serves to enrage them even more (verse 33). He insists, as he did before (4.19), that they are faced with a challenge: shall we obey God, or shall we obey the authorities? This question stands in interesting parallel to the question of Luke 20.1–7 and then Acts 5.38–39: is the movement from God, or from human initiative? Shall we obey God, or shall we obey human authorities? It is the question which Jesus still poses, both to those outside the **faith** (was he from God, or was he a deluded fanatic?) and to those inside the faith (shall we compromise our allegiance to him by going along with human instructions that cut against the **gospel**, or shall we remain loyal even at the risk of civil disobedience?). Luke, in telling the fast-paced and dramatic story of the early days, is also putting down some markers for how Christians have to think through issues from that day to this.

Interestingly, just as nobody in the early days quite knew what to call the new movement, so nobody seems to have had a single definite idea of how to refer to Jesus himself. By the time Paul is writing his letters, about 20 or 30 years after the time we are now reading about, things have settled down: Jesus is the **Messiah** ('**Christ**'), the Lord, the Saviour. But at this stage they were still ransacking various possibilities to try to say who he was and what he'd done. Peter declares that 'the God of our ancestors' (in other words, don't imagine this is a different God we are talking about, we are not leading Israel astray after strange divinities, we are being deeply loyal to the highest Jewish traditions) has raised up Jesus and exalted him as 'Leader and Saviour'. Leader, because he has pioneered the way into God's new creation, and is drawing people into that new world where **heaven** and earth overlap – as people had thought heaven and earth overlapped in the Temple, but now in a quite new way. Saviour, because he has broken through the power of death itself and is therefore ready to rescue people not only from that ultimate enemy but from such other enemies, whether sickness, oppression, persecution or imprisonment, as they may face from time to time.

Peter rubs it in: this Jesus, the one you handed over to be killed, is now offering a new start for his people Israel. He will give them **repentance** and forgiveness of sins – the very things the Temple was supposed to provide; and now here was Peter, an upstart from Galilee, telling the Temple authorities that *they* needed it and that the Jesus he was proclaiming would give it to them! Once again, we are not surprised that the issue of the Temple, and its status in God's newly unfolding plan, would come to a head within a chapter or two. But, on the way, we must note the point that 'repentance' itself is not simply something humans do, as though to persuade God to be gracious to them. Repentance itself remains a gift from God, something the **holy spirit** brings about (see too 11.18). There is another mystery here, but it's one the early Christians lived with, and indeed lived by.

What Peter said was easily provocative enough to have the authorities kill them all on the spot, if they could have got away with it. What happens next is a surprise – though not so much as we get to know the underlying story which Luke is telling, because again and again he insists that, though various authorities want to do away with the early leaders, there is a twist which brings them out safely after all. Sometimes it's an angel letting people out of prison; sometimes it's a little boy hearing about a plot just in time to thwart it; sometimes, as here, it's a thoughtful outsider who points out the disturbing truth to the people who are about to do violence.

Gamaliel is well known from Jewish sources of this period and later. He was remembered as one of the greatest **rabbis** of all time, a man of exemplary devotion and piety, who knew the

law forwards, backwards, inside out and upside down, and taught it to all who would sit at his feet – including, as we shall see, Saul of Tarsus (see 22.3). At this stage there were two great schools of interpretation of the law, which had been pioneered by the famous teachers of the generation before the time of Jesus, Shammai and Hillel. Shammai always tended to take the hard line, politically as well as in strict legal application: one had to be zealous for the law in all possible ways, and if that meant using violence against those who broke the law or questioned it, so be it. That's what Phinehas and Elijah had done in the ancient scriptures (Numbers 25; 1 Kings 18), and that's what had to be done today. Hillel, however, had taken a different line. What God wants is for Israel to keep his law. Since that is a matter of the heart, we don't need to fight people to establish it. We will follow God's law, but we will let other people do what they think is right. Live and let live.

Gamaliel was, clearly, a follower of Hillel – though at least one of his hot-headed **disciples** wasn't satisfied with that, as we shall see. On this occasion he spells out the principle clearly. There have been, he points out, other movements, other rebellions, other uprisings in the recent past. Gamaliel hasn't got it all quite straight: Theudas and Judas pretty certainly came in the other order and, though Judas' followers were scattered at the time, they regrouped, found new leaders from within Judas' own family, and continued as a revolutionary movement for another 40 years. But the principle is clear: if this is a human invention, it will fall by its own weight, but if it's from God, beware. And since at the moment you can't tell which it is (the chief priests probably thought they could, but Gamaliel's wise words won the day with the larger Assembly), you'd better leave it alone.

The church can never anticipate who will suddenly speak up for our right to exist, and to preach and teach about Jesus. Our job is to be faithful and, when a clash comes, to obey God rather than human authorities. We may have to suffer, whether actual violence as they did (verses 40–41), or simply sneering and mockery. Either way, we have to hold cheerfully to our course. If we really believe that God has raised Jesus, then the question Gamaliel left open, as to whether God is with us or not, has been decided once and for all.

ACTS 6.1–7

Problems of Family Living

[1]Around that time, as the number of disciples increased, the 'Hellenists' raised a dispute with the 'Hebrews' because their widows were being overlooked in the daily distribution. [2]So the Twelve called the whole crowd of disciples together.

'Listen,' they said. 'It wouldn't be right for us to leave the word of God to wait on tables. [3]So, brothers and sisters, choose seven men from among yourselves who are well spoken of and filled with the spirit and wisdom. They will take charge of what needs to be done in this matter. [4]We will continue to pay attention to prayer and to the ministry of the word.'

[5]The whole gathering was pleased with what they said. They chose Stephen, a man full of faith and the holy spirit, and Philip, Prochorus, Nicanor, Timon, Parmenas and Nicolaus (a proselyte from Antioch). [6]They presented them before the apostles, who prayed and laid their hands on them.

[7]The word of God increased, and the number of disciples in Jerusalem grew by leaps and bounds. This included a large crowd of priests who became obedient to the faith.

Late one night there was a knock at the door. It was a good friend of ours. His hat was on crooked and he had wild excitement in his face.

'It's twins!' he shouted as we ushered him in. 'We had no idea! Two girls! The doctors hadn't spotted it! The first one was born, just fine, and then they said there was another one in there!'

He could hardly contain his excitement. But when he calmed down he began to reflect on the new problem.

'We've only got one cot,' he said. 'There's only one set of everything. Suddenly we have to go out and get a whole second kit. We never bargained for this!'

I had the joy of baptizing the twin girls some months later. And I was reminded of the story of that night by thinking of the problem the **apostles** faced so early in the movement. Actually, it reminded me of another story as well.

A friend of mine, a famous publisher, once asked me to write a book called *Jesus at Sixty*. I was puzzled, so he explained what he meant. Jesus, he said, was a young visionary. He had a dream and went about sharing it. Everyone was excited. But if he'd lived another 20 or 30 years, instead of being killed so soon, his movement would have grown and he'd have had to get into administration. He'd have had to work out how to organize things, to delegate, to have rules and systems, and generally to do all the things that middle-aged people do which take the shine off their early vision and enthusiasm.

I refused to write the book (with some frustration, because we were very short of cash at the time and he was offering an advance). I did suggest that I write a different one, explaining why that wasn't the sort of task Jesus had in mind, but he wasn't interested. And of course, as this chapter demonstrates, it wouldn't have taken another 30 years, until Jesus had been 60, before serious questions of organization came up. Already, in these early days, Jesus' followers faced problems about how to run things.

What was the problem, and why had it arisen?

As we saw at the end of chapters 2 and 4, those who were following Jesus had, from the beginning, shared their resources. This wasn't just a primitive form of communism. Nor was it a sign (as some have suggested) that they thought the world was going to end very soon, so they wouldn't be needing property any more. No: it was, rather, a sign that they knew they were called to live *as a single family*. They were the nucleus of God's renewed Israel. (This, we recall, was why they had carefully chosen a replacement for Judas, so that the idea of 'the **Twelve**', the foundation of this renewed people, would remain firmly in place.) Like any family in that world, and many in today's world, they would all own everything together.

But how is that going to work when the family is suddenly double the size you expected it to be – like the surprising twins? How are you going to cope? You're going to have to sort something out pretty quickly. And the pressure in the early movement came to a head, not surprisingly, along a fault-line which would continue to be a problem for many years to come: the subtle distinctions between people from different ethnic or linguistic groupings, and the question of their relative status within the new movement.

The problem came to a head over the treatment of widows. This shows that already in the early church the question of 'living as a single family' had clear negative as well as positive implications: normally, widows would be taken care of among their own blood-relations, but those family ties appear to have been cut when people joined the new movement. As in some parts of the world to this day, **baptism** meant saying goodbye to an existing family as well as being welcomed into a new one. And the new one therefore had to take on the obligations of the old. That, by the way, is why we find regulations being drawn up about such things in 1 Timothy 5.3–16. Some have speculated that the problem was exacerbated, in the case of the early church, because many Jewish couples would come from far and wide in the Jewish 'Diaspora' (the dispersion of Jews all around the known world) to live in and around Jerusalem in old age so that, eventually, they could be buried in the vicinity. The husband might then die, leaving a disproportionate number of widows from different geographical origins all in the neighbourhood of Jerusalem.

Whatever we think about that, the distinction in verse 1 between 'Hellenists' and 'Hebrews' is probably one of those things with a variety of elements mixed together. Nobody had planned for a complex and intricate welfare system. It had been invented on the hoof, when there were other things (such as persecution by the authorities) to think about. It would be surprising if such a system could proceed without difficulties. And in a complex society such as that in Jerusalem, which was both a deeply traditional culture, very conscious of its historic and religious significance, and a cosmopolitan mixture of Jews from all over the world, it is not surprising that people would be eyeing one another to see if this or that group appeared to be taking advantage.

So those who were native-born Palestinian Jews (i.e. from Galilee or Judaea), who spoke Aramaic as their mother tongue, might well feel they had more in common with one another, especially in a world where many women would only speak one language, than they did with the Greek-speaking folk who had come from the wider world where Greek was at least everyone's second language and often their first. Most of these women were Jews, it seems, not proselytes (a proselyte is a non-Jew who has decided to become Jewish, renouncing paganism and, in the case of men, becoming **circumcised**). The awkward question of bringing Jews and non-Jews together in the same family would arise soon enough; the present crisis seems to have been a small-scale anticipation of it. Whenever even a small number of people try to live together, let alone to share resources, sometimes even tiny distinctions of background and culture can loom very large and have serious consequences.

In the present case, the apostles were quite clear what they should *not* do. They shouldn't at once rush to do the work themselves. Like Moses in Exodus 18, faced with an administrative crisis – and that may, indeed, be a parallel not entirely absent from Luke's mind – they must *delegate*. Jesus, after all, had shared his ministry with them in various ways, and there was every reason to draw in a wider circle of people to active and recognized work. In particular, if there was a problem about people from different linguistic and cultural backgrounds, why then it made sense to include in the work, front and centre, people who shared the background of those who had felt they were being treated as second-class citizens. And so it came to be. Stephen, Philip and the others became the first 'deacons' in the church. (That title, originally simply a word meaning 'servants', has come to have several other meanings attached to it in various later Christian traditions.)

The heart of the apostles' reasoning in all this was *the priority of the **word** of God and prayer*. Only when a crisis emerges do we see what is really important. We noted earlier that 'the apostles' teaching' was top of the list of the defining marks of the church (2.42), and that the apostles, faced with persecution, were instructed by the angel to 'go and speak the words of this **Life**' (5.20). The temptation for leaders in the movement, from the earliest days until now, has always been to heave a sigh of relief at being spared the spiritually and mentally demanding task of preaching and teaching, of explaining scripture, opening up its great narrative and its tiny details, applying it this way and that, enabling people to live within its story and make its energy their own. Running committees, though tricky at times, is not nearly so demanding. Sometimes people even dismiss the ministry of biblical teaching as a kind of optional extra for those who like that kind of thing. But the early apostolic testimony stands solidly: the task of an apostle is the word of God and prayer. Interestingly, it is at the end of this passage that Luke introduces another of his regular ways of talking about how the **gospel** message spread: 'the word of God', he says, 'increased'. He says something similar in 12.24; and Paul talks like this too, in, for instance, Colossians 1.5–6 and 1 Thessalonians 2.13. In all these cases we may suspect that there are strong Old Testament roots, for instance in Isaiah 55.10–13.

This whole way of talking about God's word is a gentle reminder that however much work anyone puts into the task of expounding scripture, into teaching the **message** of Jesus which stands on the shoulders of the biblical witness, into explaining and applying the whole thing, it is still God's work, not the preacher's or teacher's. Making 'the word of God' as it were a kind of autonomous agent is, if you like, a way of keeping the apostles in their place. They are not 'growing the church'; God is growing the church, and using their ministry of teaching and preaching as the primary way of doing so.

The fact that they mention prayer in the same breath in verse 4 is highly significant. Of course, all Christians are called to pray, to make time for it, to soak everything that they do in it. But the apostles cite it as a reason why they can't get involved in the organization of daily distribution to those in need. That implies, not that those who do the distribution can do without prayer, but that the apostles must give themselves to far, far more prayer. Here, along with the challenge to a ministry of teaching and preaching, is a quiet but explosive hint to all leaders in today's and tomorrow's church.

ACTS 6.8–15

Stephen Becomes a Target

[8]Stephen was filled with grace and power, and performed great signs and wonders among the people. [9]But some from the 'Freemen's Synagogue', as it was named, and from Cyrene, Alexandria, Cilicia and Asia, stood up and disputed with Stephen. [10]They could not, however, resist the wisdom and the spirit with which he spoke.

[11]Then they put up men to say, 'We heard this man speaking blasphemous words against Moses and against God!' [12]They aroused the people, the elders and the scribes. They set upon him, seized him, and took him in front of the Assembly. [13]They set up false witnesses to say, 'This man never stops speaking words against this holy place and the law! [14]We heard him say that this Jesus the Nazorean will destroy this place, and change the customs which Moses handed down to us!'

[15]Everyone who was sitting in the Assembly looked hard at Stephen. They all saw that his face was like the face of an angel.

Without in any way wishing to complain, I do have a fellow feeling with Stephen in this passage. He has only just been appointed a 'deacon', with particular responsibility for helping organize the daily distribution of food to the community that was dependent on the 'new family' of those who believed in Jesus. Like some of the others, he has found himself caught up, not only in administration, but also now in a wider and more active ministry of healing and teaching. (You never know, once you lay hands on people and pray for God to work through them, what new things they will get up to, or rather what new things God will do through them!) But, almost at once, he is embroiled in controversy. And all kinds of accusations start being hurled at him.

That's where my fellow feeling comes in. Far be it from me to pretend that I make no mistakes, or that all my own teaching is an exact account of what scripture says and what we

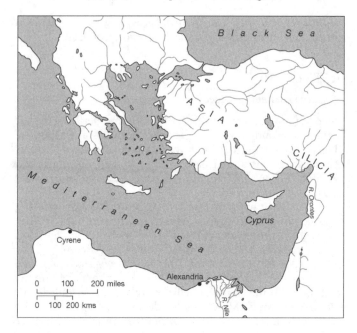

Acts 6.8–15

must understand by it today. I wish it was and am always ready to learn new things and understand the Bible better. But I have observed the way in which, in some circles, there are standard charges which are thrown around at people who dare to say things which their hearers don't expect. In my world, people of a traditional turn of mind are often on the lookout for anyone 'going soft' on the affirmation of Jesus' full divinity; on the full meaning of his death on the cross; on the promise of his **second coming**; and on some key doctrines, like 'justification by **faith**'. And, if they hear something they hadn't heard before, even if it doesn't have anything to do with any of these topics, they will readily jump to the conclusion that the speaker (for instance, myself) 'must' really be denying one of these cherished doctrines. For the record, I don't; I affirm them all. (A few days after writing this paragraph I received an email from someone I didn't know informing me that a professor in another country was going about saying that Tom Wright didn't really believe in the Trinity. That, too, is ridiculous.)

Meanwhile, people of a more radical turn of mind are often on the lookout for anyone denying some of the currently fashionable teachings about politics and ethics, or affirming anything that looks to them like old-fashioned, uncritical Bible-thumping. Offer the slightest suggestion that you really do hold to a traditional line on several key topics, and all the rhetoric comes tumbling out: you're a conservative, a fundamentalist, a reactionary, you probably hate women, you're leading us back to the Dark Ages. (For the record, I'm not.)

Now these things are unimportant in themselves, except as a sad but predictable index of the way in which, as in several previous generations, people today find real debate about actual topics difficult, and much prefer the parody of debate which consists of giving a dog a bad name and then beating him for it, and lashing out, too, at anyone who associates with the dog you happen to be beating at the time. There is far too much of that in the church, and the only answer is more listening, more actual thinking, and more careful and humble speaking. But with Stephen things became very hot very quickly; because, as any first-century Jew could have told you, there were certain key things, certain symbols of what it meant to be God's people in the midst of a wicked pagan world, and it was absolutely vital that all Jews stuck by them come what may. And anyone who started saying anything different was immediately pounced upon and accused of straightforwardly denying what all good Jews knew perfectly well they ought to be affirming.

There were (as I've said before) four key symbols of Judaism in the period. There was the **Temple** itself; the **law** ('**Torah**' in Hebrew); the holy land, focused on Jerusalem and the Temple; and the national ethnic identity, the family of all Jews (and proselytes). And, behind all this, and assumed to be involved in it all, was the question of God himself. At a time when the swirling, polyglot world of ancient paganism was all around (Judaea and Galilee were in this respect part of the general world of the ancient Near East, not a quiet haven from which pagan presence and ideas had been banished!), all loyal Jews knew they had to stick by the God of Abraham, Isaac and Jacob, and not to have any truck with compromise, with fancy new ideas which could and would only lead to following idols, blaspheming nonsenses. So, whenever Stephen spoke, out came the accusations: you're undermining the law of Moses! You're speaking against the Temple! And, behind it all, 'You're blaspheming God!'

Now of course, as we shall see in the extraordinary speech Stephen makes in his defence, there is a grain of truth in the first two at least, seen from the point of view of a hard-line first-century Jew (someone, say, like Saul of Tarsus). But the early Christian claim always was *that the God of our ancestors, in fulfilment of the purposes for which he gave the law and the Temple in the first place, is now doing a new thing.* Paul had to wrestle with this over and over again. His thinking was misunderstood in the first century, and has been on and off ever since, by people who find it easier to deal in simple, clunky affirmations and denials rather than appreciating that the **word** of God itself tells a *story* which is moving forward and, quite deliberately and necessarily, getting to new points as it does so. The story of my journey from here to London includes walking to the car, driving to the station, taking the train, and then, when I arrive in London, getting on the underground. The fact that when I get to the train I leave the car behind, or that when I get to the underground I leave the train behind, or that when I get to my destination I stop travelling altogether, doesn't mean that the car, the train or the underground were bad things, or that I wish I hadn't used them. It means that they are good things and I'm glad I did. That is the kind of point which Stephen, and later Paul, made all the time. God really did give the law and the Temple, but this was part of a great story which has now reached a new point. But this regularly fell, and falls, on deaf ears.

Stephen, it seems, was at home in the wider world of Greek-speaking Jews. Such people were by no means necessarily 'soft' on the law and the Temple when compared with their

Aramaic-speaking, native-Judaean, Jewish cousins. Far from it. As Paul found on his travels, sometimes the people who live further away from the centre geographically are all the more insistent on the cultural symbols by which they mark themselves out from their pagan neighbours (like English people abroad insisting on having tea at four o'clock even though not many people in England itself do so any more). But what has happened with the preaching of Stephen represents a new and wider venture within the early movement. Up to now, it seems (though of course Luke may well have omitted all sorts of other intermediate stages; we simply don't know), the followers of Jesus were simply taking their stand day by day in the Temple porches and teaching people as and when they could. Their main catchment area, and hence their main opposition, was within the Temple itself. But Stephen was going around Greek-speaking synagogues within the Jerusalem area, and the people he was speaking to weren't trying to defend a position of power, since they didn't have any. They were defending a worldview, a way of looking at things which coloured their whole life. And they saw the proclamation of Jesus as a threat to that whole way of thinking and living.

Luke tells us two things about Stephen in the midst of all this. We already know he was a man of the **spirit**, faith and wisdom (verses 3 and 5). Now we discover that this was put to good effect in debate, even when surrounded by hostile audiences (verse 10): they were not able to controvert him, because he kept coming up with excellent arguments, with the conviction and power of the spirit, to support what he was saying. When people are faced with this kind of thing, they have a choice. Either admit he's probably right, or throw as much mud as you can at him. They chose the latter. And soon it wasn't just mud.

But the second thing was this. Stephen was hauled before the official Assembly, the top legal body known as the Sanhedrin. But he seemed to have changed. They all stared at him. His face looked like the face of an angel. Now I have no idea how you know, in advance as it were, what an angel's face looks like. I doubt if the Assembly could have told you, either.

But perhaps what we are meant to understand is that there was a kind of light, illuminating Stephen from the inside. A kind of serenity, humble and unostentatious, but confident and assured. In the middle of arguments, controversies, false accusations, and now a serious charge before the highest court, he found himself standing, as the Temple claimed to stand, at the overlap of **heaven** and earth. The speech he was about to make, and the death he was about to suffer, were simply the final stages in his own travelling, his journey of witness to the risen Jesus, and to the word of God which provided the explanation of what Jesus was all about.

ACTS 7.1–16

Stephen Tells the Story

¹The high priest addressed Stephen.

'Are these things true?' he said.

²'My brothers and fathers,' replied Stephen, 'please give me a hearing.

'The God of glory appeared to our father Abraham when he was in Mesopotamia, before he moved to live in Haran. ³"Leave your land and your family," he said to him, "and go to the land which I will show you." ⁴So he left the land of the Chaldeans and went to live in Haran. Then, from there, after his father's death, God moved him on to this land in which you now live. ⁵God didn't give him an inheritance here, not even a place to stand up in. Instead, he promised (when Abraham still had no child) that he would give it as a possession to his seed after him. ⁶This is what God said to him: that his seed would be strangers in a foreign land, that they would serve there as slaves, and that they would be afflicted for four hundred and thirty years. ⁷But God said that he would judge the nation that had enslaved them, and that they would then come out and worship him "on this mountain". ⁸And he gave them the covenant of circumcision. So Abraham became the father of Isaac, and he circumcised him on the eighth day. Isaac became the father of Jacob, and Jacob the father of the twelve patriarchs.

⁹'Now the patriarchs became angry with Joseph, and were jealous of him. They sold him into Egypt. But God was with

IN ENGLAND'S FAIR CITY

Not long after *Headhunters* was first published, a friend of mine—Ray—
was sitting in a pub tucked into a backstreet near King's Cross station
in London. He had a pint of Guinness and a copy of the novel on the
table in front of him, and was about to settle into a relaxing, mid-after-
noon session. It was that time of day when a hush can settle over a pub
and turn it into a chapel. Sunlight filters through frosted and even
stained glass, the congregation is mainly middle-aged and over, with
the more dedicated souls sitting in solitary, prayer-like reflection. The
main difference is that these worshippers are male—retired, unemployed, self-employed, one or two on early shifts. There is contentment,
resignation and some sorrow, but none of the noise and chaos of the
night. Rough edges are smoothed and peace reigns.

Despite being close to a major rail terminus with areas of prostitution and homelessness, the passing nature of those travelling by train,
this establishment was used by locals. A big man with a shaved head
came over and sat opposite Ray. Uninvited, he was nevertheless friendly
and not stopping for long, just keen to explain that the bloke who had
written *Headhunters* drank here. He had not met him yet, but knew it
for a fact, went on to list the real-life regulars behind the novel's main
characters. Ray said he didn't think that was the case, but his new friend
was adamant and, in a way, he was right, because Carter, Balti, Harry,
Mango and Will—the self-styled, tongue-in-cheek Sex Division of this
story—do seem familiar, and they would definitely use this sort of pub.

Ray told me about this a few weeks later in The Ship in Soho, an
area at the heart of London which, until two years ago, had miracu-
lously escaped the mind-numbing gentrification that is destroying the
city. Speak, act, think the same ... Do not laugh, swear, disagree ... Spies

monitor what is said in case they are offended on behalf of someone else, too often failing to grasp the subtleties of a common English that shouldn't be taken too literally. At its most flamboyant, with the restraints loosened by alcohol, this language is loaded with double meaning and a self-deprecating humour. To understand *Headhunters*, it is important to read more than just the words.

Listening to Ray's story, it made me think how every group of drinking men has its archetypes, and others would make similar comments to the Kings Cross skinhead, recognising people they knew but I had never met. Perhaps people get on better when not sharing their beliefs too closely. It certainly makes life more interesting, and in a pub setting opinions are expressed freely and arguments can rage, but grudges are rarely held. There is a balancing of opposites—the yin and yang of the taproom philosophers; a brotherhood of the hop; the love and hate of bare-knuckle tattoos. In the harder pubs things might escalate, but there is generally an etiquette, a shared belief in free speech, the willingness to listen to the other person's point of view.

As the day progresses the chapel becomes a theatre. Evening approaches, the light fades and the doors clatter as people arrive after finishing work. That first pint slides down. The tension is eased. Night turns the streets black, lights come on and the beer has its effect, increasing the volume and intensity of conversation. The daytime drinkers drift off, followed by most of the after-work brigade, replaced by a fresh wave of thirsty people who will stay until closing time. There are no set rules, as every place is different, but most follow this pattern.

One of the best things about Britain is its pubs, and there is nothing like a proper London boozer. This doesn't mean they are all the same, as they are not, vary according to location and clientele, reflect a mass of local histories, characteristics that have passed down through the decades. Greater London is the result of villages linking as the city grew, populations changing their make-up as housing filled the gaps. The city is a jigsaw, the same as those gangs of drinking men, a mass of contradictions and quirks. Churches and pubs have long been focal points for communities, and while the buildings are modified and the people change, they offer a sense of continuity.

Short for 'public house', a pub is a licensed establishment where people of all ages, backgrounds, sexes and interests have traditionally come together. In London, they vary in scale, range from the small local sitting on a street corner or wedged into a terraced street, to grand gin palaces with their snugs and cut glass and maybe the remains of a music hall. The larger taverns and inns were where travellers stopped to lodge overnight. From The Ship in Soho, Ray and I walked for a minute and were in The Blue Posts, named after the coloured poles where riders used to tie their horses.

In *Headhunters*, The Unity is the main characters' pub of choice. Home to a 'bunch of hooligans', Denise and Eileen work behind the bar, while the resident nutter Slaughter looks on. It is here that the Sex Division is drunkenly formed, a soccer analogy that connects with the first novel in a trilogy that starts with *The Football Factory* and continues into *England Away*, as faces from the first two books join up and head across the English Channel to run riot in Amsterdam and Berlin, losing themselves in the kindred beer cultures of Holland and Germany.

A good session rinses the brain, flushes out the toxins of life, frees the imagination and releases the tongue. Love and hate become more than smudged ink. Friendships are formed and mistakes made. Ideas and opinions flow, inner lives expressed as more is revealed drunk than sober. Boundaries are broken. Every gang is made up of individuals, each person influenced by events, and as youths we are introduced to the magical world of the public house by others. It is one we soon grow to love. This is our tradition and our culture, and there is always a beginning.

•

The first three pubs I used were The Rising Sun in Slough, The Stag And Hounds in Iver Heath and The Three Tuns in Uxbridge, all of them on the margins of West London. Standing outside The Rising Sun one evening in 1977, peering through the window to see what it was like inside, if three underage boys would get served, a man's voice asked us what we were doing. Turning, we found ourselves facing our form teacher, mumbled a few words that included 'nothing,' and started to walk away. He laughed and told us it was fine to go inside, but to avoid the bar where he was meeting other teachers from the school. With its generously poured light-and-bitter and a jukebox full of 'glam' hits, we kept returning.

The Stag And Hounds was a pub I went to with my father, often at midday on a Sunday, which is a tradition in England. This was and remains a small locals' pub. It also had two bars, which made it seem even tighter inside, the space crowded with personalities that included the very different grocer and chemist, who had shops next to each other across the road. One was a big, jovial man who sold cabbages and carrots and potatoes, the other smaller and more serious, dealing in potions and plasters. Among the regulars was Dad's good friend Hughie, a Glaswegian who had run away from home to work on a ship when he was a boy, now a man with stories to spare.

The Three Tuns sits directly opposite the Underground station in Uxbridge, a mile or so from the RAF base, one of several that featured in the Battle Of Britain. In the late-1970s the front bar was used by greasers who played endless games of darts in a cloud of roll-up smoke, while a handful of younger Lurkers and Ruts kids preferred the lower back bar. The clientele here was older and more traditional, mainly retired couples, the men hunched over their jugs of Courage, the ladies sipping whisky and sherry. Walk outside, turn right and right again, and there was The Raj on Vine Street.

Pubs still had Public and Saloon bars, but this was changing fast. The Public Bar was basic, where labouring men could go in their dirty work clothes, and this probably connected to an agricultural economy, continuing in the industrialised cities. The Saloon Bar was smarter, with luxuries such as carpet and framed pictures. This was the place to sit with a girlfriend or wife, a more sedate setting where women felt at ease when they were out with their friends. The bad language of the drinking men was sectioned off, but the two bars also reflected a class divide, with the better off using the Saloon, where the prices were higher.

Those divisions are long gone, but these three pubs retain their personalities. The Rising Sun puts on bands, The Stag And Hounds remains a local, while The Three Tuns is less personal but still has low ceilings and cheap beer, the big difference being that you must turn left and left again down Windsor Street to reach The Raj. Because along with the English pub stands the balance that is the Indian curry house. And *Headhunters* has Balti Heaven to back up The Unity.

By the early-1970s, Indian food was making its presence felt in the major cities. While it is referred to as 'Indian,' in the pre-Partition sense maybe, most of the restaurants were run by Bangladeshis. Their filling, affordable, tasty meals were soon taken to by a generation of drinkers. My first Indian was in The Raj on Vine Street and my guide was again my father, who ordered a vindaloo for himself and willed me to love my Madras. One mouthful and I was hooked. A mouthful of his vindaloo and a jug of water was drained.

Three years later I was a regular, as Indian had become part of a good night out. The restaurants thrived, helped by the fact that they were open after the pubs closed, and the only place to get a late pint outside of a disco. The owner was the same George who runs the new Raj. In his eighties, he remains a legendary figure, the passing years raising him to cult status among the middle-aged herberts of the area, and these men have been keen to introduce their children to the experience, with George's son now part of the business.

To understand London, it helps to know its pubs, as each part of the city has its own flavours and they capture the differences, and reading this novel again for the introduction I was reintroduced to parts of my life spent in various locations, times that were closer to me then than they are now. When I lived in Archway with Ray in the late-1980s, the nearby pubs were all Irish-run, among them the Whittington & Cat, Archway Tavern and Mother Redcap, all serving the thirsty workers who had settled in the area.

In North London, Irish immigration was centred in the likes of Holloway, Finsbury Park, Kentish Town, Camden Town and Kilburn. Irish navvies grafted on the railways, and among other routes they helped to build the Metropolitan Line that runs out to Uxbridge, their descendents to be found in the estates that line the Uxbridge Road, moving from Shepherd's Bush and into the likes of Acton, Hayes, West Drayton and Slough. Before this, many worked in the docks of East London, and it is sometimes said that every Londoner has an Irish granny.

The Cat was the best of these Archway pubs, the landlord smart and courteous in his black suit, with folk musicians sitting at a table to play twice a week, their fiddles and banjos and mandolins setting everyone's feet tapping. Folklore says that Dick Whittington was an orphan who came to London from the countryside, believing that the city's streets were paved with gold. The truth was very different, and he eventually decided to leave, stopped at the last minute by the famous Bow Bells promising that he would one day become mayor, which he did, in a classic rags-to-riches tale.

The last time I saw Ray it was in The White Swan next to Highbury & Islington station, a few stops on from King's Cross, at the other end of the Holloway Road to Archway. Cheap and cheerful and part of the Wetherspoons chain, it is where the thinkers and drinkers head these days, with so many of the local pubs lost to gentrification. Early afternoon sees rows of old Irishmen filling The White Swan's tables, a sea of white hair matching the heads on their stout. A great place for a drink and a chat, owing everything to the characters present, these souls are the last of an era.

Headhunters, though, is based in West London, and returning to a part of the city that gave us the Fullers brewery and its famous London Pride, Brentford has long been a haven for serious drinking men. One of its best pubs is The Brewery Tap, surrounded by industrial units close to the River Thames. My father played piano here in the 1960s and '70s, and I would swap books with the landlord's daughter, Dad taking my hooligan pulp and trading the likes of *Skinhead* and *Boot Boys* for the Hell's Angels stories of Peter Cave and Mick Norman. He loved boogie-woogie, especially Pete Johnson, Albert Ammons, Meade Lux Lewis and Jimmy Yancey, and could both interpret the classics and create his own songs. He was also a regular at Eel Pie Island, a short way down river in Richmond. There was a big R&B scene in this area in the 1960s, with the Rolling Stones the most well-known of the bands to emerge.

Today, the Brewery Tap holds regular jazz sessions. Barely advertised, it pulls in an array of mavericks, and the piano he would probably have played is still there. Griffins have been spotted nearby, those experiencing these closing-time visions adamant they are not the herons that live on the Brentford Ait rookery. With its overgrown little islands, derelict boatyards and a lock that links to the Grand Union Canal, it is a fine spot for dragons. Impressions may be left in bricks and mortar, but it takes imagination to give them some sort of life, while the real hauntings are carried inside us. In *Headhunters,* the monsters take human form and are swept along in a river of beer.

•

Drink fuels all sorts of dreams. Hope fights hopelessness, shifts from daytripping fantasies to nightmares and hallucinations. Everyone wants to be loved, but some men can't admit this to themselves, let alone others, and so its physical expression is turned into a mechanical act, a way of dealing with rejection and a deeper loneliness. Sex becomes a challenge, beating it a measure of success, but unless a boaster has a very good line in humour he is soon seen as boring and then pathetic by the rest of the group. One man is an unstoppable machine, while another takes things much too seriously.

Sex has consequences. It is wrapped up in emotion, creates life and threatens death, causes break-ups and loss of family, and in this novel, despite the denials, it shapes events. Really, the Sex Division prefer eight pints in The Unity and a feed in Balti Heaven to a one-night stand. Even so, Harry and Balti keep dreaming of change, one while he is asleep and the other when awake, while Carter tries to not think too much. Mango, meanwhile, can't stop his mind racing, a ghost seeming to drive his behaviour. If there is a spectrum, then Will is at the opposite end to Mango, as he is loyal and romantic, but life is never easy, love never smooth. Yet the two are in some ways alike.

Sexism is a theme of the book, how it hurts men as well as women, and is one more way for the controllers to divide and rule. From an early age boys are conditioned. A sense of duty is drilled into them and the pressure of this obligation to one day support a family becomes more and more suffocating. The education system increases this interpretation of responsibility and self-worth, and many end up crushed, as what is expected of those outside of well-off backgrounds can rarely be achieved. They must earn good money and have a decent job in order to be respected and loved, and knowing that this is how they are valued has to make them angry. Rich men chase young women as they seek out a trophy wife, but it can work both ways. A buried resentment has to contribute to the terrible behaviour of some males. Mental and physical health are affected.

In Britain, over three-quarters of suicides are carried out by men. These rates increase in times of economic hardship. A male's average life expectancy stands at three years less than for a woman, and that is a gap that has recently been reduced. There are big differences due to social background, with those from poorer areas dying much younger, while the decrease is said to be due to the greater pressure being placed on women, which is hardly a positive. The fact so little is said about this reflects the way all men can be made to pay for the sins of some, which is sexist in itself. Few would equate the levels, but there is a fundamental unfairness there, and this novel suggests that people from the same background have more in common that those from different classes who only share a gender.

Out of work and with no money coming in, panic grips a man. The mind spirals out of control and he feels like a failure, thoughts stretching out of shape, rebounding and smashing back in to cause more damage. He sits in a park and thinks about life and wishes he had never had to grow up, as that dread he's known since he was small overwhelms him. The unemployed man remembers a bad father, someone who mistreated his mother, but he is not that person. He looks back at a lack of opportunities, the searching for self-confidence, the ebb and flow of positivity, finally reasons that despite being poor and unloved he at least has his fists. Anger plays out, while a little slack from higher up the pecking order could stop a row that leads to an escalating violence. One escape many of the poorest imagine is a win on a horse race, or a series of numbers on a lottery ticket. Or a return to childhood. He wants to run away, but where can he go?

Britain is much more than London, and there are always new pubs to discover. In Blackpool, in the North of England, The Lifeboat Inn is tucked into a small street not far from the seafront, its low ceilings magnifying the sound of an electric keyboard and a series of pensioners who step forward to sing their favourite songs, from Frank Sinatra doing things his way to Jeff Beck's silver lining. And there is The Horseshoe in Glasgow, a five-minute walk from Central Station, with its old wood panelling and etched glass and hazy interior, a cavern of murmured chat. And in Penzance, at the tip of Cornwall, there is the Lamp And Whistle, run by a Londoner who has left the city behind, built into the corner of a terrace, rows of fisherman's cottages running down to the harbour and the sea.

These were my three top finds of last year, and moving around the pubs of Blackpool I remembered being there years before and using the setting for the *Beano* chapter of this novel. Holidays are the holy days when the masses leave the hardships of their working lives behind, and in the UK people head for the coastal resorts. On the old Victorian promenades there is no great rush to change with the capitalist's idea of time. The front is lined with amusement arcades and fish-and-chip shops and bingo halls, grand shows in the music-hall style, a sense of vaudeville that runs from Liverpool's Ken Dodd back to London's Harry Champion. We all like to be beside the seaside.

Mango is at his happiest with his friends in Blackpool, removed from the company with which he has chosen to make his fortune, and these holidays with their low-cost B&B accommodation and caravan sites take us back to better days, when responsibility belonged to our parents. Millions go back to these dreamlands every year, braving the showers and freezing sea and wandering down the pier to ride dodgems as Motown booms, eating donuts and candyfloss. The Sex Division strolls along, dipping into Blackpool's pubs and hotel bars, but then their time is over and they are sucked back to London.

The daydream believer pictures the woman who will love him when he is rich, but knows that money is not the reason. It is a coincidence. She loves his personality and his soul. Because the drinking men of fiction are the secret romantics of London's pubs, and the new archetypes are little different to those who went before. Despite the language and bravado, deep down they know there is no sex war, just Us And Them. The rest of it is a game, not much more than handbags at dawn, as we are all looking for a happy ending.

John King
London, 2016

PART ONE

BEAUTIFUL GAME

Carter was first off the mark, and it wasn't much of a surprise. He walked into The Unity with a smile that didn't need explaining. The dirty cunt had been dabbling again. The others likened him to the Ooh Ah Cantona Man United side—he had flair *and* the ability to grind out a result when the occasion demanded. The lads did this on the quiet as they didn't want to give him the satisfaction. He got enough of that elsewhere.

The other four members of the Sex Division nursed half-full glasses, watering hangovers, prepared to wait for confirmation of the Carter score-line. If the result wasn't in much doubt, then there was still the small but important matter of totting up the points. But the shag man was going to take his time and passed the rest of the boys on his way to the bar. He ordered a pint of 4X and chatted with Eileen behind the counter, enjoying the warm smile, talking about electric shavers that break down a week after they've been given as Christmas presents and the odds on it snowing before the end of the week, both agreeing it would be nice to see everything painted white, though in London snow usually translated as slush. Carter finally went over to the Sex Division HQ in their usual place by the window. Will had left for the fruit machine while Carter was ordering, feigning disinterest but listening to the conversation with Eileen.

'Well?' Harry asked, forcing a note of indifference into his voice, not wanting to break rank with the rest of the service crew, but keen to get the facts sorted and filed so he could get on with life, always needing to have things straight in his head.

'Well what?' Carter settling into his seat, dipping his hand between his legs to pull the chair under the table, lifting the glass to his lips and savouring the taste, taking his time and doing his best to wind the others up.

'How many points did you get last night, you flash cunt?'

Carter smiled his Well Lads I'll Tell You When I'm Good And Fucking Ready smile and continued with the lager, exaggerating movement of arm and hand. He wondered if 4X was brewed in Australia by Australians. Crocodile Dundee's cousin giving it the big one down the brewers in between knocking off sheep in the middle of a radioactive desert, oversized wellies for the back legs just like the sheep-worriers he'd heard about on the Scottish islands; shearing the bastards then slipping them a length. Mad Max holding the poor little fucker still, rusty Harley parked up with an overheated engine. Probably not. The Aussies were all in Earl's Court and Dundee was working for the yankee dollar. Him and the yardies. He looked at Harry and Balti, the Fat Bastards, then Mango, all of who'd stopped drinking and were waiting for an answer. The season was under way with a vengeance and they had to know exactly where they stood. Perhaps it was early doors yet, as Ron Atkinson would say, but what did the northern gold merchant know anyway?

'Well lads, it was a free-flowing game as I'm sure you've already guessed, taking into consideration the quality of the opposition round here. I was up against a feeble defence trying to con its way through with a clean sheet, and I'm glad to say the old skills didn't take long to have the desired effect. I was pissed and can't remember the build up, but as you'll imagine it was quality footwork, playing it through the midfield, out to the wing, a bit of skill, dribbling and all that, end of the knob job, a bit of muscle getting past the hatchet tackle, a quick one-two, chipping the keeper. You know how it is when you're one-hundred-per-cent quality.'

'I don't,' Balti smiling despite the headache he was carrying and narked he was behind less than a day into the season, already following a leader he'd never catch. If only a self-made millionaire would turn up on the doorstep and offer to bankroll a successful championship push. But that kind of thing only happened up north.

Will came back to the table and remained standing. Carter got on his wick sometimes, but he said nothing, waiting for the mouthy bastard to get his bragging over and done with. He didn't like the idea of competitive football, turning the beautiful game into a business. He wasn't a tart like the rest of them. His sex was his own business. Even as a kid he'd never been into all the mouth, getting a couple of fingers in and running off to tell everyone. But he was signed up now and had to go along with it otherwise he'd look a prat. That's what a moment of pissed weakness did. The resolution had been made the previous night and if he bottled it he'd be branded.

He would keep his ideals, though, and wouldn't be changed by blatant commercialism. Play his natural game and bollocks to the rest of them, do an Ossie Ardiles even though Will was a Brentford man, do a Brazilian orange-juggling-on-Rio-Beach effort. It meant a place at the bottom of the table because he was no Pele and Ardiles was Argentinian, worse than that Tottenham, and they were charging over the top for oranges at the moment, vitamin C a luxury, but at least there was no chance of relegation. He could handle the tag and would live off the respect due a man with convictions, though when he left Rio and started filtering back into the pub, sucked under a dirty London sky, he knew it wasn't worth holding his breath.

'Get on with it will you,' he said, more to his Guinness than Carter. 'My pint'll be solid by the time you get your report filed.'

'It was a four-pointer.'

'Four points?'

'Four points. That's what I said. That's the way it goes. I got lucky. I was expecting three and ended up with a bonus for good behaviour.'

'You gave that bird one up the jacksie?'

'That's right. One point for a knuckle shuffle, two for a shag, three for a blow job and four for six inches up the arse.'

Will shook his head, more in sarcastic mock awe than real disbelief. Balti smiled and yawned, rolling a stiff neck. Harry sipped his drink, frowning, looking at the floor, following the faded pattern, an intricate network of faded red and black lines, a bit of yellow tucked away, holding the information for a while before storing it in his memory. Only Mango wasn't letting the unstoppable sex machine claim instant glory and further develop his cult status. If he wanted to go round shafting birds up the arse, then that was his problem. Must be a fucking iron on the quiet. He couldn't imagine a bird taking it voluntarily first time between the sheets. Not unless you paid them.

'You're a fucking bum bandit mate.'

'That's right.' Carter fixed on Mango's eyes without much humour in his voice. 'Four points in the bag and the bird's got a dose of vindaloo fall-out for the next couple of days. Serves her right as well. Do you think I'd have shit-stabbed her if there was no points in it? It's total football. I'm like the fucking Dutch. Johan Cruyff and Neeskens. A touch of Rudi Krol and Johnny Rep. Keep the tradition going. It's like that with the clogs. Bit of blow and black tarts sitting in the window waiting for their share of the Englishman's wage packet. Pride of Ajax. Cross their palms with guilders and sample the dark African continent, or at least the Dutch colonies. Have a Jakarta special with the gado gado at half-time. Total fucking football. You should try Amsterdam. The Dutch have got it sussed.'

'Were Cruyff and Neeskens bum bandits as well?' Harry asked, confused by the carpet, formation spinning and sending his head into orbit, red and black doing something to his brain, wondering what the fuck gado gado was. 'Cruyff's got a son. Seems a shame somehow, brilliant footballer like that, European Footballer of the Year and everything. I didn't know he was a shirt-lifter.'

'He's not, you cunt, it's the football I'm talking about.'

'That wasn't what total football was about,' said Balti snapping awake, big belly grin on his face. 'Total football was the whole team attacking and the goalie the only one at the back playing sweeper. It was scoring more goals than the other side. They just went out on the pitch and played the game and didn't give a toss how many they let in. Didn't follow systems and did whatever they felt like. No rules. Natural, free-flowing football. If the other side scored five then as long as the Dutch got six they won and went home happy. It was a sound attitude. Like that Brazil team with Pele, Tostao, Jairzinho. Remember the keeper Felix. Dear oh dear.'

'Didn't they have Rivelino as well?' Mango asked. 'I remember him.

Big bushy tash and always bending the free-kicks round the defensive wall.'

'We're talking total football, Dutch style. I'm a fucking Orange man stuck in Black Town, adding colour to London's black-and-white approach to the beautiful game. What do you know about football apart from how much Man U are worth on the stock exchange.'

Will sat down and deliberately placed his glass on a beer mat, Germanic lettering and a red coat of arms covered by the Irish stout. He was half cut. He still hadn't got over last night, New Year's Eve, and his right eye was murder. He'd left the party about four or so and was waiting for a cab with Mango. Fuck knows where the rest of the lads went. Pissed, stoned, useless. Except Carter on remote control looking to get his end away. Then Mango wanders off for a piss and the taxi pulls up. Three blokes appear from nowhere and try to nick it, a bunch of chancers, and when the barney started he got smacked in the head but was too pissed for aggravation and ended up in the gutter with decaying leaves for company and a kick in the head for good luck, that split second when he focused on the foot driving into his eye, like a slow-motion replay waiting for some expert analysis from Alan Hansen.

The cab left without Will, the driver only bothered about getting a fare, ignoring the body in the street. Mango returned too late, as usual, and found Will sitting on the kerb, shaking his head, pissed off that they'd have to call another car, knuckles wedged into his eye socket replaying the kick. He didn't even know what they looked like. Didn't know them from Adam. Dark shapes with dark hair. White faces without eyes, noses, mouths. Moving, living, stroppy waxworks. Any one of them could be sitting in the pub and he wouldn't have known. Will hated violence.

'I'll tell you, Carter,' he said. 'You're more like Liverpool. The old Liverpool. Grinding out a result. Going home with a 1–0. Or Arsenal. Boring, boring Arsenal. Up the arse with the Arsenal; 1–0 to the bum bandits. Tony Adams pushing up all the time playing offside then moving upfield for a ninety-eighth minute corner heading in the winner. Bad news that, getting a length off the Gooners.'

The Sex Division stopped talking and watched Denise, who'd just come in the pub. She nodded their way as she went towards the bar, dressed almost to the point of looking like a King's Cross tart; one of the girls Mango admitted shafting just before Christmas. A youngster. A nice treat for Santa. Not more than sixteen, he'd said, though he secretly reckoned she was fourteen tops. Plastic mini-skirt and six-inch heels, and the cut so short there was an inch of childlike flesh exposed, goosepimples and something extra in her Christmas stocking, just the strap of the suspender belt against innocent white skin. He'd paid his money and rolled the rubber on, knobbed her up by Regent's Park near the mosque, then dropped her off again in King's Cross. He had class, he told them. He wasn't shagging some Halifax teenybopper in the back of his car round the station, not with junkies and dossers everywhere, bloodless faces pressed up against the window screaming heaven and hell, AIDS and smack and rich punters in the blood, a dose of new-economics care in the community. He got his money's worth and said the bird offered him the night for free. She'd liked him. Will knew it was bollocks, about the girl offering Mango a freebie, but the others believed him, reckoning he was bang out of order shagging a kid that young forced on the game, sixteen still the right side of a kicking. A year or two younger and Mango would've been in trouble. He knew as much. Will reckoned they were mugs. The lot of them. Especially Harry, who pissed his wages up the wall worse than the rest of the lads, a big man with his square, shaved head and dreams. Mango was a cunt. Someone's daughter, sister, lover.

'I'd love to knob that,' Balti said, watching Denise disappear into the back of the pub. 'She's beautiful. I'd settle down and work all hours to bring her the good life. I'd give up the drink and curries and eat bean sprouts and grated carrot on crackers, lose four stone in a week, leave the coffee alone and drink grapefruit juice. I'd go and buy myself some decent gear and get my hair cut in an Italian unisex effort rather than a Greek butcher's. We'd have babies. Snotty-nosed brats puking up all over the place, shitting themselves twenty times a day for fun, dribbling like they're a minute from the grave. Anything Denise wants. I'd even change them as well. I'd take electrocution lessons and have my teeth capped, get those broken fuckers at the front mended so I look good when I get to meet her mum and dad, roses in one hand, bottle of sherry in the other. I'd do anything for that woman. Build a family and live happy ever after in the Green Belt away from you lot. And if you called up and wanted to go out for a pint I'd just have to tell you to fuck off and put the phone down, get back to the dishes.'

The others were laughing, Will pointing out that if he took electrocution lessons Denise would get a shock first time he tried it on. Denise was a cracker in anyone's book. She was also going out with Slaughter, who happened to be a Grade 1 nutter, a bloke whose jealousy wasn't worth stirring up for something as minor as sex or love. They all knew the score. Denise could prick-tease as much as she liked when Slaughter wasn't around. Winding the blokes up. Flashing her teeth and the top of her tits. Bending forward to collect the glasses and leaving it that extra couple of seconds that made all the difference, showing off her figure. She enjoyed it because they were a bunch of hooligans in The Unity. Dead lager on their breaths next day and black eyes, like that Terry watching her bum move tight inside her jeans when she arrived. She liked getting them going, knowing they'd bottle it if she offered them the business. None of them would chance it with Slaughter around. But she liked Terry, specially when she heard the others call him Carter. An unstoppable sex machine they said. Denise liked blokes who preferred women to drink and football. Mango gave her the creeps though, and Terry wasn't exactly a teetotal or football-free zone. She wondered if he had the guts. Maybe, with a bit of encouragement.

'If you settled down you'd end up bottom of the league,' Carter said. 'Imagine that, Balti. Four points maximum all season. You'd be shacked up living the life of a cunt and your mates would be on the rampage enjoying themselves, running up points while you're shovelling gerbil shit for the kids.'

'I'd never give Denise one up the arse. She's too nice for that. What kind of woman do you think she is, a slag? Denise is a solid lady. We'd make a good couple. I can see us with the trolley now, working our way through the freezers, loading up on steak and burgers, frozen peas, a nice bottle of wine to wash the meat down and some of that expensive Italian ice-cream.'

'You would mate. Believe me. A bird like that needs a good six inches up the dirt box to sort her out. Dirty old cow. No wonder Slaughter's a headcase. She must shag him rigid. Mind you, any woman hangs around with that cunt isn't letting herself in for French cuisine and vintage champagne. Must be a fucking battlefield when they get going. Can't imagine old Slaughter's into hours of foreplay and romantic meals for two. More like a quick knee-trembler and a samosa with his chips.'

'Me neither, but it's bad news sticking it up a bird like that. Mango's right. That kind of stuff's for queers, even if it is worth four points. You'd never catch me going that way.'

Eileen came round picking up glasses. She was an average looker, but friendly enough. Denise had sex and Eileen warmth. Will reckoned that meant more. He'd fancied her since she first started working in the pub four months before, though she'd never paid him much attention. It always worked like that. The women you took a shine to were either with someone else or not interested. The ones that pushed themselves were generally a bit iffy, with glazed eyes and desperation in their moves, thinking they were getting left out, craving love and affection so they'd shag anything and hope to hang on after the event. Like a lot of blokes. Will didn't think there was that much difference. Women could have babies and men couldn't. Straightforward really. He hoped Carter didn't get to grips with Eileen.

She took the glasses to the bar. It was only half-seven, but the pub was busy. Will was surprised. First day of the year and the world should've been staying home watching the game shows. Mind you, he was filling up fast enough, and would have a few more before he went home. It was like all that enthusiasm had been watered down the night before, and though everyone was going through the motions, not admitting they'd been fooled by the Christmas tinsel and extended drinking, persuading themselves it really was a brand new start, that this was the year when they'd finally get somewhere, be happy and satisfied with their lot, they knew deep down it was just going to be more of the same old bollocks.

'Where did you get to with that bird then?' Harry asked. 'Last I saw, you were chatting up Mick Gardner's sister. She's a right old slapper, even Balti's serviced it. Fanny like the Channel Tunnel. Half French by the look of the hair under her arms, but then she's gone and Mick said you'd pissed off with some decent-looking blonde which seems a bit suspect because everyone knows you're a pig-fucker.'

'Don't remember Gardner's sister. I gave her one last year. Well rough. No. I said I'd walk this other bird home so she wouldn't get mugged. It might've been New Year's but businessmen never sleep. Time's money if you're a sick cunt waiting in the shadows looking for an easy target. She wasn't bad. Lives down Ramsey Road and has her own place. Looks over the train track, but you wouldn't know it at night, just in the morning when the wagons roll through. Fuck knows who travels that early. Probably shipping nuclear waste through or pigs for slaughter. That lot don't rest. They're the real pig-fuckers. But this bird was very polite when we got back, very proper, went and turned the lamps on and chose a CD, shitty music, Mango sounds, and then when I'd had a drink, a couple of glasses of quality Scotch to warm the throat and thaw the vitals, I delivered some of the usual patter and she was away before you could say "Mango's a wanker".'

Will went to the bar and ordered a cheese roll. He hadn't eaten all day and was starving, but still had enough nous to concentrate on Eileen walking along the counter towards him, plate out in front. He self-consciously watched her breasts move gently under the wrap-around top she was wearing, long silver earrings brushing against the fabric covering her shoulders. She had a small nose-ring all the way from Rajasthan via Camden. He was feeling embarrassed just think-ing about her breasts so close to the material, nipples rubbing erect. He liked the smell she brought with her, character embedded in the face. Perfume always worked with Will. Made her stand out exotic in an everyday London boozer. He wished he'd asked for some salt-and-vinegar crisps or peanuts as well, but didn't want to send her down the bar again and make a fool of himself. Nothing turned a woman off more than indecisiveness. If a bloke stammered or didn't know what he wanted they'd look straight through you like you were scum. A man with appeal was a man who never glanced sideways. That was the way he'd been told to look at the problem. You had to have the dosh to back yourself as well, otherwise you were nothing. The rappers had it worked out well enough.

'What happened to your eye?' Eileen asked, a hard edge to her voice that he couldn't identify. 'Been getting in trouble, have you?'

'Three blokes had a go at me last night.'

'What did they do that for then?'

'Don't know really. I was standing there waiting for a cab, minding my own business, thinking about the new year and everything, wondering if today was going to be any different from yesterday, brand new life and all that, and when these blokes turned up and tried to nick it I told them it was mine, that I needed to get home because I was knackered and had been waiting around for ages. Tired and emotional like, with the end of the year and Christmas over. They just piled in. There was nothing I could do and after they'd given me a bit of a kicking they nicked the cab.'

'You should get it looked at.' She was more sympathetic now he'd shown himself the victim rather than one more pisshead causing trouble. 'They might've damaged your eyeball. You could've ended up getting blinded. The eye's very sensitive you know. It's come up quickly. You won't be impressing the women looking like that.'

She smiled and put the cheese roll on the bar and Will tried not to look at her tits, wondering whether it was a real diamond plugged in her nose. Whether she took it out at night so the butterfly didn't come out and slip into her head, working its way into the back of her skull, wishing he knew why she'd mentioned women.

Will hoped he wasn't going red, blushing like a kid as he paid his money and went back to the others without delivering the killer punch that would show he was a smooth cunt with a good line of humour. He should've followed up with a sharp one-liner, but words didn't come easy. Least not with the opposite sex. He was too much of a gentleman, that's what he told himself when confronting the truth that he was probably just shit at chat-up lines, though he'd never say it out loud. He just went along with things, they all did, expecting nothing, except for Carter always aiming to get his leg over. It was unnatural somehow, looking to get stuck in all the time, no chance for a decent chat with his mates, a couple of pints and he was off for the night sniffing round anything that moved. But she was alright, Eileen behind the bar, and maybe it was better he wasn't one of those blokes who could talk about anything and say nothing, because someone like Eileen, with a Rajput ring in her nose and classy perfume, would see through the shit and tick him off as one more brain-dead wanker thinking with his knob. One day though.

'Getting in with Eileen are you?' Carter asked, looking over his shoulder at the barmaid, talking now with Denise who'd dumped her handbag out back and was ready for the evening's work, having a smoke because the landlord was out and not due back till after closing. 'Didn't know you fancied her.'

'I was only talking to her. Why does everyone have to be looking to get into a bird's knickers just because they have a bit of a chat? She asked me about the eye, that's all. Wanted to know what happened last night. She's not going to stand there ignoring something like that bulging out of the socket at her, is she?'

'Alright Mildred, I was only asking. No need to cry about it. Here, I'll wipe your eyes. She's alright. A bit skinny in the legs but at least she's not a heifer you'd have to string up and open with a chainsaw, blood all over the shop as you hook up a rope and pull out the Tampax. I wouldn't say no if she was offering me a quick one in the cellar. Wouldn't turn her down so I could piss off upstairs and service old Balti breath over there.'

'What's wrong with my breath, you cocky cunt? Didn't even have a curry last night, though I wouldn't mind a bit of a feed right now, but I'm off them. That's my New Year's resolution, to shift a couple of stone and give those Kashmiri boys down Balti Heaven a break.'

'You're a slob,' said Mango, laughing as he rocked back in his chair.

'And you're a toerag who hangs about with nonces in pinstripe suits, sucking cock, so you can piss off back to your stocks and shares or whatever the fuck it is you do for a living.'

'I made forty-grand last year touching my cap for my betters, milking the smug bastards, getting them all worked up so they hand over their liquid assets. But at least I'm moving, not stuck in the shit like you or one of those kids in King's Cross or Streatham. At least I'm dealing in prime genetics, not the mongoloid swill kids from Halifax get shoved down their throats for a few quid. Wake up lads. It's a material world. Even Madonna knew that much. Maggie understood what it was all about. Best prime minister we ever had that woman. Gave me the break I needed.'

Balti felt himself losing it a bit, looking to smack Mango if he went on. His head was heavy and he wasn't in the mood for propaganda. He fucking hated Mango sometimes and everything he was into; the expensive gear and three-bedroom flat in Fulham, that Jag he'd bought and the holidays in Spain three or four times a year, the Jag with its five-grand stereo and automatic sun roof, Spanish resorts full of English slappers who left their knickers at Customs and collected them again on the way home; and the Jag shifted when Mango put his foot down, blowing the rest of them away. It made him sick just thinking about it all, and there was Balti, sweating his bollocks off lugging bricks around, coriander and garlic in his water, slave to a lippy Belfast cunt of a foreman, and the tosser opposite was sitting in a luxury office near Liverpool Street punching buttons on a keyboard, juggling figures and probably working out his own pay packet. It wasn't fair, and Balti was left behind in the wrecker's yard with his big end fucked while Mango cranked up the volume and disappeared down the Western Avenue in a cloud of lead-free exhaust fumes. It wasn't like Mango was smart, except when it came to maths and making money, dedicated more like, but he'd always been that way. Always had to have what he reckoned was the best of everything. Into the image rather than content. Listening to disco shit at school when the rest of them were into punk and 2-Tone, going for the soul patrol gear when he should've been wearing DMs.

The Sex Division members knew each other from childhood, sharing the same streets and school and most of the same lessons, once or twice the same girls. Like that time Balti had stopped seeing Helen Peters and Mango was straight round, filling the void. Now Carter was getting involved, telling Mango he was a wanker, that he thought he was better than his mates, that if he really thought odds and ends were all that mattered then he could fuck off to some other pub, back to Fulham and a poxy wine bar, or better still fuck off to where the cunts he worked with lived and drink cocktails and talk about the rugby, then bend over and touch his toes while he got some public schoolboy's fist rammed up his arse. You don't even like football, you tart. But Balti was giving up on the argument. It was the same old stuff that Mango dismissed as the politics of envy, turning off and drifting back to those turn-of-the-year days when he was a kid. Balti's dad would have a hangover so he'd keep his head down knowing he'd get hit if he made too much noise, maybe go see Chelsea play if there was a game on in London. Like that time they'd gone up the Arsenal, Boxing Day maybe, he couldn't remember exactly, when Micky Droy was playing and they'd gone in the North Bank, kept their mouths shut, shitting it, then there was a roar and the Chelsea North Stand steamed in and kicked the shit out of Arsenal who pegged out the other side. They were all there, everyone except Mango, even Will who supported Brentford, Mango busy with Zoe, that Iranian bird who got him into the soul music, knocking around with her Hawaiian shirt mates. He was a wanker even then, listening to love songs when any sussed kid was into decent lyrics.

They were good times. Eddie McCreadie's Blue And White Army and the Clash releasing White Man In Hammersmith Palais. That was the best song, fucking magic. Balti felt guilty suddenly, remembering Mango's older brother Pete who'd had all the records and lent them out left, right and centre, turning them in the right direction. Will, meanwhile, had always been a few years ahead when it came to music. Then one day Pete went missing. He'd walked down the tube saying he was off to Greenford and hadn't been seen since. No postcard, no letter, no nothing. The old bill had tried to trace him but without any luck. Everyone had a theory. Maybe he'd just had enough, signing on, not seeing anything on the horizon, just Maggie raving about law and order.

Balti looked into his glass and watched the bubbles popping, thinking of Mango sitting on the swings across from the station, waiting for his big brother to come home. It was seventeen or eighteen years ago now and Mango must've given up. Just before Christmas he'd seen Mango's Jag and the bloke was down the same playground, swinging back and forward. Every year he went back and didn't give a toss if the mothers down there thought he was a nonce after their kids. Maybe he cried when he thought about it all, the sadness and that, and Balti couldn't blame him. He wondered what Pete was doing now, if he was still alive, if he'd ended up on the game. Mango had told Balti that was the worst thing that could've happened, one time when he was pissed. Or a smackhead, clean now but a wreck, living in a graveyard in Stoke Newington or Hackney, sleeping rough. Mango was pissed Christmas Eve, mumbling on about Pete being a crack addict or a wino, weighing up the options. Balti had told him to look on the bright side. If his brother was alive he'd come back one day. But they were only words. Mango had never been the same since his brother went missing.

'Get a round in then, you tight cunt.' Harry was sick of the squabbling, like a load of kids the lot of them, back in the playground. 'You're the money man round here Mango, so shift yourself and go to the bar.'

'Alright. Forget I said anything. It's the change of weather, the time of year, just gets me going and everything and I've got to hit targets and keep people sweet. You don't know what it's like working for a bunch of stuck-up wankers who've got money behind them and sit there waiting for you to fall down and mess up. Forget what I said Balti. It's the pressure does it.'

'Leave it out. It doesn't matter.'

'Go on, give him a fucking kiss,' Carter said, puckering his lips. 'Couple of fucking irons you two.'

Mango stood up and went to the bar, Denise coming over to serve him, swapping pleasantries, the entrepreneur acting casual. Denise thought he was a wanker. She wouldn't trust him to water her plants. He was a right turn-off with the expensive clothes and big-man attitude, eyes shifting here and there, never following the line of conversation. His wallet was stuffed with tens, twenties, fifties, propped on the counter, credit cards jutting out. He thought he was special and she had half a mind to set Slaughter on him, take off the muzzle and let the pit bull loose. Except Mango hadn't done anything wrong really, it was just the way he stood and talked and everything about him. But that Terry, he was gorgeous when she concentrated on the back of his head and she knew he was interested. Those kind always were. She could see them getting together and though Slaughter would hospitalise them if he ever found out, probably worse, he would never hear it from her lips. Anyway, she could control him if a rumour started. She had him wrapped round her engagement finger. A sincere expression and good sex would convince lover-boy that the person spreading rumours was spreading lies and he'd be round to see them with that machete he kept under the bed looking to mend their thinking.

Slaughter was a nutter, mental about Denise and life in general, but it was amazing what a healthy bit of sex did for a man like that. It was the strippers on stage and bikini girls on advertising boards that caused problems. Agency models in sight but out of range; winding them up, taking their wages, then stabbing them in the balls for having tattoos and tatty gear, chasing wealthy fashion clones with funny hair-cuts. Slaughter would drink out of the dog's bowl if she told him. He trusted her, believed her sexual appetite meant he was major, more than sex and protection, that he was the man of her dreams or some other romantic rubbish. That Terry was smart. He was dead ahead. No complications. She'd ask him why he was called Carter when she got the chance, straight out, confirm her suspicions and learn the details. She'd blow his mind.

The man she was serving was going on about something or other, a film he wanted to see, and she was smiling and doing her job, nodding her head, raising eyebrows, but all the time she had her eye on Terry leaning forward over the table telling a story to the three others, Will and the two men who shared a flat down the road. She wished she was a fly on the wall listening, a wasp with a sting, getting hot and bothered thinking about Terry having it off with one of his girls. She guessed it was that kind of story. She felt annoyed for some reason, Slaughter getting in a punch-up with a bloke in the West End the night before, putting the silly so and so's head through a car window because he'd paid her a compliment, a bloody compliment, nice arse. Anti-theft device screeching in her ear. Slaughter ran off leaving her to follow as best she could. It wasn't the kind of life Denise wanted.

When they'd got back to her place he'd stripped off and she could see him standing there now. Covered in ink with a dead penis full of lager, body swaying side to side, head back looking at the ceiling. She'd been ready for a Slaughter special, rough sex which was okay if she was in the mood but not when he was paralytic and biting into her neck like Dracula on a bad trip. She thought of that time when she'd pissed over his face, both of them burning up. She'd covered the bastard and he choked when it gushed into his mouth, eyes wide hoping it was okay, looking to her with a kind of appeal, a dumb kid. But last night Slaughter had looked at the ceiling like he was trying to find skin in the plaster, first-year monsters in the woodwork. He fell back against the wall and sank down to the floor. Denise had to turn off the gas fire otherwise he'd have burnt alive. He didn't move till morning. Terry though, where was he last night? She watched the men laughing together, wishing she could get him on his own for a minute and arrange something.

'Here you go,' Mango was back at the table. 'Anyone want crisps? I reckon Denise fancies me.'

'Leave it out,' Carter said looking towards the bar. 'Take her on and you'll be into Slaughter as well. He'd fucking kill you. Chop you into tiny pieces and feed you to the penguins in London Zoo. Then he'd take your head and put it on a stake outside the Tower of London for the ravens and beefeaters, balls stuffed in your mouth.'

'Suppose so. Don't stare at her otherwise she'll think I'm talking about her.'

'You are.'

'What's your resolution, Mango?' Harry asked, bored with Denise, a right old slag by his reasoning. Those kind were trouble. They came in your dreams and gave you grief all night long.

'Going to get myself a Merc by the end of the year.'

'I thought you were shagging the Jag. Changed your mind a bit sharpish didn't you? Fed up creeping down at three in the morning in your boiler suit to get stuck into the exhaust?'

'I'll keep the Jag and get the Merc as well. I have to earn the money first. It's a target to aim for. You've got to plan ahead. It keeps you going.'

'Can I use the Jag when you get the Merc then?' Carter asked.

'Fuck off. You'd ruin the upholstery with all the birds you get through. It's a class motor. I don't want stains all over the leather.'

Mango regretted the comment right away because it recognised Carter's reputation. He liked to present himself on an equal footing, but never did as well as the sex machine and would have to lie his way up the table. That was okay, because Mango was good with the truth. The others wouldn't have the ability or desire to cheat, but a high position was important for Mango. He was a competitor and despite his relative wealth women didn't exactly come calling like they did for Carter. He did alright, anyone could do okay with a bit of effort, but he was nowhere near the Carter class. Sometimes it bothered him, but Carter had serviced some right old grinders in his time and Mango had long since convinced himself he was more into quality than quantity. Something stirred, the memory of that kid up in King's Cross, the girl from Halifax. Young and tender and fucked rigid by how many men he did not know.

'What about whores?' he asked.

'What about them?' Balti was feeling the strain, looking forward to a good sleep but too tired to get up and go home. He was fucked and not looking forward to getting up for work.

'Do prossies count?'

'Course they fucking don't,' Carter said.

He turned to look over his shoulder again and three Sex Division members considered the possibilities. Will wished they'd talk about something else, but was more concerned with the pain shooting through his eye than starting something off. Balti looked at Mango, then Carter, Harry catching his eye and winking as he lifted his glass and took a big swig of liquid gold.

'Why not?' Harry asked. 'After all, you're still doing the business. It's the same things you're doing so there should be the same points available. You've got to perform even when you're splashing out for the privilege. It's not that easy.'

'Don't be a cunt. What's the point having a league if you're going to pay some tart for points. It would be taking a bung.'

'No it wouldn't,' Harry was into the game. 'You look at the big clubs and football's all about how much money you can spend on players. It's like everything nowadays. Ask Mango what counts and he'll tell you money, and he should know better than the rest of us stuck down here while he's rubbing bollocks with the men who matter. Nothing else comes into the equation. You still have to buy quality players to succeed. It's not like you pay the money and everything's over with. You might not be able to get it up or something.'

'Fuck off will you. You're trying to wind me up. There's no sense having a league if you go out and pay for it. Where's the fun in that? It would be like you said, success geared by how much you spend.'

'Like professional football then.'

'We're better than that. We're in it for the love of the game, or at least I am. You lot might find it a bit of a struggle, not being into birds and all that, rather sit at home wanking over the cartoons, but some of us enjoy shafting beautiful women. Sex makes the world turn.'

'Well what about a points system for the state of the bird concerned if we can't get them for whores?' Balti asked. 'Give them a rating on looks and how much effort it takes. I mean some birds we could all have, but others are a better standard. You'll fuck anything with a dress on. Vicars, Scots, whatever. The rest of us are a bit more select. We don't scatter our DNA everywhere.'

'Is that the excuse then?' Carter was shaking his head. 'You're all going to say you're only interested in beauty queens. Next you'll be wanting points for blokes.'

'Do us a favour,' Balti said, choking on his drink, outraged. 'Any cunt does that and he's out of the fucking squad. Immediate relegation and a lifelong ban.'

The lads nodded their heads wisely and sat in silence.

'What about rape then?' Mango asked. 'What about twenty points for rape?'

'Yeah, twenty points for a rape. You fucking lemon.'

They were all laughing now, because the options were endless, and Mango was getting silly. Anyone who raped a woman deserved to be hung. They all agreed on that. It had to be the worst crime going. That and child sex. There were some fucking sick bastards in the world. Hanging was too good for rapists and child molesters.

'What about animals?' Mango asked.

'He's had a few animals in his time,' Balti said. 'Carter's not fussy where he dumps his load.'

'We all have, be honest. Get pissed and you don't know what's going on. A bit of meat would do when you're on the scent. It's programming. I mean, that's why God invented the orgasm. Nobody's going to plan kids are they, because it makes your life a misery and everything, so there's this implant wedged in the brain that makes you fancy the opposite sex, and when you're pissed you lose your reason and shag anything. A pig can still produce young, can't she?'

'I meant hamsters and stuff like that,' Mango was cracking up. He didn't normally laugh much, but was feeling spaced out. 'Some people shag animals, don't they?'

'Anyone does an animal, a four-legged animal that is, and I'll chop their bollocks off,' Will said, piping up at last. He liked animals, saw them as defenceless victims. Even mentioning rape in the same sentence as sex was bad news. That kind of stuff was all about power and control. He was a romantic and couldn't really separate sex and love.

They shut up when Eileen came round again. Carter asked her if she'd had a good New Year's Eve and she nodded, saying she'd gone to her sister's house. A few people round for dinner, and it made a nice change from the usual drunk effort, an Italian meal which her brother-in-law had made. He was from Naples and a good cook. The Italians knew how to enjoy themselves without getting pissed, though she couldn't say much seeing as how she worked in a pub. She asked how Will's eye was and he stammered a bit and knew he was going red and said fine, thanks, then changed his mind and was honest and said it hurt, real painful like, and she told him he should go and see a doctor. Harry looked at Will and prescribed another pint.

'You're in there,' Carter whispered, when Eileen had gone.

Will shook his head and felt awkward.

'How about shitting on a bird then?' Mango asked.

'Why is it always you that comes up with the sick stuff?' Harry asked. 'You've got no soul. You've sold it down the City. I bet it's sitting there in a bank vault wondering where you've gone. Why would you want to shit on a bird? You're sad even thinking like that.'

'How about shitting in their handbags then?' Balti flicked a dead match from the ashtray at Harry, which bounced off his number 2 crop before felling to the floor.

The Sex Division membership thought about this new development. It had a certain kind of appeal. There had to be something acceptable beyond a four-pointer, something nobody was going to achieve. Rape, animals, anything like that was obviously bang out of order, the mark of a pervert destined for a severe kicking. But shitting in a bird's handbag was funny.

'Five points. What do you think?' Harry liked the idea.

'What about ten points?' Carter was laughing, they were all laughing.

'Ten points for shitting in a bird's handbag then. We all agreed on that?'

Everyone nodded, even Will. It was the impossible dream, a Sex Division special that went beyond the everyday, a recognition that there was only one winner when it came to sex, unless Mango made a determined effort and Carter lost the urge. Will was negative about the league anyway and Harry and Balti would never be that bothered, maybe pulling once or twice if they were lucky, but more concerned with drink, football, food; preferring a laugh and a good wank to feeding someone a line. The handbag bonus scheme eased things and made the league more light-hearted. That's all it was supposed to be really. A bit of a laugh.

COGS

Harry was late. Well late. And that lazy cunt Balti hadn't woken him. He sat up in bed and breathed out, watching the mist form and hover, then slowly disappear, pulling the pillows high behind his back, chasing the dream running out of reach, deep into his brain where it could hide in the undergrowth. The radio was talking about a fire on the tube, Clapham North evacuated and the London Fire Brigade in attendance, a train on the District Line stuck underground packed with commuters, passenger under the carriages at Whitechapel, leaves on the line outside Waterloo threatening derailment, a pile-up on the M25 with police cutting a woman and child from the wreckage; all the normal fun and games of a rundown infrastructure. He had fifteen minutes till he was due at work and wasn't going to make it, but bollocks, there was nothing he could do now. Then Balti was sticking his head round the door saying he'd just got up, the fucking alarm hadn't gone off, that they'd better shift. He started half an hour later than Harry so was alright, handing over a cup of tea and a plate with two pieces of toast floating in a puddle of melted margarine, then shut the door and returned to the kitchen.

Harry sipped milky tea with two sugars, still tracking the dream, his head clear despite the drink of the previous evening. They'd left the pub at closing-time, though Will had pissed off about ten, wanker, and the rest of them had got soaked on the way home. Typical Will picking the right moment and avoiding the storm. He looked round the room, curtains half drawn and his clothes in a tangled pile by the chest of drawers. He needed to go to the launderette. Then he was concentrating, like he could make something click towards the back of the skull, a switch setting electricity loose, current popping and the scene sticking, colour melting inside felt-tip outlines.

He was with Balti, a tropical paradise by the look of things, both of them in bright yellow shorts. He pushed harder retracing their steps, a long winding trail through pure white sand, a bit younger, four or five years, and they must've been in the Philippines or Indonesia, somewhere in South-East Asia, because there were skinny brown kids playing in the sand looking for crabs, changing to skinny white kids building castles, then brown kids again wading into a clear blue ocean with small nets held high above their heads, up to their waists in a gently lapping sea, white kids dodging sewage and used condoms, brown kids watching for fish, wary of sharks. He saw a fin approaching, the pit of his stomach drawing back as he pictured the monster lurking, teeth razor sharp for amputation, victims drowned and mutilated, pure blue water turned to congealed artery red, a dolphin leaping then belly-flopping with a smile splitting its cartoon tab-of-acid face.

He bit into the toast and pulled the bed clothes higher. Harry liked dolphins. Everyone liked dolphins. Except the American military who'd trained the poor cunts to carry explosives on kamikaze missions. Tuna fishermen didn't give a fuck about dolphins either. Then there were the amusement parks that kept the bastards confined and taught them to perform for their supper. Life was shit if you were a dolphin in the wrong place at the wrong time. There'd been two in the Thames a while back, but there was so much shit in the water they'd got sick and their skin peeled with the pollution. He couldn't remember whether they'd escaped, the faint voice of the radio missing the end of the story. Take a wrong turn like that and you ended up boiling alive in industrial waste. But it was freezing on the mainland painting a house in Wandsworth. They had to let the gas people in first so wouldn't be starting till a bit later than normal, which gave him an excuse. Fuck's sake. He'd almost spilt the tea.

Pushing his head again, Harry was back with that line of footprints across a near-deserted beach, an exotic hideaway, sitting with his best mate, like brothers, both of them tanned and fit, bare-chested, served a nice plate of rice and a yellow pineapple dish with grated coconut, thick banana shakes in tall glasses, sliced papaya and watermelon on a separate plate. There was a brilliant green snake winding its way down a palm tree and the two men watched it as they ate, trying to decide whether it was poisonous. The old lady serving said no, that it was just a tree snake, teeth long gone and the gums bruised dark black red. There were tiny transparent geckos on the ceiling watching the dream unfold and when he looked across the sand the kids were coming back to shore with their catch, lifeless silver strips of protein. He felt happy. Real contentment. The fishermen were children, but at the same time adults. They were old when they were young, yet would hold on to a brand of innocence till the moment they died. He couldn't remember much more. The rest of the dream was fading, just out of reach, a mystery washed away by last night's drink. He was late but didn't care now. Harry's dreams usually decided his mood for the day. He dreamt a lot. He was in a good mood and knew nothing could touch him for the rest of the day.

He heaved himself out of bed and stood naked in the middle of the room eating toast, nicely done with burnt edges. Balti would make someone a perfect wife. He imagined the fat cunt in a bride's dress with a veil over his head, some old slapper from Blues carrying the train, walking up to the preacher and taking the cunt's crucifix then driving it into his head, blood on the insignia, army uniform under the holy man's skirt. Harry laughed and wondered if it was part of the dream coming up. He walked over to the window and looked round the curtain, careful not to show himself off to the outside world. He didn't want to get done flashing before he'd even got out of the house. It would be just his luck getting dragged out in handcuffs. Straight down the nick for some instant justice.

The street was damp but it wasn't raining, a gentle wind rattling the frame which was rotten and needed replacing. He put his dressing gown on and went to brush his teeth, have a wash, making a note to get the dressing gown cleaned. It didn't smell too healthy. There was no time for a shave and Balti was in the kitchen telling him to get a move on, fuck off you cunt, you should've woke me up earlier, then he was back in his bedroom considering a wank before the first day's work of the new year, a quick meeting with the five-fingered widow.

He reached under his bed for a magazine and pulled out a plum. *Red Hot Asian Babes On Heat*. He flicked through and selected Tash and Tina, who were busy servicing The Sultan Of Singh. The lager was still in Harry's system and slowed him down at first, but with a bit of concentration he was soon erect and beating out a familiar rhythm. Practice had made perfect and in under a minute he was unloading the white man's burden. He mopped up and found a clean pair of pants and a T-shirt that wasn't too bad, added his torn sweat shirt and jeans, and sat down to put on thick socks and boots. Balti was shouting he was off on his own if Harry didn't get a move on, get your finger out you fat bastard, stop banging the bishop. Just like a nagging wife.

Will worked his way through the albums, stopping at Yes. The sleeves were bent and worn, and the corners looked as though they had been gnawed by rats. He'd never listened to Yes, though he'd always been quick enough to slag them off. Longhaired hippy music. It was funny how it worked. He'd never been into Deep Purple or Status Quo as a kid, but had listened to Led Zeppelin's Physical Graffiti enough times. His first single had been by Elvis Presley, according to his old man, and later he'd found out Elvis was one of punk's many enemies. The same went for the Beatles and Stones. It was mental the way you had to act according to the rules, even as a kid. It was still there and he wanted to buy one of the Yes albums to prove a point, but if he did it to prove a point then he was still being told what to do in a roundabout sort of way. He could afford the record because it was secondhand, dusty vinyl, and he could buy it because he was older with money in his pocket. He'd pay a couple of quid, have a listen, confirm his opinion, then chuck the album out so it wouldn't pollute the rest of his LPs. But then he would have to do the same with every other battered piece of vinyl in the racks. He left well alone.

'Will? Is that you?'

Will turned and faced a woman with spiked jet-black hair and a thick red cardigan, a well-worn, multi-coloured shirt peeping through. His surprise must have registered. He tried to pin a name on the face.

'I thought it was you. Happy New Year. You don't recognise me do

you? I was in your sister's class at school. I came round your place a few
times. Karen. Karen Eliot.'

'I remember. You look different. It's a long time since I last saw you,
that's all. You were a kid then.'

'How's Ruth these days? Haven't seen her for ages.'

'She's alright. Living back round the old man's at the moment. She
broke up with her husband a year back. Took it hard, but you get over
these things with a bit of time I suppose.'

'I didn't even know she was married.'

'Bad news he was. Used to knock her about but nobody found out
till she left him and now he's done a runner. Ruth didn't tell anyone
because she knew he'd get his head kicked in. Left her with all the bills
on the flat to pay when he legged it. She's getting straight again. Must
make you feel like nothing when you've been battered and then you're
forced to cough up for the honour. There's a lot of rubbish around.'

As they talked, Will discreetly checked the albums Karen was
holding. U-Roy's With Words Of Wisdom on top, and under that what
looked like Prince Far I's Free From Sin, judging from the thick red
lines over a smaller black-and-white crisscross pattern on the edge
of the cover. Not bad. A woman with taste. Nice body and a face with
character. Classy album covers as well and they didn't go cheap, classic
reggae vinyl. He hadn't found anything he wanted and was tempted to
ask Karen if she fancied a coffee somewhere, a cup of coffee and a slice
of cake. It was too early for the pub. But he bottled out, and instead
she was saying she worked in The George three nights a week and if he
came in later she'd make sure he drank for free. There was a late-night
Moroccan cafe round the corner, so maybe they could have a coffee
after. Then she looked all embarrassed and said she'd like to hear more
about Ruth, stared at the floor, smiled a crooked smile, and was off to
the counter to pay for the records. She turned back to say she hoped
she'd see him later. When she went outside Will's eyes followed her
down the street.

Carter cut up a Rover at the lights, pulling the furniture delivery van
tight into the inside lane, his young assistant Ian, Boy Ian as Carter

called him, raising his right hand to the mirror in a peace gesture, beating the wanker sign his work-mate was about to deliver. Ian was easy-going which meant he generally got lumbered with the heavy lifting when they were on a job together. Carter enjoyed directing operations, the hard graft never much more than a double bed that the customer had to assemble, though lugging the various parts up four or five flights of stairs wasn't much fun.

Ian was a heavy-built Irishman from Donegal, though he'd lived twenty-one of his twenty-two years in London. He was London Irish, a QPR boy with a Celtic top and cross round his neck, but went against the Paddy stereotype preferring dope to Murphy's, jungle to diddly-daddly, ecstasy to whisky. He worked the cassette player as they went which suited Carter, slipping in some On U-Sound or old techno compilations. Carter specially liked Gary Clail's Emotional Hooligan, heavy bass taking him back to when they were kids into reggae, dub, punk—following Will's early interests and Pete Wilson's readiness to lend out his albums. He liked the dog barking in the background, or whatever the sound was, probably a special effect. Bim Sherman was next. Funny how music reappeared. Everything went in circles.

He kept meaning to knock together a tape of his own but never got round to it, deciding he'd get Will on the job, as the bloke had all the same records plus a thousand or so on top. Will was the man in the know. He thought about the emotion bit. Tricky that one, though if you were in Mango's shoes then maybe there was a reason. It was sad how something like a missing brother stayed with you your whole life. Fucked things up badly. Mango had never been the same, though it could've been growing up responsible for the change. He hit the brake hard for a hunchback granny walking on to the zebra crossing not looking where she was going, glancing into the mirror at the Rover he'd cut-up, a big cunt behind the wheel staring back. He put his hand down the side of the seat and felt the sawn-off snooker cue tucked out of sight, ready for the bloke to try his luck. There was a dented skull waiting to happen.

Then they were moving and he watched the Rover turn off, a nice motor worth a few bob, near enough vintage, pointing out a couple of women with kids in push chairs coming out of the bookies. He didn't think kids were allowed in betting shops. Maybe they were getting kicked out or had been in to see the old man, begging for spare change. Kids shouldn't be hanging around the bookies. Ian followed his gesture and Carter was saying the taller one was nice and well worth five minutes of his precious time, shame about the sprog, that the other bird was a bit iffy but so what. He'd fuck the arse off both of them given the chance. Ian just smiled and put in another tape, fast-forwarding to a mixture of didgeridoos and cranking metal, like the van was about to explode. Then the whole thing was taken over by some brand of psychedelic Eastern trance, Kurdish according to Ian, religious and full of nailed down sex. It was alright and made up for missing out on Bim Sherman. Ian started skinning up.

While Harry sat on a front garden wall in Wandsworth with Dave and Bob from West London Decoration, banging his heels against bricks, waiting for the men inside to sort out the gas, Balti was down in Tooting breaking his back. He wasn't in the mood for the verbal he was getting off Roy McDonald, a mouthy Belfast cunt who was going to get a brick rammed down his throat before the day was out. Balti decided on a break and set his load down, going round the back of the parked-up tippers where he could sit for a few minutes. He was shagged out. Like he was sick. Every muscle ached and his head was weighed down. There was this thud of drills from deep inside the building and he was dizzy. Then he was trying to keep his balance. He'd been on one long beano through Christmas and into the New Year, on the piss with Harry and any of the other lads who happened to be around. Harry was the top boy though. He loved his drink more than the rest of them. He could never keep up with the cunt. He tried, but failed. Harry said the lager washed away all your problems. Add a few beans courtesy of Mango and he was fucked.

'What the fucking hell are you doing?' McDonald was standing opposite, fag hanging out of his mouth, shit all over his donkey jacket, dried clay covering his boots. He spat his words and Balti looked for red flames.

Balti wondered if McDonald was a devout Protestant. There'd been a lot about Ireland on the news, history and everything, stuff he didn't understand because he never paid much attention to the details and couldn't work out the logic involved. He didn't care one way or the other, staring back at McDonald unable to speak. He had nothing worth saying. He ran his eyes towards the opening behind McDonald, the area of the site that was visible and empty of workers.

'We're behind enough as it is without you taking a fucking nap. You lazy cunts get paid on time and you want to sit around doing nothing. We've got schedules to keep. I've been watching you and you're taking the piss. Get back to work or you're out. This isn't a fucking holiday camp.'

Balti stood up slowly, moved forward with a humble expression and headbutted McDonald between the eyes. The two men were roughly the same size and the foreman liked to think of himself as a hard man; hard but fair, respected by the lads who worked for him. But Balti wasn't watching the same video. McDonald rocked back against one of the lorries and a steel toecapped boot connected with his groin, pain racing through his stomach into his mouth, down the front of his coat. Balti pulled him forward and damaged the cunt's nose with his knee. He hoped it was broken. Heard a crack.

He stood and looked at the bloke half-conscious on the ground, breathing heavily. It was the surprise that made it so easy and there were no witnesses. For a second he thought about using a slab to smash McDonald's skull in, picking up a shovel and killing the cunt for his lack of respect. But he wasn't worth the aggro murder would bring. No way. You had to know when to stop. He was out of a job but McDonald wouldn't get the old bill involved. Maybe he'd come looking, but Balti could handle that. What did he care? He didn't need his nose rubbed in shit first thing in the new year. Like everyone else he just wanted a bit of respect. That was all. Respect was essential. Without it you were nothing. You might as well give up and top yourself if you didn't have respect.

'Any time you fancy your chances, you know where I am, you Irish cunt.'

Balti kicked McDonald in the gut and went to collect his sandwich box and flask, walked to the car, and was soon driving past Tooting Bee tube towards Wandsworth Common. He smelt the fumes and felt sick, moving slow then fast, lumbered behind a bus, changing down a gear and accelerating on his way, pavements full of people, then empty, breathing slowly returning to normal. When he reached the common he parked and walked over to a bench, rich green grass stretching out in front of him, a black labrador in the distant hunched up and straining. Time to rest and calm down a bit, watching the traffic lights click red, yellow, green; double-deckers rolling slowly along, top decks full of pinprick faces; people going in and out of a parade of shops; a couple of wankers over by the pond hanging on to their fishing rods looking to catch a minnow.

Carter was directing operations, carrying screws and a couple of planks, Ian bringing up the bigger parts of the bed. They'd already brought the mattress upstairs and a well-bred woman was flicking through the instruction manual. Carter was casting a critical eye over a fit figure showing off a pair of expensive slacks. He reckoned she was over forty. There were gold rings on her fingers and a couple of silver specks in nicely-groomed but fairly natural hair. She looked up and caught his eye, turning away quickly, something wicked on her mind. He reckoned there was a good chance of picking up a couple of points if he played the game in the right way. He would have to get rid of Ian for a while, but he was stoned and open to suggestion. It shouldn't be too hard. When the woman went out of the room he had a quiet word.

'Hurry up, my husband will be back soon,' the woman gasped. 'Come on you horny bastard. Faster.'

Carter kept pumping away, the plastic cover they'd half pulled off the mattress rubbing against his knees. She was a right goer this one, but he didn't fancy her old man opening the bedroom door and catching them on the job. He wasn't getting anywhere though, so turned her round on to all-fours, trying a different angle. As he did his duty he looked around the room, a gold-framed photo of the woman in question standing next to a man in a black suit, an accountant or solicitor by the looks of him, two blond-haired, blue-eyed boys in front of their parents, smiling. Their mother was moaning and the delivery man servicing her ladyship was totting up the points. Two plus four made six and they were only a day and a half into the season. Four points would make it eight and he slipped his hand between the woman's cheeks testing the ground. He didn't really fancy the shift, but there were points on offer and Carter wanted to get a healthy lead established as soon as possible. Then he could relax.

'Don't do that,' she ordered, sucking in her breath, a hand coming back to remove his finger.

Carter was getting a bit bored, wishing he could finish and get down the cafe with Ian. His work-mate was a good boy, understanding the situation. Carter was hungry and it was time the delivery man delivered his load. He fancied a good fry-up and a nice mug of strong coffee. Meat for the gut and caffeine for the brain. Bacon and sausage smells hit home, imagination working hard, picturing the look on the faces of the rest of the lads when he broke the news. Total football. Johan Cruyff was the master, like that time out on the wing he'd taken the defender one way, back-heeled the ball through his own legs and off he went. The tradition moved on. There was no real beginning and end. There was the Gullit-Rijkaard-Van Basten mob. Now there was Bergkamp-Overmars-Kluivert. It was in the blood and the rest of the boys would be gutted. There was a tank in a corner of the bedroom, tropical fish unaware of their origins. At least they were free of predators and fed regularly. That's the way Carter looked at the situation. Next to the tank was another photograph, in an antique frame that must've been worth a bit, two girls in sixties fashion. It was probably dog woman and a sister. They were wide-eyed, female versions of the two young boys. One of them held a hoop, both with ribbons in their hair, though the picture was black and white so he didn't know what colour. There was the same expression on their faces.

'Come on, don't slow down,' the woman was panting and Carter made the effort, concentrating on the job in hand, feeling the woman shudder, trying to forget about the bacon, his mates waiting down the pub, Ian in the cafe shovelling down egg on toast, Harry and Balti,

Mango and Will the record collector sitting in The Unity, drinks lined up, having a crack, a good laugh, enjoying the show. A flash of inspiration hit the league leader, the kind of thinking that sorts the winners from the losers, championship material, the mark of genius, excitement hitting home, total fucking football. Total fucking football.

As the woman finished Carter felt the tension reach boiling in his groin, quickly withdrew, flipped her over and moved fast so he shot over her left breast then finished off in her mouth. His thoughts were with the manoeuvre, the distance between the first muscle spasm, the quick withdrawal and attempts to hold back, losing it a bit halfway, then hitting the jackpot. Calculations were all important and his tactics worked. He rolled over next to a satisfied mother and wife, the smell of pine from the bed all around them. They were strangers again in a clearing deep inside a Scandinavian forest with the trolls and lumberjacks and herds of reindeer. It had been a near thing, breaking the flow and diverting his attention, numbing the physical satisfaction. But he'd done well. Fucking brilliant. It was a three-pointer and the rest of the lads would be well impressed. The woman next to him laid her head on his chest. He couldn't wait to see the faces of his mates when he broke the news.

'You nutted him?' Harry asked, shaking his head. 'Nice one Balti, can't slag you off for the reasoning behind the action, but a job's a job you know.'

'He had it coming. I know it's not too rosy workwise at the moment, I mean it never fucking is, but he should've kept his trap shut. He doesn't pay enough to talk to me like that. He wouldn't do it off the site. No cunt talks to me like that. I should've bricked him as well. Should've killed the cunt. Who the fuck does he think he is?'

'Never mind all that. Drink up and I'll buy you another.'

'I can still get a round in. I'm not a beggar. Not yet anyway.'

Harry watched Balti go to the bar and order two pints of Fosters. Strange that the dream he'd woken up with was so positive, and now this. He tried to make sense of the beach scene, the kids fishing and everything. He must be getting his ideas mixed up. Usually he could

work out his dreams by the end of the morning, often much quicker. It
was either sorting out the past or, now and then, seeing something in
the future. Maybe it was wishful thinking. Balti sipped his lager as he
waited for the second pint. This morning Balti had been good as gold,
up with the sun and everything, then a few hours later he's giving his
boss a hiding. Maybe it was down to McDonald, fucks knows, though
it must've been a bit of Balti as well. But it didn't matter, because they
were mates and Balti's version was all that counted. If the bloke came
down looking for trouble they'd give him another helping. Harry went
back to the beach. Considered the tree snake.

'I think I'll shoot off after this one,' Balti said when he'd returned
with the drinks. 'Go home and polish off a bottle of gin then start the
new year again tomorrow. What a way to kick off.'

'Stay here and we'll have a drink. The others'll look out for me. It's
a bit slow anyway. They're still fucking about with the gas.'

They stayed in the pub most of the afternoon, drinking at a relaxed
pace. Harry was pushing a visit to Balti Heaven back home, but the Balti
king was standing firm, leaving well alone. It was a question of will-
power, something he had to prove to himself. He also needed to shift
some weight if he was going to get anywhere in the league. Harry didn't
care about such niceties, half a stone lighter than his mate. A midday
session was just what Balti needed to forget about mass unemployment, McDonald just a stack of clothes with a pool of shit inside. So
what if Balti didn't have the pleasure of killing himself hauling bricks.
There were other things he could do. He was sick of labouring. He'd
done it on and off since leaving school. Picking up the wage packet and
out on the piss, down the football, feeding his face, keeping the curry
houses going. It was a clean break. Better than a New Year celebration.
The lager was doing its job and Harry talked him through with some
expert advice. Life was good with a gallon of drink tucked in your gut.
Harry was no mug. He could see the present as well as the future.

Carter and Boy Ian were making the most of the delay, sitting in the
van behind Baker Street tube. The next delivery was due in half an hour
and they were ahead of schedule. The man buying the large double

bed wasn't due home till four. They'd tried him on the mobile but got an answerphone. Despite the fry-up, Carter was hungry, deciding it must've been that woman building up his appetite. She was a raver and suddenly keen for another portion, but he'd had to leg it. He couldn't leave Ian hanging round like a cunt all day and her husband was due back. She was mad. One minute she wanted him out, the next she wanted him to stay. It didn't matter to him, but she had a lot to lose. He couldn't work women out sometimes. Carter had a job to do, and it wasn't like he was going to add to his points total. She'd asked him to ring her and he was considering the request. He could put himself through the grinder—she'd offered to pay for a hotel room in the West End and obviously had the wedge—but the most he could hope for was an extra point, unless he saw to her handbag, and that wasn't being realistic. He would have to believe in the possibility of chalking up a bonus point before he called.

'Get us some chips if you go for a kebab,' Ian said, eyes bleary and his thoughts drifting. 'A can of Coke would be nice as well. A cold one.'

Carter made the decision and went over to the kebab house. It was different to the normal effort, a real Middle East job with Muslim girls in head gear behind the counter. Not the purdah stuff but scarves. They were in their early twenties and good-looking. Cheerful and friendly. Lebanese or Syrian maybe. He ordered a kebab and chips, two cans of freezing Coke, then sat down while the food was prepared, flicking through a magazine. Rain hit the window, Arabic script decorated the glass. It was a smart little place, big pictures of mullahs and minarets adding flavour. An old man shuffled in, smoker's cough in his throat. Too much hashish. Carter watched him, then the girls. Even the meat looked different. It wasn't the usual Greek-Turk effort he got round his way, a bit up-market seeing as this was Baker Street. He considered the girls behind the counter and whether there was any way he could top up his seven-point total. A couple of blow jobs out back, or at least a shag.

The man pissed off with his sweet cakes and Carter tried to work out whether the smiles and looks coming his way were an invitation or plain friendliness. It was difficult sometimes working things out, knowing what was true and what was fiction. The food was placed on the counter and he made the right decision, dipping his hand in his pocket to pay, leaving it alone knowing that success was going to his head, that sniffing around in kebab houses was a bit sad somehow.

'Cheers Terry,' Ian said when the chips arrived. 'I'm looking forward to these.'

Carter rolled the window down to let some of the smoke out. The wind cleared things nicely and he got stuck into the kebab, wondering what kind of meat was in the mix, the chilli sauce packing a powerful kick. They ate in silence, Ian more concerned with his chips than changing the tape. When they'd finished, he took the paper and empty cans to a bin while Carter called Mr Malik. A man's voice answered and they were in business, one more job out of the way. If they finished ahead of schedule they got off early. Carter would have a look in the pub, see if any of the boys were about. It would be a good evening if he could find some of the lads. He was on a roll.

The Lager Twins were well oiled and ready to eat, a full-scale Chinese takeaway and a couple of cheap bottles of cider to polish off the evening. Balti took two plates, knives and forks, serving spoons and the mushroom soya sauce into the living room. Harry meanwhile had the containers on a tray, leaving the lids in place so none of the heat could escape. Balti remembered the glasses and went back to the kitchen for two pints nicked from the pub. He shoved one of the cider bottles into the freezer and took the other. The telly was on in the corner, volume turned down low, a documentary on the chemicals in food packaging that were believed to be affecting male sperm counts in the civilised world. Balti said they should tell Carter.

'Look at those.' Harry had emptied the spring rolls on to a plate and was prising the lid off the sweet and sour, Balti opening the other containers. 'You get value for money down the Die Nasty. Like Carter. Value for money shag machine, always a cheap deal on offer. They're fucking huge these spring rolls.'

The doorbell sounded. Balti swore and Harry told him not to answer it. Balti looked out the window and saw the sex machine below.

It was magic. Black, evil, twisted magic. Mention the cunt's name and he turns up on the doorstep just when you're about to get stuck in. Balti was starving and letting Carter in meant sharing the food, or at least offering, but the lights were on and he'd just keep ringing till they cracked. Mind you, they'd ordered enough. Gone a bit over the top in fact. He made Carter wait a minute and helped himself to a king prawn in batter, digging his teeth into the tender flesh, then poured a glass of cider and took a few gulps. It was warm and tasted like shit but at least it was wet. He banged into the wall a couple of times on the way down, almost falling arse over tit. He could think of better ways to die. What would they write on the grave stone—'Here lies a pisshead who fell down the stairs and broke his fucking neck, the silly cunt'?

'Go get a plate if you want something to eat. We've got a chinky on the go in the front room.'

Once in the flat Carter made himself at home, filling his plate when the others had done, then another glass with cider. The drink was fucking horrible and he went to the fridge, into the freezer for some ice-cubes. He put them in a bowl and took them to the others. Then he was taking things easy, sitting back on the couch next to Balti, watching Harry in the chair opposite spilling food down his shirt. He was a bit stoned thanks to Ian, and had five pints inside him from The Unity, popping in to see if any of the lads were drinking there, having a chat with Eileen, asking after Denise who was off for the night. It was a shame seeing how he was moving, an honorary Dutchman in London, a fucking Orange man from Ajax of Amsterdam, part of the brotherhood. Then he was pissed off realising no-one was going to turn up, deciding to take the news on tour. But he wasn't getting the chance to tell them about the three points because they were pissed and into their own thing, fucking up his moment of glory. He took a ready-rolled spliff Ian had supplied earlier and lit up, passing it round.

'There's opportunities for people like me,' Balti was saying. 'Fit and healthy men in the prime of life, too good for the knacker's yard. I'm not thick you know. Just haven't had the breaks so far. I could do a lot in life, anything I fucking want. You understand that, don't you Tel? Travel the globe and create a bit of history.'

Carter wondered what the fuck Balti was on about. He nodded, his brain misfiring all over the shop, tiredness and the drink, a heavy dinner and kebab that made him feel sick when he thought about it now. There was food everywhere, everyone ripping at everyone else, cannibalism wedged in the mind, consumer society, sex consumption, bit of blow during the day, that posh old witch he'd shafted watched by the kids. It was a nasty business. The things he did for his mates, keeping the flag flying. Top of the league. Wishing he had the woman's arms wrapped round his back now. He noticed the screen for the first time with some boffin-type cunt and then these burning tadpoles that looked like fluorescent spunk under a microscope, tails banging away, sex on the brain. He had to clean his act up, it was taking over. There were other things in life. But nothing like sex. He loved it. Loved women. He wished there was someone at home when he got back, not an empty flat with cold walls till the heating got going, some tasty Swedish bird with legs right up the crack of her arse. Carter tried to work out what Balti was saying, clocking on that he'd given his boss a spanking and was out of a job. Silly fucker.

'It's alright,' Balti was saying. 'It's alright Tel. I'm fine. Don't worry about it. Something'll come up. I'm not bothered. I'm better off than most blokes, those poor bastards with kids to support. Think of the pressure. If I want I can piss off. No ties mate, no fucking ties. You should've seen McDonald go down. Didn't know what hit him.'

'That's living,' Harry agreed. 'No problems. Just keep on, full steam ahead. No surrender.'

Carter had worked it out. They were right. Fat boys in a two-bedroom flat. Looking after each other. Husband and wife. He laughed. Husband and wife without the sex to get in the way. They argued but it never lasted long. They were good mates who watched each other's backs. But Carter knew he'd always be the winner. He had his mates and kept his distance. He was his own man. He stood alone and preferred things that way. Dabbling like there was no tomorrow. He waited for the boys to finish their food and relax, waited till their heads were simmering, a late-night therapy programme coming on and the TV turned off sharpish. Then he picked his moment and broke the good news. He told the lads that their old mate Carter had pulled again and was on seven points. He watched their faces. Balti sunk his face into his hands and Harry shook his head slowly. Carter savoured the moment.

Will had to admit it wasn't a bad little place. He'd pushed himself to go down The George and Karen was right there behind the bar, like she'd said. It was a quiet evening and she fiddled free drinks for the hour till closing. When they'd cleared up she took him round the corner for a late drink that turned out to be coffee. Like she said. She called the waiter over and they paid the bill, Will waiting for the change while Karen went to the Ladies. He was chilling out nicely now, though he'd been nervous going down the pub like that, not knowing what to expect.

Karen was beautiful and he couldn't believe she was interested in someone like him. She was clever as well. He remembered her vaguely as a kid with long hair that had since been cut, and of course she'd filled out and become a woman. A real woman. He couldn't explain it properly, but it was the feeling that counted. He was conscious of mucking things up but she was easy to be with. But why him? A shabby herbert who collected punk and reggae records and made a living running a junk shop. There had to be a catch. Maybe it was a wind-up organised by the rest of the Sex Division. He sipped the coffee dregs and tried to work out the motivation. Perhaps Karen was leading him into a trap. But what kind? It could be personal. Like he could've been rude to her when she was a kid and she'd never forgiven him, showing her up in front of his kid sister. He wasn't like that though. Will was easy-going. Had she seen a chance for revenge? She could be lifting herself through the bog window at that very moment and doing a runner down the back alley, straight into the arms of the Sex Division champion who would take her back to his flat and chalk up a four-pointer. It wasn't a nice thought. He shook his head. Maybe she wasn't interested at all, at least not that way, wanting to talk about his sister who she'd hardly mentioned.

'I can't believe I've met you after all these years,' Karen said as he walked her home. 'You know I used to fancy you like anything when I was a kid. Ruth's big brother. You always seemed so mature. Funny we live so near each other, yet all these years have passed. I don't know where it goes. I shouldn't be saying this should I?'

Will wasn't sure. He couldn't work out the angle. They crossed the street and nearly got soaked by a double-decker, Karen pulling him away from the kerb. They continued and she brushed against him very faintly, but enough for Will to take notice. He saw a group of youths sitting on a wall opposite, tensing as he tried to identify whether the faces were friendly, but they were talking and not interested so he concentrated on Karen. She led the way, turning down a side street, off to the left past cars parked outside a row of lock-ups, under an old railway bridge that was dark and smelt of rotten cardboard and forgotten engine oil, the kind of twilight corner where dossers slept and rapists lurked. The type of place where Batman dropped from the rafters, opened his cape and flashed his Batknob.

'It's a short cut home, but I never come down here at night,' she said. 'It's too dangerous. It gives me the creeps, but it's much faster than going the long way round. I don't mind with you. I don't even come through here in the day. You never know what's waiting for you.'

Will was a bit narked with himself, feeling a tingle, like he was the hunter-gatherer protecting the women folk, the knight in heavy armour telling the rest of the Crusaders to leave him out of the rape and pillage. He loved women. He thought about them a lot but in a different way to the rest of the lads, or at least how he imagined the others thought. He was attracted to warmth and imagination.

'This is it,' Karen said, looking at a three-storey house, the flat she lived in on the top floor. 'Home sweet home. Do you want to come in for a coffee?'

Will was going to say no, that he'd just had one and it had been a bit strong, that he'd be up all night unable to sleep and he had to get up in the morning for work. He realised he was being soppy and smiled again. He reasoned that coffee had to be responsible for a lot of people getting together through the years. Clichés everywhere. You couldn't turn around without one smacking you in the mouth. He told himself to shut up moaning all the time, trying to dissect everything. What should she say? 'Would you like to come upstairs you dirty bastard and fuck the arse off me and if you like I'll give you a blow job so you can impress that Carter mate of yours and go back down the pub with him and the others and make yourself out to be some kind of Alfie stud.' No thanks. He told Karen coffee would be nice. Perhaps they could listen to that Prince Far I album she'd bought earlier. He had the record himself.

PIGS IN KNICKERS

Mango was the only one still in the office, but was surprised to glance at the onscreen clock and find that it had already gone ten. His eyes were aching from prolonged use of the computer. He hadn't been taking the recommended screen breaks and leant his head back, swivelling in his seat. He turned away from the machine and focused on the far end of the open plan office that covered the ninth floor of the block in which he worked. Although designed to soothe the mind and create an illusion of free space, thereby maximising potential in the work force, the inevitable kingdoms had been built with the assistance of grey dividing boards and large potted plants. Cartoons had been carefully cut from *The Times* and *Economist* and pinned up for general appreciation. During the day there was the tangible thrill of expectancy. It was the expectation of either instant dismissal or a very large commission.

Although he appreciated the unique nature of corporate vitality, Mango, or James Wilson as he was known to his work colleagues, preferred the evenings when the majority of his fellow workers had left the office. It gave him the chance to fully relax and plough through data, pinpointing potential targets. Most of the people with whom he worked took a bit of stomaching, but he bit his lip readily enough. Compensation came in the form of hefty financial rewards. This in turn allowed him to leave the poverty of his childhood behind. Mango was good at what he did, very good in fact, which couldn't be said for many of his expensively-educated colleagues who were nonchalantly trying their hands in the world of fast-turnover commodities, little resting on their success. But results counted at WorldView, a model of multinational free-enterprise, and public-school education or otherwise, failure was not tolerated. Maggie would have approved. Mango owed the great lady a great debt. He was fortunate enough to work for a cut-throat company where weakness was erased with the punch of the delete button, and he firmly believed that the WorldView set-up was at the cutting edge of contemporary economics. He had made himself competitive and was reaping the benefits. James Wilson had ambition. He was forging ahead, making money, bettering himself.

Mango pinpointed a yucca plant. He concentrated on the exotic outline, trying to readjust his eyesight to the relaxed mood of the tropics. It was the biggest yucca he had ever seen and must have cost a hundred pounds minimum. The leaves were sharp and well defined, the bark grizzled and sturdy. Each leaf had been individually waxed by a junior employee so that it would shine brightly under the office's artificial lighting. His eyes gradually adapted. It was a lot to pay for a plant, but he was quick to put things into perspective. WorldView had enjoyed record profits during the previous financial year. Talk about wealth distribution. There was no such thing in Britain. He had learnt that growing up and it was this realisation that had made Mango determined to live in a flat where there was no damp and no chance of vandalism. He didn't want to bend his head with the continual scrimping and worry that had haunted his parents. Nobody was going to give him a helping hand. Maggie had understood this essential fact and was a true friend of those people prepared to get off their arses and graft. She was a patriot ground in the realities of multinational commerce. He had taken his chance and embraced the classless society.

Mango thought about his brother. Pete must've decided on something better as well, going off like that, though in his darker moments Mango always imagined the same thing, cruising through a red light area picturing Pete selling his mouth for a couple of quid to make ends meet. Rent boy on the game tiding himself over till he made it big, letting the politicians and financiers carry their policies through to the logical conclusion. Where was he then? Mango was waiting for his big brother to come marching through the door, part of a takeover consortium, nothing less than the top boy. Pete had been trying to get ahead. Maybe that was the true story, Mango didn't know, and although it was the only way he wanted to think, he had strong doubts. Who was he to judge his brother? Sometimes he went a bit spastic and imagined himself grabbing hold of Pete and telling him what a cunt he was, not leaving a body to drain and bury and mourn, just pissing off, before Christmas as well, hitting the bloke then sticking the boot in when he hit the ground, kicking his head till the face caved in, taking a blow-torch and burning the features, melting wax.

Every year Mango's mum bought Pete a present and put it under the Christmas tree. She bought it sober, wrapped it with a celebratory glass of whisky, put it with the other presents, then got pissed. It was always the same. Every year. Christmas morning came and the family was together. The old man with the stuffing ripped out. Mango's two sisters, neither married but wishing they were, right sad cases if he was honest. They all went through the usual routine, passing presents back and forward, delaying the moment, putting it off, scouting round for something else to open till there was nothing left, just a pile of paper with red-nosed Rudolph and shepherds tending their flocks ready for the slaughterhouse, and there it was, left at the end surrounded by shredded wrapping, as per fucking usual, Pete's Christmas present from his mum. Mrs Wilson said nothing as she took the gift and hid it away in the back of the cupboard in her bedroom with all the other presents, tears running down her cheeks into her mouth, the salt of a mother's misery, one more woman ground down and battered into the concrete. It was sad, so fucking sad that sometimes Mango wanted to cry like a baby.

He always wondered what she'd bought. He asked but she said it was Christmas and a surprise, that he was still a big kid at heart wanting to know what his brother was getting ahead of time. It would spoil the surprise if she told him. Jimmy would have to wait and see like everyone else. Did she still buy for a teenager? Did she think her eldest son was the same as the last time she'd seen him, still wearing the same clothes, the army surplus trousers and Harrington, pale face and spiked black hair, suspended in time? Mango did. Off to Greenford to see about a job and there was Mango sitting on the swing waiting for his brother to come back, stood up and let down, twisting the chain round and round, spinning back to earth feeling like he was nothing.

He tried not to visualise the scene. He always saw himself in that play-ground like the spirit he didn't believe in was high above in a spaceship, looking down on the wickedness of human error. It was his own kind of death experience. He'd read about death trips. Sometimes he wished the old bill would come round, say they'd found a teenager's skeleton and DNA fingerprinted Pete, that it was his brother and no doubts remained. Murdered by a pervert and buried in a shallow grave. Found by an unemployed man out walking his dog. At least they'd know for sure. It was the suppressed hope that did them all in. It never seemed to get any easier, however many years passed.

After the regulation break Mango returned to the screen, eyes out of focus now confronted by regimented lines of white figures, digits marching in time and suddenly melting into a tangle of jagged edges. He tried to click into gear but couldn't get going. He was due in at eight the following morning, so surrendered to the inevitable and switched off his computer. He went for his coat and stopped at the drinks machine. He was groggy and tired. His thoughts were losing their clarity, the concentration essential for his success at work fading as his brother made himself part of the present. The ghost was back, ready to cause havoc. Mango chose coffee for a kick-start. It was bitter and tasted of chemicals, but would have the desired effect. He took the lift down to the ground floor and waved to the security guard, a big bastard with a starched collar and glass eye, the result of a pub fight in Bermondsey in his youth. One of the old Millwall boys. Mango passed through the heavy glass doors and into deserted City streets. The buildings towering above James Wilson were sand clean and well-maintained, architecture a fine balance of the old and new. He felt it worked well. A winning fusion of tradition and the modern element to take London deep into the new age. There was no point looking back, although the past was inescapable and had to be accommodated, so a compromise had been reached. The best elements were promoted, while those that had been ignored or pushed outside the area remained to blur the wider vision.

Mango loved the streets of the City when they were empty. He imagined the rest of the human race sucked into a vacuum, abducted by aliens, zapped by an intergalactic ethnic cleansing team. He would sit with the controllers and oversee the extermination campaign. Logic would prevail and he would be president for eternity. All around him there were buildings honed from quality masonry and shining glass, not the cheap stuff they used to house the masses. It was down to quality. If the buildings and environment were solid, then it followed that standards would be maintained. Put someone in a slum and they adapted in order to survive. He hated poverty and insecurity. It made him angry. He wanted the best on offer and fully accepted the survival-of-the-fittest dogma that had revolutionised British life. It was common sense.

The pubs were shut and most of the offices deserted. He walked down perfectly cut streets, very little rubbish to be seen, surveillance cameras on every corner protecting his interests. Mango felt safe. He went to the underground car park, paid his toll and slipped into the Jag. The smell of its interior filled him with a magnificent sense of satisfaction. He leant his head against the rest and inhaled deeply. His eyes ached and he had a pain above his nose, but the Jag was the ultimate relaxant. He closed his eyes and thought of the yucca tree. Perhaps he should buy one for the flat.

Mango drove an XJ6 3.2 Sport. It was a beautiful piece of technology. The machine oozed class and represented British car design at its finest. It had set him back a little over thirty grand, but was well worth the money. It wasn't a long trip from WorldView to King's Cross and he was travelling in style. Cleanliness and sharp design would soon be replaced by uncollected litter and inner-city confusion. Mango cut through Smithfield, past the church where Queen Elizabeth I had watched the execution of Catholics, past the market's meat racks and freezer lorries with their rows of dead pigs, ancient fields now a concrete landing pad for refrigerated truckers waiting to unload their cargoes. Mango's curiosity showed hundreds of pigs on steel hooks, deep black channels carved down the front of their bodies, from throats to missing genitals, straight through to the bone so that the insides could be hacked away, wall-to-wall, clogged together satisfying a pork-hungry public. Computers had given way to headless bodies, hard white digits to drained black blood. He put his foot down disgusted and the Jag soared through Farringdon and Clerkenwell to King's Cross. He became absorbed in the engine. The atmosphere was warm and comforting. Cold butcher's steel a mindless fantasy.

King's Cross was near to deadlock, traffic moving slowly in front of the station, paper flapping and neons flashing, cheeseburger takeaways and sex shop invitation. It was cold and dirty, the inside of the Jag the height of automotive luxury. He preferred the sound of the engine to the radio, working himself further inside the machine, feeling the power and rational precision of the XJ6 surge through the accelerator and into his body. He was part of the mechanism, naught to sixty in 7.9 seconds, cool and calculated, a top-of-the-range model beyond the tug of failure. Mango sat in traffic watching the crowds; half-drunk office workers and inter-city travellers weaving in and out of the festering scum. He stereotyped drunks, junkies, whores, drug dealers, spivs, pickpockets, pimps, muggers, rapists, hypermanics, schizophrenics, wankers. Every kind of mental disease was there in King's Cross drowning in drink and powder and lingering bouts of psychosis, too much for the clean-up campaign. He looked at thin girls and body-built men with gold watches and expensive designer gear. He thought about the girls on the game; addicts, abused kids, poor mothers. He considered the scum milking them, minor-league entrepreneurs dealing crack and selling women as a fast-shifting commodity, chopping their heads off and hanging them on skewers for roving punters. Mouths frozen and sucking devices installed. Blonde heads with bullet holes, American imports, back of the skull efforts where a man could insert his penis and fuck the pig's brains out.

Once away from the main flow Mango knew his way. He saw pros along the side street, tarted up for a cheap porno mag centrespread, caricatures leaning into cars matching the advertising billboards lining London; black and white, old and young, fat and thin, ugly and one or two beauties. Some carried handbags for their accessories, others just had the clothes they wore, making do with spit where others splashed out on lubricant. A woman got out of a car and slammed the door, kicking the wing as it pulled away fast leaving behind a heavy smell of burnt rubber, screaming words Mango couldn't hear. He looked for the kid from Halifax he'd had up by the mosque in Regent's Park, more out of curiosity than any desire for a repeat performance. There were some sorry people about, so desperate they'd do anything for a pittance, spaced out on crack, smack, fuck knows what, amyl nitrate to help them with the big payers demanding a tight fit. His eyes glazed imagining the workings of the human body. He saw blood pumped through veins powering the heart, speeding corpuscles and heaving muscles, valves straining stress, popper acceleration, his own engine expensively tuned and ready to explode down the motorway at a top speed of 138 miles per hour. But these women were the wrecks, covered in rust, scabs, burnt oil. He saw the stockings and suspenders, black white red, the thin fabric and low-cut bras, high heels and thigh-length Nazi jackboots.

A black woman approached, thick red lipstick and hot pants wedged into the crease of her cunt. He looked at the crutch and imagined her shaved clean like the pigs in the refrigerated lorries, heads cut off for Queen Elizabeth I, chainsaw mutilation in the centre of town, Jack The Ripper in the East End slaughtering immigrant workers, Irish whores, operating and hanging their insides over the walls of Whitechapel. The woman was tapping on the glass moving her hand in front of her mouth, offering to suck him off, mouthing the words cheap-very-cheap as she faced up to economic reality, fluttering false eyelashes, star of a pop music video that would conveniently avoid the cold of a leaking one-bedroom flat in Hoxton. The skin was tight against bone but the thighs were too powerful, make-up overdone and smudged, rough as fuck. Mango pulled forward leaving her behind, past three younger blondes; arms, legs, heads nailed together, mouths jabbering, powerpacks inserted. Plastic dolls on a street corner. Inflatable sex. Full of sickness battered by economy and gender. AIDS blended with herpes, syphilis, hepatitis, depression, suicide, a couple of coughing under-five black bastards waiting in Hoxton. He felt confused and thought about doing a U-turn, but kept going.

Mango moved further along the street, cars slowing down so drivers could choose from the menu. He looked in his rearview mirror

and saw Hot Pants get into a dented Granada. Then he spotted the one
he wanted, a young girl up ahead, just what he was looking for, purity
itself. She was in a doorway wearing a mini skirt, talking to a couple
of bent-looking boys. He thought of Pete. Rent boy on the game. It
was wrong, all wrong, that kids like Pete had to leave home and end
up down at the bottom of the pile, pissed on by the world, a dumping
ground for queers and sadists, the kind of people who deserved the
death penalty. The Jag came to a halt and the girl approached. Mango
pressed a button and the window noiselessly lowered, cool night air
entering the cocoon. She was perfect. The hair was cropped short and
dyed black, and she had a nice pair of lungs for a kid, not particularly
big but jutting forward with sharp nipples he could see through the
green cotton top she wore beneath an open PVC jacket. Mango imagined a red button in his mouth, digging his teeth in deep and tugging
hard, pulling the nipple off and cracking it open with his incisors. The
legs were thin but the skirt showed them off just right. The girl leant
in and touched his ear sending a shiver of excitement through his body.
Her perfume was strong, the smell of roses, resembling a sophisticated
brand of artificial beauty. Mango knew that it was cheap shit. He smiled
a paternalistic smile as he handed over his money and the girl walked
round to the passenger's side. He pushed the relevant button to unlock
the door.

Sitting next to him the girl was small and innocent, legs crooked
and half open, a kid who was probably about thirteen. He glanced
at the texture of her skin. The legs were pale white and covered in
goosepimples. He increased the heat a little, attempting to thaw her
out. She'd catch a cold standing around on street corners like that. He
remembered his mum telling his sisters to dress warm when they went
out. She'd said the same to him and his brother, but more often to the
girls. When you were young you dressed to impress rather than look
after your health. It was only when a kid got older they saw beyond all
that. But the girl sitting next to him, flicking through his CDs, she was
beyond that now. He wanted to give her advice. If he was sensible he'd
give her the benefit of his years. He should tell her to sort herself out.
Go back to school. Get some kind of an education. There were other

ways of earning a living. Stacking shelves, cleaning offices, and factory work could pay alright if she got in to the right firm. Maybe she could do something with her life, like he had, get ahead, make decent money. She could become an estate agent. You didn't need a brain for that. Just flog houses to idiots who couldn't afford the repayments, take the commission, then turn your back when it came time for the eviction. Maybe Pete went that way, but no, he'd have done better, Mango was sure of that. There was more to his brother than shuffling deeds. Pete was international. Diamonds, technology, something major. Good old Pete. He should tell the girl about the success of his brother, the short black hair and everything, pale white skin, causes and effect, but he was a man of action and would rather drive up to Regent's Park.

The smell the girl brought into the car was irritating, breaking the Jag's magical aura, yet her presence was exciting, like Halifax, bringing fresh life and the promise of pubescent sex. He drove slowly along the corridor, watching for Halifax, saw comings and goings and the exchange of currency, market forces hard at work. Once on the Euston Road he returned to the girl next to him, buckled down behind the seat belt looking out the window saying little. He found this annoying. The silence put him on edge. Fucking slag. Treating him like one more sleazy punter looking to abuse underage girls. He should teach her a lesson. Put his foot down and steam out of London, 138 miles per hour, naught to sixty in 7.9 seconds, multi-point fuel injection, power-assisted steering, over thirty grand's worth of automobile. Somewhere they didn't interrupt a man going about his legitimate business. He was solid. Doing well. He drove a Jaguar XJ6 3.2 Sport and owned a two-bedroom flat in Fulham. He snorted coke on his own late at night watching videos of German au pairs flat on their backs as queues of Italian queers ejaculated over their grateful faces, while his mates made do with more lager, blow, kebabs. The gym in which he trained was exclusive. The mirrors were floor-to-ceiling and the clientele Eton-educated or London-done-good. Mango was going places. Foot down naught-to-sixty in 7.9 seconds, six in-line cylinders, piling through North London past Hampstead, Barnet, out into Hertfordshire or cutting along the M25 to Essex.

They'd find a nice little beauty spot surrounded by black fields under a locked sky. An abandoned lover's lane. Mango was erect. Space Shuttle job. Grabbing the slut round the neck he'd drag her forward, taking the cut-throat razor from his pocket and holding her down, the blade he kept honed tight on the jugular, maybe a nick or two to see the disease in her blood. He would demand an apology for her treating him like shit, like he didn't matter, like the Jag was just another car. She'd left him spinning in circles, dizzy and confused, just a kid, sitting on those swings like a right idiot for everyone to laugh at, trapped, surrounded by losers, going nowhere, round and round and round till his mouth filled with sick and he started to cry.

He'd remember the Jag's seats and take her out into the darkness. Do them both a bit of good, breathing fresh country air, the hum of the nearby dual carriageway keeping him sane. Subhuman vermin. Drag her to a ditch scaring away the rats and foxes lurking in hedgerows. Night prowlers. The sound of survival flapping in mud. He'd pull her beneath an old oak tree and wait for the moon to burst through a crack in the clouds. He'd see the face for what it really was. He'd force her to look him in the eye. The cropped hair and black dye. The look he knew so well. Selling herself like that, beyond sex now, a boy and a girl, bisexual psychology shifting from a kid growing up playing football to a youth roaming London alone, unloved, killed by a monster and buried in the same spot, under the old oak tree, the only possible reason for a teenager's disappearance. Somewhere there was a bit of English countryside that would remain forever English. One day they'd find the bones. Thousands of years into the future, fully-developed genetic technology readily available, a society so far advanced in its scientific understanding of the creation myth that nurses would be able to apply synthetic skin to the basic bone structure and rebuild the innocent victim. Mango saw Pete in a coming world of peace and love, where people stuck together and there was no need for competition. Right now it remained a masochist's fantasy and belonged to the dole queue. Mango did the sensible thing, fitted into his world and survived. More than that, he prospered. Learnt lessons. He had the strength and the power. He had power over the kid next to him, turning her head now from the Euston Road to the punter behind the wheel.

'Where we going?' she asked.

'Regent's Park,' shaking away the thoughts racing though his brain, imagination running wild, all that death and destruction bad news, something for the TV. 'It's quiet up there. We can be alone for a bit. No risk of the old bill or some headcase watching through the window.'

The girl laughed and her hand moved to his groin. Mango felt tense and turned right. They stopped at a set of traffic lights on the edge of Somers Town. He felt awkward with her next to him when the Jag wasn't moving. The girl leant over and undid his flies. The lights changed and they continued. He cut through back streets to the edge of the park, a quiet spot under a thick covering of trees. He remembered going to the nearby zoo with his family as a kid. Everyone but the old man. Mango must've been eight or nine at the time. It sounded grand when he was small, just the name London Zoo, like the animals there represented the city. They paid to enter another dimension. Watched animals move they'd only ever seen stationary. It was mental. Lions, tigers, bears, elephants, giraffes, crocodiles, snakes. There was a gorilla as well. He didn't remember the name. The poor thing sat there in his own shit surrounded by cold steel, banged up for the duration, sectioned like a nonce, though nobody on the other side of the bars seemed to realise what it all meant.

Pete smacked some kid making faces at the gorilla trying to wind him up, and the wanker had run off crying. The face of the gorilla was in front of him now. The dimmed eyes and broken frown, controlled and paraded for the crowds, unable to appreciate the innocent love of the children outside. The size and power of his body made it worse somehow. There was an unhappiness Mango understood but hadn't been able to identify till years later, thrilled by the strength of the beast, the gentleness and pride. It was all a mess, the lot of it, and now he was all grown up sitting in a flash motor in among the wealth and prestige of Regent's Park with a teenage tart from King's Cross threatening to splash his seed all over the upholstery.

Mango was a success. He had money in his pocket. Money in his

various accounts. Savings schemes and investment plans. Now it was
time for a bit of active socialism. He was spreading his wealth. The girl
sunk her head down and started moving. He looked straight ahead,
willing himself to remain interested as he felt the emptiness of paid-
for sex, his vision quickly accustomed to the darkness. Apartments
glowed red through the trees and occasionally a car hummed past on
fresh tarmac. The girl was doing her work like the pro she was and
he felt the tension quickly build, forgetting the romantic setting and
confused motives. Mango's hands moved down to the back of the girl's
head and he pushed the dismembered head further down, doing his
best to ram his penis down her throat. She began to gag and pull back,
but he pushed harder and told her to get on with it, not to muck him
about, laughing that he was paying the wages and the employer always
demanded more work for lower pay, it was just the way of the world,
part of the boss-worker contract. Then he was coming and the girl was
coughing, Mango pushing the button so she could open the door and
clear her throat in the street, realising that the punter meant it when
he said he'd send her home in an ambulance if she dirtied the interior.
When she'd recovered they sat in silence as he did the decent thing
and drove her back. Mango made a couple of attempts at small talk
that weren't returned, one-word answers unwilling to forgive. When
he glanced at the kid he saw her brushing a tear from her cheek and
he felt like the exploiter he was, wanting to ask her name and history
but knowing it was too late.

Mango felt the Jag vibrate as the girl slammed the door and ran off,
a flash of anger replaced by a desire to get home. He needed to forget
instantly and press on as he had to be up early and needed to be at his
best. There was a big deal in the pipeline and he would have to be shit
hot to get the best for both himself and WorldView. He retraced his
route along the Marylebone Road, then on to the West Way, down to
Shepherd's Bush Corner and through Earl's Court to Fulham. He tried
not to think too much, all that stuff about cutting up kids and everything, what the fuck was going on in his head, that whore as well, the
second bird under sixteen he'd been with for a wage. King's Cross was
a cesspool as far as Mango was concerned and the sooner the police

finished cleaning up the place the better for everyone. It was disgusting. It was his last time. Something had to be done. The country was going to the dogs.

He wondered what the lads were doing. He wouldn't mind a pint and some normal company, but it was late. He knew they thought he was a bit of a wanker sometimes, with the car and flat and money in the bank, but he preferred to dismiss it as jealousy. His mates were losers but they were also his history. It was where he belonged, though he hated the blind acceptance and broken pavements, the intensity of everyone knowing everyone else's business. He wanted privacy. He believed in breaking things down and separating interests. If he wanted to bring some tart home and cut off her head, maybe leave it sitting on the living room table for a week then he could. No other cunt could do that. Not that he was going that way, not James Wilson, no chance, but it was nice to have the option. It showed he was in control. It was all about freedom of choice.

When he entered his flat the first things Mango did was bolt the door, switch off the alarm, turn on the bath and get a shepherd's pie out of the freezer ready for the microwave. It was good to be home, the flat warm and welcoming thanks to the automatic timer he'd had installed. The thick carpet was a luxurious cushion as he stripped off and went to the main bedroom. The bed was large and custom-made from the finest imported hardwood and had set him back two grand. There was a big gold-trimmed mirror at the bottom of the bed where he liked to take women from behind, able to view his actions in widescreen format. He really should've bought that girl back and shagged her properly. He was wary of disease, but imagined himself sodomising her, ripping her apart, shoving his fist up her arse and pulling out the guts. He laughed. Sick cunt he was sometimes. He'd never do it though. He knew he was alright. It was just the stuff around him hitting home. Poor little thing stuck in a place like King's Cross. Probably milked by some dago, nigger or white trash pimp. Hooked on junk. Shafted by the male population. She'd been lucky to meet a bloke like James Wilson, Jimmy Boy, good old Mango, someone respectable from the City, a mother's son, a bit-of-a-chap soft at heart, a decent citizen who wanted to help. Least he wasn't a bum bandit like Carter or some death-tripper insisting on unprotected sex. He hadn't even tried. Shown a bit of respect. He wasn't tooled-up, a knife or pliers in his coat pocket, lengths of twisted wire to dig in her skin and find some kind of silver lining under the surface. Fuck that for a game of soldiers. He'd leave that to the wankers he worked with, going on about S&M all the time. It wasn't surprising some of it rubbed off after a while.

He'd even given the bird an extra twenty quid after the event and though she took it quick enough the ungrateful slag hadn't even bothered with a thank you. He got a bit carried away, that was all, trying to get deep down her throat like a man was told to in school, just to understand what was going on inside the system. And Mango stood in front of the mirror with subdued lamplight behind him, the edge of his skin dusted with orange-tinted angel dust, an aura of invincibility protecting him from harm. He worked his penis erect, walking over to the bedside table for the KY, returning to his original position, rubbing the lubricant in and aiming for the mirror. He thought of the girl in all kinds of positions, working through the options. When he was about to come he thought of the mirror's price tag and hurried to the bathroom, entering the steamy atmosphere heavy with bath salts, hanging plants placed strategically either side of a frosted-glass window, a rainforest atmosphere for a lithe animal. Mango was in good time and ejaculated over the toilet seat and into the bowl. He watched tinsel hang, glue stretching with the weight of his heritage. He felt patriotism and pride in the DNA he manufactured, a caste away from the mutant genes dominant in red light zones and other centres of genetic inferiority. There was some kind of regret for the sperm doomed to float in dead scented water, the goal never achieved, the only possible end a torrent of green bleached water from the cistern and a one-way ticket round the U-bend. Then there was the trip through the sewers, struggling manfully to impregnate rats, creating a unique monster race that would one day rise from the underground and proclaim a new social order. Mango laughed and noticed his face in the mirror. He was looking a bit strange. Fresh from a test tube. It was the coffee. He wiped himself with a length of toilet paper, then flushed it away, swearing at the bits that stuck. Typical. He turned the bath off and was about to get in when the phone rang.

'Mango you wanker,' it was Balti. 'Where've you been? I rang twice before.'

Mango checked the answerphone and saw that two messages had been left. Balti was half-cut, but he wasn't lying. He never did, the idiot. That's why he lugged bricks around for people. He needed to get himself sorted out. Move on.

'I was working late,' he said, sitting down in the reclining armchair next to the phone, naked except for the toilet paper.

'Till nearly midnight?' Balti asked. 'You want to have a word there. I mean, it's a bit strong.'

'I worked till ten, then went round this bird at work's place. She hung about and I knew she was asking for it because she's always giving me the eye and that, and then she was still there at ten, so when she invited me round to her flat in the Barbican I thought why not? She's tasty as well. One of those professional birds in dress suits that hug their bodies. Real quality, Balti. Not some donkey from Acton or Shepherd's Bush. She comes from class. Healthy food her whole life so she looks like an upper-class model. Privately educated, went to Oxford, you know the sort.'

'Not really,' the voice laughed. 'Sounds horrible to me, but I suppose as long as you don't have to talk to her and hear all about the country estate and that, how they kill foxes and torture the servants, and if she's a looker, then why not.'

'She's beautiful,' Mango said, smiling. 'Long blonde hair and the perfect figure. You wouldn't believe it if you saw her. I reckon I should get a few bonus points for class. Carter knobbing some brain-dead whale isn't the same as what I've just been dipping my winkie in. I think I'm in love.'

'How many points did you get then?'

'Two for a shag, then I followed it up with a three-pointer. Swallowed it like a trouper. Straight down, though I thought she was going to gargle at first. She fucking loved it.'

'Dirty cow. Mind you, you didn't hang about did you? I mean, you leave work at ten, get round the Barbican, maybe say a few words or something, then you knob her, give it a while to recover and next thing you're bollock deep in dentures. Then you have to stay awake and get back to SW6. Didn't she mind you pissing off like that?'

'She doesn't care. Just wants a good bit of sex without the hassles. Pure animal attraction. She's got one thing on her mind. You know what these office birds with a decent income are like. No morals. That's how their families get rich in the first place. It goes back centuries. They rape, rob, stitch up the serfs, then set up laws so everyone believes what they're doing is right because it's been written down. It's in their history. You watch them sometime. They've got no manners. Can't say thank you or please and take what they want. It's the ordinary people who've got morals. It's them that help others and know their right and wrong.'

'You sound like Arthur Scargill. Anyway, you're part of all that now.'

'You've got to get in there. There's no other way. No point wasting your life trying to fight the system. Didn't get Scargill anywhere, did it?'

'Three points puts you second. You know Carter's been up to his old tricks again. He shafted some bird when he was delivering beds. Three-pointer as well. Puts him on seven.'

'Sounds a bit iffy to me,' Mango said, narked that the shag man had maintained the gap at the top of the table. 'You sure about that?'

'He's not going to lie, is he?' Balti sounded a bit surprised. They were mates. If you couldn't trust your mates, then who could you trust?

'I know. He doesn't hang about, that's all. What about you and that dreamer you live with? What about Will?'

'Had my first wank the other day, and I've followed it up with a couple more since then,' Balti admitted. 'As far as birds go, sweet FA. Mind you, we're going down Blues tomorrow, that's one of the things I'm calling about, so I reckon we'll be getting stuck in there. Don't know about Will. Haven't seen him. You know what he's like. Sitting at home listening to music getting stoned.'

'I'll see what time I get finished tomorrow. I'll try and get down. Where you going first?'

'The Unity, then The Hide, then Blues. Should be alright. Don't suppose you know yet, I did the foreman the other day so I'm out of a job. If you hear about anything going let us know. Keep an ear out for us will you?'

'What did you go and do that for?'

'He was slagging me off. I hated it there anyway. It's time I did something different. It's like a new start. I need something to tide me over so if you hear of anything let us know.'

When he put the phone down, Mango thought about Balti for a few minutes. Maybe he'd get himself into gear now. He could offer him a few pointers. Apply some of Maggie's infinite wisdom. Balti would be better buying and selling. What he didn't know. Anyway, it wasn't his problem, though the news that Carter had been scoring points pissed him off. But at least he was second and the office bird story had potential. She probably had some dirty mates who wanted Mango to give them a good seeing to as well. He laughed as the word spread through the bistros of London. He could be their bit of rough, riding in a limousine down to Henley or Virginia Water, rows of upper-class birds lined up waiting for a good old-fashioned dose of pleb love-making. He'd make them pay through the nose, and he wouldn't be touching any grinders either. He'd keep his dignity. Loaded by other means but willing to service the aristocracy, for a fee, considering that he was in effect lowering himself in providing such a facility. It got him thinking. Instead of hanging around King's Cross he should try one of those agencies. The birds were probably a bit more upmarket, with posher accents and cleaner gear, more into it than the worn-out street girls. It meant getting them round the flat, which he didn't fancy. Bollocks though. It was his place. He could do what he wanted. He lived in a democracy, not some communist slave state. He'd ask a couple of the chaps at WorldView. They'd know all the angles.

Sitting in the bath, Mango took the opportunity to relax. The bath salts eased the strain and he closed his eyes. Steam filled the room. The Arabs understood these kind of things. The old Turkish baths and that. The Scandinavians had their saunas. The American Indians their sweat lodges, though they went for the natural touch as well, turning it into a hallucinogenic experience. But Mango was happy with his bathroom, a

boiling cave where he could unwind after a hard day earning a crust. He
looked at his knob floating limp in the water, the paper melted away. It
was funny how something like sex became so important. One minute
he was acting like scum in some park, next he was content, ready to
support any proposed government action to clean up the streets. He
was alone. It was great. His eyes were closed and the strain of working
on computers all day was beginning to slide away. It was tough sometimes, but rewarding. He had everything material he'd ever wanted.
Rain bounced off the window, reinforcing his feelings of satisfaction.
One day, long before he was the same age as his old man, he would be
set up and retired. No financial worries. That was the crux. You were
always going to worry about money if you didn't have any, but if you
got a decent bit of wedge banked you could enjoy the finer things. It
was security. Learning from the losers. Maggie knew.

He felt tired but wanted to make his time at home last. When
the water began to cool, he topped up again with hot. The tap handles
were period brass. They shone under the light which he had dimmed.
The weather outside was getting worse. He heard thunder far away in
North London. He thought of the underclass in doorways, shafted left,
right and centre, then forced to sell their sex. His view was realistic.
Mango knew he was right. Nobody chose to prostitute themselves. The
thought struck that he was a tart himself, out of his environment, but
he wouldn't think about all that. He was living proof of the longed for
classless society. Or at least he was a representative of an early beginning. Mango didn't want to think. It was too much. Rows of figures
beating drums, pigs on skewers, women on street corners, schoolgirls
in his car, Balti on the phone, Carter on the job. His old mates. Good
blokes they were whatever they thought of him. At least when things
got too much, the pressures of achievement and all that, then he could
go back to his own manor and fall into the old ways for a night. He
didn't have to pretend. But neither did he want the pressure. He didn't
care. There was no point caring too much because you'd end up in a
psychiatric unit with the doctors pushing ECT, or on the piss like his
old girl, or jabbing needles into your arm in Finsbury Park.

Sitting in his Rest-Easy armchair, Mango's right hand adjusted the relevant handle, lowering the back rest so that he could lie out full-length. It had been expertly designed to fit the human body and was well worth the thousand-pound debit. He flicked through television channels using the remote, crisp images beaming from the screen of the Nokia 7296, surround sound supplied by the Rock Solid speakers that had been professionally placed around the room. Mango enjoyed the full home-cinema treatment, flicking back and forward through terrestrial and satellite channels without finding anything substantial to hold his interest. Trendy cult-show presenters discussed myriad forms of sexual persuasion in minute detail, a blockbuster Hollywood movie revelled in the blood and gore of a faceless serial killer without bothering with the deeper psychology behind the Razor Man's grue-some dismemberments, while the soft-porn channel to which Mango subscribed grunted and groaned its way through a by now dull routine of missionary/rear-entry/woman-on-top positions that only ever revealed bare breasts and wobbling buttocks. For a laugh he cranked the volume up full throttle to annoy the couple who lived below, a right pair of arrogant yuppies. The room was filled with the moaning passion of a full-blown orgy, female ecstasy vibrating through the bookcases he'd had specially built the previous year, shaking the books he'd never read. He did this for a couple of minutes then turned the sound down. He turned off the TV and went over to the separates system Will had recommended.

Mango was making a brave attempt with the classics. His Best Of collection included Beethoven, Mozart, Bach; all the European masters he'd heard about somewhere along the line. It was supposed to be uplifting music, the kind of thing that imaginary blonde nym-phomaniac from WorldView would be listening to as she lined the coke up along some multinational director's knob, stirring the soul. Mango skipped from one track to the next. He found it pompous and dull, failing to do anything but bore, the knowledge that it represented European history and the ruling elite's cultural values not enough to make it listenable. He had some of the best audio gear money could buy but it was no use. Maybe it was a question of being in the right mood at the right time. He should try listening with a bit of blow, or

Wagner after ten bottles of select German lager. He wished he could
get something out of Beethoven and the rest of the boys, but it wasn't
happening. He was uneducated. He would keep trying and crack it one
day. Some other day. He chose another option.

The radio was repeating news items with a breathless, speculative
presentation that owed more to the need to fill the airwaves with constant interest than qualitative news values. He moved through layers
of ragga, jungle, drum-n-bass pirate stations, French-and German-
language channels, Anglo-Indian bangra where the sitars filtered
through tablas seemingly boxed into the speakers. The clock on the
mantelpiece showed one o'clock. He had to sleep. Had to stop his brain
racing. Morning would come round soon enough. He closed everything
down, went to the window and looked outside. He had forgotten about
the shepherd's pie. He wasn't hungry. The rain slowed a little, then
redoubled its pounding. Mango pulled the curtains tight and went
to the fridge for one of the sleeping tablets the doctor had prescribed.

KICKING OFF

Harry and Balti were the first ones in the pub, landlord Len pouring two pints of Guinness to bolster their guts and line them up for the long day ahead. It was the third round of the FA Cup and Chelsea were at home to Portsmouth. The previous night had been lively, a few lagers at the end of the week, Balti knowing he'd have to start watching the pennies now he was unemployed. He'd been down the social and had his interview the following week, ready for the grief coming his way. Bollocks anyway. Pompey would bring a mob up to London, they always did, and Tommy Johnson and his mates had been in the night before, psyched up looking to bushwhack them down Charing Cross, maybe the Elephant.

Portsmouth had always been a bit tasty and would want to put on a show, the 657 Crew in their designer gear back in the eighties, they remembered that well enough. Balti laughed, thinking of the bloke in the pink tracksuit who'd gone right over the top with his clothes getting the piss ripped out of him throughout a game at the Bridge. They'd had a few punch-ups in their youth but nowadays they were older and wiser and happy to let Johnson and nutters like that do the business. It was different now, deeper underground, not such a mass thing any more, though when it did go off in a major way there were plenty of older faces ready to steam in. But it was the past. Times changed. Balti took a long drink from his glass, letting the iron content work its way into his blood, a lethal pint first thing Saturday morning. Even Harry had a pint of Guinness now and then. He was no fascist.

'There was some Paddies in here looking for you last night,' Len said, once he'd rung up and taken Balti's tenner. 'Five of them. Big bastards. They asked for you by name. I said I hadn't seen you for a couple of weeks. They ordered, hung about for half an hour, then left. The one asking the questions looked like he'd been on the receiving end. Nose blown up like nobody's business. Even complimented me on the bitter. Said they'd be back for some more. They were looking for trouble. I could tell they weren't waiting around just to buy you a pint.'

'What else did they say?' Balti asked, knowing McDonald wasn't the sort of bloke to take a kick in the bollocks, then grin and bear it and put it down to experience. He'd hoped things would pan out. McDonald wouldn't grass him up, but if he was honest then the comeback was inevitable. He'd started something that was only ever going to end in tears.

'Nothing,' Len said. 'Nothing to me anyway. They seemed more interested in the door. Who was coming in and out, clocking faces. They didn't look too healthy.'

'They're not. Thanks. What did the others look like?'

'In their forties. Hard men. They all had coats on but I don't reckon they were tooled-up. One had some kind of Ulster tattoo. I noticed that much. Another smoked roll-ups. Right stink of tobacco but I wasn't going to argue the toss. You only missed them by fifteen minutes. Looks like it was a good job. You in a bit of bother?'

'Nothing to worry about,' Balti said. 'It's a shame we missed them though. We went down The Hide, then ended up in Blues. You should've seen the skirt down there. Carter only went and pulled again, didn't he? Don't know how he can be bothered all the time. Some slack black bird. Well nice if I remember right, but I was hammered so it could've been a pig with a suntan.'

They went to their regular table by the big window at the front of the pub where they could watch the world outside. Hungover parents led hyperactive kids in and out of shops, middle-aged women lined up at the grocer's and juveniles played arcade machines, the roar of rockets and buzz of lasers filtering into humming traffic. Two alkies sitting on a wall by the bus stop shouted gibberish, sipping Tennants, ignored by everyone who passed, a regular sight. The off-licence opposite had a jagged hole in the window that had been bandaged until it could be replaced, the owner sweeping glass towards the wall. It had been ramraided a couple of weeks before for the contents of the shelves. Business wasn't going well and the owner was seriously thinking of selling up and moving out of London. Balti looked at the familiar scene and wished he was somewhere else. Carter would be along soon and Will had said he'd be in later before he met his Brentford mates and got a lift down to Swindon. The third round of the FA Cup was a big day in the football calendar. Mango might even put in an appearance seeing as how he hadn't shown up the night before.

'So what's this McDonald about then?' Harry asked, looking towards the bar, out of earshot from the landlord who was interested enough but busy serving three noisy pensioners who'd just entered, taking advantage of the pound-a-pint special offer on bitter.

'Don't know him much outside of work really. Imagine he can handle himself. I'm not bothered about the bloke. If he's looking to have a go that's up to him. We'll just have to sort things out again.'

Carter came in with a smile on his face, stubble on his chin, same clothes he'd been wearing last night. He saw the lads were on the Guinness, went to the bar and ordered, sipping his lager while Len let the stout settle, looking around for Denise who wasn't in yet, knowing she often worked Saturday mornings. Len even put shamrocks on the cream, though it wasn't that professional a job and they might've been daisies for all he could tell from the vague outlines. Carter didn't know if the governor was Irish or what, and couldn't be bothered to ask. He didn't look or sound it, but you couldn't tell things like that sometimes. He carried the glasses over.

'Straight in another bird's bush and two more points in the bag,' he said, sitting down. 'That's me on nine and no-one else off the mark yet, unless you two got the scent.'

'I forgot to tell you last night,' Balti said. 'Mango shagged some bird from his work, then he got a bonus point on top. What was she like then?'

'Indian bird. Nice body, small tits, decent shag. E'd out of her box and if she'd been strong enough she'd have carried me through the front door she was so keen.'

'I thought she was black. Into the old jungle wasn't she, jumping around and that.'

'No, Indian. Dark though. You should've told me about Mango and I'd have put in a bit more effort. That's what it's like when your game's based on flair. You do enough to get by. It's only when you're up against it that you turn on the charm. Chelsea have always been like that. Look at the teams we've had through the years. Get beat by shit one week, then go and stuff Liverpool or Man U the next. Gullit's different though. Ruud's got everything. Dutch flair and discipline. Double Dutch. That's the mark of genius. Cruyff had the same ability. Forget the Premiership though for a minute and let's concentrate on the amateur game. What happened to you two? Pull anything last night after I left, or just your plonkers?'

'Leave it out,' said Balti. 'It was down the kebab van and straight off home. I was even too pissed for a knuckle shuffle.'

'Not even one point off that Greek serving chips in the back of the van? Big flabby arse and piss flaps down to her ankles. You service that and I'll slip you a back-hander. Anyone gets between the sheets with her deserves a couple of extra points.'

'You'd have to give me more than a back-hander to touch that,' Balti laughed, spilling his drink.

Harry was watching the street outside. He was pissed off that Carter had bought him another pint of Guinness. He'd wanted lager. The Guinness was lining. He wasn't going to make a fuss. The winos were up and moving towards the swimming pool. He was thinking of flabby arses and desert islands, crystal blue oceans where the only movement was the occasional fish jumping. Except last night it hadn't been a desert island. It was somewhere on the mainland. The east coast of Mexico fronting the Caribbean, golden beaches that backed on to thick jungle and ancient Mayan temples buried so deep that the syphilis-heavy white man had never set eyes on them. On the horizon lay Cuba and Haiti. He could smell Castro's cigars and hear voodoo drums. They'd been sitting in a bar with a couple of Aztecs. Balti was on the Corona while Harry was joining the warriors in the local moonshine. There was a worm in the bottle which the older of the Aztecs said turned ordinary men into gods. Bite into the worm and they would have visions that would change their lives. But Harry and Balti didn't want to change. They were staying in a nice little place with a front porch and two hammocks where they swung back and forward watching the village kids fish in the ocean. It was similar to Harry's last dream, with a few essential differences. They were more laid back now, like they'd been there for a while, although the same dangers lurked. As he enjoyed the hemp supplied by a retired policeman, he kept his eyes on the frail little Mexicans searching for fish, knowing from his experiences in the East that sharks were present everywhere. It was a worldwide problem.

Harry woke up and went for a piss. It was cold in the bathroom and he kept his eyes half closed in the bright light. He made sure he stayed with the fuzz in his head, got back into bed and returned to the dream, preferring the heat of the Gulf of Mexico to London in the winter. At first the dream was forced and not worth the effort, but then he began sinking down and when he woke the next morning he was easily able to concentrate and everything rushed back full throttle.

It was night and they were still in the bar. An all-day session. Fireflies danced in two-dimensional blackness and there was the bark of a monkey, the screech of thousands of tiny throats that hit a crescendo before stopping in perfect unison. The Aztecs were backpacking, Spanish passports tucked into fabric money belts, visiting the land of their Mayan brothers. Harry was laughing, telling them he knew more about the Aztecs than they did about the cockney tribe, that he watched a lot of telly when he wasn't on the piss. They were chopping up the maggot. Four equal pieces. One, two, three and the four men ate the maggot. They were in the middle of the jungle. The bar and sky had disappeared and there was a heavy smell of rotting vegetation. The Aztec warriors were leading them by the hand. Harry felt the sweat on his guide's palm. He felt awkward holding another man's hand but knew it was in the interests of survival. On his own he would be wandering blind and it wouldn't take long for wild cats to smell his fear and rip him apart. The guides were old and wise and with the help of mescalin possessed infrared night sight. With this sophisticated vision they were able to cut a path through the woven tangle of the jungle, ever-present fireflies hovering just above their heads the only movement, Harry feeling the gentle pricks of settling insects on bare skin, the rough texture of a heavy snake passing over his feet. He felt no fear with the Aztecs. These Indians knew the laws of the jungle. It was only European diseases such as the common cold that could destroy the natives. Harry wore the same bright yellow shorts from Asia, but with the dead maggot his dream had switched to black-and-white.

Eventually they reached a clearing and the colour returned with a flash. He was surprised to find Frank Bruno barring the way checking tickets. Big Frank was wearing a black flight jacket more common to Combat 18 than a great British heavyweight champion of the world. His hair had been dyed white. Harry was embarrassed to see that Balti was still holding his guide's hand, even though a computer-generated fire was lighting up the clearing. A temple towered above them. Harry admired the structure, the same Mayan temple he'd seen on the TV. There were hundreds of steps leading up through slanting stone, enormous carved figures positioned at regular intervals. It was a magical moment. There was a brief silence while he absorbed this wonder of the ancient world and then he heard the music, the blips and beeps and subsonic drumming of his own culture.

Dayglo graffiti had been painted on the trees surrounding the temple and he thought it was a shame. He read the nearest message, *Congratulations, you have just met Millwall*, a few words for anyone unfortunate enough to get a hiding off the pride of South-East London. He couldn't be bothered with all that violence. It just wasn't important. He felt good and was glad to see Balti had adjusted to his surroundings and was no longer holding the Aztec's hand. He asked Frank why he'd changed his hair. The British bulldog pointed out that despite being born and bred in London, he had been a big fan of Gazza since his Newcastle days, and had always wanted to be a professional footballer. Anything that was good enough for the Geordie maestro was good enough for Frank. Wor Gazza, meanwhile, had been in training and was looking to have a go at Mike Tyson. Frank pointed out that this was what being conscious was all about. Swapping things around and blending in together. Like the music.

The maggot was fast reaching the peak of its effectiveness and

Harry found himself surrounded by a jungle that was becoming more and more distinct, a moving network of geometric patterns, complicated fractals that nevertheless made sense both scientifically and naturally, the kind of new age shit he normally slagged off. He sat on one of the steps with a girl he'd known at school. She'd been a good laugh but had been knocked down by a bus and this had left deep scars digging into her forehead and left cheek, so he'd never been able to think of her as female. She was alright though and they sat together, Harry's head held high, breathing deep and feeling content. He felt her hand in his, but there was nothing sexual going on. It seemed okay. He saw his best mate dancing around like a wanker but it wasn't important, the trimmed down beer gut still big enough to bounce. Nothing seemed to matter in a clearing deep inside the jungle. The girl whispered that the Aztecs were really Mayans. Because the Aztecs made human sacrifices they were easily understood back in London, while the Mayans had apparently invented the concept of zero and had been forgotten. The two guides just wanted a bit of respect. Then Balti was pulling his shorts down, fat arse on display, mooning for the crowd. A siren sounded and Harry wanted to tell his mate to pull his shorts back up because the Spanish riot police were on their way and they didn't appreciate traditional British humour. The feedback was too heavy so he maintained a dignified silence. He looked for Big Frank, but the heavyweight champion of the universe had taken the night bus home and Harry's alarm was sounding, a blitzkrieg warning that a wave of fighter-bombers were coming, loaded with napalm, intent on burning the ancient rainforest to a cinder.

It was daylight. Time to get up. Saturday morning. Chelsea Portsmouth. Nine o'clock. Balti's arse was the last impression the dream left as it ran back into the jungle. Harry felt uneasy. He tried to move away from the thought but couldn't let himself bottle out and pushed back inside his head to find out what had gone before. Five minutes later he was on his way to the bathroom, satisfied the dream had been a straightforward replay of events, the night out at Blues with a repetition of the desert island theme, some little gems thrown in for decoration, that bird on the Es last night. The image of Balti's arse was obviously symbolic of his attitude, showing what he thought about losing his job, but when Harry went into the kitchen and his mate was sitting there with the paper, in his dressing gown, bollocks hanging out, he actually felt embarrassed.

'You're a bit quiet,' Carter said, emptying his pint, then holding it up for careful examination, as if by staring at the glass for long enough it would somehow fill up again.

'I'm feeling a bit rough, that's all,' Harry said.

'I needed that,' Carter was prompting now with the understanding that miracles had stopped in the years BC. 'It's the best thing when you've been on the piss. Dehydration causes all the grief, and half of it's in the head, mental like, so if you start filling up again you get rid of both the reasons.'

Harry collected the glasses and went to the bar. At least he'd get a pint of 4X now. Denise came in then and served him before she'd had a chance to dump her handbag out back, Len busy at the other end of the counter. He ordered a ham roll and bit into it as lager filled glasses. Denise smelt good. Better than Carter who was carrying a mixture of last night's drink and smoke fumes and a night's broken sleep. A couple more pints and nobody would notice. He was just about to return to the table when Will walked in. Harry ordered another pint, Directors this time, and Will came over to help.

'Alright?' Will asked.

'Can't complain. Got a bit of a hangover from last night, but nothing serious. Should be a good game today if the players are up for it. You never know though. Pompey could just pull off a result.'

'It's easier than a trip to Swindon. I wonder if you'd have bought Gullit if Dave Webb had stayed at Chelsea. He only signed because of Hoddle. At least we've got Webby. The man's a god.'

'He should've been Chelsea manager,' Harry agreed, thinking of the magic maggots that turned men into immortal beings and wondering if Webby had been hassling the insect world. 'Webb was the one who brought the Cup back against Leeds. He'd have done alright and he saved us from relegation in the three months he was there. Hoddle was a great player. He'd have got into any half-decent Dutch team lining up next to Carter in midfield, so it's no wonder The Dutchman decided to come to Chelsea. Gullit's on another planet. The bloke's got so much time when he's in possession. Never loses his cool. Bit like me really.'

Will swapped pleasantries with the rest of the lads and took over Harry's daydreamer role at the window as the other three talked football generalities and Chelsea specifics. He sipped his Directors and enjoyed the ten minutes of heat a hesitant sun fired his way. He was on a high. It was funny what a woman's interest could do for you. He mustn't let himself get carried away and start behaving like a lovesick kid though. Spending time with Karen had done him good. She had an interesting flat that reflected her character, full of posters and tropical plants. She'd invited him in for fresh coffee but he'd chosen tea bags instead. A plate of chocolate biscuits and a good look through her records and CDs. They had similar tastes. They'd sat there talking about music and everything for hours, and it wasn't long before the pressure Will felt to make a move disappeared and they were having a laugh like they were mates.

Before he knew what was happening it was four o'clock and she was nodding off and he stood up and said he'd better be off. He didn't even try to kiss her and she gave him her number on the torn edge of an old envelope and asked him to call. He'd been tempted to phone right away but had held out until that same morning. A simple call to say thanks for the free drink and company. She'd sounded pleased to hear from him and he was seeing her Tuesday night. There was a band she liked playing in Brixton and he was going round her place at six. He was excited. Daft really. It was nice though. Spending time with a woman like that. Better than eight pints and a drunken effort that no matter what anyone told him was useless. You never got to know what a woman was really like and the sex itself was rubbish. Waiting a bit was another brand of foreplay, building up to something, making sex a bit special. He wondered what Karen thought about it all.

'Carter's on nine points,' Balti told him. 'It's about time we got going. You're joint bottom with me and Harry. Mango shafted some Tory princess from his work, the arse-licker.'

'Nine? You were on four last time I saw you. How did you manage five more? I thought the maximum score was four. What did you do to the poor girl to get five points?'

'I serviced this sort when I was delivering beds. It was one of those instant on-the-job demonstrations. All part of the service and no guarantee required. Three points there, and the bird at Blues last night was another two. You'd have liked her Will, but I know you'd rather get into Eileen. That Denise keeps looking over and I reckon I'll be shagging that soon. She's a right goer. A four-pointer, but I'll settle for three. Depends on the table when I get to grips with it. Total football's fine, but you've got to get points as well or you're fuck all.'

Will was going to ask Terry how the sex had been. Forget the points for a minute and consider the act itself. Still, that was Carter. He didn't give a toss about anything, just living moment to moment without a care in the world, and if that's what he wanted out of life then who was Will to say anything? He was happy and not hurting anyone. Will wasn't made that way. He wished he was because it would make everything easier, but on the quiet he was looking for something a bit more permanent. At least he was being honest with himself. It would be nice to spend time with a decent woman for a change, with ideas and views about things, even a bit of politics thrown into the equation. Carter had probably pulled some good people along the way but he never got to see more than the paintwork. Then in the morning with the goal achieved he'd be out the door. Not that it was just blokes who were like that. Of course it wasn't. Will had met enough women whose social lives and prestige among their mates revolved around how many men they'd had. It worked both ways. Anyone who thought otherwise was squatting on the moon thousands of miles into space. It was just down to people once all the decoration was removed.

He returned to the scene outside, playing the Pogues' Dirty Old Town version through his head. If you could find love in among the fumes and debris you were doing alright. He looked around at his mates and felt sorry for them. They were a bunch of kids despite the language and manners, playing their role in the greater scheme. At least they were a bit more settled these days, getting through the problem years and all that banging heads against brick walls. He hated all that. Will was a pacifist of sorts. He'd defend himself but avoided confrontation as far as possible. It was hard sometimes. Like in the First World War they'd shot those men who refused to fight or were suffering from shell shock. Condemned the poor bastards for not killing their own kind for the scum that sat miles away from the trenches in their polished havens. Stood them in a line and had other men shoot holes in their bodies.

Life was short and on special offer if you didn't work things out. He just wanted to relax, put his feet up and listen to some boss sounds. That's what he liked about Karen. She had it sussed. There he was thinking about her again. To touch her seemed wrong. He smiled. Thinking of sin as though he'd been raised with religion. It was the princess thing they'd been talking about, Mango dabbling in the City. But a princess didn't need money to make her royal. That was down to the adverts. All that consumer propaganda.

'You should've come along last night,' Carter said, pulling Will back in with the rest of the lads. 'Where were you anyway?'

'I stayed in. Had a pizza and listened to some music.'

'You'll never get off the mark sitting at home.'

'I'm not bothered.'

'What do you mean you're not bothered? You'll end up in the relegation zone.'

Will didn't want to get into a discussion on the subject. The idea of a sex league was shit. He didn't know why he'd signed up in the first place. He'd have been better off giving up alcohol instead and it was the drink in his blood that had made him go along with the idea. That's what is was. Drink was a bad drug. He'd been talking about it with Karen. It didn't mean he was going to stop, because he enjoyed a quality pint, but it only ever led to problems. They made dope illegal and advertised alcohol because a good smoke kept you mellow while drink set everyone off fighting each other. Will was gearing up for something but didn't know what. Maybe he wanted to settle down. Live with a woman again.

He thought of Bev and the three years they'd had together, though it had never really worked once they'd settled into the routine of work, food, sleep. It was two-way and they'd parted on good enough terms.

They'd kept in touch for a while, meeting up every two or three months, then every six months till she found someone else, and then there was nothing. He didn't feel bad about it, but at times he missed the companionship. She'd given him something he couldn't get from his mates. They'd been able to talk about things that he would never talk about with the lads, but they'd been too young for it to last. They were nineteen when they met. Twenty when they moved into the flat in South Acton. Towards the end it was obvious they were shifting in different directions, but they spent a year trying to con themselves. In the end it was a relief. He'd felt free again. She was a good person. He still loved her in a way. Nothing physical because that went years back, but she was a bit of the past and Will liked thinking back.

The only other Sex Division member who'd lived with a woman was Carter. Will reckoned it was a bit funny that, because they were so different. He'd been married to Cheryl for a couple of years, before the divorce. It hadn't worked out. He'd always boasted that with Cheryl nothing mattered and he was busy most of the time dabbling on the side. Will didn't know the truth about that, and when Cheryl slept with some bloke Carter had gone off the deep end. He'd been well gutted when she left but had recovered quick enough. Will couldn't live like that. He would've felt guilty lying and planning something. It wasn't in his nature, though he knew everyone was ripe when they were under the influence. Carter didn't care. He was a free man. It was his life and it was only sex and glands and nature, and he had told Will a couple of times that he should enjoy himself because that was why God had made women. Will couldn't think like that. They were miles apart, with Harry and Balti and even Mango in the middle, yet in some ways they were similar. It was like Karen had been saying the other night about party politics, that if you went far enough one way you eventually went full circle and ended up on the other side.

Carter and Will were the only two who'd gone all the way and moved in with someone. And Carter had gone right in and got himself married. Big wedding and everything. They'd all gone. He looked at Balti and Harry and wondered where they'd end up. Living together when they were forty? What did they think about it all? Probably didn't know themselves, so how could Will? Living day to day. Then there was Mango. He had enough ambition for the rest of them but somehow Will felt most sorry for him. Even though he had a bit of wealth it was a dead-end world, without soul or morality. Carter had few traditional morals but was honest and no harm was done, while Will was so moral he had to admit he sometimes verged on the self-righteous. He hated himself for that. Harry and Balti were decent blokes, but Mango lacked something, like a slit had been made and that part of the brain converting the relevant codes had been rewired. Will wondered if he was getting religious or whether that bit of blow he'd had last night had set off a forgotten circuit, turning him into a raving fundamentalist. He was smoking a lot these days.

Will saw Mango coming out of the bookies, walking with his head up for a bit, then bent forward focused on the pavement. Like he was proud, then ashamed, then proud again. Will thought of them playing that game as a kid, it didn't have a name, avoiding the cracks and lines, the slabs land and the cracks rapids that would drag them away. One day he'd ask Mango if he remembered. A car stopped at the zebra crossing and Mango was on his way to the pub. He often came down on Saturday to see his mum and dad, then have a pint with the lads if they were about. It was one of those loose rituals. He saw Mango stop and talk with a group of women, friends of his mum. When he stopped his face had been creased like he was thinking too hard, but now it had smoothed out, back in the community. When he left them and continued Will saw him stop by the drunks standing outside the swimming pool, begging, and hand something over.

'Alright?' Mango said, going straight to the bar to get a round in. When he'd brought the drinks to the table he sat next to Harry who shifted up a bit. Mango looked happy enough.

'What happened to you last night?' Balti asked.

'I had to work late.'

'On a Friday night? You must be joking. You were round that bird's place sipping champagne with your caviar.'

'Wish I had been. I was working my bollocks off till three. We had a big job going through.'

'She didn't want another portion then?' Carter asked. 'Once was enough, was it?'

'I'm going round tomorrow night. She's a real cracker. Seems like I'm in second place. How was it down Blues?'

'Not bad. I'm on nine points now so you'd better get out of first gear, but don't worry about these three. Will stays in these days listening to his records and these two are always so fucking pissed they can't get it up.'

The talk drifted back to the football while Mango started bending Harry's ear about dreams. Mango never remembered his dreams and wanted to learn the secret. He'd tried eating cheese because he'd heard from his old man that a good bit of Cheddar worked wonders, but nothing had happened. He couldn't get to sleep without his prescription, and then when he managed it the next thing he knew the alarm was sounding and he was getting up with nothing but a blank filling the gap. Without chemicals he would lay there for hours with his mind racing, the same thoughts that came in the day when he wasn't busy, but which his work helped him avoid. Mango was sensible enough to know that it was only his imagination speeding, but he didn't want to think when he was alone because the later it got, the darker the pictures became. He didn't mention his tablets or thoughts to anyone.

Harry thought of the siren and the bombing raid on a Mayan temple. Remembering your dreams proved you were alive, that you weren't just a machine put on charge overnight. They'd talked about it before and Mango agreed, but he wanted a bit for himself. He liked the idea of symbolism and another part of his head working free-style. Harry told him about his dream, about the bar and Frank Bruno, the Mayan temple and the music, how the whole thing had started in colour, shifted to black-and-white while he was in the jungle, then returned to colour. The others were talking football and he kept his voice down so nobody took the piss. He was selective in his account. Mango nodded. It sounded good. He wouldn't mind some harmless home cinema for himself rather than the late night horror shows he never spoke about. Hallucinating in the tropics would be better than running around North London with some kid next to him thinking of ways to chop her up.

'Harry, you remember that Cup game against Tottenham in the sixth round?' Carter was already getting pissed, topping up. 'The yids were coming down from Sloane Square and the old bill pulled up. We were down by The Black Bull, remember, and then they started running horses into Chelsea.'

'Course I do. I went under one but it was going so fast it didn't land on my head. Went right over me without doing any serious damage.'

'The rider didn't even look back. Just kept going.'

'I could've been brain-damaged. Sitting here now with a nappy on that you'd have to change for me.'

'Fuck that,' Balti said. 'When was it? Early eighties, something like that. The pubs were packed by twelve weren't they and everyone was looking to have a go. The Shed was full an hour and a half before the fucking kick-off.'

'Only because the old bill cleared the pubs and pushed everyone inside, closed the gates so they could get Spurs past.'

Will had to admit it had been a lively day out. Hoddle had scored for Spurs but he wasn't going to remind them. The North Stand had been empty and when Tottenham piled on to the terrace they got a warm reception. It had gone off in a big way outside afterwards and they'd nearly got battered by the old bill as the two sides clashed. It was a long time ago. He'd gone to a few games with the others when Brentford weren't at home, or playing a shit team. Chelsea had always been a bit of a cult side. Things were better now. Peace was better than war. Sex instead of violence. Bollocks, he was thinking along Sex Division lines.

'What are you lot doing tonight?' he asked. The drink was having an effect and he fancied a few more. It was fine meeting a decent woman like Karen, but he wouldn't mind a decent drink as well. He was thirsty after a quiet Friday sitting at home listening to records.

'Have a pint somewhere,' Carter said, considering the options. 'Pick up a Miss World and give her a good servicing. What I normally do. What else?'

'We'll probably come back here,' Balti said. 'Have a beer round Chelsea after the game and get back by eight at the latest. At least it's a short walk home.'

'What about you?' Will turned to Mango.

'Don't know yet. Might come down here if you lot are around. I'm shooting back to Fulham first.'

'You giving us a lift then?' Carter asked.

'Long as you don't piss all over the upholstery like you were threatening to do last time I let you in the car.'

Will left at twelve and the rest of them stayed till nearly one. Mango had a couple of pints and then stopped while the others started working their way into a session. He wanted to get back and go through some paperwork. He was toying with the idea of phoning one of those home-delivery services, a call girl in leather with stilettoes and high cheek bones. Like that bird in the Barbican. The others were pissing about pleading for another pint before they left. Mango stood up, took out his keys and the rest of the lads fell into line. It was still early enough to get down to the Hammersmith roundabout without too much hassle and then slowly roll along the Fulham Palace Road. He felt good behind the wheel. The Jag purred, though he doubted the others appreciated just how good the engine really was. They appreciated the luxury and interior, but with a bit of drink inside them the finer edges were blurred.

'You shagged anything in this yet?' Carter asked, sitting in the front passenger seat, Harry and Balti in the back.

Mango almost answered more or less, that the bird from the Barbican had been down on him the other night, sitting in the same seat as Carter, then remembered the story, confusing the down-and-outs with those who helped put them there.

'No.'

'You've got a stain here,' the unstoppable sex machine pointed out. 'Thought it might be spunk, that's all.'

Mango took his eyes off the road to look and almost went up the back of the car in front. He looked at the spot Carter was pointing to, a small blob ground into the seat. The fucking slag. He'd warned her. Fucking whore. It was typical. You couldn't trust anyone these days. That was the problem with England, the sorry state of the industrial base. He had forked out hard cash and received a shoddy service in return. That sponging cow should've taken a bit of pride in her work rather than falling down on the job. He was disgusted with himself for allowing such a thing to happen. Next time he wouldn't be so generous. He would make the woman perform in a doorway or under a tree. That's what happened when you tried to help the less fortunate. They were rabid and quick to bite the hand that fed them. The thought struck that the girl might have infected his knob, that soon he would start frothing at the mouth and go on the rampage, biting and breaking skin until he was shot down in the street by a police marksman, shot down like a mad dog.

When they were kids Kev Bennett had gone mental and held his girlfriend hostage with a shotgun nobody knew he had. Mango remembered it well. It was a major occasion. The neighbours had reported screams coming from his flat and after the old bill pulled up there'd been a stand-off. The area was sealed off. It had been quite exciting being a kid and that, with everyone talking about what was going to happen next, about the negotiators they would bring in to try some psychology. Bennett was nothing out of the ordinary, just went off his rocker one day. He'd been in there for ages and everyone expected a happy ending when he got his head straight. They said he was pissed up. Then there was a bang from inside the flat and the old bill shot him. It was unreal, the pop of gunshots. Nobody ever knew the reason why Bennett did it and his girlfriend moved away. He wondered what she was doing now. Whether she thought about the boy who'd threatened to kill her all those years before. It was funny how things worked out. But he wasn't thinking of guns.

'Did you use a rubber with all those three birds?' Mango asked Carter.

'Course I did. Well, I did with the first one, but I was a bit pissed last night and let it go. I'm not bothered though. Wouldn't want to do it too often but she seemed clean enough, not some smelly hippy or scrubbed trendy who specialises in queers. Mind you, I didn't bother with that woman I was delivering to, but she was married so she must be safe enough.'

'What about when a bird gives you a blow job?' Mango asked, worried. 'Do you use one then as well?'

'Leave it out. What are you going to catch that way?'

Mango felt relieved.

'You should do,' Balti said, leaning forward. 'I read that if a woman's got a cut in her mouth then AIDS can spread through the end of your cock. That's the weak spot.'

'They're not going to get stuck into a lump of stinking rubber, are they?' Carter laughed. 'It's all to do with blood and that. I mean, it might be possible to get it from a cut like you said, but the chances are small.'

'It would be a fucking horrible way to die,' Balti muttered from the back, his eyes closed and head leant back. 'Getting HIV or AIDS, whichever one it is that comes first. Withering away like a skeleton. I feel sorry for people forced to die like that. Poor bastards. No-one deserves that.'

'You could die of anything though, couldn't you,' Carter said. 'As long as you're careful you're alright. I mean, you can't stop having sex just because it might kill you. How would the human race continue? It would be a bit boring as well.'

'It's a time bomb waiting to go off,' Balti said. 'It's blokes like us who are next on the list.'

He sounded like something from a documentary. Mango checked the mirror, Carter turned round and Harry moved back in the seat and looked sideways. Balti just sat there with his eyes shut.

'You miserable cunt,' Carter accused, not appreciating the tone. He didn't like thinking about AIDS too much because he'd been through a fair number of birds over the years, and if the propaganda was true, that it wasn't just queers and junkies condemned to a miserable death, then by rights he should be shitting it. But it wasn't in his nature to think like that. You had to live right now. Forget the past and not worry about the future.

'You could die under a bus tomorrow, or that lorry over there could skid and wipe us all out. How many people die of cancer, heart attacks, blood clots? It's only because it's sex that they go on about it. Fucking hell, lads, live and enjoy it while you can. At least if you die on the job then you've gone out with a bit of style. I mean look at that bird over there. You're not telling me you wouldn't risk death for a poke at that.'

The other three looked at a tall, thin blonde, moving at the same speed as the traffic. Carter rolled down the window and hung his head out, trying to attract her attention. She smiled his way and went into a shop.

'I was thinking,' Harry said, once they'd got past the lights and were moving again. 'Maybe we should get Balti to write a report, like Taylor did for football. He could look at the safety aspects of the game and make certain recommendations.'

He saw Mango's eyes move in the mirror and a smile on the side of Carter's face.

'It would be for the good of everyone involved in the game. Look at Carter. He picks up some bird in Blues, goes home with her and gives her a good seeing to, but the main problem is that he's a bit casual about the whole thing and doesn't take any precautions. He's putting himself at risk, not to mention the woman concerned. Not that he's carrying any tropical diseases or anything like that, but he's taking a bit of a chance. Now say the Balti Report insisted that points couldn't be registered unless the person concerned had used a rubber. Carter would be about to get stuck in when suddenly he'd realise he was going to lose out in the league and make the effort, tell the woman to hang on a second, walk to the other side of the room, go through his clothes till he finds the custom-made, pigmy-size condoms, coated of course, chinky spare-ribbed efforts, then slips one on his knob and returns to the business in hand. That way he would be looking after himself and doing his bit for the human race at the same time.'

'Makes sense,' Balti said, 'but I don't see why I should have to write the report. Let Will do it. He's the sensible one. He'd enjoy doing it as well. I'm shit at writing.'

'You could limit the kind of birds as well,' Mango said. 'No junkies or those ones who go with dodgy blokes. No slags either.'

'Hold on, you were the one who wanted points for shafting prossies the other day,' Carter said. 'That's interfering with freedom of choice. I mean, I can see the point of rubbers and all that, maybe even avoiding junkies, that's common sense, and I mean, anyway, they're not going to be walking around with a sign round their necks, but just because a girl puts it about shouldn't be enough to cancel the points.'

'You're only worried because it would put you bottom of the league,' Mango said, turning off the Fulham Palace Road.

'Fuck off. You're slagging off some dirty old tart for shafting anything that moves just because she's a woman. That's sexist. I fucking hate sexism.'

The others laughed.

'Dear oh dear,' he said. 'Look at the tits on that.'

Mango parked and waited for the others to get out. He had a quick look at the passenger seat. He was thinking about the stain and whether to clean it himself or get it done professionally. All that talk about death and disease had put him off the idea of an escort girl, though to be honest he didn't have the nerve to get someone round the flat. He was tired. It was all catching up with him and he wouldn't need his prescription. The thought of curling up in bed like a kid, getting into the foetal position again with the doors locked and everything shut out, that's what he fancied more than anything.

'Come down The White Hart after the game,' Carter said, 'and you can give us a lift back. You can doss round my place tonight if you're coming down The Unity. We'll be in there till seven or thereabouts.'

Mango went indoors and Carter kicked a puddle of water at Harry who told him he was a fucking donut and tried to grab him, but the sex machine was too fast and ran ten yards down the street, then kept his distance till he reckoned Harry had forgotten about the wet jeans he was wearing. They turned towards the ground and a pre-match pint, building up for the kick-off.

BLACK VINYL

There was a break between bands and the DJ was busy mixing sound effects. Will had ordered two pints of snakebite and was weaving his way through the crowd towards Karen. There was a thin film of sweat covering her face and arms, red cardigan wrapped around her waist, black mascara very slightly smudged. The snakebite had been her idea. Will hadn't had the potent mix for years. A lot of pubs had stopped serving it, though Club Verbal didn't seem too bothered by the bitter-cider potential for aggravation. But it was a peaceful, largely anarchist gathering. He handed Karen a plastic pint and sat down next to her on the stairs, returning to their conversation as she folded the copy of *Two Sevens* she had been reading.

'My mum died three years ago today,' Karen said, Will noticing the mist in her eyes. 'She had a hard life, you know. All women her generation had hard lives. They say it's different now, and I suppose it is in some ways, but it's still a world built by men for men. My mum had to graft almost till the moment she died. She had a faith, though, that never left her. She was raised a Catholic. Believed in God and heaven and a better life in the ever-after, bearing everything as though it was her fate. Like an all-loving God would invent something as wicked as cancer.'

Will nodded. He couldn't disagree, though he didn't go along with the line that every male in the country had an easy ride. He thought class was more important, sexism one more element in a strategy of divide and rule. But he didn't want to argue. Will loved women. Maybe he even loved Karen.

'You take a man and if he has sex with lots of different women he's admired, but you catch a woman doing the same thing and she's a slag.

Where's the sense in that? Why shouldn't a woman be able to go off and have sex with whoever she wants, when she wants?'

Will agreed. It was nonsense, but try as he did there was still something there in his head. He'd heard that it was to do with the male's in-built biological function, the need to keep his genes flowing through the generations. It was like a computer chip. A basic battle for survival. Genetic programming buried so deep in the circuits that any amount of reasoning and self-disgust would never be able to remove it entirely. Maybe there was truth in the theory. Will didn't know. But it was something worth considering. A woman could always be sure the kid in her belly was her own, but what guarantee did a man have? He vaguely remembered publicity surrounding the marriage of the century between Prince Charles and Lady Di, rumours of royal checks on the future princess's virginity. In the bad old days that kind of thing had been up front. Kings had their wives-to-be examined because they didn't want any doubts about parentage when it came to succession to the throne, no tainting of the divine DNA. He couldn't really believe that kind of stuff still went on though.

There had to be some kind of logic behind jealousy. Either that or men really were chauvinistic slavers. He was glad Karen didn't hear the way his mates spoke about women, birds, slappers, whores, tarts, grinders, slags, whatever. He tried to imagine her sitting in on a session with Carter and the rest of the Sex Division crew. At least they'd tone it down a bit if she was around. It was all about respect. She would have to put a bug somewhere, in the bottom of Carter's pint maybe, and record everything without moral constraints. Karen was right. She was beautiful as well.

'Don't get me wrong,' Karen smiled, the odd crack splitting her face, something Will was already used to and which seemed to fit her personality, a lop-sided grin that cut through her right cheek. 'I'm not into sex with strangers like some people. I mean, what's the point of having sex with someone you don't know when you're drunk or stoned or whatever drug's flavour of the moment, because it's not going to be much good, is it? I mean, this friend of mine, Leoni, she goes through two or three blokes a week, but she never gets anything out of it except a hangover and when she's careless too often a visit to the STD clinic.

'I went down the hospital with her once and the unit was just a mobile home on the edge of the hospital grounds, like something off a rundown caravan site. It put it all into place. It was raining and we got soaked, and the nurse was a right old hag, and I was just thinking all the time what a waste of something that should be full of feeling. Even so, there shouldn't be any judgement, should there? We should all have the freedom of choice. There shouldn't be all these religious relics weighing people down, covering up the truth. We'll all be dead one day, whether it's from cervical cancer or old age.'

Will nodded and said nothing. He had never had a venereal infection, at least not as far as he knew, but Carter had been down the STD a few times. He was a regular customer in fact. He should get himself a season ticket. Then there was that time Balti shagged some bird at a party, his first bit of sex in seven or so months, and it was just his luck that he picked up a dose. It was the lack of alcohol that almost killed him. Leoni sounded like a bit of a raver. Carter's long-lost cousin following the family trait, spreading peace and love and one-on-one masturbation techniques through the community. If Will was feeling generous he'd fix them up and let them bang each other into the next century, but he wanted to keep Karen separate from his mates. The drink was obviously going to her head a bit, because she kept talking without waiting for a response, as though he wasn't really there.

'I'd rather make love with a man. One day I suppose I'll find someone who's the other side of the same coin and we'll live happy ever after in our own little flat, and when we're together there'll be nothing like it in the world. It's the difference between making love and having sex. I suppose it sounds old-fashioned to you, but that's the way I look at things. You get more out of something if you build up to it and have some emotion. I mean, we're not machines are we, and we're not animals just interested in reproduction.'

It was strange, but all this talk about love and romance and emotions wasn't turning Will off. It didn't even sound that dated. If anything it was drawing him in. It was turning into a bit of a lecture but he stayed with her as she got scientific. He wondered what exactly pro-gestogen and oestrogen did to a woman. Thrombosis was something to do with blood clots, but he didn't see how that connected with babies. She was ahead of him. He watched Karen's mouth move and thought how feminine she was, yet she had a punk look about her and was no damsel in distress, no frail caricature in a frilly dress picking wildflow-ers on her way to church. She must've thought things through a bit further than the usual kneejerk reaction. He felt his eyes drift down to her T-shirt and focus on her breasts, then down to her crutch. He tried to imagine what she would look like naked, and whether he would ever see her in that state. Maybe tonight would be the time, but he doubted it somehow. He didn't mind. It was nice to keep the thing going.

'What's old-fashioned anyway?' she asked, leaning her head back. 'Things are never how they appear. What's conservative and what's liberal? You look at the people here, and you could say that a good number of them are liberal in their outlook, whatever liberal is sup-posed to mean, but when it comes to an argument their views might be just as entrenched as those stuck-up bastards passing laws for them-selves in Parliament. How many of the so-called alternative preach free sex and everything and dismiss love and faithfulness as conservative values? They wouldn't be able to even talk about the subject without sinking into worn-out rhetoric. Their own locked-in approach makes them the real conservatives. It's just another version of materialism. Communist or fascist, what's the difference. Where's the soul?'

Will nodded his head. He thought he understood what she meant. He was beginning to feel like a puppet having his strings pulled in time to Karen's words. He wondered where it was leading. It was a line of argument he didn't mind hearing because it added to her attrac-tion, gave her strength of personality and independence, but he could guess the reaction of the rest of the lads. Carter would shake his head listening to such blasphemy and piss off, not bothering to waste pre-cious seconds on a dead end, back on the trail of a quick knee-trembler. Balti and Harry would go along with a bit of the chat, liking the virginal princess angle, which would probably be the way they'd misinterpret Karen, a bit of a novelty, before getting bored with it all, just wanting the quick presentation and an instant succumbing to the fine love-making skills of the beer-bellied elite, or preferably a visit to Balti Heaven. Will didn't have a clue what Mango would think. He'd either walk away in disgust or set the woman up as a piece of prized property worth pursuing purely for the pleasure he'd get from charming his way past her resistance. Maybe he'd even fall in love with the imagery.

'This stuff makes my head go funny,' Karen said, leaning into Will. 'I haven't had snakebite for a while. Last time I drank five pints and threw up in the sink at home. That was soon after my mum died and I haven't had it since.'

The lights went down and the band came on, and a mixture of punk and rap kept them going for the next hour. They didn't wait around for the encore, hurrying to Brixton tube to catch a train to Victoria. The buildings were rundown and dark, the pubs kicking out, police vans patrolling the back streets. The wind screamed as it blew over dustbins and scattered flyers. Further along and a young ragga-muffin had been stopped by a patrol car. Will was glad he wasn't black. The poor bastards didn't have a chance. Then they were in the sharp light of Brixton station past the Nation of Islam boys preaching fun-damentalism and the avoidance of chemical distraction. The escalators dazzled under their feet, churning up warm snakebite, running for a train about to depart, the carriage almost full with people from the Academy. The blend of sweat, drink and happy faces made it a quick roll to Victoria where they had to wait ten minutes. There was more room and a different mix of office workers on the train, pissed and loud. Once in Hammersmith they took a bus to Karen's flat. Will followed her up the stairs. She fumbled with the key and then they were inside.

'What do you do for a job?' Karen asked, once she'd made two cups of tea and was sitting on the sagging couch next to Will.

He wanted to pull her forward, but had to be careful, all that talk about making love instead of having sex. It made sense right enough, but it also made him hesitant. That's probably what it had been like in the old days in high society. The gentleman had to go through the routine and get things just right for the lady. They must've spent a lot of time making themselves blind; morning, noon and night. At

least that's how period dramas presented life. Will couldn't stop his
eyes straying and felt guilty because he was sure Karen could read his
mind. She was peering into the place where his soul should be, deciding
whether his intentions were honourable, reading the cartoon bubble
above his head, words etched in scratch black ink. He looked away and
her words connected.

'I run a shop, halfway between junk and antiques. I make a living
and do my own hours. You soon know what to buy and what to ignore.
Before that I worked for a cab firm. I saved up enough to buy some
secondhand gear, rent premises, and I haven't really looked back. I'm
my own boss, though it hurts when the tax bill comes round. I do the
odd market. It's a good life. I've been lucky. What about you?'

'I work in the housing department at the council dealing with
benefits. I get to help people at least.'

Will stood up and went over to the singles stacked next to the
two long rows of albums he'd examined on his first visit. Karen had a
good five hundred or so seven-inches. He sat down and pulled a few
out at random. First was Gary Gilmore's Eyes by The Adverts. Next
Penetration's Don't Dictate. He remembered seeing both bands when
he was a kid. Gaye Advert speeding through Bored Teenagers. Pauline
Murray fronting Penetration at the Roundhouse. Female vocals fitted
punk to perfection. That had been a night out that one. He'd gone along
with Mango's brother Pete, lying about his age to get in, taller than his
mates then. Black Slate and Fusion had opened the bill and the place
had been stacked with skinheads all going on about the forthcoming
Slade reunion gig, the original skinhead band. Sham's barmy army was
definitely mental. It had taken Pete twenty minutes to work his way
through the shaven heads five deep at the bar.

Wooden terracing led down to the dancefloor and Will had been
bundled aside during Penetration's set as a big crew of skins piled
through the crowd. Black Slate and Fusion had been okay, but Pauline
Murray stood out. Will had wished he was a bit older and that the
Penetration vocalist had taken a shine to him, spotting the boy in the
crowd. Pete was at the back of the terrace during the break between
Black Slate and Fusion, snogging with some punk girl with peroxide

hair, torn fishnets and a PVC mini-skirt with a silver zip up the back. Pete was pissed and leant over the back of the terrace to puke on those down below, then went back to the punkette who didn't seem bothered by the new flavour. Will kept his eyes ahead most of the time, young enough to mix embarrassment with curiosity. A stream of Clash tracks blasted through the speakers. Pete had been wearing his Snow White and the Seven Dwarves shirt at the time. Poor old Snow White was getting a regular servicing from the sick midgets, stumpy erections jammed into every available orifice. Happy, Grumpy and Doc were doing their best to give the girl a night she would never forget. Disney's caring image had been given a gangbanging punk rock reinterpretation, a tribute to consumerism which the righteous majority condemned. Will looked at Karen sitting on the couch sipping her tea and smiled as he linked Pauline Murray and a similar look.

He pulled out the Sex Pistols' Anarchy In The UK. It was the EMI pressing and worth a bit. Will went into one, the snakebite hitting, telling Karen that nobody had ever matched the Pistols, the best working-class London band ever, despite the latter-day revisionism of middle-class journalists who insisted that punk was nothing more than an example of Malcolm McLaren and Vivienne Westwood's manipulative powers. Will told Karen that it was the natural progression of boot boy culture. That the new-wave term really got up his nose. It was always like that. History was written by a certain element in society and that was the only version left behind. Johnny Rotten was the top man, hearing that voice when he was a kid in school striking the right chord. The Pistols were an obvious development. Simple really. One hundred per cent boot boy music with a chunk of non-party politics thrown in which he had been able to appreciate because it came from his own experience. Paul Cook and Steve Jones were sound as well, West London boys. He liked picking up the records, looking at the sleeve designs and then pulling the vinyl out. Funny really, but he'd never been into the coloured stuff, the yellows and pinks and reds. He preferred black vinyl. Beautiful stuff.

He wanted to put the record on, preferring the B-side to Anarchy In The UK, but it was midnight and it wasn't the right time for good old-fashioned lyric-heavy listening. He was sitting with a classy woman and needed something a bit more mellow. He switched to the albums and asked Karen what she wanted. She didn't mind, so he took out a King Tubby collection and was back on the couch with the volume low and Karen leaning into him again. He stroked the back of her hair, looking at the perfectly formed ears, three earrings in the left, two in the right. She wore a silver necklace and the pendant had worked its way to the side, some kind of pagan latticework with a hidden meaning. He could feel her breasts against his stomach. The heater was working and the room was warm. Karen sat up and twisted her body, taking off the cardigan. Her breasts pushed forward against the top and Will could feel movement between his legs, noticing the line of a low-cut bra. He tried to think of something else, playing the gentleman. He was getting into the swing of the thing, deciding he would play hard to get. He went back to the records, back to the music, back to the Lyceum.

He'd been to quite a few gigs with Pete. The Lyceum had been a good Sunday night out. Like that time when the UK Subs had been due to support Generation X. The Subs had a hardcore following and for some reason Charlie Harper's band hadn't played, so the Subs element of the crowd was well wound up by the time Generation X were due on stage. Billy Idol was the cowboy of punk, with his pretty looks and plastic leer, and the Subs fans hadn't exactly welcomed him. But it was afterwards Will remembered most. Coming out and finding a hundred or so skinheads lined up across the road, a lot of them with bottles, waiting for the UK Subs mob to appear. He was with Pete on the Strand when the skins steamed in and then the old bill had arrived and broken things up. They'd walked towards Trafalgar Square and the skins were given a police escort along the Strand behind them towards Lord Nelson waiting with his press gang and the short sharp shock of naval service. A couple of stray German tourists heard the skinhead chant and shot off into Covent Garden. Pete had been good like that, taking a kid along with him to gigs. He'd been a nice bloke. Nothing was too much trouble. He didn't have to bother with his younger brother's mate who happened to be into good music at an early age. Most people wouldn't have made the effort.

Karen got up and went out of the room. A blast of cold air hit when she opened the door. Those gigs had been brilliant, the DJs either playing solid reggae between punk bands, or maybe throwing in one or two punk singles, playing them a speed too slow to take the piss. It was all the same tradition really. Ska and skinhead bands. Punk and reggae. Soul and mod. Then there was the techno and scratch, rap, jungle, drum n bass, all the colours of the rainbow. But he knew where the roots were. You couldn't beat music. Anyone who didn't like music wasn't alive as far as Will was concerned. It was something to be proud of, the way cultures had blended so successfully in music. That was the way racism broke down. Living and growing up with black kids, Asians, whatever. That's how they'd been raised. The whole skinhead thing owed its roots to the ska bands and all that old Jamaican dancehall style. Classic sounds. Boss sounds. And it was best heard on vinyl, with all the rough edges. CDs didn't compare, and they lacked the sleeve artwork and overall feel. CDs were convenient and polished and part of the technological age, and more sophisticated reproduction methods were on the way. New formats would be marketed and software pushed, then the hardware, raking in the cash. Will had a CD player, but whenever possible bought vinyl. Like Karen had said, soul was more important than mechanics.

He stretched out on the couch. The room was so warm with the gas fire burning. King Tubby soothed him. He was relaxed but far from tired. He heard water running and Karen stuck her head round the door to tell him she was going to have a bath. She felt dirty and smelly with the sweat frozen to her skin. She wouldn't be long, and Will was bending his head back just seeing the head detached, wondering what was behind the door. When she was gone he closed his eyes, concentrating on the music. He was okay for a while, then started thinking of Karen. He heard the water shut off.

He had finished his tea and fancied a biscuit. He went into the hall. It was icy. A lamp shone in what he imagined was the bedroom. There was a strange pattern on the whitewashed ceiling. The door was half-ajar. He heard Karen splashing in the bath, King Tubby in the living room. He poked his head round the door, peering into the woman's private world. He felt a bit guilty. It was a plant creating the shadow. A teddy bear drew his attention, sitting on the bed's pillows. There was a purple duvet and Islamic-patterned pillowcases, a pine chest of drawers and a small stack of clean clothes on a chair. The carpet was red and the curtains black, pulled together. Light from a streetlamp highlighted the material's texture. An electric fire had been plugged in and was beginning to have an effect.

Will went into the kitchen, remembered his manners and returned to knock on the bathroom door. He asked if he could have a biscuit. Said he was feeling hungry. Karen's voice was slightly muffled, and he knew the answer, but wanted her to know where he was. He went to the biscuit tin and took four custard creams, then sat at the small vinyl table. He heard the plug pulled and water rushing away. The bathroom door opened and Karen went to her bedroom. It was an odd situation and Will didn't know what he should be doing. Usually, you went back with someone and that was that, but here he was the second time round her place sitting in the kitchen eating custard creams while she was having a bath and, for all he knew, wandering around naked. He finished the biscuits and wondered whether he should go home. He was nervous. Something wasn't right, yet a little while ago everything had seemed perfect. His old paranoia started to return. What could she see in him anyway? What if it was a stitch-up by some of the lads? It would've been easier staying at home listening to music, then going straight to sleep. But here he was sitting in a strange kitchen.

Eventually he turned the light off and went towards the living room. King Tubby had fallen silent and the light had been switched off. He heard Karen call him from the bedroom. He stopped outside the near-shut door and felt his confidence go. It was the build-up that was doing it to him, the time to think and imagine. Then he was through the door and the light was right down low, the atmosphere friendly and warm, this stunner naked in front of him. Will hardly had time to look at Karen before she was up against him showing that it was no pisstake.

An hour later and Will was looking at the effect the street light had on the curtain and far wall. He'd played the same game as a kid at night when he couldn't get off to sleep, trying to create scenes in fabric or on wallpaper. Karen was asleep and breathing deeply. Her right arm was over his chest and her breasts against his side. He felt like something major. There was no way to describe it really, just the best shag he'd ever had, and yet it wasn't a shag at all. He needed another way to describe it. Making love, that's what it was. Like Karen said earlier. It was probably the first time since Bev really, but much better. He had to be honest that he'd never really satisfied Bev. He'd wanted to talk about it but had never been able to find a way into the subject. He'd just felt useless, but reckoned things couldn't be that bad because she seemed to enjoy it sometimes. She never complained or anything. Never said a word against him.

With Karen, though, they'd just merged in together. He'd felt her spasms and heard the groans and reckoned it had been alright. He hoped so, but somehow knew that the love-making had worked right away. Maybe that's what love was all about. Not the sex so much, more the feeling. Will didn't know about love, didn't want to think that far ahead. He was getting soppy. Acting soft. He had to keep himself in line and not give too much away, just go with the flow and hopefully things would turn out okay. Karen shifted a bit, murmuring in her sleep. She pulled in closer. He felt great. Really happy.

The clock on the radio said it was three and Will wasn't getting anywhere. He wanted to sleep but couldn't. The curtain was made from fairly thick material and the light created different levels. He saw lines of men marching across an empty desert, off to war, travelling thousands of miles just to get their bollocks blown off. He thought about the teddy bear. Karen could have had it since she was a couple of years old. His own teddy bear was long gone. It was a shame really, and he wished he could remember the moment when it was forgotten. All those years and it gets dumped in the dustbin or given to the jumble. It was sad somehow, that kids had to grow up and have those kinds of things taken away. Peter Pan had the right idea. Peter Wilson forever young.

Half an hour later and Will gently removed Karen's arm from his chest. The movement disturbed her and she turned round, curling into a ball. He looked at her back for a while in the vague light, following the gentle ridge of her backbone from below the neck, between small shoulder blades to the base of her back. He pulled the duvet down, looking at the curve of her buttocks and the shapely legs, while she slept soundly, suspended in time, somewhere far away. He thought of Harry briefly, the dream master, that ability he had to remember so much the next morning. Will pulled the duvet back up and positioned it around her neck. He got up. The electric heater was still on so the room was nice and warm. He pulled on his shirt and jeans and went into the hall, then into the living room. It was cold. He put on the gas fire third go and rolled himself a healthy spliff. He laid back on the couch with his bare feet up, feeling the burn of the flames. He was doing well. Inhaling deeply and watching smoke spiral towards the ceiling. He looked at his surroundings with no music to distract his attention, moving from the records to a row of books, past a couple of prints on the wall towards a small, crooked pile of videos.

He went over and knelt down, looking at the titles written in pencil. Most were films from the TV or comedy series, mostly *Black Adder* and *Dad's Army*, one marked *Family* in black felt pen. He inserted the last cassette in the VCR and returned to the couch, remote control in his hand. He did the business and inhaled as the picture flickered and faces began to appear. It was old cine footage converted to videotape. Will was surprised by the instant close-up of a man's face, the camera zooming-out to show what he identified as Karen's old man. He looked like a decent enough bloke. He wore an oversized collar and sideburns and had the same crooked smile Will had seen on the face of his daughter. Karen's dad turned and walked across a small lawn to a woman sitting in a deck chair. Karen's mum. Had to be. The likeness was obvious. She seemed happy, waving at the camera and laughing, then turning her head away. He rewound and pushed the freeze-frame button. The face stuck in time. He leant forward and inhaled, the blow hitting home. He suddenly felt bad, like he was trespassing in a private zone, seeing the dead woman's face and looking for clues to the future. There were lines across her forehead, but that was nothing unusual. She was dignified-looking, her hair dyed blonde with an absence of make-up on her face. Natural beauty in a rough sort of way.

It was mental freezing a bit of personal history like that. Will couldn't imagine being able to watch a film of his own parents once they were dead and cremated. It was too much. It made death look irrelevant when in reality it was the ultimate degradation. Was she a bundle of bones in a rotting coffin or the woman he saw on the screen with a smile splitting her face? Will reached for the remote and pushed Play. It was bad news that frozen image. The frames flashed past and there was Karen running around with the brother she had spoken about. He tried to match the six-year-old on the video with the sleeping beauty next door. She was all grown up with the reproductive urge added to the equation, cleverly disguised as recreation. It was odd to think of making love so many years into the future with that small kid busy shouting and jumping up and down, without any kind of care or worry. He felt uncomfortable. But it was making love, not sex. Was that all sex meant, adding another division to male and female when you reached puberty? Was it possible to carry that innocence on when you grew up, or did it have to be destroyed with the toys that became childish?

What would Carter think, in his unbothered way, taking some bird back and finding Teddy sitting there on the pillow waiting for his mistress to come home from a hard night's entertainment? Probably try and mount it into the bargain. He'd think it was soft. But it wasn't. Will didn't see why there had to be such a big divide. Why couldn't sex just be loving and everything, like Karen was saying at Club Verbal, a bit of romance without the materialist hard-sell? He watched the kids run and play and Mum and Dad kiss for the camera, holding hands, and he drew on the blow hoping to get to sleep. He stopped the video and rewound, pushed Eject. He replaced the cassette in its case.

For the first time he noticed a vase of flowers by the window. Every year Karen bought carnations on the anniversary of her mother's death. They'd been her favourite. The flowers were red and white and pink, and though he didn't like flowers much, at least not out of the ground and indoors, the ceremony made them worth something. At least the memory was preserved, a bit like his punk records, though he knew he was a bit of a tosser comparing vinyl and death. He'd bought Pete's

records off Mango five years after Pete went missing. It bothered him
a bit at first, but it was Mango who'd made the offer. Will had been into
the idea of owning lots of records and paid the asking price, Mango
using the money to go out with a millionaire's daughter from St John's
Wood he'd been trying to impress. If he remembered right, Mango had
taken her for a meal, got her pissed and then been blown out. He'd been
well fucked off about it, but wasn't bothered about the records. It was
a bit bad somehow. The whole transaction lacked dignity, even though
the records were only objects.

Will finished his smoke, coughed, and went for a wee. He was
halfway through when the fire alarm in the hall started sounding, a
high-pitched scream that cut through the dull throb in his head. He
splashed his jeans but was straight in pushing the right button. He
sweated a bit listening for Karen. Silence returned. It was the smoke
that had set off the alarm. Talk about touchy. He went back to the
bathroom and tried to wash the piss out of his jeans, then returned to
Karen's bed and crept in. It frightened him that she hadn't heard the
smoke alarm. She hadn't even shifted her position since he left twenty
minutes before. She turned in her sleep and cuddled up to him again.

Will lay on his back listening to his heart, her heart, both hearts
together. The bass was deep and contented. His eyes were open and
he became used to the faint light once more, thinking of the video
and what a shame it was there was no film of Pete. It was probably for
the best. It was better just to erase that kind of thing. He felt sorry for
himself and Karen, whatever happened, even if he never saw her again.
His heart beat had always worried him as a kid. It seemed so easy to die.
A valve could go just like that, or a fatal disease appear and you'd be on
the dissection table with your guts in a plastic bag and an attendant
eating his ham sandwiches. That worry was in the past now. He was
positive. He thought of his time with Bev. They'd been close at first, like
this, but gradually the bed had been separated down the middle, especially in the summer when it was hot and sticky and touching another
person made you feel clammy and dirty. In the winter it was different,
closing up for body heat. But it was okay, because this was what life was
all about, getting attached for a while and enjoying intimacy before

moving on. A lot of people missed out. Couldn't make the connection because they were scared of the pain later on. Loads of blokes he knew didn't get the chance, whether the fault was theirs or a bit further down the road. You couldn't get the same fulfilment wanking your life away, even if it was in the shape of one-off sex.

Then the sun was forcing his eyes open and Karen was in her dressing gown next to the bed, a purple effort that rode above her knees, saying she had to get to work. She kissed him on the mouth. A long, warm kiss. She said she could always phone in sick if he wanted. She'd never done that before. It wasn't the right thing really, because she had responsibilities, but maybe staying home one day wasn't that bad a thing to do if there was a good enough reason. Will didn't need much persuading and was awake now, sliding her dressing gown apart. Karen pushed herself into the bed and for the next couple of hours everything centred on the bedroom.

Will sat up sipping his coffee, the smell of the soup Karen was making in the kitchen working its way under the door. It was raining out. The wind was blowing and the sun had been hidden by thick cloud. He was starving. It was yesterday dinner-time when he'd last eaten, apart from the biscuits, and the drink had made him even more hungry than normal. It was a good day to be shut indoors. It was the right weather for chips with brown sauce, crumpets with melted butter and jam, a nice tin of soup with the toast. He was tired after just four and a half hours of sleep, but beyond it now. His balls ached. After months of sexual inactivity, Karen's enthusiasm was a shock. He started wondering how long it was since she'd last had a shag, he meant made love, then dismissed the thought. There was no need to ruin things thinking like that. Maybe after the soup he'd be able to rest up a bit. The shop would just have to stay closed, but there wasn't exactly going to be a flood of eager punters braving the weather to spend their fortunes on his collection of tatty furniture and chipped ornaments.

The teddy bear, who Karen said was called Ted, sat next to him. Will was sure the expression had changed. There wasn't the same non-committal grin he'd noticed before, more a knowing leer with a bit of resentment thrown in as a bonus. Will stroked the bear's muzzle without response. It was just a toy. The blow was sticking around longer and longer. He turned quickly to see if it was watching him, but Ted hadn't moved. Poor little fucker, forced to listen while his childhood sweetheart made love with a strange man. Next time he would have to go and sit in the living room. Will laughed at himself and lobbed the bear in the air, catching him by the right ear. He held Ted out in front at arm's length. The expression hadn't changed. He was giving nothing away.

'Talking to Ted, are you?' Karen asked as she came into the room. 'What was he saying to you, Teddy dear?'

She gave Will the tray she was carrying and lifted the bear to her head. She looked at Will, then back at the bear. She frowned.

'Ted says you threw him in the air and made him feel sick, and that you caught him by the ear. He says that his ear is hurting. He thinks you don't like him, and if you're not careful he'll get you when you're asleep. You should treat him nice or he'll make you sorry.'

Will looked at the bear, then down at his soup. It was homemade and vegetable and a bit too healthy-looking for his tastes. Thick brown bread was buttered on a plate. He preferred his bread white and ready sliced, but said nothing. And you couldn't beat soup from a tin. Just get the old can-opener working, dump it in the saucepan, give it a few minutes over the flame while you buttered the toast, and there was a four-star meal ready and waiting. His mouth watered at the thought. He looked back at Ted, then Karen.

'Don't look so worried,' she laughed. 'Ted and me don't have any secrets from each other. We tell each other everything.'

Karen went to the kitchen for her soup. Will looked at the bear. It must've been a lucky guess. But he was beginning to dislike the toy, with its cocky grin and glass eyes. She came back and got into bed.

'How did you know I threw him in the air and caught him by the ear?' Will asked. 'I wasn't talking to him though.'

'I saw you through the crack in the door. You looked scared when I told you what he said. Toys can't talk. They're just toys, nothing more. Something for when you're a kid. Ted's a memory more than anything else.'

Will nodded. He was tired and his brain was misfiring. It was nice putting emotions into things which could never have that quality. That was what religious icons came down to really. Karen's mum shifting her feelings somewhere they couldn't do any harm, avoiding debate, hearing the sort of answers that made everything alright. If it helped her accept her own death then maybe it was okay, even if it was a con.

'They were fine when I phoned up and said I wouldn't be in,' Karen said, blowing on her soup and waiting for it to cool down. 'I was a bit nervous lying like that, but they told me to go to bed and rest. I said I had the flu. I said okay, that I'd go back and spend the day sleeping, but they didn't know I had a man waiting for me.'

She rubbed the inside of Will's leg and he was glad they both had trays on their laps. He didn't fancy sex again right now. He was a bit worn out. Karen had enough energy for them both.

'You didn't sleep well last night, did you?' Karen asked.

'I'm usually alright,' he answered. 'Just one of those nights.'

'Thanks for staying. Sorry I was going on a bit. I was depressed yesterday thinking of my mum. It was a nice night out. And it was even better when we got back, wasn't it?'

Will guessed he was going red and sipped from a spoonful of soup. It didn't taste bad for something homemade. He stirred it and noticed chopped carrots, mushrooms, onions, and a couple of bits of what must've been potato. He didn't fancy the bread much. He made the effort seeing as how Karen had fixed it for him, treating him like a king. It had to be the first time in his life since he was ill as a kid that someone had made him food in bed. The bread was alright. A bit chewy and that, but nothing he couldn't handle.

'It was a great night,' he admitted, feeling the enthusiasm in his voice but reasoning that it was okay to be open.

'What do you think of the soup? I made it with miso.'

'It's great.'

Will wanted to ask what miso was, but felt a bit of a prat. He'd ask one of the lads, and if they didn't know he'd go down the library and look it up in a dictionary. He was getting into the soup now, not pushing himself any more.

'I made the bread yesterday. Do you like it? You've only had a couple of bites. I don't like all that processed rubbish. You don't know what shit they've put in it and I never touch anything that's been in a tin. It's unnatural. I'm sure cancer comes from tinned food and preservatives. It seems a bit of a coincidence it's such a big killer in the West. My mum should've had a go at the food corporations rather than putting everything down to fate and trusting in God's mysterious ways. It was just easier for her to believe all the propaganda she was fed as a kid.'

'The bread's good. I've never met anyone who makes their own bread before. Never met anyone who makes their own soup.'

'It's easy enough, nothing special. Just a bit of DIY.'

Will wanted to tell Karen that he knew a couple of blokes like that. His old mates the Lager Twins. They were DIY merchants, preferring a J Arthur Rank to sex with a woman. You'd never catch VD that way. It was on hand any time of day, literally. Karen might have laughed but it wasn't the kind of humour he was going to introduce at such an early stage. He wanted things to be perfect. Romance, love, all that kind of stuff. Karen understood better than him. Maybe the Sex Division should split in two. Balti and Harry could form the Skin Flute League, where each wank scored a single point. It would be a local derby really, because they lived in the same flat and would have to constantly outdo each other in the quantity stakes. Quality wouldn't even come into the daily Skin Flute derbies. It would be non-league football, but would be better than constant battles against relegation where the beautiful game would be corrupted and reduced to a coarse scramble for points.

Will chewed the homemade bread as Karen went through the details of how she had made it, thinking of the Sex Division. If she ever found out he was in something like that she'd probably send him packing. Will felt righteousness take over. Karen would look at him in another way. Gone forever would be the caring, gentle Will she was obviously attracted to, and in his place a pisshead would rear up, or worse than that, a Carter cut-out. As for the Sex Division, he would never be able to claim the points of last night. It would ruin everything. But bollocks to all that. He would keep Karen away from the others for as long as he could, but eventually they would probably meet. Not that anyone would say anything, but he wouldn't feel good about it all the same.

Will had to get out of the Sex Division. Had to go into liquidation. A loss of assets. Sell his ground. Whatever it took. He didn't want to belong. He'd never liked the idea in the first place. Imagine meeting Johan Carter in The Unity when he was a bit pissed, maybe going into one, Karen telling Will what a wanker he was and that he could fuck off. It had to be done. He was getting paranoid. He'd been smoking too much blow. But it was only exaggerating things he already felt.

When they'd finished eating Karen took the plates away and washed them. She came back soon after, smiling, asking Will if he had anything left for desert. She took her dressing gown off and he admired her body. Despite himself he was aroused and the woman he thought he was probably going to fall in love with pulled the duvet back and got in next to him. He noticed that one of her earrings had fallen out. He was on for a three-pointer that would never be entered into the statistics. Will was with Karen for pleasure, not points. They were together for the purest of reasons.

PART TWO

DREAMSCAPE

The Hide was heaving and the boys were steaming, Carter well into a blonde number, her two mates waiting for Harry and Balti to show a bit of interest. Harry leant back against the wall and considered the options while Balti remained tucked into the side of the jukebox. One Step Beyond by Madness was playing and usually they'd go into a bit of sax imitation, maybe do a Suggs or something, but knew the girls would think they were a couple of muppets. Harry was thinking of saying something but couldn't really be bothered, and he'd had a good wank that morning before the football, sitting back in the bath with the water scorching hot burning the week's paint and turps from his pores, lager dregs melting away, his first chance to bang the bishop since Monday. Balti was weighing their chances up, thinking they looked okay but were a bit too fucking trendy for his liking, too fucking cocky for their own good. They were obviously out of it or they wouldn't be eyeing up a couple of herberts. He'd had a skinful and the last Saturday of the football season was always a sad time.

'Where'd you get the earrings then?' he asked, leaning forward and almost falling into the woman's chest, the support of the jukebox removed forcing him to stand on his own two feet, instantly regretting a shit chat-up line. When he looked more closely at the face in front of him, he realised she was the same age or older, that she had probably heard of Madness after all.

'A mate of mine brought them back from Goa. He DJs over there. They're silver and the stone in the middle's a ruby. They cost a tenth of the price you'd pay in London.'

'I used to wear an earring, when I was younger like, but every time

I got in a row someone pulled it out trying to rip my ear off. Nothing special mind. Just a silver hoop.'

'I was thinking of having my nose pierced but everyone does that now,' she said, eyes widening, circled with slightly smudged eyeliner. 'I've had my right nipple done, and my friend's got a stud through her lip.'

Balti looked sideways and saw the ring-free mouth, then thought about it for a moment. He wondered what it was like shagging a bird with a butterfly tucked in between her legs. A bit rough probably. You'd have to be careful. The one doing the talking was looking round like Mango did, checking for a reaction, a bit of recognition. She was nice though, despite the pose. The gear was a bit expensive and fashionable in that naff way that left him cold, all designer dago bollocks. But that was her trademark and if she'd been a heifer, or not paid him attention, just ignored the shit line and made him look a cunt, then he'd have been forced to dismiss her as one more dyke who didn't know what she was missing. One more dyke in a brave lager culture suffering from mass outbreaks of lesbianism.

Harry was moving now, uneven on his feet, feeling the effects, Madness replaced by some industrial effort neither of them could identify. For a second Balti wished he was back home where he could decide what music he listened to, like Will, who was sitting in with Karen again, the miserable git, but bollocks, he was having a laugh and if he'd been in Will's shoes, with a cracker like that on the go, a bit of class, then he'd be doing the same. At least he'd remembered to set the video for *Match Of The Day*. The Dutchman had played another blinder for the Blues. He wanted to see it again. All the flicks and feints, the surging runs ghosting past the opposition with an ease that made his team-mates look like Sunday league players. Even Carter had ditched Johan and was going on about Ruud's genius. Next thing he'd be growing his hair and wearing dreadlocks.

The idea of Carter in Gullit-style dreadlocks set him off. With the football season at an end, and that riot in Birmingham having run its course, the papers were looking round for a new public enemy. As ever, summer meant hippies, ravers and travellers were about to take the strain. Balti had always dismissed white blokes with dreadlocks as wankers. He didn't hold an opinion about Stonehenge and pagan rights of worship, though the media usually went into one when the summer solstice came round, denouncing the anarchist threat to democracy and the Christian way of life. The tabloids were comics anyway so he didn't take them seriously. He was starting to see the logic. Karen had set him straight, following the line of descent back to punk, the way the anarchist movement had rearranged and developed itself. She was alright Karen. And it showed what could be done. He didn't believe in all that nonsense, witchcraft and everything, knowing that it was too much drugs that did their heads in, but getting away made sense. He'd been signing on for five months now, going for jobs he never got, just sitting around. That was no life. He wasn't talking about Glastonbury either. That was just more wank. Paying through your nose to stand in a field. Playing at being something you weren't. They should bomb the part-timers. Like the football. All those cunts who came to five or six games a season and sat in the most expensive seats. Going walkabout for a couple of months would be a laugh. It was supposed to be alien, like it couldn't be part of your life because of the pictures you saw and the interviews you heard, but when Karen cut through the prejudice then it made sense. Like it didn't have to belong to someone else.

She was great Karen. He wouldn't mind meeting someone like that. None of the lads had seen her for the first couple of months and then Will brought her down the pub and everything was sweet. She got her round in. Everyone liked her. She had her view and could make you think things through. It was another angle. She wasn't some sloppy cow giggling the whole time, or some flash case rabbiting on trying to boost her ego. Karen was solid. Hundred per cent. She came down quite often now and none of the lads complained like they usually did when a bird tagged along. She wasn't a mother figure, nothing like that, more a sister. But even that wasn't right. Just a mate really. She had a different slant. Made them think. Most of all she was honest. She fitted in perfect with Will. Balti didn't like posers. Mango pissed him off. Something chronic. This bird was pissing him off as well. But she was a good-looker. He didn't know how important that was, the sex appeal and everything, whether he should play the game and bite his lip, hoping to get his leg over. Act all impressed because she had a ring through her tit.

'I started stretching my bollocks last year,' Balti lied. 'Had the weights nailed on and my sack soon began sagging. Once I'd gained a couple of inches on the old scrotum I added more weights and my balls are down round my knees now. It took a while, but they got there in the end. It's something you just have to stick with and force yourself through the pain. I'm suffering for my body art. All you need is the time and a bit of patience. I've got time at the moment, being self-employed and that, though you get a bit impatient because you're so keen to see the end result.'

He patted his left leg. She looked a bit wary. Like she thought it was a wind-up but wasn't sure, trying to picture a stretched sack and a couple of chestnuts floating in the void. She powered into his face looking for an answer, but Balti kept his dignity and refused to crack a smile. She seemed a bit pissed off now. She sipped her drink and looked past them, then meaningfully at her mate, then her shoes which Balti reckoned must've left a serious dent in her wages. A waste of money you saw more clearly when you were living on pennies.

'I keep them tucked down my left peg because I'm right-footed and don't want to strain the veins. I can swing them side to side. My mate's the same. We're the Bollock Brothers. Surprised you haven't heard about us. We're famous round here. Balls down to our knees and now we're working on the guts, filling up nicely.'

'Nice one, Scrote,' Harry shouted, grabbing his mate by the knee, pretending to squeeze his bollocks. 'Just like knicker elastic. With all that weight attached it means the skin stretches and when you let it go again it snaps back to the body. It's like playing ping-pong.'

Doesn't it affect you when you're with a woman?' The second of the two asked, moving closer and taking him at face value, maybe taking the piss, while her friend adjusted her stance. 'Doesn't it make things a bit difficult with all that skin getting in the way?'

'It takes a bit of imagination, that's all,' Harry laughed.

He was taken back to last night with the two women on top of the hill. He hadn't slept well, the weather hot and humid, summer arriving early with the effects of global warming and city pollution. The confusion of the seasons was mucking up his sleep. Everything was shifting around. In the winter he dreamt of the tropics and psychedelic jungles, where his surroundings were bursting with life and sound, the natural world mixed with futuristic technology, Mayan Indians disguised as Aztecs and Frank Bruno on the door. Now it was almost summer and he was stuck on a moor, without shelter, with seven thousand shades of black and white for company. He was part of a line drawing and there was a coldness about everything, the cracks in the sky cracks in broken bone china. There'd been a woman in a white gown laying on a horizontal stone, a woman in a black dress in the background next to a fossilised tree. It was a dead oak and the only tree to be seen. The woman on the slab was alive and tripping on special-offer button mushrooms. In a semi-conscious state with her brain frying from all the things she'd seen. Somehow it was up to Harry and Balti to show her that it was worth going on with life, that just because she'd seen a crow flap its wings and been able to follow the vibrations through the air, it didn't mean that boring everyday life wasn't worth living.

They were old men. With long beards and slight hunches. Merlin wizards without the magic. The end was near and they were dressed in rags. A couple of tramps on top of a moor surrounded by ancient stones not knowing what to do next. They'd lost their way. Balti leant forward and the woman's eyes opened. Harry remembered the black circles, the emptiness; eyes without pupils. A thin white arm pulled Balti forward. The woman turned sideways and Balti slid onto the stone. Harry turned his head away but heard their moans. She was a witch and was draining Balti's resistance. Harry tried to say something but no sound came from his mouth. He left the moor, the footsteps of the second woman right behind as he hurried towards the orange glow of London. He turned once and saw that the second woman was dressed in worn-out rubber and had the head of a giant insect. London was on fire. He ran from the moor, covered in a thick sweat that soaked his mattress.

The two women made their excuses and went off to the Ladies, and Balti and Harry had a laugh, not expecting them to return. Fuck it anyway. They were enjoying themselves, Carter well away with the blonde. Not a bad-looking bit of skirt if they were honest, but the music was loud and they were pissed and nothing could touch them, no fucking way. It was May and they'd been to a goalless draw in front of a full house. The Sex Division had gone a bit quiet as well, with Carter so far out in front now, Mango in second place with those posh numbers from his work, while Harry and Balti were in serious relegation trouble without even a sniff of a point. Will, meantime, had gone underground since he'd got all serious with Karen. They didn't even know how many points he was on, and Carter had stopped winding him up about it because Will wasn't shifting. But Carter liked Karen as well and didn't really want to know, just felt he had to ask. It was expected of him. Will said he wasn't in the Sex Division any more, which was fair enough really, when you had class like that, but they still included him. Who needed dodgy old boilers when a decent bird paid you attention?

'You in there or what?' Carter asked when the blonde had followed her friends to the toilet.

'If they like their bollocks hanging free,' Harry said, filling him in on the details.

'I don't understand you two.' Carter was unamused. 'There's two fit-looking birds obviously up for it, gagging for a good servicing more like, with studs in their tits and fannies, and you two start feeding them a line about having Plasticine balls. I mean, what's the game? Don't you like women or something?'

'Not Plasticine balls,' Balti said. 'Elastic sacks.'

The Bollock Brothers were cracking up. Balti looked like he was going to have a heart attack. He was doubled in half and there were tears in his eyes.

'What's the fucking difference?' Carter was getting excited now. 'Don't you want to get in there? I'm not surprised your balls are down to your ankles. It's the middle of May and you're not even off the mark yet. It's spring-time lads. Make an effort.'

'There's a lot of difference,' Balti insisted. 'We're not choirboys with our balls bit off by the vicar. You couldn't produce much with Plasticine balls, could you? But just because you've stretched your sack doesn't mean you can't bring pleasure to a beautiful woman. That's the problem today, nobody appreciates differences. We're unique. We're the Nut Crackers.'

Harry was laughing and didn't want an argument. It was good to see Balti enjoying himself. After five months signing on he was coiled tight. It was a long time living on a pittance. He thought about the desolate moorland and the rags they'd been wearing. Maybe it was a warning. He should watch out for his own job. That's what happened to you in the end. On a slab of concrete with blind birds the only ones willing to spend time with you. There was no helping hand when you went down. Mango had that much worked out. He'd said he'd be along later, they were meeting him in The Unity. Harry had forgotten about that, but Mango had been blowing them out a lot recently. It was his WorldView commitments and those posh birds he was into at the Barbican. It was another world. Harry knew it wound Balti up when Mango went into one, the fact that they came from the same backgrounds making unemployment something personal. The propaganda fired through the TV and radio, covering the front of the papers, that didn't do anyone any good either. Just made the likes of Balti feel more useless than ever.

Balti saw the three women come out of the bogs. He pointed them out. They stood for a minute talking, then left the pub together.

'Couple of fucking lesbians,' Balti said. 'Don't know what they're missing.'

'Dykes, mate,' Harry agreed. 'Fucking dykes.'

'Probably off to some queer club,' Balti said, knocking back his drink. 'Some place that costs twenty quid to get in just so they can pay three quid for a bottle of foreign lager surrounded by a bunch of fucking shirt-lifters.'

'More like fat birds with short hair and beards.'

'They didn't like the old stretched bollocks routine much,' Balti noted. 'Couple of posers. Seems like it's alright sticking a ring through your clit, but stretch your sack and you're an outcast. Where's the fucking equality in that?'

'Didn't fancy yours much anyway,' Harry said.

'Didn't fancy yours either,' Balti agreed.

'Lesbians.'

'Dykes.'

'Fucking horrible.'

'A narrow escape.'

'Fuck knows what's been up those two.'

'Right old slappers.'

'Another pint?'

'Don't see why not. No need to be uncivilised, is there?'

'What about you, shag man.'

'They just pissed off,' Carter said, stunned. He wasn't used to getting blown out. 'They went without a word. I was well in there. It's you two going on about your bollocks the whole time. You fucked it up. I was on for a minimum three-pointer.'

'Do you want a drink or what?' Balti was getting narked now, took the glasses and muscled his way to the bar.

'You ballsed that up badly,' Carter told Harry. 'You should play the game. Talk shit with them for an hour or two because that's all you've got to do and then you're in. Show them you've got a bit of a brain and think they're the cream and before you know it you're away. Birds are easy to work out. Flatter them. That's all it takes.'

'Can't be bothered,' Harry laughed. 'We're pissed. Who cares? We're having a laugh. If she starts off talking about piercing her tits then what does she expect? You've got to have a laugh. It doesn't matter, does it?'

'What about relegation?'

'Fuck that. I'd rather have a laugh and go down than say things I don't want to say just to get a few points. I'd rather have a wank than waste my time talking gibberish with some poser.'

Carter stood in silence looking around the packed Hide until Balti returned. Time was standing still with the music blaring and Harry couldn't get his thinking straight, that miserable dream of last night confusing things. He liked everything in order. Neatly filed and understood. The dream was all mixed up with what was going on around him. He was losing the thread and when Carter suggested going down The Unity he remembered Mango. They drank up.

They walked slowly and Balti stopped to get some chips. The door was open but it was still a pressure cooker inside, with the oil bubbling and fat frying and some skinhead on his way out with a half-eaten roti. There was a woman in front with a couple of small kids buying the Saturday night special. They waited while the chips were wrapped and Harry watched the woman disappear. Kaleidoscope patterns of passing traffic pulsed inside the window, light caught in blasted sand. He was feeling the effects of the drink and last night's dream still wouldn't go away. It bothered him. He was trying to think back but the winter setting kept getting in the way. He was sweating heavily. The weather forecasters said it was going to be a hot summer. Long and hot. Balti took his chips and they continued down the street. It was half-nine.

The woman's white gown had been almost transparent, but there was no warning that she would pull Balti towards her, that she was interested in anything other than what was happening inside her head. She belonged to a different tribe, with her long hair and weathered features. She wasn't ugly, but not exactly state-of-the-art Modern English. She wasn't what she seemed and Harry couldn't pinpoint what she represented. Those eyes must mean something. The scenery was sparse and brutal. It was going back to a primitive environment. Somewhere on the coast of Scotland or Ireland perhaps, though there was nothing to show they were outside England other than the barren landscape. He thought instead of the woman in rubber, the insect head that made him nervous. It wasn't much fun when you started dreaming of bondage insects, giant fuckers who would suck your blood and kick your carcass into the gorse. Past and present. Maybe that's what it was. It didn't sound right somehow. The stones were obvious, magic and druids, but what about rubber woman?

'These are fucking shit,' Balti moaned halfway down the street. 'I should take them back.'

Harry tried one. They weren't cooked right. He threw the chip in to the gutter. Even the chippies were going down hill these days. Balti ate a few more and put the rest in a bin. The Unity was up ahead. It was an odd feeling, the end of the football season and the start of summer. There would be a hole for the next few months. At least with the football there was something solid at the end of the week. They were all season ticket holders and averaged thirty or so games a season. They'd been going since they were kids. Older and wiser, they avoided aggravation, back into a second childhood of team selection and tactics discussions. The eighties had been a bit mental with Chelsea on the rampage week in, week out, but they'd got older and couldn't be bothered. Things had changed. All of them had the odd flashback to childhood, carefree days growing up.

'Alright Slaughter?' Carter asked as they entered the pub.

'Not bad mate,' the nutter replied, and Carter had a subtle look towards the bar where Denise was serving.

Unknown to the rest of the lads, Carter had been shagging Denise for the last month and a half. Dirty Denise. He'd been right about her, she was a right goer. The best bit of sex he'd had for years. She seemed to get off on the knowledge that Slaughter would kill them if he found out she was doing the dirty on him. Carter didn't like that part of the arrangement, but he kept going back for more all the same. He'd had his eye on Denise for ages and knew she was interested, but it had been an accident how she'd ended up round his flat. Carter and Ian had finished delivering early and he'd bumped into Denise in the street. She'd invited herself round for a drink and he'd been nervous in case they were spotted and word filtered back to Slaughter. They'd got pissed on vodka and Denise ended up staying. She was mental. There was passion there alright, but it boiled near to violence, which Carter wasn't keen on, but he didn't want to put her off, just keep it in line a bit. There was no way some bird was going to tie him up. No fucking way. He'd heard a story like that from some bloke down Chelsea, about some other cunt nobody seemed to know personally who'd picked up this bird down a club in Brixton, gone back with her and let her tie him to the bed. Next thing he knows a six-foot nigger turns up, shafts him up the arse so hard he needs thirty stitches, and then the poor cunt gets robbed into the bargain. Not that Carter reckoned Slaughter was an iron, but you never knew what else Denise might have planned. Trust might've been the basis of all good relationships, but he wasn't looking for any of that from Denise.

It was iffy, though, with Slaughter being a headcase and Carter slipping his missus a length, Denise a bit suspect. He didn't feel guilt or anything like that, it was just that he enjoyed life and wanted to die in his sleep or from old age, not under the fine edge of a machete. From the first time she'd come round, Carter had thought about knocking it on the head, but he still kept going. The longer it went on the harder it was going to be walking away. He would keep his head down, but knew he was asking for a kicking. She was a good ride though. He switched back to their last session as he worked his way to the bar, Denise with her vibrator and clitoral stimulator spilling out of her handbag. The dirty cow.

'Three pints of lager please Denise,' he said, avoiding the bar-maid's eyes, then watching her move along the bar. She had a lovely arse. Eileen was back there with the landlord and his brother-in-law, who helped out sometimes.

'There you go Terry,' Denise smiled, eye-to-eye contact for a split second as he handed over his money.

'I thought you were coming down at nine,' Mango moaned, appearing from the mass of people crowded into the pub.

'Thought you'd be blowing us out again,' Balti said.

'I've got the night off,' Mango smiled. 'It's a bit quiet at the moment. That Saudi deal kept us up late for ages and now it's over we're left playing with ourselves.'

'What about that Penny you're always going on about?' Balti asked.

'She's alright. I saw her last night.'

Mango was moving forward in the world. He'd given up on the degraded scum haunting King's Cross and moved up market. The old bill were cleaning up the area, moving the problem on with the help of the council which was looking for a bit of inner-city rejuvenation, and Mango was pleased. It was an eyesore and not exactly conducive to economic growth. A couple of the chaps at WorldView had opened his eyes to that one. Being men of commerce and in the peak of physical condition, training at a Mayfair gym which Mango was considering joining, they had little time for women and found chance meetings a waste of resources. Time was of the essence. Ridley and Hetherington would have been appalled at the thought of picking commoners off the street. They had outlined the best approach over a working lunch, and Mango had accepted the card Hetherington put on the table.

James Wilson was better than King's Cross. The agency supplied quality acts, and while he paid heavily for the privilege of shafting women with nice accents and expensive gear, he considered it money well spent. There was a selection of nationalities available. Models from Zurich, Paris, Copenhagen. They would do anything for a price. Mind you, a pro was a pro, but they weren't so desperate somehow. Kids from Halifax were definite victims while at least Mango could feel the cold steel of a financial transaction with the call girls. They weren't even called whores. It was so much more sophisticated. Corporate sex. It felt international, with none of that Anglo-Saxon bawdiness he had grown up with. It was Eurosex. Multinational business transactions. There was a lot of religion at WorldView and the likes of Ridley and Hetherington had been educated in public schools rigidly controlled by the Church Of England. Perhaps it was being a Christian, making money and respecting wealth. It was the next stage in Mango's development. He reminded himself that he was a Christian. Fucking right he was.

'Penny's into it alright,' Mango explained, lowering his voice. 'She's got all the gear and I'm not talking your everyday stockings and suspenders either. Wanted to know if I wore hoods. Whether seeing as how I was a Tory voter, did I follow my masters and need a good caning and a night behind bars?'

Harry smiled and felt a bit better. Carter shook his head and marvelled at the workings of the female mind. Balti felt like he was going to throw up. A nightmare situation. It was bad enough the ruling class beat you into submission day after day, year after year, grinding you down and then screaming that you were a sponger for accepting benefits you'd paid for a hundred times over during the previous decade and a half. They humiliated you every day of your fucking life and then their women wanted to put a hood on your head so you didn't even have a fucking face, whipping you like they did in the Middle Ages. Fucking slag, and there was Mango, accepting the dogma and pissing on his own kind. Balti remembered those two kids he'd told them about. The bird from Halifax. He was on the verge of headbutting the cunt but held back. A year or two years younger and he'd have done him no problem. Mate or no mate. You had to have morals or you were fuck all in this world, but it was choosing the right morals and sticking to them that was hardest. There were plenty of wankers around who wanted to define the rights and wrongs for you. Karen had been right about that one. They'd had a long talk about it and Balti saw it more clearly. She was telling him that he was the victim and not the criminal. It was hard to see yourself as a victim, it made you look like a wanker and everything, like you were another castrated cunt on the box going on about the suppression of women and the white man's guilt. You had to work according to your own standards. Funny really, but Will had told him more or less the same thing, soon after he'd lost his job. But it had been presented in a different way. Not so direct. Karen got to the point. He respected her but he was no victim. No fucking way. He downed his pint and went to the bar for a refill, the others way behind, spending money he didn't have.

Nothing could compare with Saturday night. Except Friday maybe. And they usually had a few beers on a Thursday, warming up for Friday. Saturdays were good though. There was more of a mixture in The Unity whereas The Hide was a younger pub, pre-Blues drinking, people from all over West London, The Unity more local. Carter seemed less rampant than usual, enjoying a drink with the lads. He pissed them off sometimes, sniffing around anything that moved. Slaughter passed them with a grin and went to the bar and kissed Denise on the cheek, leaving with a couple of his mates. Carter smiled to himself.

'Will, what the fuck are you doing down here, you cunt?' Balti shouted, wrapping his arm round the new arrival's shoulder. 'I thought your liver had given up now you've gone all romantic on us.'

'Fancied a pint,' he answered, a bit sheepish.

'Hello,' Karen said.

'Alright darling?' Balti said, more quietly. 'I didn't see you there. What do you want to drink?'

'I'll get them,' Will insisted. 'We're only having a couple.'

He went to the bar. The rest of the lads shifted a bit so Karen had some room. Balti was hammered but felt embarrassed all the same. It was bad manners mouthing off in front of a class bird.

'Didn't expect to see you tonight,' Carter said.

'I fancied a drink. I had to give Will a bit of a kick to get him moving. We got a video out but it was rubbish. We're going back for the football. I heard Chelsea was nil-nil. Brentford won though. Beat Cardiff 3–1.'

'It was a good enough game,' Harry said. 'Typical end of season match when you've got nothing to play for, but at least The Dutchman was making the effort. Earns enough mind, but I'd rather he had it than some wanker in Westminster. We were thinking of going over to Amsterdam for the weekend next month. Terry's spiritual home, isn't it mate.'

'Sort of.'

'Why's that then, Terry?' Karen asked.

'Just love Dutch football, that's all. As soon as I got into football I remember watching Holland playing when Cruyff and Neeskens were around. I love the idea of total football. Look at the team they've got today. Overmars, Kluivert, Davids. Brilliant players.'

'Have you heard of St Pauli?' she asked.

'What's that then?'

'It's a football team in Germany, in Hamburg. It's in the squatter's area and the police are banned from the ground. Most of the fans are anarchists and instead of the national flag they fly the black flag. When there were riots against the police in Hamburg some of the players were even supposed to have taken part. I read about it. It sounds good. It's not that far from Amsterdam, though I suppose the season would be over by the time you go.'

'I wouldn't mind seeing Ajax play,' Terry admitted. 'What are they called, the German team?'

'St Pauli. They're in Hamburg.'

'That sounds alright as well. Depends on the anarchists of course. If they're like some of the ones you get over here it wouldn't be much. Students playing politics for a couple of weeks till they get a decent job.'

'It's probably better than that,' Karen said. 'It's just something I read about, that's all.'

Will came back with two pints, Guinness for Karen, Directors for himself.

'We were thinking of going to Amsterdam for a weekend during the summer,' Balti told Will. 'You don't mind him coming do you?' He turned to Karen.

'Course I don't. Why should I?'

'Don't know. Some women don't like their boyfriends or whatever going off on their own.'

'You're a traditionalist at heart, aren't you?' Karen said, laughing.

'You coming then, Will?' Mango asked.

'Don't know. I'll think about it.'

'Plenty of dope over there.'

'Plenty over here. It depends on the money.'

'Mango's going to try and put the train tickets through his work,' Terry said. 'It'll be worth it just to get his company to pay for something like that. Mind you, can't see being able to put the drugs through, and the red light's a no-no as well. Not that I'd be into it anyway.'

'You lot aren't like that, are you?' Karen asked.

The Sex Division shook their heads. Mango most of all, though he was the only one who'd ever paid for sex. He was looking forward to seeing Amsterdam's famous red light district, though from Carter's and Terry's descriptions it sounded like shit. Then there was the Reeperbahn in Hamburg. But he was up-market now. Call girls. He moved the conversation on, feeling uncomfortable. It was something you wanted to keep quiet, a failure really, and he wished he hadn't mentioned anything to the others in the first place.

'Will was saying you might be going down to Cornwall for a week in the summer,' he ventured.

'I've always wanted to go to Tintagel,' she said. 'Ever since I was a kid. It's beautiful in Cornwall. There's less people and the landscape's the nearest you get to Ireland in England.'

Harry was happy. He had the gift. Maybe he was psychic. Seeing things in the future. Of course, it was only now and then, but it gave him a buzz when it happened. Like he was above fate and in control. If he could get it a bit more accurate, control the gift, then he'd be away.

Imagine being able to predict the future. You'd make a packet with the horses and win the Lottery every weekend. They wouldn't be able to stop him and he'd keep on taking their money. The world would be his.

'I dreamt about a moor with stones last night,' he told Karen, who seemed impressed. 'I've done it a few times now, seen things that happen later. It's never really clear at first, but when it happens I know right away.'

'Are you a lucid dreamer?' Karen asked.

'That's when you're in a dream and know you're there, isn't it, so you're able to control it and make it go the way you want. That wouldn't be a real dream.'

'Of course it is,' Balti said, aggrieved. 'It's like daydreaming. You can have dreams when you're awake. They don't always have to be buried.'

'That's alright if you can be honest with yourself, but the thing is, you're always going to be turning them your own way. It's better to be straight and let it sort itself out. Then you've got the problem of working out what it means and making sense of what you've dreamt. That's the part that does me in. But when you finally understand, you're made up.'

'Who says you can trust what happens when you're asleep? Anyway, everything's natural.'

'I'll tell you what's natural,' Terry said, getting a bit fed up with the dream shit, daydreams or night dreams, it was all images and airy-fairy hippy bollocks. 'What's natural is getting a decent pint down your throat.'

They all laughed. Karen liked Will's mates. Mango interested her. To see someone like that change their stripes, when inside he understood how things worked. He was aware, but had given up. Will insisted that deep down Mango was still the same person as when he was a kid, that it was to do with Pete.

'I'm going home to watch the football,' Balti announced twenty minutes before closing-time. 'I've had enough.'

'You're recording it,' Harry said. He had his second wind and fancied a few more. Carter knew he was in with Denise.

'Hold on and we'll walk back with you,' Will said.

They drank up and moved through the pub. Will was always surprised when he went into a drunk pub sober. It was mental, watching the deterioration, the conversation and behaviour. Unless things got nasty it was a good laugh, though there was always an undercurrent in pubs like The Unity, though The Hide was worse, with regular punchups and now and then someone getting glassed. That place was a tinderbox, packed with geezers ready to start tearing up. He didn't like the place. It was ugly. But The Unity was fine. And it was a nice evening. He was really going to enjoy this summer.

Will, Karen and Balti turned off the high street, sharing some of the short journey home. Televisions created patterns through net curtains and men and women sat watching life pass by. Everything was fine. Business was picking up after a slack period and Will was in love with Karen. They'd even told each other as much. She was going to move in with him soon. Will felt the best about life he had done for years. The streets were quiet and he could think straight, a couple of pints enough during hot weather like this. Now and then a car passed, and when Karen bent down to stroke a white cat it made a noise then hurried off. They came to their street and Balti turned down the chance to watch the football round Will's. He was knackered and didn't want to move again that night.

Balti checked his watch. He was pissed but the air was clearing his head. He breathed in deeply and enjoyed the oxygen. As he was beginning to exhale he felt himself spun round and for a second thought he was a kid's top and wanted to laugh seeing the flash of a familiar face from five months back, his last memory of the working world, five months for someone to pick his moment and bring his head into contact with the space between Balti's eyes, that spot where there was supposed to be a secret gland that told the future and everything there was to know about everything else, he'd heard about that from some Indian at work, but the pain wasn't mystical, just a dagger through his skull rattling the brain's suspension and that moment of happiness, of breathing in and out in silence, shot out the hole, though maybe the drink had dimmed the sensation a bit but not enough, he should have had a couple more down the pub with his mates who were back

there enjoying themselves, and he was bouncing back and that cunt
McDonald was there in the flesh with big black eyes, where was the
fucking blue, that's what they said about Paddies, their blue eyes and
tin whistles and Balti was spinning remembering in slow motion his
own headbutt down in Tooting, putting a man on his arse all that time
ago, another world now where you got a pay packet at the end of the
week and didn't have to search supermarket shelves looking for special
offers and could have a pint whenever you wanted not worrying about
pounds and pence rather than saving it up, and he reckoned the kicking
was going to be a bit of lynch mob justice for the five car stereos he'd
nicked for some pocket money that's what happened when you got
fuck all off the social the only way to survive was to start acting like
a juvenile again, thieving small time, McDonald something he'd forgotten about after the night the Irishman came calling knowing that
revenge was going to take an exact course and waiting for the kick but
trying to pull himself into shape, swinging a punch that didn't connect
then feeling his arms pulled behind him up tight in the base of his
back with a heavy smell of tobacco and McDonald was saying something that he didn't get and there were another couple of shapes, one
on either side like birds on his shoulders, massive fucking vultures
waiting to pick at the remains of the dead, the dustmen, nature's bin
men those Orangemen, waiting for the kick thinking about the old
stretched scrotum and then it dug in deep with the pain jetting up
through his body sending his balls racing in pure agony and he was
sinking down and felt his arms released and they were kicking him
on a patch of grass and he was wide open and he saw these legs in the
air as one of the cunts, he wasn't sure which one, it didn't really matter,
tried to stamp on his head and connected with the side of his face and
they were sticking the boot in, stretched out, and he was in and out
of it thinking about everything taken back knowing now why he was
on the dole surviving on forty-six quid unable to live like a human
being while the world around him insisted he was a sponger, politicians who spent that much on their breakfasts, that's what they did,
they hired prostitutes and the prostitutes got you on the floor and
kicked the shit out of you, stuck the boot in good and proper, and it

was just being work shy that stopped him getting a job and those who lived by the sword died by the sword except that it wasn't a sword and he was shouting some kind of insult at the four men around him like they were vivisectionists or something, and he remembered that conversation with Karen saying what would it be like to have your arms and legs nailed down while some old cunt, no, she didn't use that word because she'd said once that it was insulting to women, some old sod with a scalpel half blind drooling into his tea not using the anaesthetic right trying to slit the rabbit open, carve it up, and Balti had no sympathy for himself because you had to have personal responsibility and everything and there was no forgiveness from your enemies, the fucking Belfast cunt and his scum mates, for the first time in his life he wished the IRA would blow the fuckers away because he saw the heavy hammer coming and he knew his legs were going, but then it all stopped for some reason and he heard shouting and the running of feet, one last kick in the head and a laugh saying the score's settled you fat cunt and then there were slamming doors exhaust fumes burning rubber and there was this black face right up against him with Ruud Gullit dreadlocks tight to the scalp and a thick West Indian voice, but he was alright, still conscious, and he sat up against a wall and tried to see straight trying to work things out, but bollocks, it was fine now though he was probably concussed and the three men around Balti were helping him up saying they'd call an ambulance on their mobile, but he said he was alright, he could look after himself and stand on his own two feet, and there were more strangers around him talking among themselves and now and then asking him if he was okay, so he stood up a bit unsteady feeling embarrassed getting a spanking on his own manor, but they were bad odds four or five on to one, and he was angry with himself getting slack thinking things like that would fade away and he was going to get the bastards, the first reaction was revenge, living the nightmare, fucking right, no surrender, no turning the other cheek, who the fuck did they think they were, and then he went down on the pavement and sat there for a long time getting his strength back.

SCUM OF TOYTOWN

Hammers echoed deep inside Churchill Mansion, the dull thud of steel on concrete filtering along tunnels and walkways, through broken security gates and across the common to where Balti sat on a park bench. By the time the vibration reached him it carried little of its original force. Music sounded further inside the building, thumping bass matching the hammers. Consciously he heard nothing. Just felt the gradually dimming pain in his skull and the sun on bare arms. The lion tattoo was worn and tired, a faded ghost of its original glory. The ink had been ground down over the past fifteen years and the Union Jack wrapped around the king of the Stamford Bridge savannah had lost the defining edges of its red, white and blue grooves. The skin had healed and absorbed the graffiti. It was two weeks since Balti had been on the receiving end of McDonald's anger and the breaks and bruises were still mending.

'Mind if I sit with you for a while son?' the man asked.

Balti shook his head. The old boy with the trolley had turned up at the same time the past couple of days. At first Balti was annoyed, but kept his mouth shut. It was a free world and they lived in a democratic society. One of the oldest on the planet. With the best judiciary and finest armed services, a sense of fair play and profound love of decency.

George wasn't as barmy as he first seemed. He was in his fifties with bleary labrador eyes and creased clothes. This morning he was clean-shaven. It was something the younger man had let slip. Normally he wouldn't go more than a day without a shave. He made sure he got his money's worth from the plastic razors. But the last couple of months he'd been going two, three, four days. His best mate had even accused him of turning into a hippy, a long-haired wanker who needed a good scrub. His hair needed seeing to, the number 2 crop filling out a bit. He was pushing past grade 4 and pissed off with his own laziness. He would visit the barber soon. But four quid was four quid and not to be thrown about when you were hard up.

That's what happened. You let your standards slip. Yet it didn't matter. Not really. That's what you realised. It changed your ideas being on the dole for months on end. Single mothers took a battering from politicians who screamed they were sponging off the state. You wondered if there was a bit of truth in the official hate campaign when you were in work looking after number one, no smoke without fire mentality. Like a kid would get herself up the duff for an extra tenner a week. The politicians got you thinking their way. Constant assault and battery. Assaulting your intelligence and battering you about the head soon as you hit the deck. But it brought you back to reality. Opened your eyes again. Got rid of the selfishness. Those cunts down the social, some useless but well-meaning, the others arrogant scum who only escaped a good kicking because you needed the button on the computer punched so you'd get your cheque on time.

'It's a fine day,' the man said. 'Feel that heat on your head. Nothing can beat a sunny day. It's easy to understand why they used to worship it on a day like today. There were sun-worshippers all over the world you know, and I'm not talking about boys and girls sitting on a beach trying to turn themselves into darkies. We make fun of the sun-worshippers now, but it's understandable really. Without that ball of burning gas none of this would exist. No photosynthesis, no energy, no life. We'd live in a world without colour if the sun ever burnt out. Think of that. Just consider it for a moment, won't you? We wouldn't last very long. We'd be nothing more than notions. Undeveloped ideas floating through the universe. That's all we boil down to at the end of the day anyway. Energy and notions. Some we call good, some we call bad. You have to take your pick, that's all. Make your choice and claim your reward. Please consider what I have just said.'

Balti raised his head and shaded his eyes. He was sweating and it was running under his eyelids. He couldn't get near the sun. George wore cheap sunglasses. Balti wasn't bothered. He knew the sun was up there and didn't need to burn a hole in his eyeball to prove the point. There was no need to blur your vision. He leant back on the bench. It had been dedicated to a Mrs Someone Or Other, the name of the dead woman cut by kids with no respect for memories.

It was easier having nothing to do when the weather was like this. In the winter you stayed in and kept your head down, a hedgehog buried in leaves, waiting for better days. Staying patient. Now Balti was outside making the most of the sun. It would've been nicer being on a beach somewhere, like the old boy said, but beggars couldn't choose. You took what you got and were grateful. What would the point be anyway, without a bit of cash in your pocket to go and have a drink now and then? He didn't want to listen to George wax lyrical about the nature of the cosmos, rambling on about the beauties of nature and the sheer wonderment of it all. He was on a different frequency. Probably didn't even hear the hammers. Balti wasn't slagging him off, because it was fair enough if he was on some head trip. It was just he'd rather enjoy the sun without a lecture, before a cloud came along and blocked the fucker out.

'Did you get down the bookies in time yesterday?' he asked.

'I lost a tenner,' George admitted. 'I lose a tenner a week. It's worth the expense and it's a hobby, getting to know the nags and the form. If I'd won I'd have been fifty quid better off. It's a chance you take, but it means you've always got something to look forward to. It gives you a stake in society. If it doesn't happen then that's fine by me. I could as easily spend it in the pub. The money's dead then. You piss it out half an hour later. With a horse you have a chance of getting something back.'

He moved his trolley level with the end of the bench. The contents rattled. He took out his pipe and tin and prepared a smoke. The smell of tobacco reminded Balti of McDonald. He looked at the trolley. The mesh was precisely sectioned and ordered. The old man lit up. He deserved a reward for his efforts. A patrol car slid along on the opposite side of the common, then turned into the flats. The banging stopped. Balti had noticed the old bill a lot since he'd been signing on. Like he was a crook. True, he nicked some car stereos now and then, just to tide himself over, when he was short of cash, but he wasn't making a habit of it. Breaking into cars was kid's stuff. If you were going thieving you should do it properly. If things got really tight, then he wasn't going to sit back and think of England while he got shafted by the exchange mechanism. He'd line something up and fight back good and proper. He was being looked down on. An expectation of guilt fired his way, that he didn't feel, not really, but which was force-fed and stuck in his throat.

'You have to have an aim,' George said, revelling in the contents of his pipe. 'That's what's wrong with the world today. Too many people drifting. There's no point coasting along hoping things will get better. They never do. That's one thing I've learnt from life. You have to go out and grab the opportunities. Spend to accumulate. It's important to try and better your situation, while at the same time doing something worthwhile for the community. Above all, though, it's vital to remember your place and your limitations. There's no point getting too big for your boots. Leave the more complicated problems to those with specialist skills.'

George was moving into a speech. Like he was on a platform. Balti waited in silence. It had been the same the last two days. He was worth listening to for a bit before he started losing the thread of what he was saying. It helped pass the time.

'Look at my situation, for instance. Not that I'm blowing my own trumpet. Far from it in fact. That's not my style. Anyone who knows me will back me up on this. It never has been and never will. I'm an average man of average means. I've suffered from severe depression and been treated by psychiatrists. They've fed me with drugs and recommended various therapies, but I feel no guilt. It happens to everyone at one time or another. Mental collapse. It's part of the human condition. I refuse to feel guilt. But that's because I have a purpose. And I also have hope. Always remember that young man. Whatever you might hear, I have a purpose and I have hope.'

Balti smiled as George leant forward, looking for the go-ahead. He sucked on his pipe and let his gaze scan the common, surveying the land stretching before him. There wasn't a great deal to see. The kid's playground and a few trees. Rows of houses to the left, flats to the right. The sound of hammers once more.

'People look at someone like me and what do they see? What do they imagine? I'll tell you. A well-turned-out man of middle-age pushing a trolley around. What do they think? An eccentric perhaps. An environmentalist maybe. But I don't care about the labels people pin on me. I have a purpose. My own agenda. Simple in itself but a purpose nonetheless. My goal each morning is to fill my trolley with cans, as you can see. This goal has been achieved. Coca Cola, Pepsi, 7-Up, Fanta, Lucozade; whatever the name of the corporation involved, I will collect its cans and take them to be recycled, thereby saving resources and avoiding unnecessary exploitation of the planet's resources. You see, it's nothing dramatic when compared to famine and war, but it fills my time and if everyone was the same as me, doing their bit, then many of the problems of our society would be solved. Extend this attitude on to a global scale and the world would be at ease with itself. We would have an everlasting peace. I have my reasons. I move from A to B and follow a path. If everyone followed after me, what a society we could create. Just try and imagine it for a minute.'

Balti tried. He saw men in expensive suits pushing supermarket trolleys across the common. He imagined the Pope and other European leaders, mullahs and naked fakirs heaving their cargoes past the adventure playground. The dictators and owners of the multinationals were there as the kids on the slide took the piss raising their right hands in wanker signs. The arms manufacturers and monarchy. They were all there. Thousands of them. Following some nutter across the common, dodging the dog shit and squeezing over Mugger's Bridge, on their way to the recycling bins in the swimming pool car park.

'Serving the common good is not enough. I have learnt that. A man must have hope. Women also, in this age of equality between the sexes. One day I will strike gold. A nice winner on the ponies which is only the first part of my plan. I will spend this jackpot on the Lottery. This in turn will increase my probabilities of ultimate success. It is a simple mathematical equation. The more I spend on the Lottery, the better chance I have of becoming a winner. One day my number will come up. It is a simple chain reaction. I have calculated my chances of becoming a millionaire in this way. It is many millions to one, yet it remains a real possibility. It is a chance not to be spurned. The more I try, the shorter the odds. When the cheque is deposited in my account I will be satisfied. I will be comfortable for the rest of my life. That is how democracy works. I think you will agree that it is a fair system. We all have a chance to make a claim. There's no need to become angry and bitter at the system. After all, we are nothing in comparison.'

Balti thought George was a sad bastard. It was true what he said, in a roundabout way. Balti had been putting more than he should into the Lottery. It did give you something to dream about. That moment when the phone rang and there was some bingo master on the other end insisting you were no longer eligible for unemployment benefit, some smarmy showbiz cunt talking through clenched dentures clogged up on jealousy. Saying that you were a multi-millionaire with the tabloids hot on your trail. Would he want to remain anonymous? Fucking right he would. A cool ten million wouldn't make everything perfect, at least that's what they said, but it would certainly help. If news filtered out somehow, then bollocks, Balti had what it took to handle the pressure. It wound him up hearing people who'd come into a fortune moaning that the winning millions were making their lives a nightmare. Whoever said something like that had obviously never lived on forty-six quid a week. He was ready to be a winner. No problem. But George was a nutter. He really was. Balti wouldn't end up like that. He'd top himself first. Pushing a trolley around trying to save the world.

Balti thought about the first thing he'd do once the cheque was in his hand. He'd be straight down the bank to deposit his winnings. Wait for the expression on the face of the clerk. Next he'd be down the social to tell them he was signing off. It wouldn't piss him off standing in line wasting time because he'd make sure he got that cunt who'd forgotten to punch the button on the computer. The cheque hadn't come through and when he'd gone to find out where it was there was no respect, no apology, no nothing. This was with him being a customer now as well. A client. With a set of aims on the wall telling him how much they wanted to help you. One day he'd work out how much he'd paid into the system. He'd get the same person. See if he could get a bit of respect that way. It wouldn't matter how he became a millionaire, as long as he had the readies. Nobody thought that far. It was like if you had the money then there was some kind of divine justice about it all. Put a fiver in the collection bowl and you were away.

'I tell you this in confidence,' George shifted nearer, looking round and holding his pipe away from Balti so that the smoke from the burning tobacco didn't get in his eyes.

'When I was made redundant I pocketed a few bob. A couple of thousand pounds if you're interested. This is between you and me and mustn't go any further, because the kids round here, they'd be through the window and murder me in my bed for a tenner. Anyway, with careful management, using one light at a time at night and keeping the heating bills down to a minimum, even in the middle of winter, I've been able to hang on to a few hundred pounds. It's for a rainy day you understand. It's good to have a few hundred behind you in case of emergencies. You never know what's waiting around the corner. Plan ahead, that's my motto.'

Balti admired the self-discipline. George had been told by the doctors that his mood swings were related to the seasons. He'd talked quite openly about this on the first time they'd shared the bench. With the shorter daylight hours and overcast skies, he went into himself. He spoke little and remained indoors. When spring came he began to stir, his mood shifting full throttle when summer arrived. He was pure energy. Following the sun. The doctors had given their opinion. He was like the Aztecs, but without great pyramids and a need for human sacrifice. It was official.

'Well,' George said abruptly, after they'd been sitting in silence for five minutes watching the kids in the playground. 'I can't hang around here all day. There's work to be done. Must press on. I have to deliver these cans. I've given myself a deadline and it must be kept. Goodbye.'

Balti watched him go. He was a squat character with a balding head that would burn if he didn't get a hat sorted out. The sunglasses didn't match the overall impression. Balti thought about what he'd said about energy and sunlight. It was common sense really. You always felt better when the sun was shining. You had to have a bit of hope as well. Worshipping the sun was probably the obvious thing if you lived thousands of years ago out in the country and depended on the seasons for your food. In London all you needed was money in your pocket and a bit of respect. God was redundant these days. Signing on.

He stretched his arms and wiped the sweat from his face. He was losing weight. It was cutting down on the drink that did it. Not getting pissed as much as before. He was only able to manage thanks to the stereos. He wasn't going to hit rock bottom. If his Lottery numbers came up he'd be laughing the last five months off. Like George said, you had to invest to accumulate. He hadn't thought it would take this long to get work. He was bored. Well hacked off. Having all that time during the day got you thinking. It got you down and his motivation had gone. Dumped on his arse by four slags from South London. He'd thought it was the IRA that specialised in hammers, not Protestant militiamen. Time to think. It was deadly. You had to keep busy. Will slipped Balti a bit of blow now and then, specially after that night. It helped keep the lid on things. It had done him a lot of good if he was honest. But Balti wasn't going to get all emotional. He was logical. Holding back. Doing the right thing. Keeping his dignity.

Except when they got you down knocked off balance then there was no such thing as dignity because once your legs went you were another piece of shit just one more animal without a name without any say-so no tears no nothing just the violence that showed you up and when you thought about something like that like when you were tipped on your arse on your own manor round the corner from where you lived your whole life where you fucking grew up and walked and played when you were a kid so near home that if the telly was turned up loud enough or the music on it would've drained out the sound of the kicks and breaking bones the thud of hammers so near home kids getting murdered on the news youths going missing Pete never came home did he and it was mostly in the summer every year it seemed like it was more regular now living in the technological age when more and more you were plugged into the mains and pumped up with all that voltage pulsing through the skeleton up the backbone into the brain cracking across the room and all that radiation was deadly what was it Karen had said the other day about there being no strength in the unions any more

telling him to think about the word union when they were arguing
about Scargill and that and how the mines had been closed down just
like Arthur had said part of a bigger plan maybe even worked out in
advance a blueprint for a Britain where nobody knew their neighbours
and there were no organisations to fight for your rights no solidar-
ity with everyone scratching out their own boundaries even the street
markets were being sterilised because the authorities wanted to erase
community and turf the stalls off the street and they built shitty little
shops and charged high rent selling mass-produced shit from China
where the slave labour was cheaper free in fact so the capitalists were
in bed with the communists and it was impossible to know who was
shagging who and it all tied up because there was no such thing as
unions in China and you weren't safe to walk down your own streets in
London because they could do you any time they wanted the outsiders
waiting late at night down a side street picking their moment when you
were pissed and unable to fight back and the old bill could come into
your home and the bailiffs would be banging on the door because that's
what happened when you failed when you couldn't pay your way and
it wasn't the old family firms and new-age gangsters and nutters who
lost their furniture no fucking way like would the paper shufflers and
magistrates put themselves out that was a laugh they were shitters who
preferred the easy targets the honest people with their defences down
not ready to fight just wanting to live quiet lives and it was always the
small people the trolley-pushers of the world who did what they were
told and swallowed their tablets and wanted to do something worthwhile give something back grateful for a bit of analysis from some
stuck-up cunt who treated you like shit as he mended you but the sad
old bastards never got the chance of a bit of dignity and it was the old
and the young and the sick who got hammered because like Karen said
it's those cunts in the cattle trucks were the ones who ended up stripped
and naked because they couldn't fight back and Mango was right in that
respect because he'd have been in with the guards looking after himself
fuck everyone else like he was fucked and Balti wasn't going to be one of
the losers even if it meant doing a bank one day and he could reason the
thing out play the white man and say that McDonald was out of order

with the verbal but he'd been more out of order kicking the cunt in the balls head gut a bit naughty that McDonald was working for a boss higher up and had a family to support and his own pressures getting his ear chewed job on the line investment and all that nonsense and if he was honest really straight with himself and there were times to be honest and times to lie and now Balti was being honest as honest as anyone ever could be but it didn't matter because he was telling the simple truth when he reminded himself that the thing wasn't over, not yet, no fucking chance pal.

Balti stopped walking and looked in the window of Will's shop. There was a picture of Jesus in a black frame. The face was dark, Arabic-looking, Jewish probably, but he knew it was Jesus because there were thorns in his head and blood gushing from the wounds. It was an ugly picture. There was no beauty. No warmth. It was cold pain and misery. Self-sacrifice the vicar would say. Balti couldn't imagine anyone paying good money for something like that. Especially seeing as how Jesus looked different. You had to be able to connect. There was a bowl full of cheap jewellery, odds and sods, and some bronze ornaments that were a bit more up-market with price tags turned the wrong way so he couldn't see what they said. He saw Will in the shop serving someone. When the woman turned to leave Balti entered. She carried a picture under her arm and he stood aside to let her pass. It was another Jesus. An identical twin in an identical black frame. They must've come from the same egg.

'Religion selling well?' Balti asked.

Will looked puzzled, then understood. He pointed to a row of frames. The first showed the same picture. They were part of a batch. He'd bought fifteen at a car boot sale in Wimbledon. Against the odds, they were selling. Once he sold two he started making a profit. He'd sold three already. It must've been the novelty value of seeing Jesus looking like that.

'You always think of Jesus as a white man, don't you,' Balti said, sitting down in an old armchair next to the big desk from which Will ran his business.

Will went to the chair behind the desk. It was worn wood but quality all the same. One day he would sand it down and give it a varnish. There was a big mixture of gear in the shop, something to satisfy most local tastes. It was junk with a touch of quality, according to the owner. The inside of the shop was musty and warm.

'That's because they make the pictures in their own image,' Will said. 'Jesus would've been dark, maybe black. Who knows. He wouldn't be Anglo-Saxon, that's for sure. No blond hair and blue eyes for someone from the desert.'

'Still looks odd though, seeing Jesus H looking like an Arab or yiddo.'

'The Nazis used to teach their kids that Jesus was part of an Aryan tribe that took civilisation to the Middle East and that they were slaughtered by the Jews. If you're taught that you're going to believe it, aren't you? We always believe what we're told, just depends on who does the telling. But we think like that any way. Make everything fit in. Draw him like he's a Viking or something.'

'It doesn't matter, does it,' Balti said. 'I mean, whatever he looked like it's what he said that counts. I know it's supposed to be history and all that, but a lot of it's made up isn't it, to suit the kings and the censors. Mind you, I don't know what he had to say anyway. There was the Good Samaritan. Dead man laying at the side of the road. Hartlepool fan comes along and eats the heart. Liverpool fan turns up and eats the liver. Arsenal fan arrives, but he's not hungry. Remember that one?'

'I remember. You still wouldn't go thieving from a church though, would you?'

'Don't know really. Probably would if you were desperate. I was thinking that walking over. If I was really skint, right down the bottom, I'd do a bank. I think I would anyway. Maybe not. Probably bottle it. No-one wants to go down do they? Don't suppose I'd do a church. No reason why I shouldn't. Don't suppose they've got anything worth nicking. I'll stick to petty crime, breaking windows and thieving stereos.'

'Most people wouldn't rob a church. It's a built-in fear of retribution.'

'Fear of getting nicked more like.'

'The magistrates would make sure you paid the penalty. They're all in on it. The old bill, vicars, magistrates, lawyers, judges, journalists, big business, politicians, necrophiliacs. It's a self-help club.'

'Divine retribution.'

'I reckon you can play at being God in two major ways,' Will said, putting his feet on the desk and skinning up. 'Either you use chemicals to get up there with the superhumans, or you're born with a silver spoon up your arse. Trouble is, the chemicals are mostly man-made so you end up with the after effects, whereas in the old days you could find something natural and, provided there were no witch-hunts on, you could get into the flow. Now it's different. More mechanical. Material society with a materialist religion. Trick is, you get the power, with the old bill backing you up, and you can play God that way. A certain kind of God. Lots of wrath and indignation. One that likes healthy profit margins.'

'You were alright with the old witch-hunts if you were a bloke though, weren't you?' Balti said. 'It was the women that got burnt and drowned. Like, which way do you want to die, darling?'

Balti thought about it for a minute as Will concentrated on his task. When he was young he'd wanted to be part of a midfield trio that had included Ray Wilkins and Garry Stanley. That was as near as he wanted to get to immortality. To be on the pitch bossing the game with Ray and Garry. He thought about that sort of stuff even now. He supposed most blokes did. In that world it didn't matter how old you were, or how unfit. It didn't matter if you couldn't kick a ball straight or you were the same age as those players approaching the end of their careers. He wondered what Harry thought about. He'd have to ask him later when he got back from work. Probably playing up front with Steve Finnieston keeping Kenny Swain out of the side. If Eddie McCreadie hadn't been forced out of the club then who knows? Balti remembered how upset he'd been when McCreadie left. He'd heard that Eddie was somewhere in the States. A great man.

It was the glamorous way out of the gutter. Running round kicking a ball. Either that or doing a Frank Bruno. Keeping yourself fit and building up for the big fights. Nobody pushed Big Frank about. He demanded respect. And if you were in that midfield with Wilkins and Stanley, then you were major as well. He didn't know what career he'd choose if he had his time again. Midfield genius or heavyweight champion. Probably the football. There was less chance of brain damage that way, though he'd read something about footballers who headed the ball a lot, how it rocked the brain on its suspension. In midfield you could keep your head and play it on the deck. That's what everyone wanted to see. Creative football. Seeing The Dutchman in action showed how far the English game had to go. The young kids coming through were lucky to work with someone like that. Funny, you got past a certain age and suddenly you looked at the young lads, the nutters and that, or the footballers, that's what he was thinking about, and they were like school kids, all wound up doing things wrong, getting booked, getting nicked.

Mind you, it was all in the hormones. He thought science had proved something along those lines. Birds didn't cause the problems that men did. If women were in charge things would be a lot better. Mango was always going on about the first female prime minister. How she'd done the business, in the Falklands and for the economy. But for blokes it was a time of life. He had to admit they'd been a bit naughty till their late twenties. Then they'd slowed down and the new talent came through all larey and tearing up. But you still had respect because you'd been there already. Nobody was going to give you unnecessary aggro. That's what it had been like at football. Things had changed a lot and the new mobs coming through were smaller in number but more vicious. He couldn't work people like that out really. Having a punch-up at football had just been part of the Saturday landscape till the politicians got involved. The new era was fine by Balti. He wanted to watch the football again. His second childhood had come around, though he didn't mind the odd punch-up for a classic fixture. But using knives, that was out of order. It was only a bit of fun, after all.

When you had time on your hands you thought about the past, but he also found himself shooting off into the future. It was easy to reinvent the past, but it wasn't so good somehow. There was always the truth nagging at you, or at least a version of that truth, telling you it wasn't that great. It was okay playing about with history, but when you planned the future you could be anything you wanted. The more you thought, the more unreal you could become. That's probably what was happening with that sad old cunt with the trolley. One minute he was stuck in the past ready to top himself, all the missed opportunities, dead loves, whatever, the next the sun starts shining and he's off, making plans and marching forward. But the thing was, whatever extreme he was into, there was always the chance of a controller in a white coat lining up an upper or downer trying to bring him back into the middle. It was like Harry was saying about the colour in his dreams. The past was usually black and white but confused, whereas the future was all about new technology and crystal clear vision. It was mind games. You went through life keeping busy, getting pissed and that, doing a few substances, but once you had time to kill your mind was straight into one.

Balti had a puff. Sweet as a nut. Carefree whoever he may be. With Will shutting up shop for a while so they could relax. They sat buried in old furniture and prints, a kid's doll sitting on a shelf, horse brasses and rows of yellowing books. There was some good gear knocking about. If you knew what you were doing and had ambition you could make a packet. Balti wondered if his mate needed an assistant. He doubted it. Kept quiet. Business was slack. Enough for Will to keep ticking over but that was all. Will was a diamond now Balti came to think about it. He'd always had that bit extra with the music and slower pace, and now he had Karen as well. They were made for each other. He wondered if one day he'd find someone like that. It would be nice. Harry was a sound bloke, another diamond, but he didn't want to spend the rest of his life shacked up with the cunt. There came a time when you had to move on. Find a woman and that.

Harry had been acting a bit strange. Balti couldn't work it out. At first he'd thought it was to do with him signing on, but reasoned it out and had even asked his mate up front. It wasn't that. Why should it be? He wasn't a beggar. He stood on his own two feet. There was something though. He couldn't work it out. Maybe he was going through a change. Everyone had slow periods. It would be alright. He was better than a brother.

'Me and Karen are moving in together,' Will said, after they'd decided to go down Andy's Cafe, the door locked behind them as they walked down the street.

'You leaving the flat then?' Balti asked, Will nodding. 'Why doesn't she move in with you. It's big enough for both of you. Just clear out some of the shit round there and you could turn it into a barracks, you've got so much room.'

'She wants to start somewhere fresh. You know. A new beginning. Something of our own. You know how women are. They get their minds set and they like the romance. I can see her point. I mean I wouldn't want to move in somewhere she's lived. You'd always feel like the lodger. It's better off starting together, then everything's equal. Nobody's in charge.'

'Do me a favour. She wears the trousers. Not that I'm slagging it off or anything, but Karen's in charge. Everyone knows that. You've got to put your foot down or the woman will run the show.'

'It's half each.'

'Alright, whatever you say. But someone's going to be the boss, aren't they? It's only natural.'

Will shook his head. Balti was winding him up. He did tend to go along with what Karen said a lot of the time, but that was because he wasn't bothered. She was sharper than he was. He hated the idea of being hen-pecked.

They ordered at the counter and sat by the window. The fruit and veg market was busy, Phil from The Unity on his stall outside. He waved when he noticed them, serving a couple of old women. Balti could never understand the bloke. He was one of the old-time Cockney Reds, born and bred in West London but choosing to follow Man United around the country. Where was the sense in that? His main day had been in the Seventies when Tommy Docherty had been the manager with crowds near-enough sixty thousand. There'd been regular aggro between the Cockney Reds and other sections of the Stretford End. He didn't go much these days, being older and everything, a time and a place. He preferred remembering Old Trafford how it had been in its heyday, rather than the satellite accessory he felt it had become. He went to a few aways and slagged off the club for making the ground a home for part-timers. When the club messed up then the thousands like him wouldn't be going back to fill the gaps.

Two teas arrived and Balti thought of the 4–0 Cup Final. It was funny, because they'd been gutted after the game, but it didn't bother him now. Just getting to a Cup Final had been a bonus, seeing the teams come out and everything, even though Wembley was a shit ground and thirty-five quid for a length of plastic with no back was a lot to pay. They saw you coming and shafted your loyalty. And there was no Vaseline on hand to ease the pain. At the end of the day though Chelsea had given Man U a good hiding outside the ground before the game. They'd been coming up the hill lobbing bottles at United who legged it, hid inside the pubs, or tried to have a go back but ended up getting a kicking. It was a good day out, Harry smacking some cunt with a flag, Tommy Johnson and his mates going mental. Balti was honest enough to say he'd rather Chelsea were in charge outside the ground than on the pitch. Getting a pasting off someone was the end of the world. You didn't want people taking the piss. Chelsea had a reputation to maintain. Balti had his self-respect. That fucking cunt McDonald.

'You hungry then?' Will asked, when the food arrived, Balti's plate loaded with sausage, bacon, beans, chips, toast.

'I'm getting too thin. I'm down to fourteen stone. People will start thinking I'm dying of AIDS if I'm not careful.'

'Not for a while they won't,' Will said as he put ketchup on his plate only for the top to come off and half cover his chips. He put the lid back on and did his best to use it up.

'So what are you going to do about Slaughter then?' Will asked, once they'd finished and ordered more tea.

'What do you mean?'

'About the work he's offering,' Will said, seeing the expression on Balti's face. 'You told me Friday night when you were pissed. Dangerous talk costs lives.'

'I don't know,' Balti admitted. 'I mean on the one hand it's a chance to make the kind of money I'm not going to get anywhere else. On the other, I don't fancy ten years banged up. Depends on what it is, but once he tells me I'm going to have to say yes, aren't I? I mean, Slaughter's not going to want too many people knowing what he's doing.'

'You should leave it alone. That's what I reckon. Anything he does is going to be dodgy. He could tell you one thing, then the next minute you're too far in, stuck in some bank with Slaughter waving a shooter around. It's not worth the risk. Being skint's not as bad as killing some bank clerk.'

'I don't know. Maybe it's worth taking a chance sometimes.'

'What if he does that though. Takes his machete along and does someone. Or he gets a shotgun and the old bill turn up. It's not just him is it? Everyone goes down. ABH, murder, who knows. Nothing's worth going down for.'

'Say I made a couple of grand, maybe more. I'd be able to live well in the summer till I get something sorted out. Maybe it's worth it.'

'You go down and you'll crack up. What are you going to do for five years, maybe twenty, who knows. You go in and come out an old man. Eat, sleep, shit, piss, wank, get a bruising. What sort of life is that? You'd be better off dead.'

Balti thought about it as he sipped the hot tea. He might be a bit out of order now and then, but he wasn't a robber. Not that it was the rights and wrongs or anything like that, but Slaughter stunk of trouble. There was a kind of justice about it in a way, doing a bank or building society, because they were the system that ground you down, everyone wanting their share. They charged high interest and milked people. Going in there with a shooter would be alright. Then he thought straight. It was like McDonald. He was the small man. The representative. Those behind the counter weren't getting anything out of the interest rates and repossessions. Just earning a crust. It wasn't their fault. Why should they get their heads shot off? Why should McDonald get a kicking? Balti knew why. Because he didn't show respect. There was no excuse for that. The same as the cocky bastards behind the window in a bank. Except most of them were alright. And that cunt down the social. The one who'd forgotten to punch the button. He deserved a slap but there again he was nothing. Earnt fuck all for a boring job. But he was stroppy. That was the problem. It was the arrogance that got to you. Who the fuck were these little people holding the purse strings? But he would listen to his old mate Will.

'You look at the crack dealers and the bank robbers and everything,'

Will said, 'and they're just small-time Mangoes, except that they operate in a different field. You get caught selling crack and they'll do you. The courts won't hang about. There's no glory.'

'But you do a bank or something like that and you're getting at those bastards, aren't you?' Balti said.

'You could even dress up in green tights and pretend you're Robin Hood. It's not worth it. Leave it. If you want to borrow five hundred quid till you're set up again, ask. Behave yourself in the meantime, that's all. Poor's in the head.'

When they left the cafe the sunlight had faded. Will went back to work and Balti headed home. He stopped in The Unity for a pint. He was surprised to see Carter sitting at the bar talking with Denise. She gave him a free pint with Len out for the day and he pulled up a stool. Carter was pissed, his eyes following her arse down the bar.

'She's a good-looking woman,' he said, lowering his voice. 'Looks better naked, I can tell you.'

He winked and Balti put two and two together. The silly cunt was taking a risk. Slaughter would kill them both. Maybe start on the rest of the Sex Division as well, if he thought they knew.

'Three points, but don't tell the others. I don't want word getting round. I put it down as that bird from Blues last week. She wasn't interested. But I counted her as Denise. No need to let points go to waste, is there?'

Balti agreed. Smiled. Said nothing.

'She wants me to take pictures of her. You know what I mean. But what's the point. Who am I going to show them to? I reckon she's pushing it. Send one to Slaughter in the post. She's dangerous. One word out of place and I'm dead. We're both dead. You're the only person I've told, so keep your mouth shut.'

Balti nodded. Slaughter was a headcase. There was no way he was doing a job with the bloke. There were more important things in life. You could be poor but have respect. It depended how you looked at things. Will understood that, though there were the basics to contend with. It was the fear of going down that made up his mind. You had to be a nutter to go that far. Those were the real hard men. He had respect for blokes who could push things. You had to be a bit mental and not give a fuck what the old bill did to you. That was how they kept you in line. Sheer violence kept the thing going. The old bastards who ran the show were nothing without the army, police, secret service. Take them away and any cunt could walk in, have his say, blow them in half. You were better off sticking to small scale thieving. Nobody cared about that. He'd work. Sooner or later. Earn a living and take his place in the scheme of things.

He tried to think how long it was since he'd last had sex. Must've been about eight months. He had to get his leg over soon. That would do him good. Maybe he'd borrow the cash off Will and go with the rest of the lads to Amsterdam. That's what he'd do. They said they'd chip in and pay his way, but he had his pride. At least taking a loan made the money his own.

Carter was off to Spain for a couple of weeks in the summer, but whispered to Balti that it was only half a holiday. You might as well be at home, and the birds weren't all that. Amsterdam was really going overseas, though they might have to put it off for a while because Mango reckoned the most he could get through his card was a trip to the seaside. They'd decided on Blackpool. Not Amsterdam. But it was better than nothing. Next year they'd go to Amsterdam. Next year Balti my old mate.

Denise came back down the bar and after she'd had a quick glance over her shoulder at the old boys at the other end of the counter, involved in some argument about the number of Asians who'd died building the Burma-Thailand railway, she refilled Balti's pint. She was more friendly now, with nobody about, and even if Carter hadn't let him in on the secret Balti would probably have guessed from the way she looked at him. Balti settled into his seat and started thinking about Blackpool as Denise told them how Slaughter had got himself nicked the night before for drunk driving. It was lucky he'd left his machete at home. Otherwise he'd be getting done for murder as well.

BEANO

The Jag was spotless. Cleaned in one of those valet efforts staffed by Eyeties. It was a flash motor, nobody would argue about that, but there was nothing flash about Mango's CD collection. A right pile of shit. Luckily there was a cassette player and Will had done them proud, saving their souls and delivering a decent soundtrack. They were humming north with Harry's electric soup doing its duty, fucking up their heads, the man himself in the back seat with Balti and Carter, half-asleep.

Will was up front next to Captain Mango, playing the selector, and it was classics all the way. The Jam were stuck on the Underground as the Sex Division ran a bombing mission over Birmingham, the throb of the engine racing straight up Mango's right leg and tickling his bollocks. Will waited for the song to fade and slipped in a collection that included the Blaggers ITA, bringing the tradition forward with a bang. This Jag was no ramraider special though, not the kind of Made In Britain topnotch precision engineering model some hip-hop cunt was going to drive through the off-licence window. Not with the anti-theft gear Mango had splashed out on anyway. No fucking way.

The lads in the back were getting pissed quick enough on the electric soup, food of the people, Mango a bit nervous in case one of those mugs behind him decided to puke up, and Harry thought he'd have a laugh telling the cocky cunt at the controls, Captain Scarlet, that he felt sick, with his guts about to do the old heave-ho. He didn't know whether he could control those saveloys from last night, the pickled onions, wally and chips, that he might have to spread his breakfast over the upholstery as well, a bacon and eggs special.

Mango looked in the mirror and caught the fat boy's eye and told him, all serious like, with a cutting edge Harry and the rest of the lads hadn't heard before, real Jack The Ripper stuff, bit spastic, a tang that made them sit up and take notice—Mango saying that if Harry messed up the Jag he'd pull on to the hard shoulder and leave you behind you tart, this is my fucking car and I'm paying the fucking petrol. I'll drop you off and keep going and there's no U-turns on the motorway so I won't be coming back. I'm doing you a favour and there's no second chance. Behave yourself.

Harry wanted to get to Blackpool in comfort, enjoy the ride, the suspension and everything, not hitch-hike on the hard shoulder choking to death. He wanted to enjoy the weekend. Have a laugh. Maybe get his end away. That was only natural. I was joking Mango mate, where's your sense of humour you miserable git. To play things safe Mango pulled into the next services and parked up, the lads going for a piss, in another world now, an outpost in the wilderness.

This was the real England, not London, that was full of blacks and browns and yellows and all the colours in the rainbow, with every food and type of music, a cockney bazaar where the cockneys were a minority from Bengal. No, this was flat-cap land. Up North. Where they fancied their pigeons and shagged their whippets, five pence a pint and mushy-pea butties for dinner, four-bedroom houses that cost five grand and mining villages living with a hundred per cent unemployment. Balti nicked a couple of CDs from one of the shops for a laugh. He bought himself a chocolate bar that he scoffed in the car park, then got back in the Jag with the others, Mango sweet again, back in command, commander of his jet fighter—precision machine.

They quickly picked up speed filtering back on to the M6, putting his foot down knowing he could do naught-to-sixty in 7.9 seconds, six in-line cylinders, thirty grand's worth of XJ6 3.2 Sport sex on wheels, hardcore British technology second to none. And it was patriotic to buy British. Fly the flag. He was laughing again enjoying some old-time pre-revolution Ted Heath generosity, helping people out, the kindly benefactor, Will skinning up sitting back soothing things, Balti in the back taking the CDs from inside his jacket, one a Country and Western greatest hits effort with a Dolly Parton lookalike on the front. Look at the lungs on that lads. The other a marching band with soldiers in busbies and red tunics, lots of brass on display. Must be hot, the silly sods, walking to slaughter.

Will was coming under pressure from the Bollock Brothers and Carter, the sex machine wide awake now and knocking back a can of Fosters, telling Harry that the electric soup would do him no favours. They wanted to listen to Land Of Hope And Glory, but Will said in a minute, hang about, and they soon forgot about the marching band because Carter was telling the lads that if they didn't service something this weekend he was giving up on them. Non-believers you lot.

Northern birds were alright and didn't pose like the women down south. Salt-of-the-earth, high-heeled tarts hunting in mobs twenty and thirty strong, inflated tits out on the counter. Girls who were ready for a good time, and all Northerners were like you saw on *Coronation Street*. But it wasn't a patch on *EastEnders*, though Carter reckoned the Mitchells were bottle merchants because you never saw them getting stuck in, not really, it was all front, and they were always mouthing off. Said it was like West Ham used to be, remember that time they came in Gate 13 and Chelsea gave them a pasting, and Balti asked the shag machine if that was the time he got his nose broken when some ICF cunt nutted him, and Carter shut up because it was and West Ham had the nous to get up the ground early and buy tickets for that area of the East Stand where they knew Chelsea's main faces would be.

Harry weighed in saying leave it out, I hate West Ham as well but you wouldn't have seen the Mitchells anywhere near the ICF, and Will was passing the puff round, Mango shaking his head keeping himself on the straight and narrow because he was doing the driving and the Jag was thirty grand's worth of sheer automobile heaven, cruising at ninety miles per hour, working himself into the machine, feeling the energy. The rest of the chaps should show a bit of respect for the power and the glory, a Best Of British factory working overtime turning out the purest kind of machine.

They gave wanker salutes to the Liverpool and Manchester signs, all those games at Anfield and Goodison, Old Trafford and Maine Road, ice-cold Saturdays playing Oldham, on their way to Blackpool Friday afternoon. It wasn't much further now as the miles clocked up and then they were pulling off the motorway rolling towards the town centre where Mango had lined up a place on the seafront. He was fiddling it on his expenses, feeding the accounts department a line. Amsterdam would have to wait. He could only do so much. And the rest of the Sex Division wondered where they'd end up, whether Mango was just giving it the big one again flashing his credit card around, if he really had the say-so, but the bloke was a con artist of sorts and they had to agree that he was a good bloke sharing the wealth around like that. Not his own, mind, but ready to use WorldView for his old mates.

They were watching the streets. Houses plastered in bed and breakfast signs. Polished toytown brickwork. Wondering if they were going to end up buried in one of the terraces. Blue-rinse grannies and Glasgow bouncers sick on candyfloss. Then Mango was pulling up outside a smart hotel. A real quality effort it was too, and they were standing in the entrance, the foyer, whatever the fuck it was called. Mango steamed right in with his WorldView confidence, no problem, and the staff even wore uniforms.

None of the lads had stayed in a place like this before, except Mango of course, but they didn't feel out of place because corporate cards counted and made you something with the weight of a major firm behind you. Numbers mattered. They were going up in the lift with some spotty Lancashire youth showing them the way. They had two rooms side by side. Carter was in with Mango, and Will was sharing with Harry and Balti.

They dumped their gear and Mango went into the attached bathroom to wash his face in the sink, taking his time with the hot water and soap. Leaving the door open, Carter throwing his bag on to the bed nearest the window. The old sex machine magic was bound to rub off. Mango was tired. Carter sticking his head round the door—you fucking ponce, what's the matter with you, wasting time when we could be down the bar having a few sherbets. Mango was brushing his teeth— don't worry about your breath you slag, because you won't get near a bird tonight—and he laughed it off, but Mango was hoping he'd pull.

It was alright knocking off pros, a simple business transaction with both parties happy, but he'd like something for free once in a while. A bird who didn't need a backhander to open her legs. Genuine affection, or at least attraction. Shafting whores all the time made him feel ugly. As though he was rotten inside. He was in the mood, with WorldView left behind for a few days, but in a strange way he wasn't too bothered about sex, there wasn't the same frantic need to dip his winkie, because once you got out of the City, outside London, things eased and you could do whatever you fucking wanted. Blackpool was his first decent break for ages and he wanted to forget everything and relax.

The Sex Division were soon back in the lift on their way downstairs, piling into a bar that was nicely done up with big old paintings on the walls and a new carpet on the floor. There was some greasy scouser behind the bar pouring pints. They all hated scousers, because you had to if you came from London. It was written down somewhere in the rules. Everyone except Will that was, because he didn't hate anyone. But the scouser was alright when he came over and started talking. He had a sense of humour to go with his Terry McDermott tash, because they asked him where Kevin Keegan was and he said upstairs clearing one of the bogs that was blocked, making the most of the dodgy haircut. There was no preferential treatment in Blackpool. That fucking toilet needed clearing and King Kev was the man for the job.

They liked the barman straight off, so that meant they hated all scousers except the one they'd spoken to, and that was probably in the rules somewhere as well. They moved over to a table by the window, looking out to sea. The waves were grey and white in the drizzle that had started, the sun bright through grey clouds, a slow-motion strobe effect, the wind kicking-up and battering a tram carrying a fucking great Goofy cut-out. They all laughed. There was a word for it. They sat back and watched Goofy vanish.

This was the life. A chance to have a drink and breathe in healthy air, even if it was in the bar. The first round went down quick enough, Will ordering more lager. The prices were cheaper than in London even though this was a hotel so fuck knows what it's going to be like down the town lads, Carter lifting the glass to his lips. These Northerners are thick as shit, don't forget we're going back in time, that Jag's a fucking time machine.

They were kids on a beano, Will telling the others he was going to phone Karen to let her know they'd arrived safe and sound. They started taking the piss as he went to the end of the bar, Terry Mac moving the phone over so he could sit on a stool and take his time and have a bit of privacy. Will talked for a bit and Carter, Harry, Balti, Mango were having a good laugh, taking the piss something chronic, ball and chain and all the normal stuff. Who the fuck is it wearing the trousers? Look at that thumb print between his eyes. His head's nodding like he's giving Mango a blow job. Fuck off you cunt. Karen was a cracker though. Shame she didn't have any sisters. What about her mates? That was one to think about when they got back. Nice one Balti. Fuck off Carter, it was my idea, you keep your hands off. Don't want you infecting her with a tropical disease.

Will came back and took his glass, keeping up, and one or two older couples were coming into the bar and ordering from Macca and his dodgy tash. A husband and wife sat by the window, nodding as they passed, and the Sex Division had to admit that Northerners were friendly.

It wasn't just the mobbed-up brass either. They admitted this on the quiet, because you had to maintain the pecking order. An old geezer, a right northern slaphead, and his wife, a big postcard woman rabbiting on the whole time, sat at the next table. The slaphead took a shine to Carter and asked him who they supported. Were they into the football? When he heard Chelsea he laughed and called them a bunch of hooligans, because he read his papers and stereotypes were essential to the nation's well-being.

He was a Leeds man himself and had never forgiven Chelsea for beating them in the Cup Final in 1970. Will chipped in, saying Webby's at Brentford now, and the old boy went into one about Tony Yeboah and how Leeds hated Man United. Leeds were Yorkshire and Man U Lancashire. That was enough. It would've been interesting to know some of the history, but that kind of thing just kept going century after century, and then it was ingrained, and then it was all down to Eric Cantona.

When the Sex Division membership left the hotel they were on a roll. The electric soup had worn off, but the lager gave them a kick. They laughed at Goofy, the silly cunt, back and forward all day, and went in a big fish shop on the seafront. It was full of Jock tattoos and families, but there was enough room for everyone. The batter was crisp and the chips well done. They ordered and ate quickly, ready for a decent drink.

They had a couple of pints in a pub full of old-timers, then went for a wander along the front, legs eleven and intergalactic shoot-em-ups booming from speakers, the Sex Division standing back laughing as a mob of youths pegged it round the corner, a bit of a row going on, followed by a bigger mob, blokes done up in suits and ties like Northerners dress when they're out for the night, the dozy cunts. They were well thick the old Yorkshiremen, or were they from Lancashire, it was one of the two, and the locals would've been well pissed off if they'd heard that one, because there was the Wars Of The Roses to think about. Pikes and axes thick with blood. Men had died in the fields fighting for their county, and there were a few bottles flying without much chance of contact, a lot of shouting, the sound of breaking glass, and then it was all over and it was more than Leeds against Man U. Will would ask the Leeds man if they saw him again. Get some details.

It was like they didn't belong. Just spectators watching someone else's battle. But they didn't give a toss either way, with a gentle breeze blowing in off the sea, quite nice really, and Balti said Ireland was straight ahead over the horizon somewhere in the dark, and McDonald would be on his way home for a bit of rehabilitation in his Belfast slum soon enough. That was the best place for him with ten pounds of semtex shoved up his arse.

The Blackpool Tower was in front of them now, and there were crowds of people everywhere, a bingo town full of grannies. There was a bit of crumpet about as well, but so many Jocks you could've been in Scotland. Big extended families wandering around loaded up with donuts and the smell of chips in the air mixing with candyfloss.

They saw a decent-looking pub that was packed solid and were soon inside on their way to the bar, right off the Bollock Brothers chatting up a couple of birds, blondes done up very nice thank you with their tits stuffed tight inside boob tubes, heavily painted faces and sparkling

eyes. They were friendly with it. Well fucking friendly. Drinking pints.
And the rest of the lads were talking with some of King Billy's boys
when Carter mentioned Chelsea, and the Rangers boys were sound
enough, well fucking pissed, singing some battle hymn telling Will
how much they hated the Fenian bastards, how Bobby Sands could do
with a chicken supper, the dirty Fenian fucker, and Will wasn't going
to argue the toss. He wouldn't get involved in a discussion on Ireland
because he didn't fancy getting glassed.

A DJ sat in the shadows at the far end of the pub, togged-up
bouncers on the door, a view through the bodies and glass to the sea,
and Will was gagging for a decent drink, the same as Mango who was
smiling and looking all laid back. Even Carter didn't seem that bothered about pulling, and the time was going fast, getting stuck into the
lager-lager-lager, and before they knew it the fat northern cunt behind
the bar was calling last orders, just like the fat London cunts at home,
no fucking difference. They were tired, rolling back to the hotel with
the two birds who'd linked arms with Balti and Harry on the seafront,
drunks wandering around talking to themselves, people shouting and
laughing at each other, laughing at two drunks trying to smack each
other but swinging and missing and ending up on the ground.

They piled into the hotel bar lining up the drinks and Carter was
apologising to Terry behind the counter for that game when Newcastle
got thumped 6–0 at the Bridge and every time McDermott went near
Gate 13 they'd been offering him ciggies and it was like Gazza and the
Mars bars, winding them up, they earnt a decent enough wage to suffer
a bit of verbal, and Terry said not to worry, it was all part of the game,
he'd laughed all the way to the bank, and they were back by the window,
same table, getting stuck into the drink, and then Mango asked where
the Bollock Brothers had gone and the lads realised they'd pissed off
upstairs.

Who cared anyway? That geezer from Leeds had appeared and
was winding them up, and his wife was howling, red in the face, such
a dark red that Will thought she was ready to pop but kept quiet, at
least he hoped he did, he could feel the hangover coming, and above
them Balti was turning off the light, with the door locked—Will would

have to sleep next door—and he took off his trainers and jeans and was between the sheets and he could hear Harry and the other girl whispering in the next bed.

The bird Balti was with had his knob out and he hoped he wasn't too pissed, too drunk to fuck, so he ran his hand back from her pants and made sure, the old confidence returning, and then he hoped he wasn't going to blurt before he got inside because it had been a long time, too fucking long, and he had her pants down, bra off, naked now except for her stockings, and Harry was taking his time, his head spinning round and round the mulberry bush and the same ideas were there, and then he heard his mate in the next bed banging away and the bird moaning, the cunt didn't waste any time, and the girl was whispering about using a rubber, just my fucking luck to pull a sensible bird, and then she was sitting up and the curtains were so thick they couldn't see a thing, so she turned on the lamp by the bed and the first thing Harry saw was Balti on the job.

It was a right royal turn-off that, and the dream came back, hitting in a massive rush, and the thought of that flabby arse made him laugh because he was relieved. He'd been wondering about that dream of his, why he'd dreamt of his mate's arse. The experts on the telly said that you didn't even know sometimes if you were a bum bandit. They said that social pressures made you keep that kind of thing buried. It had been on his mind for a while. Imagine that, Harry a shirt-lifter. Horrible. It had been worrying him, and Balti had even asked if there was something wrong, and now he knew it was just a premonition of this very moment.

Everything emptied from Harry's mind. He was in the clear and wasn't going to end up a queer. Thank fuck for that. But Balti didn't like performing in public; what the fuck are you doing the fat cunt said and the bird underneath him pulled the covers up, the one with Harry saying sorry, but there's no need to swear is there love, reaching for her handbag and then turning off the light.

She pushed Harry back on to the bed and he heard her messing about and then felt her slipping the rubber on his knob, and before he could sing IF SHE DON'T COME, I'LL TICKLE HER BUM, WITH A LUMP

OF CELERY, she was on top of him doing the work, hanging her tits in his face and he reckoned that if he was going to die then this was the way he wanted to go. Her body was so warm and she smelt good, smelt of rum and perfume, pure heaven, this was the kind of dream that was better than real life.

Downstairs in the bar Leeds was telling Carter what a great player Eddie Gray had been. A couple of younger men came over with Leeds crests cut into their arms. They were the same age. Big bastards who asked if the London boys were at the 5-0 thrashing Leeds got that year they smashed up the scoreboard and Chelsea tried to get in the North Stand. Carter remembered well enough, with the old bill steaming into the Leeds mob, Chelsea on the pitch at the final whistle trying to get in as well but forced back by the truncheons, then that time up at Elland Road when Chelsea had gone mental outside, but Mango was turning off the football.

One of them was a mechanic and somehow they were talking about Mercs, and everything was sweet, having a good laugh, with Will getting chatted up by the old woman wondering again how a face could get that red. She loved Elvis and she'd been to Graceland in Memphis with her husband. Did he know that you could buy an Elvis model that was battery-operated and would move around? It's true dear. Her husband leant forward and said Memphis was alright, but the black areas were very poor, the younger Leeds saying it sounded like Chapeltown because there were too many niggers in Leeds, and you went to Bradford and you might as well be in Mecca. Combat 18 would sort things out, and they asked Carter about the C18 presence at Chelsea, Carter saying he didn't know about all that political stuff.

Will felt sick from the drink and went to the bogs. He stuck his fingers down his throat. Nothing happened. Back in the bar he got the keys off Mango and went upstairs, banging into walls, falling into Mango and Carter's room, nicking a pillow off one of the beds. He crashed out on the floor, felt himself spinning for a while and then everything went blank.

Next morning when Will woke up his head was fine, and there was a narrow ray of light hitting the wall next to him, a laser threatening to burn through to the next room for a view of Harry and Balti, the sound of Mango snoring, Will turning his head and going back to sleep. A second later the curtains were open and Carter was scrubbed and ready for the day ahead, telling Will it was eleven and Mango wouldn't budge, wanted to sleep a bit longer. Mango said he was fucked, and Carter said fair enough mate, I'm going down for breakfast. Will said he'd catch him up.

Carter walked into the restaurant and found the others half way through a quality breakfast with two women opposite. He remembered last night, sitting down ordering orange juice, bacon, sausages, eggs, tomatoes, toast, coffee. The birds were scousers. He hadn't realised they were from Liverpool. They weren't bad either, the one with Harry carrying a healthy pair of lungs if he was honest. They were having a laugh going on about some techno club they'd been to a couple of nights before where they'd done well, five Es each and the neurotransmitters rioting, and maybe they'd see the lads later down the same pub tonight, about nine, because they had to meet a friend.

They left money for the food and pissed off, and Carter wanted to know the scores. It was about time the Sex Division got into gear again, with the boys off the mark and looking well pleased with themselves, well fucking pleased. Two points each. But more than that it was a good feeling after so long wanking, and there was Carter on thirty-eight points with Mango on fifteen, or was it sixteen, they'd have to check that one, but at least they were off the mark. Carter said they should get down that boozer tonight and pick up a bonus point, who knows, maybe two, and Balti smiled and knocked back the coffee, sweet as a nut, out of the chicken run, away from London, free as the proverbial.

Harry had slept a deep sleep without the sniff of a dream, and it was great sitting there listening to Carter, thinking how that bird had ridden him last night. She'd wanted it another couple of times as well, and he was tired. He fancied a kip. But then Will arrived looking fresh and raring, and if that cunt could do it then so could Harry, Will ordering and going to the phone again with the others taking the piss, again, coming back happy enough telling them Terry was behind the bar. Newcastle obviously weren't paying him enough if he had to work here as well. You'd think they would've worked something out wouldn't you? Next thing you knew you'd have Les Ferdinand and Peter Beardsley in black mini-skirts serving tables. Will ordered Cornflakes and toast from a bored teenage girl with chubby legs and black slacks.

At twelve there was still no Mango so they left the hotel and walked along the seafront. The sun was sizzling and Blackpool was burning up. They went down the pier for a go in the arcade. Mango was the one for space games but the sloppy cunt was probably wanking as they spoke. Thinking of England. They'd go get him later. When he'd finished.

There were a few anoraks at the end of the pier with their fishing rods out and Carter led the way into some dome effort where you stood holding crash barriers and an aerial film of forests in Canada passed by and the idea was you felt like a bird, an eagle or hawk maybe, fucking daft this, the sex machine said, but they were serious forests. Think of the amount of bear shit there must be in that wood, he said. It was his only comment. The others had been impressed by the size and beauty of the landscape.

They went down the beach, strolling along taking their time, past white flab turning a deep tandoori red and kids building castles and kicking balls. With the pier and beach done they fancied a pint and found a pub further along the front, ordering four lagers. It tasted different, the water heavier, or lighter, noticing it more now without the electric soup. They should really go and get Mango, though, and Will said he'd do it and left quickly. Balti and Harry were going on about the two scouse birds like they were in love or something and Carter was telling them to leave it out, it was getting right up his nose. The Bollock Brothers laughed at him saying that's a bit rich coming from you, all you ever think about is fanny.

They'd finished their drinks when Mango arrived with Will, so they bought him a pint seeing's how he'd seen them alright with the transport and accommodation. He screwed up his face. This lager tastes different, have you noticed, we should stick to bottles, you know what you're getting, and the others told him it was the water. They had a few more with men coming in and out, one or two women, and they hadn't heard another London accent yet which they didn't mind really, seeing as they were on holiday.

Mango showed them a postcard he'd bought on the way to the pub, so stupid it was funny, some fat old boy going through a tunnel on a train with a dolly bird in a short white skirt next to him, a mis-understanding involving a couple of geese, and they asked him who he was going to send it to. That bird from his work? Penny? He said no, he didn't have her address with him, he'd keep it for himself. She was above all that, a class act. Everyone smiled and nodded their heads.

Mango had to admit he was the happiest he'd been for ages, having a drink with his mates, a long way from home. They could do anything they wanted to you in this world, but if you had a few good mates you'd always get through. People you'd known for years. Grown up with. Got pissed and kicked to fuck with as juveniles. Three Brummie birds came over from the bar and sat nearby, Carter giving them a line of chat and two were into the old jungle, the other preferring punk, and the jungle girls shifted over and were chatting up the Bollock Brothers, which was a turn up. Carter wondered if he was losing his touch, and before Will knew it he was the music expert and the third girl was sitting next to him as he told her how he'd seen The Jam at The Rainbow and The Clash at the Electric Ballroom.

She was younger and well impressed, and he was tempted and knew he should stop drinking otherwise he was going to do some-thing he'd regret. It looked like the afternoon was going to end up in another session, which seemed to suit everyone, but then Mango said he wanted to see a bit of Blackpool and off he went. Carter told the girls to get a round in, which they did, and the Sex Division were on their sixth pints already. Things were going very nicely, no cares in the world, even Carter wasn't that bothered because, after all, even though the Brummies were fit enough, three right little ravers if he was honest, they were right old slappers. They had to be, blanking him like that. If the rest of them wanted to fuck pigs, then that was their problem. It was a free world. They all had a vote.

Eventually the lads decided to go for some food at a curry house they'd seen earlier. They'd stopped to check the menu and it seemed alright. They left Will in the pub with the girl he was chatting with, while the other two Brummies went to the pier, saying they'd be back later after they'd been over the forest.

Will was more pissed than he'd thought. He was giving the woman the once over and he knew he was in if he wanted. He couldn't help playing the thing through his mind. Taking her back to the hotel. Up in the lift. A bed to himself. Stripped off and having a good time together. He wanted her, but fought hard and said he had to get back and meet Mango. He'd see her later maybe, if she was around. She looked disappointed, a bit hurt even, which made him feel bad, but said that would be nice. They walked some of the way back and he shot off and found the lads in the Blackpool Tandoori, sitting in the back near the bar with the waiters.

The Sex Division members present stood up and clapped him in, because they knew he'd been on for a shag but had come through the test in one piece. None of them wanted to see him do the dirty on Karen. It was easy saying yes, so fucking easy to just say yes all the time. It was much harder saying no. Will had shown quality and self-discipline, controlling the beautiful game and keeping possession, showing patience and reserve, choosing the highest footballing values above kick-and-rush. It was just what they had expected, though Carter, Harry and Balti would have taken the easy option and gone for a great big yes please darling, if you could just go easy with the teeth on the helmet, but Will was his own man. He wouldn't meet her later, even though he wanted to. It made Harry and Balti happy because it showed there were people around with morals. Not many, mind, but one or two. It was temptation and all that.

They were single men, and Balti and Harry were interested in the Brummies, Carter reminding them of their responsibilities with the scousers, and he had a point. Bollocks did he. He just didn't want them getting cocky and scoring too many points. Look who it was giving it all that. But it was fucking typical. You wanked yourself silly for near enough a year and when a shag came along, right away it was followed by another portion, by more sex on a plate. Like tube trains.

Why couldn't it be spaced out a bit? It wasn't right. Did they go back to the scousers, or try and knob the Brummies? A difficult decision.

They were soon into a feast, filling up nicely, the tikkas and vindaloos washed down with Carlsberg, and the waiters all had northern accents which was fair enough really, telling them Bradford was the curry capital of Britain. Maybe even the world. The owner had moved over to Blackpool, extending the family business, and Mango emptied the chutney dish leaving the lime pickle and onions to the others. It had started raining heavily outside so they had another pint and when it stopped they paid up, left a tip, and went back to the hotel.

Will left for a few zeds, and the others joined Mango in the bar. The drink was making them a bit tired, delayed reactions, but Terry was pleased to see the boys, the afternoon floating past easy enough, and next thing Will knew he was being kicked awake by Mango and Carter who'd both had a bath and a shave, and were looking spick and span ready for a decent night out. Next door Harry and Balti were still trying to decide whether they should service the scousers again or go for the Brummies. Harry was thinking of the warmth of the scouser, a million miles from his dream's harsh moorland. They were unable to make their minds up, but bollocks anyway, they just fancied a laugh. No need to take life so serious.

They turned off the light and went next door, banging to be let in, sat on Carter's bed waiting for Mango to hand out the Buddhas. It was pure stuff, or so he said. They were downstairs for a drink and Terry Mac was there behind the bar. Waiting patiently with his selection of lagers and beers at the ready.

They had a couple of lagers and, giving Macca a wave, were outside in the night air, a real buzz to Blackpool now—and they watched the colours and heard the sounds and stood in a pub bumping into the Brummies more by chance than anything, having fun enjoying themselves, not expecting anything, not bothered, and they had a thirst on, Will ordering, then they were off down the road paying their money and taking their chance indoors, lights popping, everyone together in the dark and there was no North or South now and the music made sense getting inside the feel of the bass and football was a beautiful game—it really was—and there was no hatred because you realised that everyone was part of the same thing and even something as naff as sex meant nothing—what was the difference?—mostly a bird could carry a sprog in her belly, there didn't have to be rules and regulations because slagging people off because of what they were was a nonsense—they were part of the same thing—and you could feel it now, like what was a Scot except someone who lived in another part of the country and had a different accent, a few different customs, a history that was all in the past, and if any one of them had been born in Glasgow, say, rather than London, then they'd have been Jocks as well, it was so simple, but sometimes you couldn't see things clearly because you were in this multi-storey car park looking for the ticket machine watching the clock all the time because you had to spend your money, but when you came out into the light then it was there waiting, because it made some kind of sense that everything was connected somehow—a long line of DNA that went back to Java Man—back to Lucy in Africa—some Stone Age primitive world—and when you listened to Aboriginal music it could've been made in a factory so there was a connection there and they looked at the birds around them and there was no need for sex or points there was no difference now and it was all decoration like lucky charms and jewellery something to play with and pass your time and it didn't matter if you died tomorrow or if you were dirt poor because when you got into the clearing with the lights and everything—right inside the fucking dream, that was just like life—then you could do what you wanted—if you wanted to drop your kegs—but what was the point, you could never escape the conditioning that was part of what you became and it was like the wild children you read about who lived like the apes that raised them so if someone dumped you on your arse then what was the point of killing them for it because they were the same as you (deep down inside) and there was no reason to stitch people up and use prostitutes because every porn actor was a human being as well and money meant something but not everything (it was worth remembering, it would be forgotten) and the dreams made sense (perfect sense) now they were all in the clearing together with the jungle in the background—Big Frank on the door checking tickets—and time didn't matter with Karen back home and punk and reggae black vinyl relics of the past, everything was how it should be.

The connection was obvious, but the women were tasty, maybe he (Carter) was losing his touch, they were in shorts and bra straps, something like that, but they weren't that game, must be the effect of the Buddha, and you couldn't be bothered talking let alone talking shit and even the Bollock Brothers were tapping their feet, big men with cropped heads, the volume seemed to be moving through the ceiling shaking the foundations but the house stayed standing no problem there with the scousers of last night and the Brummies as well, the whole of Blackpool in one place and London seemed a long long way away.

The Buddha was breaking down their attachments and that was what it was all about really because you didn't want to suffer and all life was suffering because you were going to die, so you did something about it and considered the problem with the pulse running through the building and there could be no regrets because history was rewritten, but for the individual it wasn't going to matter, and who knew what would happen, only Harry the dreamer, they all had a glimpse, he was no saint no prophet, religion was a mug's game the Buddha made that clear enough and they could've been in a crowd on a Saturday thinking of The Shed singing together with a rougher edge, but there were similarities, some kind of fanaticism, and where were the fascists and where were the communists?

It was like time flashed past outside in the street with the music shut off but still echoing through their skulls, fading away, ears toasting, the lads wandering home, buying chips with curry sauce, sitting down on the beach, looking out to sea, with the Brummies and the scousers, nobody talking much, it wasn't that cold, five o'clock, they were shagged out, wandering off home, the lads alone back in the hotel, Terry McDermott nowhere to be seen, none of them fancied a drink, sitting around having a smoke, eventually fading off to sleep.

Carter opened the curtains and walked back across the room. He went into the hall and banged on the next door. Come on you lazy bastards, it's time to get up, we've only got half a day left. The rest of them were taking their time getting sorted out so the shag man went for a walk along the seafront, breathing in the air and watching the gulls hover. He found himself thinking that it would be nice to live by the sea one day, when he was older. Maybe run a little shop. He shook his head. That was a soft way to think. He'd been born in London and that was where he'd die.

When he got back to the hotel, the others had almost finished breakfast and the papers. They were quiet and thoughtful. Two days wasn't long enough. They went down the pier and played the arcade, then down the pubs of the last couple of days for one or two civilised Sunday pints. Everything was different now. It was a bit of a disappointment.

Mango unlocked the doors and the Jag purred. They were on the move, leaving Blackpool behind. It was the warmest day so far and no-one thought to put any music on. They were dozing or thinking their thoughts, with the driver back inside the machine enjoying the smooth ride, doing a ton in the outside lane. He pulled into the middle to let the cowboys past. Usually he'd blow them away. Thirty grand was a lot of money for a car. He couldn't be bothered right now.

The countryside flashed past and you could understand the road protesters, even though motorways made life a lot easier. They were early enough to miss the major jams, two and a half hours later at the Watford Gap approaching London. Nobody was saying a thing, the lads in the back asleep with Will looking forward to seeing Karen again because it was nice to have someone waiting for you. He was glad he'd had enough sense to leave that girl alone. The traffic got heavy around Brent Cross and it was a slow haul down to Hanger Lane and on to the Uxbridge Road.

BALHAM ON TOUR

Balti sat in The Unity with Harry and Carter. Mango had refused point blank. He had too much to lose getting involved in petty squabbles, scratching around in the gutter getting his hands cut. It was bad news Balti getting a kicking like that, but he should pay someone to do the job on his behalf. Get a whip-round going in the pub and send some hard-up headcase down to Balham. A spanking by proxy. If it came to money, simple pounds and pence, then he'd be first to dip into his wallet. There was no problem there. He was willing to back his old mate with cold hard cash, putting his money where his mouth was. Now he couldn't do better than that, could he? But Mango was missing the point. And Balti had been spending a lot of time slagging him off.

Will tried to talk them out of the idea. They were making a big mistake in his opinion, picking his words carefully, because he understood the logic well enough. This was fair enough in Balti's eyes, because Will was no bottle merchant and had always been a peace-lover, though not the kind of pacifist wanker who'd lay down on the pavement and let some psycho jump on his head for fun. Will reckoned bad blood had to settle sooner or later, otherwise everyone involved would bleed to death. That it took a stronger man to walk away from trouble than it did to keep the thing going. Will was true to his nature. They couldn't fault him, that was his belief, and though Balti and the others disagreed, thought it was bollocks if they were honest, that was his genuine view so fair dues. Mango, though, was always giving it the big one and now he was counting job opportunities instead of friendship.

Carter and Harry sat with Balti, Slaughter staring into his glass examining the fizzy reflection, near enough care in the community that bloke, a liability in his combat fatigues. But it was better not to wind up a bloke who had a glint in his eye and a machete under his pillow.

Mark, Rod and Tom sat at the next table. The Sex Division knew the younger men from football and the pub, and the news that it was an Irishman, a season ticket holder at Millwall no less, who'd given Balti a pasting had got them interested. Johnson owed Balti one, an incident that went back years to when he'd been a kid and Balti, Harry, Carter and the crew they'd knocked about with at the time had saved him from a kicking in Cardiff. It had been a good day out, with Chelsea going mental before, during and after the game. They'd even gone in the Cardiff seats where their main mob had been and the Taffs had needed a police escort back to the terraces. Talk about getting your noses rubbed in it, and it had made things worse when it went off outside. Balti had helped him out in the town centre.

'I'm the only bloke drinking am I?' Slaughter asked, as he necked his fourth pint, fed up with the ugly mug staring back.

He'd been having a hard time lately and looked towards Denise serving behind the bar, raising his empty glass. She didn't notice. She was demanding sex all the time and he'd had a lot of overtime and was shagged out. Denise was killing him, treating him like a dildo on legs. Not that he was complaining mind, but he was going to ask her to marry him and wanted to get into a conversation where he could lead up to the big question nice and easy, without having to perform like a speeding chimp. He hadn't got the proposal worked out yet. It took a lot of bottle doing something like that. It was funny, really, because he'd kick someone's head in but wouldn't propose to the woman he knew and loved and trusted with his life. She was getting a bit kinky as well. Wanting him to use cucumbers and carrots. He had to be up at six-thirty in the morning and wasn't a fucking market trader. If she wanted cucumbers and carrots she should go down the market to one of the fruit and veg stalls. Mind you, if he caught her shagging some barrow boy she was dead. Denise and the cunt giving her a portion. Slaughter loved Denise. Wanted her to be happy. But only with him. Anyone else started sniffing round her and they were history. He knew he shouldn't complain about the sex, but he really was worn out. Least she wasn't some old slapper though, and he wasn't pumping his right hand like a lot of blokes he could mention. Denise was classy alright, though he didn't think much of the cucumbers and carrots. He was a lucky man.

'Right, drink up lads, and we'll get going. Me and Harry in the motor, you lot in the van.'

Balti knew McDonald's habits. You didn't work with someone like that year in, year out, listening to the non-stop patter, without learning how he lived. The habits and everything. That's why the Irish toerag had been able to bushwhack him. Just showed up at the right time and place. The car was slow starting, but Balti pumped the accelerator and it fired up. Just his luck, the fucker. He set off for South London keeping an eye in his rearview mirror so Carter could stay with them.

Balti was looking forward to the trip. You could say what you liked, about turning the other cheek and letting things go, that the needle had to end somewhere so why not with you, but that kind of thinking was shit. It was like at school and the first sign of trouble from another kid and you hit him hard. That way you were left alone. Show weakness and you became a punch-bag. Let McDonald get away with it, and the next thing he knew Balti would be getting a slap everywhere he went. It would take his self-respect away. It was inside him. Self-respect was even more important than respect you got from others, and the people who tried to persuade him otherwise would still think he was a bit of a wanker if he didn't hit back.

There was nothing you could do about it. Alright, Will was different, but that was nature and genes talking and, fair enough anyway, he didn't want to go on about his views. Will spoke his mind and was straight. Mango, though, was nothing. He'd shag some kid and take the piss in King's Cross, but drew the line at helping a mate. That's where sex and violence got mixed up. It was another kind of violence, taking advantage of runaways like that, treating women like shit. It was worse than giving a bloke a kicking, shafting a frightened kid. He'd sort Mango out one day. Priorities—that's what it was all about. Look at the blokes in the van behind. They were up for it. You didn't hear them whining about jobs and the old bill. They understood what it was about, or at least Carter did, the others along for the ride. Never mind, you needed numbers.

It was almost ten and the roads weren't too bad. It didn't take long getting down to Balham, taking the South Circular to Clapham Common then off down the High Road. Carter was tight behind them all the way keeping himself happy getting right up the car's arse. The memories came back, Balti shovelling shit for slave wages, blood on his hands and the smell of concrete, dust in his eyes and pennies in his pocket, though even that was better than what he got on the social. At least you had pride at the end of the week and the hard graft stopped you thinking. He'd sell the car if he could get anything for it, but truth be told it needed an MOT and tax, and the clutch was starting to slip. Another week or two and his acceleration would be fucked. Maybe he'd torch it and pick up on the insurance. He'd take a chance and spend fifty quid on the Lottery. He'd done a tenner of his forty-six quid last weekend on the numbers game. Mental really, but the fever was everywhere. Everywhere you looked there was some poor cunt standing in line. You had to wait ages just to get a paper in the morning there were so many no-hopers going without their protein.

Ten million in his account and Balti was taking a week to think things through. He'd sit back and laugh himself sick. Delivery pizzas and crates of Fosters straight to the front door. Enough to keep him and Harry happy till he decided on the next move. Keep the cunts waiting. Carter could come round for a big slice of the extra-large deep pan Hawaiian and a couple of chilled cans, Will too with Karen, but Mango would have to stand outside with the scum from the papers. His old girl would be there with his sister later on, aunts and uncles, everyone he knew and trusted, and when they were stuffed and went home happy he'd let the dolly birds in. Blondes, brunettes, redheads. He'd have the lot queueing up down to the end of the street and round the corner. Put Harry on the door checking tickets. In bikinis next to the telly. They'd flock to Balti with his ten million in the bank. Anything he wanted they'd do it for him. They'd be stunners, no down-and-out street girls dying from the cold and malnutrition and AIDS. He wasn't taking those girls for a ride, no way.

'Run the bath for me, will you darling?'

'Right away big boy,' Pamela Anderson said, shifting herself from the cushions by his feet, collecting the clipped toe nails and scurrying away.

'Make us a cup of tea, will you love?'

'Milk and two sugars, beautiful?' Liz Hurley asked, stroking his tired brow one more time and hurrying to fill the kettle.

'Get us some chocolate biscuits would you? When you've finished.'

'My pleasure,' beamed that scouse bird from Blackpool, speaking with her mouth full.

Ten minutes later, when he'd fully recovered from the sheer pleasure of expertly performed oral sex, Balti tied his dressing gown together and went for his bath. He sat in the middle of the bubbles with his mug of tea while Pam shaved the stubble from his face, Lizzie massaged his shoulders, and the scouser operated the taps, making sure the bath was kept at the right temperature. He'd put on his new jeans and shirt, call a cab and steam down to Balti Heaven, leaving the crumpet at home to keep his bed warm. The lads would be there waiting and he'd get the Kashmiri boys sitting down to enjoy the feast and have Mango serving. He'd send the wanker back to warm up his kulcha nan as well. Make the big-shot bangra bastard work for his tip. Serve the flash sod right. His mouth watered. They'd drink and eat till they couldn't move, and when Mango came round with the mints and Buddhas he'd buy the fucking lot.

They said the Lottery was a bad thing. The old queens in their gold-crusted churches banging the holy book and the bishop, denouncing gambling as evil. But Balti didn't see them signing on. Didn't see them going through the rotting carrots and mushrooms on the special-offer table down the supermarket. Moral guardians said the Lottery was a sign of a society in serious decline, a culture with the threading picked bare spilling its guts, well, everybody knew that was the truth, too obvious even to talk about really, but it was still freedom of choice. You couldn't argue with that. At least it offered you one chance in sixty million or whatever it was. He didn't know a person who didn't want to win a fortune. It was something to look forward to. You had to have your dreams. What else was there? Without dreams all you were left with was the reality.

'Deeper, Balti, deeper,' Pam screamed, legs wrapped round his shoulders.

'Harder, Balti, harder,' Liz begged, head banging into the wall.

'Shut up will you, I'm trying to get some fucking sleep in here,' Harry shouted from the next room, covering his head with his pillow to get rid of the horrible sound of Balti servicing the entertainment industry.

Balti had taken the Carter crown and was an unstoppable sex machine with an industrial drill for a penis, standing on the side of the M4 by Heston Services flashing the cars in the inside lane laughing his head off, catching the startled look on the faces of the blondes in their Jags as they realised he was that multi-millionaire Balti Heaven Playboy on the front of all the papers, the one that scouse bird had found in bed with Pam and Liz but even so stood by her man and forgave him his sins, face plastered over billboards, a wealthy man who didn't give a toss if the neighbours knew he was loaded. According to the grudging editorials, he was a winner with a heart, ploughing a cool million into homes for the homeless. It added to the attraction. He had conscience as well as soul.

Carter had lost his way, unable to compete with the new boy, but Balti knew it could never be as good as with that scouse bird in Blackpool. He was seeing her regular now he'd got a private detective to track her down and put him in touch. It was a shame it would never happen. Mango with his Buddhas had messed things up. The chance was there for another portion and it had turned to spit with the vague image of some bald guru with big ears sitting in the full lotus position, taking sex out of the equation. It was nature. The birds and the bees. And with ten million quid you owned the fucking hive.

When Balti calmed down a bit, he knew his ideal woman. Ingrid Bergman would meet him in Copenhagen. Everything would be crystal clear. The air would be pure and the food healthy. Even the lager would taste different. They'd sit outside by the harbour, surrounded by classic buildings, holding hands across the table. Ingrid would tell him about her life and times, and listen fascinated as Balti revealed his hopes for the future. It was a shame she was dead. But you never knew. With ten million you could achieve a lot.

'Mind out.'

Balti hit the brake just in time. Harry laughed. Balti was back in Balham doing a right and a left and pulling up thirty yards from The Carpenter's Hammer. It was a small pub with blind windows and a dark interior. McDonald was down there most nights. Sometimes for a session, usually for a few quiet pints. He'd sat in back streets with his mates waiting for Balti, hiding in the shadows like a nonce, so Balti was going to do this in style. There was no need turning the pub over. That was asking for publicity, lining up witnesses. It would be quiet, Tuesday night, and it should be easy enough to shift things outside. He was marching straight in. Carter was behind them under a big, overhanging tree. There was nobody about. The street was dead.

'Right, when I come out, you lot steam in.'

Harry walked back to the van, everyone on the pavement. Slaughter was standing there like Action Man, having a slash. Mark was giving him a wanker sign behind his back. Carter shook his head sadly. They had a nice collection of cricket and baseball bats, Slaughter told to leave the machete at home. As Johnson had pointed out, they weren't a posse of fucking niggers, were they? No need to go overboard. If McDonald was in there with a few mates they'd need the numbers. If not, then Balti would do the cunt on his own. Harry watched Balti walk over to the Hammer, then disappear inside. It was a shame you had to grow up. Things were easier when you were kids.

It wasn't long till Balti was out in the street again moving fast along the pavement, away from the light. The only sound was the bang of the pub door. There was a short pause then the door swung open and three men came running out. Balti was twenty yards off now, on a bit of wasteland, and he had an iron bar out from under his jacket slapping it into his hand like he was in some budget gangster production, cheap video rental, third-generation video nasty. McDonald and his mates were concentrating on the silly bastard who'd strolled in, given them the come-on, then walked out again like he owned the place. Didn't the cunt understand? A bit slow in the head was he? The boy hadn't learnt his lesson. He was going to get some homework for his trouble. He should be locked up, but if that's what he wanted then that's what he was going to get. The punches and kicks couldn't have registered first time. It was those jungle bunnies spoiling things.

Bill Docherty was a Glaswegian and had known Roy McDonald for more than twenty years. They were good Protestants, though Bill was more dedicated to the politics than Roy. They'd been working in Highbury and dossing along the Holloway Road when they first met up. It was a hard life and there were enough Fenians around to make you nervous, but when you were trying to earn a crust you had to put your differences on hold. They'd eaten in the Archway Cafe after work, then drunk till closing in the local boozers, many of which did lock-ins. They'd stayed mates after Bill saved his nest egg and moved into the car trade. He was an alert bloke, his eyes keen and his mind ticking, but he was getting on and the five pints of bitter dimmed his awareness, the first thing he knew about the West London boys the thud of Slaughter's cricket bat against the side of his head. He wouldn't feel the kicks till the next morning and then it would be aches more than pain. Alcohol was a great anaesthetic.

'You and me, come on you cunt,' Balti shouted, lunging at McDonald who stopped dead and shifted back, the bottle in his hand still in one piece but ready to make its mark.

McDonald heard the noise behind. He turned but only partially. There was little light and he could see something crashing down. Doc stumbled forward and Roy tried to hold him up. Balti caught McDonald a beaut across the bridge of his nose, misting his eyes and smashing the bone. Slaughter was after the bloke he'd just hit, cracking McDonald in the balls in passing, Balti pulling his old foreman forward and dumped him in the rubble. There was the stink of rotting paper and wet mud taking Balti back to the reek of shit he remembered so well. Now it was his turn. Tit for tat. Hide and seek. Throwing the dice, one after the other playing the game of chance. They had the numbers and the Balham lot were getting a hiding. Balti kicked McDonald, then kept going, again and again, continuing till long after the Irishman had stopped moving. The others had backed off and were standing around waiting in silence. Not a bad result. Piece of piss in fact.

There was no colour to the scene and the whole thing had lasted a couple of minutes. Still there was nobody about. It was a dead part of the world. Balti felt empty. The tension gone. There was no pleasure kicking McDonald now. It was just something needed doing. Everything was still as a graveyard. He didn't feel good or bad. It was over. McDonald was one more bit of rubbish. He wasn't a person.

Balti remembered going down the Hammer a few years back. He'd forgotten about that. It was after work and Roy had taken a few of the boys along to celebrate the birth of his first grandson. Bought them drinks till closing. Funny how he'd forgotten that. The kid had died. Leukaemia or something. It all came rushing back, how McDonald had gone sour, but Balti couldn't let himself think like that. He was on top again and had to stay unemotional. Everyone suffered. You couldn't waste time on other people's problems. You still deserved some kind of respect. He stopped kicking. The kid had only lived a year and then they'd buried him. Given him back to his maker. What a waste, the poor little bastard.

McDonald didn't groan or move. He was very still. Maybe Balti had killed him. Kick a bloke in the head like that enough times and they could go under. He bent down and shook the figure. There was a moan. He'd live.

Balti noticed a wedding ring. It was a darker outline and he didn't know whether it was silver or gold. He pulled it off and was about to throw it as far as he could into the distance. Send it into orbit. But he stopped and thought and then dropped it next to McDonald. If the others hadn't been there he'd have put it back on his finger. Enough was enough. It was personal and had nothing to do with family. He was in a street full of ghosts, a sad world south of the river. Balti turned and the others were hurrying back to the van now, Harry telling him to come on and stop pissing about, that they shouldn't hang about riding their luck. Only Slaughter remained. Pissing on one of the unconscious men.

'I saved a bit,' the headcase laughed. Balti looked at him and was glad Carter was shagging his missus.

Back in the car and Balti hoped it would start. No problem. God was on his side alright. A just God who understood revenge and retribution. An eye for an eye and a tooth for a tooth. It was so easy he wanted to laugh. Balti had the last word and from now on he was going to be careful where he walked, wouldn't get careless like before. He'd take precautions and look after himself. As long as you were smart you were in the clear. It was when you got cocky and thought you were special that you suffered. It was God said the meek would inherit the earth. Or was it Jesus? One of those Bible boys. They'd done it in school. Why was he thinking of God anyway? And Balti was meek and mild and signing on, and McDonald would let it go now. Balti knew he would. He had a wife and kids. He'd taught the man a lesson. Best yet. That was it. Top of the totem. Finished. There had to be a winning line and he was the one drawing it here in Balham. End of story. Nobody took the piss out of Balti. Maybe the other two they'd done had been with McDonald before, maybe not. Who fucking cared anyway? They were up for a bit of five-onto-one so deserved everything they got. It was a neat package, wrapped and sealed with a kiss.

It was strange though, because the thing had been eating away at Balti and then when the pegs were put in place he felt empty. Not in a bad way, but like something was over and there was nothing to take its place. He felt that for a bit, then he was a man again, with mates to back him up. He was worth something. He might have to sign on and talk nice to some tart with a computer button to punch, but when it came to the crunch it was your fists and feet that counted. That and an iron bar. See, the thing was that nobody listened to you unless you showed a bit of violence. They talked about the ballot box and the great democratic experiment, about putting your cross on a piece of paper once every five years or so, giving you the chance to vote for some tosser from Oxford or Cambridge, Tory or Labour, it didn't make much difference, they were all the same, but the thing was that they never listened to anyone but their own kind.

Balti was riding high, crest of a wave, somewhere off a Gold Coast beach skimming thirty-footers trimmed down with the beer gut tight and under control, pizza under his arm, thinking the thing through, not listening to Harry talking about the aggro. Because it was only the violence of the old bill that kept you in line and some kind of idea that there was justice in the legal system which everybody who had ever dealt with the law knew was shit, so when it came down to it, if you had the front to use your fists then you could get things done. It was like the IRA and that, and he hated them like most people, but they wouldn't have got anywhere doing things peacefully. Or like the Poll Tax riot in Trafalgar Square tearing up the West End and scaring the tourists. That was the only way you could ever change things, but most people were scared shitless. He'd been listening to Karen and Will, though they talked ideas and weren't about to go out and plant a bomb to back them up. They were alright those two. It must be nice to kick back and not give a toss, but still know what was going on, get wound up in your head but be able to control things. Turn it all round somehow and make sense from the chaos. But that was them and Balti was Balti and fuck it, he'd had enough of South London, a right shithole, crossing Wandsworth Bridge returning to the civilised world. Bollocks, he fancied a pint.

'Your round then?' Harry laughed as they entered The Unity.

Carter was at the bar with Slaughter. The sex machine was sharing a joke with the machete man, Denise filling glasses with extra strong refreshment. There were minutes till last orders, but they were on for afters. Balti muscled in with a tenner and Denise completed the round. Slaughter blew his special girl a kiss as she went to the till, winking at Carter, who was thinking about the night before with that old scrubber in her red gear wanting him to stay longer. He'd had to get going, with work in the morning, and didn't like hanging about in case Slaughter turned up. He was a bit nervous about it all, because though Slaughter looked a joke, with the fatigues and everything, he was seriously off his head and Carter didn't fancy having his balls hacked off and shoved down his throat. It was well dodgy, shagging that mad woman behind the bar, but he was in too deep and, anyway, she was a great ride, rough as fuck taking it like a trouper.

Carter had to be careful. That was all. Denise hadn't been too pleased when he'd left, her face twisting around and in on itself so he wondered if she was a nutter as well, which when he thought about her and Slaughter made sense, a marriage arranged in hell, acid bringing out the toxins, leaving purple scars. It was a shock when he put two and two together because he could deal with most things, missing limbs and pictures of lepers rotting away on the other side of the world, but mental illness was different. He couldn't handle that sort of stuff and Denise had enjoyed telling him before they'd gone down Balham how she rang Slaughter and he'd come straight round to take Terry's place. Fair enough, Carter wasn't complaining, but he couldn't look the bloke straight in the eye with the fresh image of his bride-to-be naked with a cucumber up her fanny.

'You see that film last night?' Harry asked. 'It was about this bloke who came back from beyond the grave. This witchdoctor jets over from Haiti, takes the shekels, digs up the coffin and gives this mug the zombie treatment, blowing some kind of angel dust in his face. Then the zombie kills the witchdoctor for interrupting his beauty sleep and goes on the rampage. Steams this pub full of yokels and wipes them out.'

'When did you watch that then?' Balti asked, enjoying the lager and good company.

'About three. I woke up and couldn't get back to sleep. But I was thinking, imagine being dead like that granny the other day on the news who the doctors sent to the morgue and it was only luck that they saw her varicose vein twitching and realised she was still alive. I mean, how many people do you reckon that happens to? Bit naughty, isn't it? Waking up six foot down.'

The lads shook their heads. It was shocking. A sign of the times. The failure of the state to protect its citizens from premature burial. They paid their taxes and were entitled to accurate diagnosis.

'This zombie, big fucker he was, and it only took a bit of the dust. It's supposed to be true. They use that kind of magic in Haiti. They say voodoo can bring you back to life.'

'That's a load of shit,' Carter said. 'Once you're dead, you're dead. That's the end. Heaven and hell is here. There's nothing afterwards. You've got to enjoy yourself right now.'

'You think though, if you could live forever. You wouldn't be bothered about anything, would you? It's only the thought that you're running out of time, that your best years are flashing past and you're going to end up with a shit pension, freezing to death, that does your head in most of the time.'

Harry stopped to think. If you could dream then it showed there was something more. It was imagination that made it all click into place. If you were asleep, but the brain was still ticking over, then there had to be something extra. It was the same with instinct. That had to come from somewhere. It was alright saying it was built-in, but that didn't explain anything. If you could get a good dream going then why wasn't that real in its own way? If you were pissed or charged-up, then you saw things different, and that was real as well. There'd been a few times when he was stoned that he knew what the others were thinking, and they agreed, so how did anyone explain that? Nobody really tried. Maybe they knew deep down. In their dreams.

'The only zombie round here is Slaughter,' Carter said when the nutter had gone for a piss.

'He's alright. Just a bit sad.'

Harry thought about it. Even Slaughter must have dreams. He wondered what he dreamt about. Whether he took them seriously. Maybe he didn't remember anything the next morning.

'And dangerous,' Carter mumbled.

'You should leave his woman alone then,' Harry grinned.

'Why don't you shout it out,' Carter snarled. 'Let the whole fucking pub know.'

'Calm down girls,' Balti said.

They moved over to an empty table once Carter had got a round in, leaving Slaughter talking to Denise at the bar. Balti stretched his legs out and noticed blood on his trainers. There wasn't much. Just a black smudge that had congealed. He'd wash it off later. But he wasn't thinking about all that now. It was history, and the image of ambulances and nurses was fantasy.

'My granddad had one of those out-of-body experiences when I was a kid,' Balti said. 'He snuffed it and next thing he knows he's looking down on his body laid out with this nurse banging his heart. He said first off he saw his mum and dad standing there waiting for him, all his old mates, his gran and granddad, everyone who was dead, outlines he recognised against this brilliant light. Then the next thing he knows he's off down this tunnel and finds himself floating around the ceiling like a balloon. Except he didn't feel like a balloon because there was no feeling at all. He was there, but not there, if you know what I mean. An out-of-body experience.'

'Leave it out,' Carter said. 'You're winding us up. Dead is dead. There's no second chance.'

'Straight up. He told me. He's not going to lie about something like that, is he?'

'You never told me about that,' Harry said, interested.

'You don't like to, do you? People would just take the piss.'

'So what happened next?'

'He was up there looking down watching this nurse trying to revive him and he said he felt the best he'd ever felt. Really happy and everything seemed perfect and it was like he understood why his life had gone the way it had, even though it wasn't the details so much as one big hit. None of it mattered any more. He said everything was suddenly alright. There was nothing to worry about. Then he was sucked back into his body and he was alive and felt like shit for months after. Once that was over, he was sweet as a nut because he knew there was something waiting for him and he could go to sleep one day and see everyone again. He knew there was a happy ending.'

The lads sipped their drinks and thought about this for a while. Carter knew it was nonsense. It was a nice enough idea, but impossible to believe. Still, he wasn't saying anything. After all, it was Balti's family and you didn't slag off a mate's family. Harry was amazed and trying to get his head round it all.

Balti wondered why he had come out with that story about his granddad. That's right, it was the zombie film Harry mentioned. Word association. Football association. And for some reason he was in the dark on a patch of wasteland with these three men laying in the mud and there was a big flash of light like a bomb going off, except it was more like a searchlight because it wasn't doing any harm. It was so bright it made him blink, but there was no sound because someone must have pulled the plug, and when he looked around the banks of speakers had been removed and there was just dark concrete lit up by this light that came from nowhere. He could see his foreman floating about, or at least some kind of ghost outline, and there was this Ulster accent telling everyone that it was alright and that there had to be peace because they were just acting their parts and keep that nurse away and send the ambulance back to the hospital because there's this little boy waiting for me and we're going to have all those football games we missed because of bad blood.

'Alright Will?' Balti asked as his mate pushed through the doors looking a bit nervous.

'You did it then?'

'No problem.'

Carter watched Eileen pouring pints. She wouldn't cause the kind of grief Denise was capable of bringing down on his head. He saw Slaughter lean over and kiss his woman on the cheek. Carter wondered what she would say when he popped the question. He had to laugh. Slaughter with his hair longer and styled, the tattoos removed and bitten fingernails grown and manicured, a five-hundred quid suit and shiny new shoes, down on one knee with a close shave and quality after-shave swamping the pores, a fine speech prepared in front of the mirror and not a drug in his system, seeing things clearly, ice cool, down on his knee with a bouquet personally selected from that expensive flower shop on the high street, building up to the big moment, a subtle line of chat, four-grand diamond ring in his breast pocket and a suite lined up at the Mayfair Hilton, dinner at the Savoy, the vintage champagne chilled, asking for the hand of the queen of West London barmaids, the look on Denise's face as she realises what's going on, that gold-plated machete in a shoulder-holster, James Bond making a comeback.

More like a tab of acid to get his night vision focused on the job in hand, a few pints and a couple of burgers on the way home, giving her a take-it-or-leave-it offer just as he was about to dump his load. Because that was something birds forgot. That sex was personal, even with strangers, though no bloke was going to admit as much. It was better than talking shit for hours on end, girls lined up in the bogs applying their make-up and discussing the men they'd shagged, giggling like they were back in the playground, the stupid fucking slags. Carter wouldn't get caught out. Not like Slaughter. Not like Will. Not like before.

'You heard, Chelsea are trying to sign Gazza,' Will said.

'They're always going on about Gazza,' Harry replied.

'He couldn't play in the same team as the Dutchman,' Carter insisted. 'You can only have one major play-maker in a team. It's like me and you lot. There's only room for one shag machine.'

'Mango's still within striking distance,' Balti said. 'At least mathematically anyway.'

'What about when Osgood, Hudson and Cooke played in the same side?' Harry asked. 'They were all quality players.'

'That was different,' Carter insisted. 'They were out on the piss night after night and didn't have to worry so much about their fitness levels. Football's more athletic now and there's so much money at stake nobody's going to go out and let themselves go when they've got ten years at the top creaming it.'

'I don't see you sitting at home keeping fit,' Will laughed.

'I'm different. A throwback to a golden age. When footballers were men and the crumpet down the King's Road was well fucking nervous.'

'I bet you The Dutchman isn't getting hammered every night. It's not like he can't afford a pint. He earns more in a week than us lot do in a year.'

'It's good work if you can get it.'

Harry was thinking about the death trip. It sounded like the old boy had been at the Buddhas. Burning away the weeds and leaving the ground clean and full of carbon. There was no pressure weighing you down and everything seemed perfect, though you couldn't work out why. There was no reason or rhyme, you just felt good. He'd have to have a word with Mango. It had been a good night out. The memory was still there and it was easy back-pedalling, but it was different. Strange how Blackpool and the jungle dream had come together, walking into the clearing where the lights were brighter and Frank Bruno was keeping things in order. Maybe they were nothing more than chemical reactions. He didn't know if it was a good thing or not. None of them had been raised with any kind of religion.

Harry knew from the telly that the Mayans had been into peyote and mushrooms thousands of years before the righteous majority stood up in Parliament and pointed the finger. Most places in the world had their own version. Like the Christians getting pissed on blood. No wonder they feared vampires in the Middle Ages. But they were all at it, all over the planet, whether it was magic mushrooms in the shires or sweat lodges on the American plains. Everybody needed a holiday. The brain had to loosen up sometimes and he reckoned the old witchdoctors understood these things, picking plants and mixing potions, collecting the fungus and reaping the harvest. They fixed up the strobe lights and created ceremonies, added a bit of music and some costumes and away you went. That's why they got pissed sitting in The Unity. Easing the tension, though Karen was right when she said lager was a violent drug. But they lived in that kind of world, so it was natural enough.

It was the fucking hippies that got acid banned, with their long hair and noncy dress code. The Sex Division came from a punk/herbert generation that identified hippies as sell-out merchants. Until they started making a big noise acid had been legal. It was before their time anyway, and the Christians lived a material life without visions or imagination, so nowadays it was all synthetic stuff. Pills and powder. Badly brewed lager shifted down the assembly line. Scientists in backrooms juggling formulas, creating reactions, maximising profits. But mention death experiences or dreams too loudly and you were in trouble. There was always some cunt around ready to slap your wrist. Telling you to get back in line and stand up straight.

'Did you hear about the new sports centre they're going to build?' Will asked. 'There's going to be a swimming pool, weights room, sauna, squash courts.'

'Where's that going to be then?' Harry asked, fed up with mind games.

'Over by the library.'

'What about the swimming pool down the road then?'

'They're knocking it down and building a DIY shop.'

'Bit daft, isn't it?'

'You know what they're like. It never makes much sense. Suppose the swimming pool's a better site for a shop. The sports centre isn't definite yet, but the finance is more or less in place. They reckon it will be a luxury effort.'

'Probably one of those fun pools. Plastic dinosaurs slides and a maximum depth of two feet.'

Denise was in charge of the pub with Len away and had called last orders. Before long, the pub had emptied, leaving Carter, Harry, Balti and Will at their table. Slaughter passed them on the way out, knackered.

'See you lads.'

'Thanks Slaughter.'

Eileen and Denise came and sat at the table once they'd cleaned up. Denise sat next to Terry and slipped her hand between his legs under the cover of the table. Eileen was beside Will. He'd noticed her looking at him the last few times he was in the pub. Ever since he'd started bringing Karen along. Maybe she was interested, or perhaps it was his imagination. He thought hard about Karen as Eileen started going into one about the hard evening she'd had.

'Have a nice night out then?' Denise asked.

'Great,' Harry said.

'Where did you go?'

'Nice little pub in South London.'

'Anywhere's better than here. I'm fed up with this place.'

'It's alright,' Balti said. 'Free beer after closing-time then?'

'In your dreams,' but Denise hadn't charged them for the last round.

Will wondered if Carter was getting to grips with Denise. She was sitting quite close to him and there seemed to be something between them. Carter kept looking away and Denise seemed cocky. He'd ask him later on. He didn't like her much. She was a real turn-off. Not so much the looks, but the attitude. Eileen was different, but he had Karen and was a one-woman man. Like Balti and Harry, probably, if they had the chance.

Will had had a good day. It was a bit morbid sometimes going round the houses of old people who'd just died, making offers for their furniture and various odds and ends. The stuff had to be shifted, though, and it made things easy on the relatives. The house he'd visited that morning had been full of good stuff. The furniture was old and sturdy, built to last. Nowadays it was pinned together and the wood was cheap and cheerless. He'd told the son and daughter they could get more than he could offer them, if they sold items on merit and went to a bit of trouble, but they didn't care because they were in mourning and he'd done well for himself. Will believed in being up front with those kind of things.

Karen had come round the shop later on, admiring the furniture and china. He had to find space to display the stuff and he'd been wrapped up in the thing, not really listening to her, then picking up on what she was saying, about how they could use the furniture and he should put it aside.

'Anyone want another drink?' Denise asked, and Will was sure she was touching Carter up.

'Go on then,' Balti said.

He watched Denise as she went to the bar, Eileen following.

'That Eileen's gagging for it, Will,' he said.

'Leave it out. I'm a married man.'

Balti watched the girls behind the bar, then turned and looked down the street. The wind had picked up. He wondered how McDonald was doing. Getting stitched up as he sat there enjoying a free pint. Sitting in Emergency while Balti sat in The Unity. The bright light of a sterilised hospital and the warmth of a friendly pub. Life was good sometimes. Taking the pint Denise placed in front of him. Tipping the magic liquid down his throat. Letting the lager take the strain.

DEATH TRIPPING

The vicar was consulting the holy book and delivering his words of comfort. The mourners listened in silence. Mango sat next to his dad. To his right was Debbie, to the other side of the old man Jackie, who was holding a tissue to her eyes. Now and then she lowered it tentatively, but never for longer than a few seconds. Mango looked at his sister with a dull throb of irritation. Her hair was freshly dyed and the roots that normally showed through and annoyed him were gone. At least she wasn't sobbing out loud, sending echoes into the rafters, embarrassing him.

The Wilsons were together in their grief. Mango had bought a new suit. The material smelt good. The cut was perfect and elevated his already heightened sense of worth. His gear was new and alive and boasted prosperity and success, in a church that was old and musty and stunk of death. Flowers added colour to the dark interior, but were doomed to wilt in the next couple of days and only served to increase the morbid atmosphere. The best thing was the stained-glass windows.

The scenes incorporated the usual classic imagery—Christ as a child with his mother and father, Christ as a young man drinking with the saints, Christ dying nailed to a crucifix bleeding from his head and chest, myth and history rolled in together, promoting self-sacrifice and resurrection. The heart and lungs had been crushed by the weight of the dying man, the sadism of the Romans right there above the congregation, detailed in black and white, red and yellow. It was the colour that dominated. The images melted as clouds shifted outside. Glass trapped sunlight and filtered it through a prism, thousands of precious stones converging in raking shafts of light that cut through and highlighted floating dust, illuminating the epitaphs carved into grey stone walls.

Margaret was the beloved wife of Nicholas Young, and the loving
mother of Emily and Patricia Young. She had died in child birth in 1847,
and though she was greatly missed by her husband and children, they
were content in the knowledge that she sat with God in a kingdom of
eternal light, surrounded by angels and saints, with their son James
who had died with his mother, an unborn spirit that would rest forever
in the heavenly realm, a celestial world where there was nothing but
love and eternal joy.

Mango tried to ignore the effects of the stained glass and concentrate on the vicar. He didn't want to read the memorials. They were
depressing. He'd never seen the vicar before because, after all, the
Wilsons weren't exactly a churchgoing family, but even so, this was
the correct ending. Having a man of the cloth, someone trained and
educated in the Christian mysteries, delivering the final tribute made
things official. But Mango was finding it hard following the vicar. He
was lecturing them about blind material values and a new spiritual
order, about good and evil and the bliss that followed the long, hard
struggle. Materialism had swamped humanity and at times like these
it was important to remember that there was a spirit that needed
nurturing, that death should be seen not so much as an end but as a
new beginning. Mango wondered whether the vicar had ever heard of
shares and bonds and the profits available when a man with business
acumen invested wisely? The vicar had obviously never felt the tug of a
brand new Jag eager to soar past the hundred mark. Now that was living.

Mango concentrated on the sky behind the Christ Child, keeping
his eye on the shepherds and all the other potential animal-worriers
in the background going about their hopefully legitimate business.
There was straw for bedding and no room at the inn, which wasn't
surprising when, even today, with technology racing ahead and the
materialist ethic firmly established, thousands slept on the streets
of London. Mango was glad he hadn't been in Bethlehem at the time,
because he would have put his foot down and passed the pregnant
mother roaming alleyways, heading for the orphans that the priests
sold to men of means. Because, when you had a hard-on and listened to
the priests in charge, it wasn't really prostitution if the girls were cared

for by holy men and protected by God. And the girls remained virgins in the eyes of the creator. The synagogues were charging through the nose, and those shepherds caught his attention again. He had to keep them under constant surveillance. Never turn your back on a sheep shagger. He was back with the light losing the images. Back inside a grey church. A religious sanctuary where his most private thoughts were no longer his own.

Mango's dad leant forward and his son started. Was it a heart attack? A stroke or something? The shock of realisation? No, he was smiling, the old sod. He was actually smiling in the middle of a funeral service. Maybe not. No. He was sitting up again. It was a trick of the light. Because Mr Wilson was a decent citizen who, though he never went to church, nevertheless respected the sanctity of religion. The church may no longer have been a focus for the community, but Mr Wilson would have been shocked by its destruction. It was an old building that went back hundreds of years and there had to be something like that around, even if the congregation was tiny. Birth, marriage and death were all worth celebrating. It was something that had to be done. And done properly. Speaking of which, they were going to have a good drink after. Destroy a few brain cells and do it in style. It was what the deceased would have wanted. It was a chance to wash away the sadness.

The light in the sky over Bethlehem consisted of various shades of purple and the star marking the occasion was a brilliant yellow that left an impression. Mango saw the spaceship hovering, recording the miracle birth for later study. A peephole through time and all you had to do was lift your head and blank the words fired by the cross-dresser in the pulpit. No, that was out of order. He couldn't think like that in God's house, bringing everything down to the gutter. He had to keep his mind focused. He was fine at WorldView because his attention was centred and he could listen to his colleagues and the clean thoughts and cleaner language rubbed off. It was true that some of his colleagues were far from angelic, but it didn't matter really because they were proper and confident. There was pure colour and light flooding through the window, a focal point within the church. He should be able to appreciate the place for what it was, rather than wondering how much it cost to enter, or whether the smile on a dodgy-looking shepherd's face was genuine, or what kind of benefits Mary could expect as a single mum.

Mango was tired. He wished he was alone and able to enjoy the sunlight. Just sit in total silence for a few minutes, with all the radios and TVs turned off, the cars still, everyone deep asleep minding their own business. Nobody preaching, telling you what to think and what to do. He wasn't hearing much of the service, now and then returning to the vicar's words, making an effort, and then he was off again. Moving from the colour to the pictures and back to the colour. He had to pay attention. A small boy at school with the teacher shouting that if he didn't pay attention to the mathematical equation on the blackboard he'd end up stupid and on the dole and never do anything with his life. But the coffin the Wilsons had chosen was top of the range and Mango felt proud putting it on his credit card. His old man and uncle nodded their heads solemnly and thanked Jimmy, the kid they'd seen grow to be a man and make his fortune. They were proud of the boy. Mango smiled and looked at the mouth moving in time.

The vicar had a kind face and seemed sincere enough. Mango made a last effort and realised the vicar was telling a story. Something personal from his own life. An event that had come to pass a few days earlier. At seven in the morning in fact, because, you see, the vicar was an early riser. Every day was a new beginning. He was walking his dog around the common when he'd found a purse belonging to one of his parishioners. An elderly lady with little money, who was a regular at the church—it would be nice to see some of the people here today come again because religion had an important part to play in everyday life—and he had made a detour. This wasn't a problem. He'd tucked the purse through the woman's letterbox as he didn't want to bother her. Maybe she was still asleep or valued her solitude. The curtain twitched and before he knew where he was he'd been invited inside for tea and biscuits, and Reggie the labrador sat at his feet and was patted on the head and given a Digestive. That was the most important thing in life, fellowship. Everyone gathered here today should rest assured that this feeling of unity and giving continued beyond the grave and in to the next world. This was truly the greatest comfort.

Mango agreed, but had been distracted as the story drew to its happy conclusion.

He saw a new face in the stained glass. The mouth was moving and filled with a pulsating red light. It was a young mouth drowning in blood and wine, and sometimes the edges curved up, then down. Mango recognised features in the face. It had been in the window for hundreds of years and the expression was changing all the time, clouds covering the sun before relenting and letting the light through. He understood why it was so dark inside the church, and why the atmosphere was sombre and why stained glass had been invented. It forced you to lift your head and look towards the sky, towards the sun, like plants that always found a way towards the energy source. At WorldView the layout of the office meant he was without sunlight during the day, the windows a mark of seniority and superiority reserved for his betters.

When the vicar concluded the service the mourners left the church and trouped into the graveyard. The earth was freshly dug and black against moist green grass, the yew tree still in the wind and the bark rock hard and bleeding. Mango looked around and the stones were older to his left, chipped and touched by moss, the inscriptions battered by rain and pollution, the dates more recent where they stood.

Mango breathed in deeply and smelt the richness of the soil, studying the earth, the shades of stones and white roots ripped and exposed. He watched a worm. It was thick and juicy and trying to dig back down under the surface, hurrying to escape predators. There were more words and tears, the vicar a good man at heart who was respectful towards the deceased, helping family and friends find solace in this dark hour. As the box was lowered Mango felt another flush of pride in the fine wood and quality handles. The first handful of earth that hit the lid of the coffin made a crisp sound that gradually dulled as people came forward to take their turn.

Will stood at the gate watching from a distance. He could see Mango and the rest of the Wilsons. Mango stood out in his new suit. Will hadn't known the dead woman very well, but she'd been friendly to him when he was a kid and that was enough. He wouldn't stay long because it was a family occasion and he didn't want to get in the way.

Will wondered where Mrs Mango was. He looked at his watch and left, leaving the Wilsons to get on with it.

'Do you want lager or bitter, son?' Mr Mango asked, when they were back home.

'Lemonade's fine,' Jimmy smiled.

The old man was looking sharp. His eyes were shining and he was standing tall. Jimmy Boy watched him pour the lemonade from a two-litre All White's bottle. It was quality stuff. None of your own-brand rubbish today. His old man was standing straight and fighting the sadness he felt at losing his sister.

'Thanks Dad.'

Mango went over to the table his sisters and cousins had filled with food and took a sausage roll. He wondered what it would be like when it came time to bury his own sisters. How would he feel? Jackie an old woman carted off to the morgue for the butchers to prod and cut up. Youth drained and replaced with whatever it was they put in your veins once you were dead. Top of the head sliced open. Inspecting the brain of a little girl playing in the street in summer, skipping with Debbie. He couldn't think about it right now.

'Your aunt was a fine woman,' Uncle Ken said, standing next to Mango.

'She was Ken. She was.'

'Shame your mother couldn't be with us at the church.'

'I know. She was upset. It hit her hard.'

Ken lifted his tankard to his mouth and gulped down three healthy mouthfuls of the Chiswick bitter. It was a bit of an expensive drink, but Jimmy had been more than generous. The lad had certainly done well for himself and didn't mind sharing his wealth around. Uncle Ken smiled at Mango and patted his nephew's shoulder with a huge hand.

'You're a good lad Jimmy.'

Auntie Stella came over.

'I've just seen your mum Jimmy, and she'll be out in a minute. I gave her something for her headache. She feels guilty not turning up for the funeral, but I told her she shouldn't worry. It's only the ceremony. We're family.'

Mango smiled.

'You can't beat family,' Ken said, putting his arm around Mango's neck. 'Family values, Jimmy. Look after your own and you won't go far wrong. That's the problem with this country. Too many selfish bastards only thinking about themselves.'

Mango nodded. His uncle was right. He'd finished his sausage roll and leant forward for a couple of egg sandwiches. Stella had her head on Ken's shoulder. Mango smiled at Ken and Stella and said he was going outside for some fresh air. Ken asked whether he was okay, because he was very quiet, are you alright son, except Ken was Jimmy's uncle, not his son. He was fine. Just sad. It was natural enough. Mango went out and sat with his back against the wall, by the door, below a slightly-open window. Someone had put on a CD. Irene always said she wanted music after her funeral. That she didn't want people to be sad.

'Irene loved John Lee Hooker. We should put some of his stuff on instead of this rubbish. She was mad about his music. She never could stand Elvis you know.'

'Strange that. I thought everyone loved Elvis.'

'Not Irene. John Lee Hooker was her favourite. Sonny Terry and Brownie McGhee were up there as well. Muddy Waters and Blind Lemon Jefferson. She loved the blues.'

'She didn't like Elvis at all? What about Gene Vincent and Jerry Lee Lewis?'

'No. None of them. She said it was watered down English folk music. She'd go to a session in an Irish pub if she wanted to listen to native music, but she preferred the blues.'

'Why do you think that was then? We all liked Elvis when we were young.'

'Wasn't black enough.'

'Elvis wasn't black at all. He was a white boy. A truck driver who loved his mother and decided to surprise her with a record.'

'I know Elvis wasn't black, it's the voice I was talking about. He sounded black but his face was white. That's why Irene never liked him.'

'But if he sounded black then why didn't she listen to him.'

'Because he wasn't black enough. He was copying the originals and

Irene didn't like that. She thought it was wrong nobody would listen to black music unless it was sung by a white boy.'

'Everyone likes Elvis.'

'Irene didn't.'

'Everyone except Irene then.'

'Pete didn't. He hated Elvis.'

'I don't remember that. Did he really?'

'All the kids his age did. The ones who liked punk hated Elvis and the Rolling Stones and the Beatles.'

'I can understand the Rolling Stones and the Beatles, but Elvis? How could they hate a dead man?'

'He wasn't dead then, was he? Not at first anyway. They said he was fat and old and that his money was as bad as how he looked.'

'That's a shame. I liked Elvis. Still do in fact. I was playing that Twenty Best collection I got for Christmas last night. You know, I never think of him as being old or fat. I always see him as a good old boy. Some kid in his pick-up truck driving along just minding his own business eating peanut-butter-and-jam sandwiches.'

'I don't suppose they cared once he died.'

'Who's that?'

'Punks.'

'They died, did they?'

'I suppose so, or at least the ones with spiky hair, but I mean the punks, or at least some of them, probably wouldn't have cared about Elvis if he'd been dead at the time, but then he died and they forgot about him I suppose. Now all you see is pictures of Elvis when he was young. It's like Marilyn Monroe. Once they're gone, you want to remember them at their best, don't you? No kid's going to pay good money for a picture of Elvis with a massive beer gut and side burns. You can go down The George if that's what you want.'

'Why do you think Irene liked blues so much then? I always found it too slow.'

'It was in her blood maybe. I don't know. Everybody has their own tastes. Human nature. Suppose it would be a bit sad for right now, when I think about it.'

Mango listened to the conversation. He could smell cigarette smoke and hear a pop tune he didn't recognise. The voices drifted away and he found himself listening to the song. When it stopped there was a lull, the sound of people talking rising up to fill the gap. The music restarted, this time low and respectful. Mood music that was trying to shift everyone sideways. Irene had told her family they should have a party and get pissed when she died. That's what everyone was going to do.

'I remember when we were kids. When the school got bombed and Irene was upset about it and started crying. She was the only one who did that you know, because the rest of us were chuffed. She loved her lessons. Especially geography and art.'

The voices had returned.

'It's a shame they closed it down, isn't it?'

'No they didn't, they repaired the school. It didn't take the teachers long to get us back in our classrooms again. They were dedicated.'

'They closed it last year and shifted the pupils. A cost-cutting measure.'

'Do you remember when Irene and Ted got married? I'll never forget that day. She was so drunk by the end of the reception that he had to carry her to the taxi, never mind through the front door. Mind you, Irene did like a drink. She lived life to the full, didn't she? Always laughing and enjoying herself. Nothing was ever too much trouble.'

'Salt of the earth, Irene. She had a good run, though sixty-nine's still a bit young.'

'At least she lived that long. Some don't, you know. She's alright where she's going. She was a believer. Mind out, here comes Ted.'

'You two alright?'

'Fine, Ted, fine. How about yourself?'

'Bearing up.'

There was a silence and Mango leant his head back straining to hear what was being said.

'Poor old Irene. She was the best woman ever walked the earth. We had a lot of good times and that's something to look back on and smile at I suppose. I've got lots of memories and everything, but God knows what I'm going to do without her. I can't believe she's dead. It's like this person is with you most of your life and then she's gone. And there's nothing you can do about it. I'm going to miss her so much.'

There was another silence and Mango felt awkward. He wanted to move away from the window but was stuck. It wasn't right sitting there listening to other people's conversations.

'Come on Ted. It's alright. I'll get you another drink. Come on mate.'

Someone seemed to have turned up the music. Not a lot, but enough. Mango could feel the vibration moving up his spine. The walls of the flat were thin. Right along the nerve endings into his skull. He tried to concentrate on the good and the positive. He thought about his car, the power and the glory of the Jaguar. Named after a wild cat, a killer, fleet of foot and lithe of form. It was the first time he'd made the connection. Of course, the jaguar was covered in fur and had a mind of its own, while his Jag was a brainless machine built to obey orders. Jaguars could shift a bit, because he'd seen wildlife programmes on the telly with all kinds of big cats running down gazelles, or whatever it was they ate.

'Give her another half hour and I'll get her up,' Mango's dad said. 'She's gone back to sleep again. She's had a bad shock. We all have. Except with her she just goes and gets pissed.'

'Never mind. Let her sleep.'

Mango couldn't place the voice. It was a man. That was all he knew. It was the music distorting things.

'I don't know what to do sometimes. I mean, the boy's gone, but there isn't a day goes by that I don't think about Pete. Where he is and whether he's still alive. Sometimes I think he'll turn up one day, and the next moment I know there's no chance. She's been drinking all these years and it doesn't do any good. It doesn't solve anything and she only feels worse the next day.'

'Maybe she'd drink anyway. You don't know. Everyone has their crutch. She must get something out of it, otherwise she wouldn't do it, would she?'

'I know all that, but it makes her unhappy. The more you have, the more you want.'

There was silence and Mango reckoned the two men had moved away from the window. Maybe he should talk to his dad about Pete. Funny thing was, he'd never really gone into it with the old man. At least not for a good few years. He couldn't remember. The door opened and Jackie came outside, surprised to see her brother sitting there on his own. She shut the door and lowered herself down next to him. She was average-looking and a bit shabby the way she dressed. Her appearance was okay now, but she needed to take more pride in herself. She wore cheap clothes and cheap perfume. Everything about his sister made Mango think of cheapness.

'You alright, Jimmy? You're very quiet. That's a nice suit you've got. Irene liked black suits.'

Poor old Jackie. Working in the baker's earning three quid an hour.

'I'll miss Irene. We used to meet up every Thursday dinner time in The Bull for a drink and a chat. We took turns buying each other sandwiches. She was so happy all the time. Whenever I was feeling miserable she'd cheer me up. Just being around her made you feel better somehow. She never seemed to worry about anything. Not that she didn't think, but she never let things bother her. She always told me that life was too short. That one day we would all be dead. Now she is.'

Mango had never known Irene and Jackie were close, though she went along with Irene and his mum to the bingo sometimes. He didn't know a lot about his sisters really. He'd never liked them much. He stopped himself. It wasn't that he didn't like them, it was something else. He didn't know them. At least not as grown-ups. It was his fault. They'd done nothing to him. But he remembered them going on and on when Pete went missing, crying and worrying, while he suffered in silence. They were common as well. He hated the thin walls of the flat and the cheap perfume they wore.

'Auntie Irene was one of the best. It's strange how it's always the good people who die, isn't it? You'd think it would be the other way round. It's like Pete. He was a good person, what I can remember about him. Not that he's dead. I don't mean that at all, but, well, you know what I mean don't you? I didn't mean he's dead. I know he's not.'

Mango knew what Jackie meant. She was right as well. Maybe she wasn't as thick as he'd thought. Just because she worked in a baker's. Perhaps she enjoyed it. He'd ask her.

'I always liked baking. Mum will tell you that. It's fine. They're good to me there and I can walk to work. I know everyone who comes in and we have a laugh. The pay could be better, but that's the same for most people. At least I've got a job and that's more than a lot of people can say. You've got to be grateful for what you've got. There's no point wishing for things you know you'll never have.'

It wasn't the same for her brother. Her poor, hard-working, loaded brother. He knew that the pressure was on and if he messed up one day he'd be out on his ear. There was no generosity at WorldView. There was no real happiness there because you were only as good as your last deal, and there was a balance sheet in operation that once it shifted away from the black spelt trouble. There was no room for passengers because the rewards at the top were good so you didn't want to fall off and you gave more and more of yourself. Every morning Mango had to haul himself out of bed and get dressed, and drive through the greatest city in the world to the greatest multinational, in his eyes anyway, and the best reward he had (and he almost wanted to grab one of his colleagues and shout it in their face), the best reward was that he'd sent Irene off in a top-of-the-range box and paid for the drink and spread afterwards. It was the first time he'd put decent money into his family, and it was all for a woman who he'd never really known, not properly, not like poor old Jackie who was rich in a way because she got to go down The Bull with her aunt who made her happy. Mango had never known that his chubby aunt with the dyed hair had gone to a school that had been bombed during the war and had grown up liking John Lee Hooker, that old blues man in the beer adverts.

'I didn't tell you, Jimmy,' Jackie was saying, looking away from her brother, then staring into his eyes. 'I've been seeing this bloke for three months and he wants us to get engaged.'

There was a silence. He had never really seen his sister's eyes properly and they were brilliant blue and sparkled as though made from stained glass, burning with a light that seemed to come from inside her skull. It was frightening. He wanted to look away. Mango thought he should say something, but didn't know what. Why was she looking at him like that, as though she could read his mind but still wanted approval?

'What do you think, Jimmy? I mean it's not a long time, is it, three months, but we get on well and he treats me like I'm special, which I know I'm not. I mean I'm not good-looking and I'm not clever—I don't think I'm thick, but not really smart. Thing is, he treats me like I'm special and he makes me feel good. That seems like enough for me. What do you think?'

'I don't know.'

Mango was confused. Why was she talking like this? Why was she slagging herself off? Why had he never noticed the blue eyes that swamped her clothes and perfume and made a three-quid-an-hour job in the baker's unimportant? He slagged her and Debbie off in his head, he knew he did, but that was because he was a wanker and those kind of values rubbed off after a while working at WorldView. You couldn't help but be affected. It was the price you had to pay, selling yourself, a prostitute in an Italian suit. It didn't mean Jackie had to think like that as well.

'I mean, yes, I do know. Give it a few more months and see how things go and then, why not? If that's what you want then get engaged, or don't waste any time, go and get married now. You don't have to ask me. What do I know about it?'

'I just wondered what you thought,' Jackie said, smiling and holding her brother's hand, and Mango was so surprised that he didn't even have time to feel awkward.

Jackie was off on a marathon sprint telling Mango how she'd met Dave when she'd been out in the West End one night with her mates and he'd been very polite and he'd phoned her up and they'd gone to the pictures together and he was very proper and they went out again to a pub in Ladbroke Grove and then for a pizza and he lived in Westbourne Park and was a mechanic and did alright for himself, and everything had gone on from there. They got on fine and he was very respectful and he reminded her a bit of Will because he was thoughtful and kind but not poofy or anything like that, and would you meet him one day? Of course I will, and Jackie threw her arms around Mango and gave him a hug and he felt a tear in his eye but luckily she didn't see because she was on her feet and going inside saying she was going to tell Dad about Dave now she'd told Jimmy, and Mango felt honoured that he was the first to know. Or at least the first of the two men.

Mango closed his eyes and leant his head back. He dozed a bit, but it was a shallow rest, thinking about his sisters. Family was important. He felt sad and happy at the same time. He was glad Jackie had spoken to him. Pete was gone but Debbie and Jackie remained.

It was getting dark. Mango wondered how long he'd been sitting outside. Nobody bothered him. He thought logically about the girl last night and tried to work out why he'd gone back to King's Cross. It was far easier picking up the phone and calling for home delivery. The girls were women and in far better shape, though they had a confidence about them that put him off a little, but there again, they weren't as stroppy. He felt better with call girls because somehow it all seemed more above board and business-like, and they came recommended by the chaps at WorldView. Their bodies were often tanned and usually toned, and the extra he paid for his sex was made up for by the gear they wore. They were clean. The street-walkers were full of disease, but he'd gone back to King's Cross because the girls made him feel important. His car was better than those of most of the other punters and he could be generous. He was helping put food in their mouths while the call girls were earning big money and probably servicing far more important clients than the likes of James Wilson. But never again. He was finished with all that. He was second in the Sex Division, but if the proper rules were applied he still had to get off the mark. The others didn't know so it would never really matter, but in this brief moment of clarity he admitted that it was pretty sad finding himself behind Balti and Harry. They couldn't even be bothered, not really anyway, preferring to dedicate their attention to the finer things in life.

'Why don't you come inside Jimmy?' his dad said, standing over him. 'You'll catch a cold out here. Come in and have something to eat and a proper drink. You've been out here on your own for ages.'

'Alright. I was having a think, that's all.'

'You know what they say about too much thinking. It's not good for your health. Look at me. Never had a thought in my life and it hasn't done me any harm.'

They both laughed.

'Here love, fill a plate for Jimmy will you?'

Mango watched Debbie load a paper plate. He was feeling better. It had done him good being on his own.

'You heard about Jackie's bloke then?' his dad asked.

'Sounds alright.'

'You think so? Good. That's what I thought. As long as she's happy. That's what's important.'

'A bit early to get engaged, but give it a few months and why not? Suppose you've got to let yourself go sometimes.'

'Exactly what I thought. She told me you'd said that. Sound advice. Get him round and see what we think. If he fits the bill fine, if not we'll sort him out. Only the best is good enough for my daughters.'

Mango saw Jackie and Dave sitting on the Wilson couch, lights dimmed and a spotlight shining into their eyes. The interrogation team wanted to know about Dave's background. His schooling and certificates. Whether he'd done well at university and served his country. How he would develop the family estates and his views on the encroaching environmental lobby threatening the local hunt. There would have to be blood tests and a line of heredity drawn back at least two hundred years. After all, the Wilsons didn't want poisoned blood seeping into the family line. They themselves didn't have certificates, medals, estates, and like every normal human being they hated bloodsports. They had fuck all in fact. But that didn't mean they lacked breeding. Far from it. They were keen on breeding. At least Mango was.

'It's funny having kids, Jimmy. One minute they're babies and it's almost like you blink and there they are all grown up living separate lives, threatening to have kids of their own. I'd be a granddad. Imagine that. Jackie will be getting married and getting pregnant and sitting around thinking of names for her kids just like me and your mum used to do.'

Mango bit into egg and bread. He thought of the name Jackie

Wilson and how his sister shared it with a singer. He wondered if Irene had been involved. So close and yet he had never realised. Jackie had soul, he knew that now. He supposed there was a link between blues and soul. He'd ask his old girl.

'You okay Mum?' he said, when the old man had gone for a piss and he'd spotted her across the room. She was sitting in a chair with a glass of Coke in her hand.

'Of course I am. Just a bit tired. Me and Irene were close.'

Mango sat next to his mum on a hard chair that rocked on unsteady legs. Her skin was pale and she was getting old. There was no colour in the face, but she was a tough woman all the same. She would live forever. He knew she'd never die and felt sad trying to imagine himself as a baby in her arms, wrapped up in the white blanket he'd seen in the photos. He hadn't had much hair and looked like a chimp. He thought of the ape in the zoo and how Pete had got angry when that kid started winding it up. Pete was always ready to help the underdog. He missed his brother more and more. You'd think things like that would dim with time, but they didn't. Pete had been close to his Auntie Irene as well.

Jimmy listened to his mum as she told various stories about his aunt. She emphasised the fact that she hadn't been feeling well and that was why she hadn't gone to the funeral. It had nothing to do with drink. Mango nodded his head and offered a few encouraging words, while around him everyone drank and told stories, voices merging together into a wall of noise that grew louder and louder. He saw Ted patting his eyes, trying not to cry. Mango's cousins stood together pouring lager down their throats, the language straying now, and he hoped they'd remember where they were. There was no reason starting a punch-up at their mum's funeral.

Mango stayed till after eleven, feeling more sober as those around him slurred their words and spilt their drink on the carpet. Debbie came to talk with him. His other sister didn't have anything amazing to say, no coming marriage, but as they spoke he realised she was okay as well. He smiled and she seemed happy enough given the circumstances. He looked at her eyes, and though they were blue like Jackie's he couldn't find the fire. That's what love did for you. He felt bad for Debbie. Everyone should have that fire. Something extra. He thought about that bloke she'd been set to marry. Years ago now. He'd let her down. A week to go and he called it off. Joined the merchant navy. Wanted to see the world. She never heard from him again, or at least not as far as Mango knew. He wanted to hug Debbie and tell her it was alright. He wondered if it still bothered her. He couldn't ask.

When Mango left he did the rounds and was hugged and breathed on, his hand shaken by the men and his cheek kissed by the women. Jackie hugged him and said thanks.

Outside he was alive and free. The sky was heavy and the glare of the city meant the stars were invisible, but he felt happy. He was suddenly relieved to be away from everyone, yet glad he'd spent time with his family and spoken with Jackie and Debbie. Somehow everything had worked out fine. He walked towards the car juggling keys, flicking the electronic lock and buckling his belt. The engine started first go and Mango marvelled at the smoothness of the Jag as he reversed and then straightened up. The interior smelt clean and was revitalising after the smoke and alcohol. He was moving in different circles now.

It was a short drive back to Fulham and he watched the drunks on their way home stumbling over broken pavements, kebab houses full of customers, a tall woman in black leather trousers and a red jacket standing at a bus stop. Her hair was swept back and she had thick lipstick that matched the jacket. She was a real cracker and shouldn't be hanging around late at night on her own. He pulled over and reversed. The window opened automatically. He leant across the passenger's seat and asked her if she wanted a lift.

'No thanks.'

He asked her if she was sure. It was late at night and London was full of muggers with their eyes on her handbag and men who would follow a woman home and cut her to ribbons.

'I said no thanks.'

Mango wanted to help and told her that it was okay, he'd just been to a funeral, and did she understand that there were some very sick people around. She shouldn't be travelling by public transport because it was dangerous and the buses were full of perverts with skinning knives tucked into their coats.

'Why don't you just fuck off,' the woman shouted, her face contorted.

He was shocked by the strong language and about to respond when he noticed a bus approaching in his mirror. The Jag eased forward and Mango shook his head sadly. Perhaps he was being a little naive, because after all the woman didn't know who to trust. She didn't know that he was an upright citizen who earnt a decent wage and had helped pay for a first-class funeral. How could she know? But the language really was a bit much and the woman needed a lesson in manners, though he blamed it on the parents really, because if sound values were applied early enough in life children grew up to be decent citizens able to contribute to society. It was too late for the woman, and he mustn't really blame her because he read the papers every day and there were so many cases of people going missing and unprovoked assaults on ordinary men and women just trying to live honest lives, on the way to the cornershop for a carton of milk when they suddenly found themselves covered in blood, slashed across the face, cut to the bone. It should have been obvious from the suit and car that he was safe.

Pete should have been more cautious. If he'd been determined like that woman then perhaps he'd still be alive. It was a fine line between trust and plain rudeness. It was better not to take chances and they'd had a great day at the zoo. Pete had been amazed by the polar bears. A man standing next to them said the bears loved to travel big distances. They roamed for thousands of miles through freezing conditions. It must've been hard for such a proud and powerful creature to be confined in such a small artificial world.

Back in the flat Mango turned on the TV and moved through the channels. There was a documentary he'd seen before. Johnny Rotten was snarling through the screen and then Joe Strummer was talking to the camera. It was old footage and the narrator was telling the story of punk. Mango wondered whether Pete was in one of the crowd scenes. He'd never shared his brother's interest in the music, and it was a shame really because Pete had taken Will along to quite a few gigs. Maybe he'd missed out, but he'd still been close to his brother. He missed him so much. It was like Jackie said. It was always the good people that died, or went missing. Everyone had their story. Those kids up in King's Cross had their lives and he knew he was a bad man and wanted to do something to make things right, but didn't know what, and soon the natural chemical balance would shift and he'd be working to another agenda.

He made up his mind that he'd give Pete the best send off possible if they found the bones. He'd spend thousands of pounds. People said it was a waste splashing out on funerals, because the person who'd died was gone, but ceremony was important. If you couldn't do things properly then, when could you? It made him feel better and he was listening to a girl with jet black hair and heavy mascara and she seemed very young and sincere, so he switched channels to a mindless Miami cocaine-smuggling story where the men carried Uzis and wore pigtails and all the women were blonde-haired beauty queens in tiny bikinis that showed off their perfect figures and their sparkling dead eyes.

PART THREE

SKIN-BONE-DRUM-BASS

The brown sauce bottle was empty, so Balti leant over the back of the chair to the table behind. Nice and full, he squeezed the plastic container and added a generous helping to his plate. A full English breakfast with chips for two-pound twenty, and Andy the Turk always gave his regulars an extra cup of tea on the house. You couldn't beat it for value. Balti only came in two or three times a week, but it filled him up for the rest of the day and probably saved a few bob in the long run. It was tasty food as well. Freshly cooked and served with a chat and a smile. Sausage, bacon, beans, egg, two slices and the chips he always ordered on top. Andy's was a good place to start the day, watching the world yawn and stretch and get itself in gear as he sat on his arse going nowhere. Least he could let his breakfast sit. He was in no hurry watching that Cockney Red bastard outside selling tomatoes and peppers on a fine August morning.

Balti's paper stayed at the back page as he got stuck into his breakfast. Funny thing was, not working he thought he'd be eating less, but found he was as hungry as when he was grafting for McDonald. It was the boredom that did it. He'd never realised how much he relied on work to fill the gaps. Going home knackered had its benefits. When he finished he leant back and savoured the warm glow in his gut, reaching for the tea. He sipped the magic brew and turned from the back page focus on an Italian international who'd reportedly soon be earning twenty grand a week in England. The star striker was said to be collecting an undisclosed signing-on fee, moving expenses and a loyalty bonus if he could be bothered to stay with the club for more than two years. His agent was earning his cut and the player a crust. More like the fucking bakery. It was crazy money. He flicked through sports pages filled with cricket reports and athletics meeting results. When he hit the racing results he flipped to the front page and another sex murder. They all came out in the summer. All the nutters and pervs. He skimmed through outraged tales of sexual violence and violent sex, past the saucy photos featuring well-endowed blondes who loved holidaying in the sun, looking for something to get his teeth into.

When he was working he wanted a paper he could flick through and laugh at, but signing on he was looking for a bit more. A few articles that would hold his attention longer than five minutes and help pass the time. There was fuck all here. He gave up and stared out the window waiting for something to happen, Phil the Man U fan rearranging his yams and cabbages. After another slow cup of tea Balti paid Andy and left. He walked through the market and turned down a side street, past the construction yard towards the common. He'd sit in the sun for a while. It was going to be another scorcher and Balti was already sweating. It was the car fumes that did him in. Down a back street it was better. When he came out of the shadows he was hit by the fumes. He waited for the lights to turn red and crossed with the mums, kids, pensioners, unemployed men and women using up time.

The billboard overlooking the zebra crossing was new and boasted a blonde in a short red skirt. She was young, or at least made up to look young. She must be ill. Almost a child when he concentrated on the picture. The advertising industry seemed obsessed with thin, pale-skinned girls as it flirted with anorexic child-sex. The girl was so skinny that at first he thought it was part of an AIDS warning. It took him the length of the crossing to see that the billboard was promoting a fashion house. Fucking horrible. AIDS and bulimia. Like shagging a fucking skeleton.

The girl reminded him of the kids you saw in TV documentaries on child prostitution in the Philippines, Thailand, Cambodia. All around the world. Virgin life-savers. Anywhere but England. Nepalese girls drugged and shipped to the knocking shops of Bombay, and the television crews went undercover and recorded eight- and nine-year-olds on sale to sick old cunts on their way home from work. The yanks were another favourite target, because though they filled up the viewing schedules with shit sitcoms and the music charts with middle-of-the road tunes, the researchers still liked having a go. The big shock, apparently, was that *middle-class* kids were on the streets, lining up outside the shopping malls and drive-in takeaways. It was a big bad horror show and there was a happy, warm feeling that England was in the clear. That it didn't happen at home. Until a crew zoomed in on Bradford and Leeds and even London itself.

Balti thought about Mango. It made him sick, all that sort of thing. Undercover video shots of small girls in a windowless Bombay whorehouse. He didn't know how a bloke could fancy girls that young. It was unnatural somehow. You had to have standards.

Balti sat on his usual bench and skinned up. Will had passed a bit of blow his way the week before and he was making it last. Taking things nice and slow; clock ticking, detonator disconnected. Mind you, he'd nicked five car stereos and sold them down Audio 5 the week before. This was an easy place to dump nicked gear. He was thinking ahead and hitting the jackpot. Fifty quid on the Lottery and he was a winner. He'd soon be laughing. No more sitting on park benches rotting away. No more haggling with that slimy old cunt Stan in Audio 5. He'd be straight down Heathrow and into the departure lounge, sitting at the bar sipping a bottle of Becks waiting for take-off. A month in the sun and when he got back he'd hire some posh financial adviser and invest wisely. A month in the sun at a classy resort. None of your everyday Ibiza packages. Fuck that. No, he'd go somewhere in the Caribbean. A real luxury hotel that looked after your every need. He fancied Jamaica. One of those paradise hotels in the brochures where you could eat and drink as much as you wanted and then swim it off in a crystal-clear ocean. There'd be no radioactivity or sewage eating into his skin. No candyfloss and processed chips to weigh him down. He'd trudge back up the beach and crash out on a sun bed. He saw the massage girl rubbing coconut oil into his back, easing the tension and getting rid of the knots in his shoulders. Heaven on earth with nothing to worry about. No dole queue, bills or loonies. Pam and Liz would have to wait till later. Maybe he'd blow them out. Fuck it, he had the readies so he could do whatever he wanted.

Balti inhaled deeply and watched George on the far side of the
common pushing his trolley. The old boy had a goal in life and was
serving the community, but Balti was no mug. He was playing the
numbers game and confident of his chances. He deserved a bit of luck.
It would make a change. Life had to get better and when he was in the
West Indies he'd be strolling along golden sand and turning off into
the jungle. Through the palm trees to a natural waterfall where he'd
buy best quality herb from a local rasta. A day in the jungle wandering
back to the hotel for his evening meal of lobster and sweet potatoes. A
few chilled Red Stripes to wash it down. He'd sit on the verandah and
get talking with the massage girl. A Kingston woman training to be a
doctor, using her knowledge to earn a living. She'd sit on the porch and
they'd talk till midnight and then she'd leave. They'd meet the next day
and romance would blossom. Maybe he'd invite her back to England
when he returned to face the press. No, he didn't want to spoil things
bringing her to London. He could see the scene now. Pam and Liz at the
airport throwing themselves at his feet. He didn't need it. What would
she think seeing him in Jamaica and then back in London? It would
spoil the image. He'd get things sorted at home and move to JA. Spend
the rest of his life in wedded bliss growing pumpkins and sitting on
his porch. Natural respect and no aggro.

Balti inhaled again. Will was a good man. So was Karen. A good
woman. They were good people. Diamonds. It was all about people.
Men and women were from the same egg. Different chromosomes
and he would've been a bird. He laughed at the thought. That was all it
came down to, the difference between X and Y. He was glad he wasn't a
bird. It had been a narrow escape. It was bad enough being a bloke, let
alone a bird. Or a black woman from Kingston fighting the prejudice.
That would be harder. He'd move to Jamaica and tell them all to fuck
off, McDonald and the social and the old bill in their crawling patrol
car watching George on the other side of the common, but he wouldn't
forget his mates. He'd set up in business with Will and Karen. They'd
come over and get into the import-export game. Shifting old reggae
and ska over to London. They'd fucking love it. And he wouldn't forget
Harry. He could come over as well. He'd buy him a nice little place on

the beach, something with a swimming pool, a couple of miles away so Balti had a bit of breathing space. Carter could visit, but he couldn't have him staying, because he wanted to get away from all that competitive football, the dog-eat-dog of it all. Strictly for fun in Jamaica, and anyway, he was a married man now with pumpkins and responsibilities. Sitting on the porch breathing fresh air, a different world to London.

He'd come back regular. Especially for the big games. He could see it easy enough, a sixth round Cup game against Spurs. Land at Heathrow at ten, meet the lads by eleven, a few beers and then turn the bastards over 5–0, with Ruud at the controls and Johnny Spencer scoring a hat-trick. Chase the yids down the Fulham Road after the game, then round off the day with a full session and a curry down Balti Heaven. England at its best. Welcome home Balti. But he knew the reality was different. Tony down the pub had been back and forward between Kingston and London since he was a kid and he reckoned it was well rough. That the poverty made England look rich. It could be a violent place and even music-wise ragga and jungle were more important than reggae and rocksteady these days. So maybe he'd have to go somewhere else. How could he know? He was waiting for pay day, when the numbers would rack up right and give him his due. He saw George catch sight of him and change direction, glad he'd found someone to talk to, and Balti didn't mind his company these days. With an Andy special tucked away and a nice bit of blow, everything was sweet. He had his dreams and the chance to make those dreams come true. He was used to George now. He was a sound enough bloke, even if he *was* a nutter. Least he was harmless. The world was full of nutters.

'Hello son,' George called, his trolley packed tight.

'Alright George? You've been busy. It's only ten.'

George sat down and wiped his face with a rag. There were wet patches under his arms and a strong smell of sweat. He needed a bath. You had to look after yourself.

'I woke up at five and felt like I'd been given an electric shock. I was raring to go and was up and out by half-past. It was such a beautiful morning, walking through empty streets with just the cats for company. One or two cars, but otherwise a city empty of life. The air was cooler and the engines hadn't started up yet. I was ready for the big push and here I am with a heavy cargo and an early finish. I'm going to dump this lot and start again. See if I can do two loads before midday. I won't stop long. There's work needs doing. Why don't you give it a go? We could work together. We'd make a fine team.'

Balti tried to imagine himself working the bins with George. He didn't fancy it somehow. The bloke was speeding and Balti was taking things nice and slow. George needed to hit the brakes. He shook his head. He didn't like the idea that George saw this younger man as similar to himself. Balti was passing through. He wasn't a dosser.

'Is that drugs you're smoking?' George asked, looking over his shoulder and then back at Balti, lowering his voice.

'Sort of.'

'Can I have a go? It won't get me hooked, will it? I don't want to end up an addict with no idea of what's going on around me, living in a fantasy world.'

Balti laughed.

'It's harmless. Drink and fags do more damage.'

'What about that ecstasy stuff you read about then? Now that's a real killer. Kids dropping dead like flies. I've heard that their brains explode. I wouldn't want any of that, though the way I'm feeling now I don't think I need it. I've got so much energy I could shoot off into space. I feel like Superman.'

George inhaled and sat back. They were silent for a while. Balti looked towards Churchill Mansion. He was thinking of that scouse bird up in Blackpool. He wondered what she was doing now. She was alright.

'That helped,' George eventually said. 'It happens like this. I don't feel like doing much for months and then I'm off when the sun comes out. I have to slow down a little. Did I tell you that once I was out walking early and I saw a fox coming down the road. He was big as well. Probably thought he had the streets to himself, but he didn't mind that I was there. He kept going on his way. I shouldn't sit around talking though. I know what people think. They think the old man is eccentric, a bit of a character, maybe a little strange. But I have a purpose. I have an

aim. I have ambition. That drug helped. I'll give myself till twelve and
have a nap maybe, if I get another trolley done. I'll be off now.'

Balti watched George struggle with his load. The poor bloke
needed to knock himself out, but sometimes you didn't get the chance.
It was easier being sedated than trying to fight back. Balti thought
about fighting back but wouldn't have known where to start. There
was nowhere to go. Nothing that could be done. He was white trash
like they said. Scorned by both the Right and Left. Judged by silver-
spoon commentators who didn't understand the complexities of
English culture. The behaviour and use of language. You couldn't win.
Whatever you said or did was going to be wrong. So you gave up instead.

He hung around for ages, watching people pass and the pure white
clouds above play kiss chase with the sun. He was hot and fancied a
pint. A cold pint of lager. Maybe he'd treat himself, seeing as he had the
money from the stereos. Just the one though. He didn't want to end up
getting pissed every day like the winos you saw year in year out, rotting
their livers and brains. He'd top himself before he ended up like that.
He was a social drinker. He had to keep a firm hold on things.

Will sifted through the racks, searching for the vinyl that would give
him that special kick, the intense feeling that discovery brought. He
was meeting Karen in half an hour for a drink during her break, and
using the time wisely. It was funny to think that eight months ago
he'd been in this same shop and had first spoken to her a few feet from
where he was now standing. It was pure romance, a mutual interest
in good music bringing them to the record shop at the same moment.
Now they were living together and he couldn't imagine anything
coming between them. They were made for each other. It was one of
those things you know is right the moment it happens. It was a fresh
start for a new year and it had all happened so fast. Now they were
sharing a bed and that was perfect as well. Will was happy. More happy
than he'd ever been. The balance was just right.

A Blackbeard album passed under Will's fast-moving fingers and
he paused over Two Sevens Clash. Now that was real culture. The Clash
had understood. He flicked the yellow cardboard and stopped dead.

Heavy Duty Manners by Keith Hudson, and the sticker said it was in mint condition. Will was well chuffed and lifted the album cover from its polythene sleeve. He inspected the cover and hovered for a while, before half-heartedly completing his inspection of the rack. The bloke behind the counter had just put on a ragga track. Will hated ragga. All that macho guns-and-bitches bollocks. He hated violence. He paid for Keith Hudson and hurried out into the street. He couldn't wait to play the album. Maybe he could make it home before he met Karen. He checked his watch. He didn't have time. There was a small record player at work that he sometimes used, so he'd give it a spin there. Better still, he'd shoot off home after he'd met Karen. He'd just have to open the shop a bit later. The punters could wait. He wanted to hear the record on some proper gear. Usually he listened to tapes at work, only using the dodgy record player when a customer wanted to hear one of the shitty old albums he kept by the door.

'You're early,' he said, walking into The Crown and finding Karen already sitting at the bar.

'I punched out a quarter of an hour ahead of time. I thought I'd find you here already. I've really missed you today.'

'I saw you this morning.'

'I know, but I still missed you. Silly isn't it?'

'No, it's nice. I missed you too. Do you want a half in that, or another pint?'

Will paid for two pints and ordered a couple of Ploughmans. They went to a table and worked their way into the corner. The Crown was a steady kind of pub and didn't get flooded during the day. It was a hard-drinking, middle-aged pub at night and they must've been coining it behind the bar.

'Look what I found,' Will said, opening the plastic bag and pulling out the album he'd just bought.

Karen smiled and kissed his cheek. He was like a school kid with his enthusiasm for music. It was a quality she found attractive. It meant their life together would never be sad. They were solid and there was an understanding she'd never known before with a man. He was as open as anyone she'd known and it meant they could live together.

She was happy with Will. They were great together. It had been love at first sight, though that wasn't strictly true, because she'd known him when she was a kid, but then it had only been a childish crush. She'd met the family, her old friend Ruth, and it was natural and easygoing. Will had his shop and mates and interests, and she had her job with the council and her friends and interests. They were into a lot of the same things, while their friends were separate, which was healthy. They both hated the idea of happy couples going out in groups of six and eight and any even number under the sun. It gave them room to breathe. Independence was important. So were the Ploughmans coming their way, because Karen was starving. That last case had built up her appetite. If she could change anything, it would be the amount of dope Will smoked, but he was a laid-back bloke and it was only an extension of his character.

'What do you want to do this evening?' Karen asked.

'Listen to this record.'

'Nothing else?'

'That's enough.'

'I thought I could make us something special for dinner. Don't look surprised. There's no reason, I just thought it would be nice.'

It was fine by Will. Sometimes it seemed unreal how he'd met Karen and how everything had gone so well for them both. He'd start thinking that it couldn't last, that she was too good for him, but then Karen was with him again and everything really was fine. It would be something to look forward to while he was in the shop. There was nothing better than a good bit of music, a decent smoke, a drink or two, some home cooking, and quality time with a quality woman. That's what love and comradeship was all about. That's the way men and women should be. You couldn't ask for more.

Balti had only planned on the one, but he'd got the taste and was on his fourth pint. He'd had a chat with Len behind the bar and Eileen had said hello, but The Unity was near enough empty except for a few pensioners sipping halves of stout and bitter. He sat at the bar and Len asked if he'd ever met up with those Paddies who'd come in that time looking for him. Balti smiled. It was a couple of weeks since he'd thought about McDonald. He shook his head. It was funny, but something happened and it was important for a while, and then it was sorted, and before you knew where you were it was forgotten. It was months ago when they'd gone down Balham. Balti tried to remember the details, but it was blurred now. An old video ready to be recorded over. It was history. When Len went out back he moved to the window. He'd been on his toes for ages, but nothing had happened. McDonald had learnt his lesson. Don't fuck with Balti. Even so, he shouldn't get sloppy even now. He saw the van speeding down the street, indicate right and park up outside. Carter jumped out and came into the pub.

'Alright Balti?' he asked, looking toward the counter.

Balti watched Carter go to the bar. He said something to Eileen and she shook her head. Balti liked Eileen, but knew he didn't stand a chance. Maybe he'd take her over to Jamaica. She could work in the bar at the hotel while he sat on the beach getting oil rubbed into his back. At the moment she wouldn't look at him. Birds expected you to be doing well. It was a power trip. Whatever you said, it was the law of the jungle. Most of them looked at blokes as a provider, the old lion-out-on-the-prowl-hunting routine. It was in the fucking genes. You never saw a dead-end bloke with a quality bird. No chance. You needed to be flash and drive a convertible to pull the models. The real hundred-carat crumpet. You had to have something to offer. They weren't interested in your mind. They wanted to be looked after. Not when it came to one-nighters, but long term. Slags were like blokes, just wanted a good fuck. The best you could hope for was someone on your own level, though if you accepted that yourself then maybe it wasn't surprising others looked at you the same way.

Balti couldn't be bothered about it all now. There was no way out. More jobs lugging bricks. Sitting on his own drowning his sorrows staring into a glass. He'd finish this drink and go see his mum. He couldn't remember the last time he'd been round the old girl's. Carter came over, said a few words, and went back to work. He seemed wound up. Balti finished his drink, took the glass to the bar, and left.

It was a fifteen-minute walk to his mum's. As he went he started thinking about her and how he should go round more often. His dad had run off when he was fifteen and they'd never heard from the cunt again. For the last five years his mum had been living with a retired copper. It was hard to take at first. A fucking copper. Everyone hated the old bill. They were fucking scum. It had been a few years ago when she met him, and once he got talking with the bloke he'd found that he wasn't that bad. He would never forget he'd been old bill, but you had to go along with things sometimes. Bob treated his mum well. That was the most important thing.

Bob could tell a story. With his tales about the Krays and Richardsons. Mad Frankie Fraser who was on the telly these days. Now there was a bloke who'd never given up, no matter what the system did to him. You had to admire people like that. Balti never knew if Bob was telling porkies or had really been involved with the top gangsters of the day. When he reminisced he spoke of the Met as though he and the force were one. After serving his time he'd set up in the security business, made a packet to go with his pension, and was willing to share it with his new love. Balti's old girl had peace at last and a four-bedroom house, money in her purse and all her old friends. She'd done well for herself and Balti realised that he was thinking the same way, that he was seeing her as a woman who needed looking after. But it was different, because his old man was a cunt and he loved his mum. His dad had knocked her about and treated them like shit. It wasn't even like he was an alkie, and he'd made good money on the trains. Till he lost his job. There were no excuses. He was a cunt pure and simple. If Balti ever saw him again he'd give him a good kicking. The old man had slapped him around enough when he was a kid. A fucking sadist. Slapped the old girl. Black eyes and missing teeth. Crying children. A mother's love and sobs. No wonder some women hated men. Maybe he was little better. He didn't know.

Balti stopped outside the house. He didn't like thinking about the past. At least not that part of it. You moved on. He opened the gate and walked between flowers lining the path. The grass was cut and the beds weeded. It was a nice house. His mum had done alright and she deserved her happiness. Everyone deserved to have some kind of happiness. Who cared if Bob was a former copper? None of it mattered when you got old because you should have your bit of peace and quiet. It showed there was justice in the world and gave everyone else something to look forward to, knowing that things could turn around.

He flashed back to his mum battered and bruised, and when the old man left Balti remembered her sitting in silence, and he remembered thinking that she had turned into a witch. The expression on her face said it all. Her face cracked in half and she went all spastic. She'd been like that for a year, not looking after herself and crying all the time. She began to smell and he was ashamed of her. Didn't invite his mates round any more.

Then she suddenly goes back to being his mum. Has her hair cut and buys some new clothes. Just like that. She said she was a better person for it because she'd been through the mill and got rid of old rubbish. Sometimes he wished the old man would stroll up cocky as fuck and Balti would put him in Emergency along with McDonald and all the other cunts who didn't show respect. He was big enough. All grown up and filled out, through the courts when he was a kid for all that juvenile nonsense. He smiled. When you had fuck all else going for you then blokes like him were better off than most, because at least you had your fists. That was something.

Up down, up down, making sure the paint covered evenly and filled in the odd crack, maintaining a steady flow. A big oblong of pure matt white with a cut of gloss to frame the south side of the room. The wall was straight and the work steady. The ceiling might be a bit tricky because it was covered in small shards of hanging plaster, but he'd take his time and dip the brush into all the nooks and crannies. Harry was into the rhythm listening to a DJ crack half-funny jokes in between a blend of lightweight guitar sounds and classic semi-hard rock. There was a cassette Will had lent him and he would play it when he finished the wall. The paint was going on a treat and the minutes slipping past. The room would look smart once it was finished. He was going with the motion of the roller. These were the best days, when everything went to plan.

His only regret was that his old mate Balti couldn't seem to sort out his head. He'd been signing on for months now, and while he felt bad for him, Balti needed to get his finger out. When you went back to nicking stereos from cars you were playing a loser's game. He was no snotty-nosed hooligan sciving off school. If he was going thieving, then he should be thinking big. Either that or find a job. Breaking into cars was for kids and junkies.

Harry laughed and wondered if his dream of last night would come true. They'd been back on that Mexican beach and it seemed they'd settled in for a long stay. They were living a lazy life swinging back and forward in their hammocks and had given up on the all-night raves. That last bit of aggro with the riot police had been well out of order. You went abroad to get away from all that. Balti had been spending a lot of time in front of the small mirror he carried in his rucksack. He seemed lovesick. The focus of this interest was the village school teacher. Harry hadn't noticed her before and was surprised to realise she looked like Karen. It wasn't Karen, he knew that well enough because Will was a mate and Balti wouldn't shaft his mates, but when he'd been on the psychedelics he looked across the beach and saw her there talking with the kids, her face shifting shape, and for a few seconds she was the spitting image. He wondered where Will was. Over the sea in Jamaica sitting in a shanty town with Scratch Perry blowing his mind, leaving Karen to educate the people.

It was late and Harry was walking home alone, stopping when he saw a light on the front porch of their hut. Karen was swinging back and forward in his hammock talking politics with Balti. He closed his eyes and listened. He was floating gently. She was telling Balti that he should fight back. Look at the Zapatistas and what they had achieved. Nobody could say they weren't real men. Maybe the real men were the men who spoke up and didn't get conned the whole time. Balti was nodding his head and Harry smiled. It was all words and his friend was like a kid in the classroom with a crush on the teacher. He waited for his best mate, his old friend the Balti king of West London, to reach over and hand Karen an apple. Standing in front of the class grinning at the blackboard. Karen was giving a lesson on English rebels, from the Diggers to the Suffragettes, to the streetfighters of Cable Street and the Poll Tax Rebellion, rows of skinny kids in the background asking whether it was true that Henry VIII had died of the clap.

Harry was carving his name into the desk with a clasp knife as Balti dozed next to him, head in his hands. His old man had been rioting the night before and his mate had a black eye. The history teacher was telling them about the Industrial Revolution and factory conditions before the formation of unions. They weren't interested. They were kids in The Shed, packed in tight so you could take your feet off the ground and let the mass of people carry you up and down the terrace. Every so often the old bill would form a wedge and try and get into the middle of The Shed and chuck a few of the young herberts out, but when the place was full they didn't have a chance. The whole end was having a knees up as it piled down the terrace taking the coppers with them. Nipple helmets bobbed over the heads of the crowd and were thrown towards the dog track.

Balti walked out of Stamford Bridge and bought himself a burger. He stood in a pub doorway waiting for the revolutionaries to arrive and together they were heading for the hills. Harry went back to the hut. He heard the sound of hooves and knew Balti was gone. He wasn't bothered because he wanted some time on his own. He felt no panic at the dangers facing his mate as he had realised he was inside a dream and because he had the knowledge he was able to turn the tables. He was lucid. Fucking right he was. Not only could he see the future, but he could take control. A whole new world was there for the taking and he understood that the argument about control was about to start all over again. He opened the paper and read about the Lottery win. The high court had decreed it valid, so Balti was in the clear. Balti had issued a statement saying he was going to settle down and marry a scouser he'd met in Blackpool. The hunt was on. She had to be found.

It was an easy, stupid sort of dream. Up down, up down, applying a nice even coat. Waiting for the DJ to tell a joke he thought was funny. It was the first time he'd been inside a dream and really known what was going on. Even then, though, there was some confusion, as he'd seemed to wake up, but was still asleep. He didn't know how often it would happen in the future, but it really did open all sorts of windows.

If he could take charge of his dreams he could do whatever he wanted. There would be no more limits and no more boundaries. Roller applying an even coat.

Carter slammed his foot down and yanked the hand brake into position. He jumped out of the van and ran back to the Sierra. The driver was getting out as well, but the dozy cunt was too slow. Flash him, would he, the fucking cunt. Carter hit him with the sawn-off snooker cue he kept under the driver's seat. He felt the hatred surge. There was blood splattered across the bastard's face and the man staggered back. Carter pulled the door towards him and rammed it home, brought the cue down on the back of the cunt's head. He fell into the car. His eyes were rolling. Carter looked around and hurried back to the van. He released the hand brake and shot off. Who did the cunt think he was? He'd had it coming. Flashing him like that. The fucking cunt.

Sometimes you had to be hard as well as skilful. With women you had to show your good side, pile on the charm and avoid aggravation. The goal was the most important thing. Flatter a bird and eventually she'd let you in. This constructive approach to the beautiful game rarely failed. If you could show them you were open to things they'd keep an eye on you. Find their interests and then connect up and you had it made. The next thing you knew you were slapping your balls against some bird's chin, chalking up points as you shot a wad of salty duff over their tonsils. Stroll in the pub and the rest of the Sex Division wondered how the old charmer had scored yet again. It was simple when you knew how.

When it came to cunts like that getting up your arse and flashing his lights just because you'd cut him up, then you couldn't fuck about with pretty talk. That was a mug's option. You had to get stuck in. All the great teams were like that. They could knock the ball around sweetly, but they were also able to stick a foot in when they needed. It made sense. Compete at the physical level and then let the imagination flow. You had to have a plan. The more straightforward the better. That's why the rest of the lads didn't get their leg over more. They were too busy with other things. You had to focus your attention.

Balti and Harry. A couple of fucking donuts. If they made the effort they'd be alright. Balti sitting in the pub on his own like that. He'd have to have a word. Shame he couldn't get him a job on the vans, but there was nothing going. You never knew. But he couldn't let him sink down like that. It was all in the head. Harry was doing alright, but how long since he'd done the business? Carter couldn't live like that. Fucking Will shacked up. Fair enough. As for Mango, he didn't know how much of what he said was true. All those points and nobody ever saw him with a bird. Still, he was way out in front so why should he bother? No complications. That was the way he lived. The trouble with blokes like Harry and Balti, though, was that they didn't care enough. Give them a few pints and they were happy just having a laugh. Where was the sense in that? They thought they were letting themselves down talking shit. They'd lost sight of the goal. With the points in the bag you could relax. The Sex Division was important. Carter loved women. He wanted them all the time. He loved the chat and the sex. It was like being a salesman really, giving them a line and reeling the catch in. Except it was all friendly. Nobody got hurt. Except cunts who tried to shove their bumper up your fucking arse.

Balti's mum poured two cups of tea. These cups sat on a tray. This tray rested on the coffee table. She sat on the sofa. Her son was in the chair on the opposite side of the table. The furniture was new and smelt fresh. She knew that her son had been drinking. Not a lot, mind, but he'd been drinking all the same. He wasn't drunk. She could smell the drink. She felt sorry for him being out of work, but felt that it was simply a case of him hanging on. Things changed. She had an optimistic approach to life. She handed her son his tea. He was a lovely boy. She thought of him as he was seconds after she had given birth. Smacked into the world. Opening his lungs to cry out and choking on the air. Covered in slime. A nearly-bald, peanut head. Pure virgin skin and frail little bones she could have crushed with too strong a hug. His eyes saw nothing. She held him tight against her chest. She tried to feel his tiny heart beating against her, but her own heart was like a drum deep inside and they blended together. A rhythmic pounding. Her son.

A beautiful boy who would grow and be anything that he wanted. The possibilities were endless. Floating on a cloud. She was a mother. He was so fine and honest and totally dependent, how could anything bad ever happen to him? Nursing her little boy, changing his nappies and wiping his nose, seeing her son grow, happy-go-lucky as a little boy kicking a football around, wanting to be an engine driver. He wasn't that much different now. Not really. She wished she could turn the clock back and her kids could stay six years old for ever. That had been the best age. Old enough to talk and communicate but still innocent and excited by life. He was all grown up. Her baby had become a man. She wondered if the boy's father had ruined it all. Seeing the violence and unhappiness. How could anyone know. The man had turned and she hoped her boy wouldn't go the same way. Something in the genes. But her boy seemed fine. He made jokes sometimes like all the men felt they had to, but inside he was still pure. She knew he was clean. But she wished he'd settle down with a nice girl. If he could find a decent job and a woman who would love and cherish him, then Balti's mum would be able to rest easy. She worried about her son. Every mother worried about her children. It was natural. She knew him like nobody else in the world. Drunk or sober, he was always her child. Things would get better. She knew things would get better. They called it a woman's intuition, but it seemed obvious enough. Things always got better eventually.

RENT BOY

James Wilson left WorldView early, his hasty departure causing a few raised eyebrows and a great deal of whispered comment among his colleagues. The excuse was vague, a mumbled line concerning family matters. A doctor's appointment for work-related insomnia, or perhaps long-delayed dentistry would have sufficed, but no, Wilson had spoken of family matters in a broken delivery that, while comforting in the weakness it revealed, had also shown a peculiar forcefulness. His fellow workers didn't expect this from such a dedicated employee as, of course, the corporation came first, but he was determined and the surprise lasted at most a few minutes. It was out of the ordinary, but his colleagues were more concerned with the various tasks facing them. Time was most definitely money. When he disappeared through the door, James Wilson was neatly indexed.

Jimmy sat in the front room, his Rest-Easy chair pulled across to the window where he could watch the street below. He sucked the leather's treated fragrance deep into his lungs, held it for a few seconds, and then slowly let it go. He felt the air tickle the end of his nose. He shut his eyes and repeated the process. This time white light crossed his eyelids. A tingle remained in his throat and he felt calmer. He had changed into smart but casual clothes, and had taken twenty minutes in the shower, liberally dowsing himself with his most expensive aftershave and deodorant. He had been to Dino's Delicatessen on the Fulham Road and purchased two types of fresh tea, caffeinated and decaffeinated coffee, skimmed and full milk, four kinds of biscuits. But perhaps they would go to the pub. Or maybe for a meal. Fulham was packed with up-market restaurants, though Mango rarely visited them. Italian, French, Greek,

Thai. Whatever money demanded there was always a well-bred entrepreneur on hand to supply the goods.

His mum had phoned and told him the news. Her words were
warped as they passed along the line linking two very separate worlds.
It was the first time she had called him at WorldView. It had taken
Mango several seconds to tune in properly and realise he hadn't
drifted over the edge. The words filtered through and were distorted
by the receiver, the message trapped and disjointed, turning to a fuzzy
echo. It had taken him those vital seconds to understand the sense of
his mother's message. Then he was asking questions and receiving
answers, finally putting the phone down and going to collect his coat
in a daze. The details of the office were of little consequence, his direct
superior no longer a key player in the thrilling game of international
finance but a small-minded wanker with BO, dandruff and a boring
tendency to transfer *The Times* editorial into self-aggrandising lectures. WorldView melted into the background, the people around him
shadows. He went to the lift and waited for the doors to open, unaware
of his noiseless descent. He drove home at a relaxed speed, the radio
silent.

Jimmy strained his eyes and sipped a glass of mineral water. He
was nervous. The deep breathing exercises the doctor had suggested
worked up to a point, but his brain refused to be totally sedated. It
was more than nervousness. That was natural enough. He was alone
in his flat and terrified. Actually terrified. Of what he wasn't sure.
Expectations. That's what it was. He tapped his foot against the skirt-
ing board and looked around the room quickly, making sure everything
was in place, trying to distract his attention, fear coming again, flicking
back to the street. He could have stayed on at work for a few more hours,
but knew he wouldn't have been able to concentrate. He had wanted to
leave immediately his mother's words kicked home. Property, wealth,
status; what did it matter when your brother was coming to see you
after eighteen years buried in a field? What did any of it mean? His head
was buzzing. His brain playing games again.

He thought of the churned field, thick black mud and thick brown
worms. An ancient battlefield filled with the corpses of Danes and

Saxons and all the tribes who had ever landed in England and fought over the land, artery blood absorbed by the soil. Men had been hacked and chopped into ragged pieces, shining gold axes rusted and blunted from the constant hack hack hacking of Jack The Ripper and M25 murderers with their vans and cars and razor-wire erections. Jump on the ring road and observe the speed limit. Dump the evidence. Spade in the boot. Silver clean. Fresh from the superstore. Brand new wellies. Green rubber padding. Out for a stroll bird-watching on Sunday morning listening for woodpeckers in the copse in the distance but only ever hearing crows and seeing ravens with their jet black feathers and peck peck pecking beaks sharp and merciless ripping the heads off smaller birds, pulling the neck tight, cutting into the skin, decapitation headless bodies rotting blue from the rain thunder lightening flooded England, draught-stricken England. Black soil, black birds, black mummified hand pushing through the soil reaching out for Jimmy, grabbing him around the neck feeling the pressure of finger bones on his throat making him want to throw up, gasping for air, inhalation/exhalation restricted, muddy fist pulling him down into the mud, into the sewer, into the sordid backstreets of homelessness and psychiatric disorder, care in the community beyond the streetlife blockbuster romances showing at a five-screen deluxe cinema, popcorn backseat masturbation as a kid spunking up over the velvet chairs and black stockings and suspenders of a girl from school. Back from the dead. Back from the grave. Back from heaven and hell on earth, high-rise office blocks and high-rise flats where the views are the same. Clogged earth reeking of insecticide, washed away by acid rain, burnt off by sun, watered again until it's clean and rich and ready to give up its dead in some kind of resurrection. And classroom history lessons forget the men in the field, content with kings and queens and their sons and daughters, ignoring the raped sons and daughters of the peasants buried alive.

Seven o'clock his mum had said.

Pete Wilson had been hit by guilt. It connected with the bridge of his nose sending blood over a bare-breasted Snow White. His guilt was natural rather than something conditioned or manufactured, an ingrained notion of justice. Looking straight ahead he'd ended up in bed with Jill Smart, and his biggest mistake was that he kept going round knowing full well she was living with a boy who loved her and would be heart-broken if he ever found out about her infidelity. But he didn't care. Didn't give it a second thought. It was help yourself time and everyone out for themselves.

Then one day they were unlucky. Playing with people's emotions. All so he could have it off with a fucking soulgirl. Kev Bennett walking in and finding them on the job, naturally enough going off his rocker as he took in the scene, Pete behind Jill, the woman Kev loved on all fours, turning her head to see her fiance in the doorway snapped in half, snapshot disaster, faces registering shock and a stark realisation of what the moment meant. All because of glands. Natural urges. Then there'd been the inevitable punch-up, Pete's head racing from the speed and his reason wired as he stumbled out of an unhappy home with his clothes tucked under his arm. He'd left Jill to sort out the mess. He dressed in a doorway hoping it wouldn't be opened by a middle-aged bodybuilder who hated flashers. With his clothes on he'd hurried home to hide. A bottle job, but he hadn't known what to do. Couldn't think straight. Just didn't want Bennett banging his head on the bedroom wall or passersby seeing him naked, laughing their heads off. Jill had been game enough and he didn't want any aggro with Bennett because Kev was the one getting stitched up. Pete didn't blame him. Anyway, Bennett would've slaughtered him if he hadn't got away, Kev turning back towards Jill looking for some kind of explanation, something that would make everything alright. He was waiting for the magic excuse knowing there was nothing left to say. Actions were more honest than words. Pete rolling home and waiting for sleep to come and turn the engine off, willing his brain to close down, tapping his fingers impatiently with a pillow burying his head. It was a long, tormenting wait and when he finally slept he didn't wake until the next morning.

Pete had a bath and washed away the filth. Stared at his face and into battered eyes—red veins and stunned pupils. Dressed slowly feeling sore where Bennett had punched him in the ribs and head. A kick in the back as he legged it out of the bedroom. He was walking into a nightmare as he sat down and took the Cornflakes box. Filled his bowl, pouring milk from the bottle. Sat silently with Mum and Dad talking excitedly about the police siege of Kevin Bennett and Jill Smart's flat. Young Kevin holding Jill hostage with a shotgun, pissed up threatening to blow her away and then top himself.

He'd made no demands, that was the strange thing. There seemed no reason for the madness. No request for a fast car to the airport, a suitcase full of cash and a private jet to a mystery destination. Nobody could understand why he'd gone mental like that. What else could the police do when they arrived and tried to talk him into handing over the gun? After hours of patient, logical discussion things were getting worse, with Bennett swigging from a bottle of whisky. The reason they were trying to apply only wound him up. Mr Wilson wished he knew what was behind it all. Then Kev fired a barrel into the wall and the old bill had taken him out. Blown his head in half according to hearsay. Splattered spirit-pickled brains all over the new wallpaper Kevin and Jill had put up together, laughing and joking as the paper peeled and the paste stuck to their hands. Imagine that, Mr Wilson said—being the marksman with Kevin Bennett in your sights. He remembered Kevin when he was a young lad, a nice enough kid who loved motorbikes. He shook his head sadly and wondered how his family felt. Didn't know what the world was coming to. Wondered what Kevin was doing with a shotgun in the first place.

It was a sin, playing with people's emotions. Pete returned to his room and laid on his bed until midday before venturing out. He felt as though people were staring at him, but in truth nobody knew why Bennett had gone off his head like that. It was just one of those things, now and again someone cracking under the pressures of living. Thing was, he was only nineteen and had the whole of his life ahead of him. He had a good job as an apprentice electrician and a nice fiancé who'd done a typing course, and it wasn't like they didn't have anywhere to live. It was a crying shame, it really was, and when Pete went into the newsagents they all seemed to be talking about the shooting and he wondered where Jill was, the first time he'd thought about her properly. His skull was creaking and he had to sort things out. He needed to justify himself, but was unable.

He tried to imagine Bennett's face after the marksman had done his job. Did he get it between the eyes like the Westerns, those spaghetti efforts where the eyes stayed open and blood covered the walls, or did the bullet go straight through an eye and leave a neat wound in the socket, exploding deep inside the brain. An earthquake sending tremors down the spine. A police horror show. More likely half the head was blown over Jill. He wondered if Bennett had let her get dressed. Whether she had stood there screaming, naked, with grey matter plastering her hair. He went home without buying anything and sat on his bed, everyone out. He hung his Snow White T-shirt on the door, watching the sick midgets go about their business, Snow White with a big smile on her face enjoying the attention of her seven lovers. He propped the pillows behind his head and stretched out. What would Snow White's prince think when he walked in after a hard day finding the love of his life on all fours with a spiky-haired freak banging in and out of her? Only Bennett knew the answer to that one.

Later that day he heard that Jill was staying with her mum and dad in Uxbridge, and after a week sitting around wondering what to do he looked up the family name in the phone book and took the tube to the end of the Metropolitan Line. He found the Smart house and sat on a wall down the road waiting. It was a warm day and he was conscious of being on his own, but eventually he saw Jill come outside, a bent, wrecked version of her old self. He followed for a while and then caught up with her. Jill's eyes took time to focus and it was obvious she was sedated, the bruising on her face only now beginning to fade. It took a little longer for her to register who he was and then she was scratching his face with blunt fingers, long red nails bitten down and the skin ripped to threads. She was screaming that they were murderers. Why hadn't Pete stayed and taken his punishment like a man? He'd shifted his share of the blame and left her to die.

She ran home and when Pete phoned a couple of weeks later a harsh male voice said she'd slashed her wrists and been cremated, that her ashes were in the rose garden where Kevin was at rest. Then the line went dead.

Mango went to the cupboard in his bedroom and took out a box of photos. He'd had the doors specially made, hardwood from an Asian forest. He ran his hand over the surface. Strong and beautiful with centuries of life ahead, until a chainsaw brought the tree back down to earth. The doors were built to last. You only lived once and he wanted the best. You had to look out for number one because that was the first law of nature and England was a nature-loving country, where the land had been deforested and carved up for the various business interests guarding the nation's heritage.

He held a picture of Pete in front of him and studied the face. Thin and pale with black hair and bright eyes dominating the face. He was smiling and wearing a Harrington, T-shirt, moleskin army surplus trousers and DMs. He seemed happy enough, though who really knew what went on inside someone's head. It was hard enough working out what went on inside your own at times. The next photo showed Pete juggling a football in a pair of shorts. Winter and summer images. Dark skies and bright sunshine.

Mango sifted through the snaps stopping at a family photo of all the Wilsons together. Mum and Dad in the middle with their four children. Two on either side—boy girl, boy girl. He looked at the faces, how they had gradually changed so you never noticed. Then he was staring across the room unfocused trying to imagine what Pete looked like now. It was something he often found himself doing. All his family admitted to doing the same thing. Now his mum said he'd become a farmer in East Anglia.

Mango laughed out loud. A farmer? The dream had been a top international financier riding the high seas in a luxury yacht and the nightmare a smack-addled boy prostitute. For some reason a farmer seemed about right. How could any of them have guessed something like that? The imagination took you to the far corners. The best and worst options. Extremes always seemed more attractive somehow, as though there was no middle way. How the fuck had he ended up in East

Anglia turning earth? Mango pictured a broad character in wellies and overalls, with a ruddy complexion and cow shit under his nails carrying a pitchfork. He laughed again despite himself. Pete the farm hand building a scarecrow and then hanging his old Harrington around its shoulders. A head full of straw for nesting birds. Squire Wilson.

He thought of thick English soil again, but this time he was away from the ring road, the M25 overgrown and reclaimed. Rich earth and healthy crops. None of that intensive farming shit. Pete living a clean life away from London on an organic smallholding, and what would his big brother think of Jimmy in a flash office block in the City, taking the lift to the ground and then slipping into his £30,000 XJ6 3.2 Sport, foot down, naught to 60 in 7.9 seconds, six in-line cylinders humming, rolling through King's Cross picking up runaways. The bloke was driving a tractor home while Jimmy lowered his window and solicited juveniles. Moving on to call girls shifting up-market while his brother strolled through the fields on his way to the local. A Green Man sign over the door and East Anglian ales lining an oak bar. Pipe loaded with tobacco. Country and Western on a jukebox that was rarely used because it broke the calm. Watching stars burn in a clear sky as he walked home.

On the one hand, vast wealth would have offered some kind of justification for the family's loss, while the role of victim would've allowed Mango to condemn the exploitative system which he himself had so successfully embraced. But a farmer? It didn't suggest success or failure, just everyday life away from London and the satellite towns. It meant that Pete could have walked away without a care in the world, unbothered by the misery he was causing. That would be worst of all. The final insult. It would mean that he hadn't given a toss about the rest of the Wilsons, leaving his brother to fend for himself and his mum, dad, sisters to grieve. Year in, year out. All that wasted time. All those Christmas presents hidden away waiting for Pete's return.

Pete Wilson walked slowly. After so many years in East Anglia, the tight London air was a shock but at the same time so familiar. It brought everything roaring back, adding colour and movement to dreamtime imagery. There was less wind and the same artificial, carbonised warmth with which he had grown up. The concrete beneath his feet was harsh and unforgiving with none of the softness and flexibility he had found in Norfolk. Buildings smothered the sun and blocked the wind to which he had become so accustomed. A deep chill had long since worked its way into his bones and would stay there till the day they lowered him down. It was part of him now. The dark soil and barren winters, when the flatness of the land made his ears ring and his mind twist in on itself, when the days shortened and he had time to sit alone and remember Kate. He had spent almost as much time in the country as the city, but eighteen years of his life was compressed as soon as he got off the train at Liverpool Street and stood on the escalator taking him underground to the tube home. It seemed a month since he ran off. He still called London home despite everything that had happened.

Pete had met Kate two months before leaving. She was twice his age and had grown up outside King's Lynn. She had a bumpkin accent and the worn features of someone born and raised on a farm. Her hair was frizzy red and she had a straight, slightly mocking manner. She also had cancer.

He first spoke to her at a Clash gig at the Electric Ballroom in Camden Town. He'd been to see the band the previous night as well. Mickey Dread on stage beforehand toasting, while Joe and the boys had been at their best. The first night he'd gone with a mate and Will. The second time he was on his own standing at the bar listening to the records the DJ was playing. Reggae and punk. Minding his own business. Then this woman had started talking to him in an accent he could hardly hear above the music, let alone identify. He found it hard to understand what she was saying at first and had to lean in close, noticing the way her perfume and sweat mixed in together. The Electric Ballroom was baking hot and she was also there on her own.

Kate was in London for a month enjoying the bright lights, because she might've been in her late thirties but she loved the music and ideas, and had been a mod when she was younger, going on the runs and living the life. But punk was better because of the strength of the music, the Jamaican-inspired bass and the everyday political

lyrics. She was staying with her cousin in Greenford, and then The
Clash were on stage and Pete forgot about everything else. The place
was full of dehydrating bodies and the thud of Topper Headon's drums
and Paul Simonon's bass, Joe Strummer in control of the microphone
and Mick Jones doing his guitar hero bit. It was one of the best gigs
he'd ever seen. He noticed Kate again at the end as they came down
the steps into the street, a line of police helmets through the sweaty
mist and a young skinhead in a sheepskin standing on a white Merc.
He got the tube some of the way with Kate and he was conscious of her
age at first because he'd been told age was a bad thing and something
to be sneered at, old and boring, all that stuff that he soon labelled as
another brand of prejudice.

He'd seen Kate again, a week later. They'd gone to The Ship in
Soho and found a corner in the busy pub. Chelsea were playing at the
Marquee and they'd thought to go along and see Gene October's Right
To Work encore, but started getting into a conversation and when it was
time to leave they stayed behind as three-quarters of the pub filtered
away. They got pissed and took the tube towards West London together,
but there'd been nothing sexual. She was attractive, that was all. They
enjoyed talking about bands they'd seen and records they liked and
anything at all really. He'd got off the train and said goodbye and it
didn't seem strange not going home with her. Anyway, he had Jill Smart
on the go and there were no complications there. Love didn't come into
it and they were both satisfying themselves with easy sex.

He had nothing in common with Jill, a soulgirl into the bargain,
and punks and soulgirls weren't supposed to mix. All those tribes that
made up England in the late Seventies. Jill was the opposite to Kate.
They didn't talk much. Just went to bed and had the sex which was
good and uncomplicated and that was all there was to it. No emotion
or feeling except for what happened between their legs, and when it
was over Jill always wanted to put some twelve-inch American import
on the record player and talk about her Kevin and their plans for the
future. That was a real turn-off because it made Pete think of the
silly sod working and trusting her, and he started telling himself he
shouldn't be there in someone else's bed taking their place. It wasn't

right, but he'd been so into his music and sulphate that he went along with everything and dismissed any kind of morality as old-fashioned.

He saw Kate a few more times and then the nightmare began. Kate told him she was going back to Norfolk and invited him round for a goodbye drink, that she knew of a job if he was interested because he couldn't stay on the dole for the rest of his life. They'd gone down that pub in Greenford and drunk till closing and ended up in bed together. Watching the older woman striptease in front of him throwing her bra in his face and peeling off her panties. It had been different. Another kind of sex. More warm and human. The next morning she told him there was work on the farm if he wanted it, that she would have to hire someone anyway now she had inherited the place. It wasn't big, but too much for Kate on her own. She also told him that she had cancer. She didn't want to hide anything away and didn't want Pete feeling sorry for her either, because maybe she would live to be an old country lady, or if she was unlucky she would last a few more years. She was being upfront. There were no ties. He could come and work for a couple of months and save a bit of cash and then leave without any hassle. He should know about the cancer though. Just in case.

Pete wanted to ask questions but was embarrassed searching for details. So he left with her. Just like that. His head getting to grips with the sex and the work and the illness that would kill her one day. Just like that. Because he needed the money and because he liked her.

Sin and retribution they called it. He didn't believe in the dogma, but he had been guilty. If you were able to pay for your sins and achieve some kind of redemption, then he was in there with a claim. If there was a God responsible for everything, and if he operated how the preachers insisted, then he would be there with gold stars next to his name. The idea of justice had to come from somewhere. Natural justice. And he felt these things free from any kind of indoctrination because he had only ever been to church a couple of times in his life and didn't come from anything near a religious family. Maybe it was built into his culture. Your everyday person had a greater morality about them than the rich and powerful. It was natural to feel remorse and guilt. There weren't enough people learning from their mistakes. But he had suffered. Nothing but cancer eating Kate away for the last year, the visits to the hospital and treatment, the hopelessness. Making arrangements. The years spent mourning. Then the obsession with death. Kevin Bennett, Jill Smart and now Kate. He was paying his dues. For all the good and bad sex and endless attempts at procreation, there was only ever going to be one end to the affair.

Finally it got to the point when he had to push himself, with Kate dead for four years. He decided to phone his Uncle Ted and ask about the family. He wanted to test the ground. He became scared when he couldn't find his old address book, digging through cupboards and finding it wrapped up in a decaying Snow White T-shirt. He held the shirt up in front of him. Snow White enjoying an orgy with the seven dwarfs. He couldn't believe he was the same person who used to wear that shirt. He threw it across the room and opened the address book, sat down on his bed. Pete flicked through the pages that had turned yellow with the passing years. He saw Jill's number in among the names of people he'd once known. The reality hit home, making him realise that eighteen years was a lifetime for some people. His mother could be dead. Or his dad. Perhaps both of them. His sisters. And what about Jimmy who would've been waiting for his big brother to come home. How could he do that to the boy who'd looked up to and admired him? He was a selfish bastard wrapped up in his own misery. Self-centred and full of himself, and that was what had gone wrong in the first place. He'd had no sense of responsibility, following his knob straight up Jill and then running away. But living with a dying woman had taught him respect and humility. He appreciated the world now. Working on a farm brought you back to some kind of starting-point. He was disciplined and had picked up Kate's honesty. She had changed him for the better.

Pete ran through the book again and finally phoned his uncle, found out that his aunt was dead. His mind was made up. He had to go back. He had shut that other world away in a cell pretending it didn't exist. He'd exhausted himself working the land, pushing his body through the hard, miserable winters and busy summers. He'd spent his days either shivering from the cold or sweating in the sun. His muscles ached yet he pushed himself. His body was healthy but at the expense of his head which he wanted to keep numb. Others would have turned to drink, but Pete worked until he was too exhausted even to get pissed. Now and then he would have a pint, but more for the walk than the alcohol. In the evenings he mostly sat in front of the fire thinking of how the woman who had sat opposite him gradually lost her grip on life and faded away, tortured by chemotherapy. When she died East Anglia seemed alien. For four years he had kept going until the worst was over and he had to move again.

He started looking back, examining where it had gone wrong. First there'd been the guilt of Kev Bennett and Jill Smart, that was obvious, and he had submerged it caring for Kate, but with her death any sense of atonement had been replaced by guilt for what he'd done to his family and friends. The longer it went on the worse it became. He hurt everyone he came into contact with. He was a disaster and wasting time. His uncle was so excited to hear from him that it filled Pete with shame, explaining that their greatest fear was that he'd been murdered. If only they'd had some news that he was alive and well. Why hadn't he phoned? Written a letter. Got in touch. But now he was alive. Back from the grave. Some kind of resurrection. Ted said it was a miracle. When was he coming home? He couldn't wait to see him again. Everybody would be excited.

Pete phoned his parents. Amnesia was the excuse, the only explanation with which he could come up. It would cope with the bitterness and prevent him having to explain things in too much detail. Sickness had claimed him one day and he had drifted away and become a farmer in the country. He wasn't sure of all the details. Then his memory had gradually returned. Very slowly over the years till one morning he woke up and remembered his life in London. Imagine that. Without memory you didn't exist. You were nothing. Amnesia would make everything much easier to handle. All those years away and it was sex that had led to his downfall and the guilt that came with the consequences of fucking people about. Kev Bennett and Jill Smart, forever together.

Mango checked his watch again. It was a quarter to seven. Normally he would be hard at work burrowing into rows of letters and numbers pushing himself to identify a good investment. Instead he was hurrying to the bathroom and arriving just in time. He leant over the toilet and was sick into the bowl.

That girl last night. A woman. Sophisticated with exotic eyes and eyebrows that stretched up and away towards her temples. She was beautiful, with a nice voice and a slight tilt to her head. Black hair cut in a bob like thousands of Cleopatra office girls. Except she was no office girl this one. Hetherington at WorldView had recommended her personally. Mango sat in awe as she drank the gin he'd poured, her gaze wandering around the flat. Her legs were long and shapely and he imagined Hetherington with the whip turning her back into a mass of lacerations. He had paid heavily for the privilege, the sight of blood costing extra. After all, she would need a few days to recover and it wasn't as if Hetherington didn't have cash to throw around. His colleague had explained it to James. That it was the desire for power that drove people to the top of the pecking order and that once you joined the march you had to crush everything in your path. Sex was nothing but a display of power. Hard sex. Wilson should think of his pecker as a weapon. Women loved it. They really did.

When Monica arrived Mango sat there wondering what would happen next. Whether he would chop off her head in a fit of free expression or merely thrash her to within an inch of her life. He had never been interested in sadism, but Hetherington and Ridley from WorldView were always encouraging their colleague to give it a go. They had painstakingly explained the mechanics of power, and how sex could be inverted. He had ended up with all that class in front of him and what had Mango done? Bottled it. That's what. He could remember the look of scorn on the woman's face as he asked her to leave. It withered him and he was sure the chaps from the office would find out that he didn't have what it took.

The water stopped spinning and he remembered Hetherington telling him to thrash her but treat her with respect, telling him about a cheap whore he'd picked up with a friend, how they'd fucked her both ends and how Hetherington had lubricated her and tried pushing his fist up the slut's arse. She'd screamed and his friend had helped secure her, Hetherington stretching her sphincter until he had three, four fingers inside, easing the pressure, then inserted a full fist. The dirty fucking whore. His eyes and smile widened as he explained things to Wilson. The only way to treat the workers was to bend them over a barrel and fuck them rigid, then shove your fist in and pull out their guts. The women were the easy targets, but they'd do the men as well, but in a roundabout sort of way so half the time they didn't even know what was happening to them. That was the beauty of democratic politics and people like Wilson were there to be educated.

Mango was lonely. To be reduced to sadism was the end point as far as he was concerned. He knew he had been thinking mental thoughts with under-age kids and that he was scum taking advantage of them, but faced with a willing victim he didn't want to know. Loneliness must have driven thousands to perversion. He was sure of this. He understood the difference between right and wrong. He wasn't some misfit freak without morals or decency. He wasn't like Hetherington and Ridley, however much he tried and listened to their bragging, because he understood what it was like to be part of the majority. He knew what it was to struggle and have those you loved taken away. But he'd been taught to respect his betters. He couldn't hurt the woman with the clipped tones. He needed his own kind because they were rubbish and he was rubbish.

Mango puked again until the tears stung his eyes. He was sorry for everything wicked he had done in the name of his brother, in the name of himself. He could blame things on Pete but it was a con. He was okay. He would be alright soon. With his brother back everything would be like it was when he went away. Life would be simple and bursting with youth and vitality. It didn't matter if he was rich. Mango could open up again. He flushed the toilet and watched the water twist away with the sickness. He straightened himself up and brushed his teeth, rinsed his mouth with mouthwash. He was fine. And when he went back to the chair by the window for some reason he thought of his first serious curry with the rest of the lads when they were teenagers and how he'd been cocky and ordered a prawn vindaloo. He was pissed and went straight into the food and was halfway through when his mouth caught fire. He'd knocked back a pint but it only worked for a while and then he'd steamed into the mango pickle and emptied the tray trying to cool the fire in his mouth. He still had the nickname today, after everything that had happened. He had a good job in the City, a posh flat in Fulham, and he drove a £30,000 XJ6 3.2 Sport with six in-line cylinders, which did naught to 60 in 7.9 seconds, yet his mates still called him Mango after a night in the long-closed Ganges. His mouth had tasted of curry and mango for a couple of days after. Now mouthwash and toothpaste masked the sickness.

Pete stood at the end of the road and prepared himself. So far everything had gone according to plan. He had spent the afternoon with his mum and dad, and then his sisters when they arrived. There had been tears and kisses from his mum and arms thrown around his neck, squeezing him tight, and then a firm handshake and watery eyes from his old man. Debbie and Jackie ran at him and almost knocked him down they were so excited, crying and laughing at the same time. He felt the tears in his eyes, but men didn't cry. The words came fast and he sat everyone down and slowly explained the amnesia. It made all the difference. He knew he was doing the right thing. He was letting himself off the hook, true, but at the same time sparing them the truth. They didn't want to know that he was shit. Lies were important sometimes. They kept things going. Pete wanted to see his brother alone. After all, it was Jimmy who he'd been supposed to meet in the playground.

What did the kid think as the minutes and hours passed and night began to draw in? Why hadn't he returned? Pete knew why well enough, the drink he'd shared with Kate and a heavy mating session that took them well into the night. It was easy to run away in the short term, but long term he had made things worse for everyone. He had hated himself, and maybe deep down he still did, but he couldn't think that way any more. He had to make amends. Had to see his kid brother on his own and try to put things right. Just thinking of Jimmy on the swings, going up and down the slide, getting worried by his brother's absence, looking into the shadows as the darkness came down, scared as he ran home. What had his mum and dad told Jimmy when he got in? That maybe Pete was out with a girl or had met someone and gone down the pub? His dad would've told Jimmy not to worry, that Pete was a growing lad who was late for everything.

Pete didn't want to think about it now. There was a stack of Christmas presents that his mum had brought out and she said that tomorrow they'd have Jimmy round as well and they'd all sit down and have a proper dinner together. Pete could open them then and Jimmy could watch with the rest of the family because every Christmas that boy had wanted to know what his brother was getting. He was a big kid at heart, though he'd done well for himself. He'd done them proud. Pete sat with his cup of tea and listened and didn't really notice how much his parents had aged, though his sisters were women now rather than kids.

He walked down the Fulham street with its precisely spaced trees and top-of-the-range, polished cars. The pavements were clean and small patches of grass well maintained. He was hot and the fumes filled his head. He stopped outside the address he'd written down and looked up to the floor where his brother lived. He thought he saw a face move back from the window, but couldn't be sure.

The Wilson brothers sat in a corner of the pub. They were on their fourth pints. Mango drank Fosters, while Pete had opted for London Pride. He found the prices high and the beer lacked the flavour he was used to in Norfolk. Still, he wasn't concentrating on the quality of the drink. He had avoided his brother's eyes at first, but with the Pride inside him he was able to look Jimmy in the face. His kid brother was all grown up and filled out, and while it was obviously going to be the case the reality took time to absorb. It was the same with Debbie and Jackie. They were adults. Jimmy's features had filled out but the bone structure was how he remembered. He certainly dressed well. Pete felt scruffy, despite the new shirt he was wearing. But it was good to see Jimmy again. Pete was glad he had decided to meet him on his own.

Jimmy was floating above the clouds. Amnesia meant there had been no rejection and his brother was a victim without the degradation he had feared. They were together again. Pete was late coming

home, but had made it in the end. One more pint and maybe they'd
go for something to eat. Anything his brother wanted was going on
the Gold Card. Life was good. Life was fucking brilliant. Feeling the
drink at the back of his throat and studying his brother's face. He had
really aged. Looked older than his years with a bit of a receding hairline,
creases in his skin, and a weathered face. He looked healthy enough,
but tired. Exhausted more like. It must be the hard living. That and the
strain of not knowing who you are.

Pete wasn't bothered about food so they stayed in the pub. The
more they drank the more the barriers faded and it could have been
yesterday when they'd seen each other. Even so, Mango couldn't ask
too many questions. He was pissed but still bottling things up. The
details would come later. They drank until closing and were the last
to leave the pub, swaying as they walked back to the flat. Pissed-up
brothers strolling home at peace with the world on a perfect summer's
evening. Mango's thoughts were jumbled and simmering while the
Pride that had at first made Pete confident now kicked back and made
him ashamed. Their emotions had been chopped up and put through
a liquidiser.

Pete couldn't get over at how much Fulham had changed. It was
really posh now. Not how he remembered it when he was a kid. He
heard his name.

Mango hit his brother in the side of the face and Pete rocked
back against a parked car. His kid brother followed up with a kick that
bounced off his thigh, then a flurry of drunken punches that either
missed their target or half-connected. They staggered in and out of
the cars. A wing-mirror smashed. Pete didn't respond, just staggered
back from the impact. He wasn't even that surprised. It seemed right
somehow. There was nothing he could do. He faced up to Jimmy and
the London Pride made him keep eye contact as he felt the fist connect
with his nose. The punch was straight and it hurt. He wondered if his
nose was broken. There was a lot of blood. It pumped from his nostrils
and spilled over his shirt. A white Fred Perry he'd been given by his
mum as a Christmas present. She'd even got the size right. She'd let
him pick one present to open now, but the rest would wait for Jimmy.

It fitted him, but there was no way of knowing when she'd bought it. She hadn't bothered putting dates on the tags. He would have to ask. It would need a good wash. He hoped the blood wouldn't stain.

'Mum gave me this shirt,' he said.

Mango stopped. He blinked as he focused on the shirt, his vision hazy. He saw the red pattern covering his brother's chest. Pete had always liked Fred Perrys, but they were expensive.

'Mum gave it to me before I came round. It fits perfect. She let me open one present without you and this was it. All the rest I've got to open when you come round for dinner.'

Mango stared at the shirt. It was a good fit. His mum was a smart woman. He started laughing. Shook his head. Looked at the pavement for a bit and turned. The brothers continued walking back to the flat, Pete laughing as well.

BURNING RUBBER

Will had said little all night and the rest of the lads were starting to notice, though Carter had been keeping their attention as he entertained the Sex Division with his latest exploits. It was hot and humid and he was talking as much to himself as the others, trying to forget about the aggro he'd had with Denise the previous week. He'd been looking to wind things down, regular sex breeding contempt and an appreciation of the finer things in life—such as freedom from hunger, poverty and the fear of Slaughter's machete. But Denise wasn't taking hints. She was acting strange and Carter was worried. There was something about sickness in a woman that turned him right off. All that pervy sex stuff was okay, something you had to laugh about otherwise you looked soft, but insanity he didn't even want to consider.

Slaughter had asked Denise to marry him and it had done something to her head seeing the bloke on one knee acting the poet, with a bunch of roses in his hand and a tear in his eye. She told him she'd consider the proposal and seemed to think Carter was planning something similar, as though she had a choice to make between the two men. A decision that was going to stay with her the rest of her life. That moment when she'd reached the crossroads and had to go one way or the other, all that destiny nonsense. He was shitting it because she kept telling him she was a single girl and staying that way, that life was too short for major attachments, which was fine by Carter, but he didn't like the new way she was looking at him. He'd turn his head and her eyes would be drilling into him full of possession. It was like she was trying to convince herself. Then there'd been that business when she'd gone off her trolley, smashing plates in his kitchen and punching him in the mouth. For no reason. Well out of order. He'd pulled his fist back ready to drive that pretty little nose into the slag's brain, then stopped. He'd never hit a bird before and wasn't starting now. End up like that and they'd done you good and proper. Made you into a prize wanker. It was a load of bollocks and he was bailing out soon as he saw his chance. These things needed timing and tact, especially when you were dealing with a headcase who could put a word in the wrong ear and cause you some serious grief. Women were dangerous. Never mind all that weaker sex propaganda.

He must've been mad getting involved in the first place. He was a relaxed bloke and wanted a simple life. But that's what happened. You followed your knob and ignored the messages coming through from the brain, and then it ended in tears. His fucking tears. Even so, he'd given her one up against the fridge for good luck after she'd calmed down and said how sorry she was about hitting him, that she'd replace the plates and was his lip alright? She was mad enough to get the hump and tell Slaughter. He had to be careful. If he wanted Denise then he'd be up front with Slaughter and get it over with, but the thing was he just didn't care. All he wanted was to get his leg over. He felt no guilt about shagging Slaughter's woman. He didn't give a toss. Guilt was for wankers.

'That bird last night was pure class,' Carter said, trying to wash away the problem of Denise and concentrate on the football. 'She worked as a bouncer for a while in King's Cross, but you wouldn't believe it looking at her. She's tall, but not exactly made of muscle. At least she doesn't look that way. She's got a black belt in karate and keeps herself fit. I met her down Blues when I lost you lot. Very nice. Anyway, we had a good chat and everything and then she invites me back, and there I was with a smile on my face lining up a few more points. That's the mark of a champion, the ability to keep churning out results even when faced by quality opposition. I only managed a swift one off the wrist though, because she doesn't drink and eats healthy and doesn't put poison in her body unless she knows where it's coming from. That's her words, not mine. Like my duff's toxic or something. Still, can't blame her I suppose. Anyway, I'm on for another point tomorrow. I've got these curry-flavoured rubbers from The Hide. I'll be unstoppable with these beauties.'

Carter dipped his hand in the right pocket of his jeans and held the condoms up for inspection. The pack was a mass of colours and Balti leant over to sniff the wrapping.

'Doesn't smell of anything to me. What kind of curry is it?'

'It just says curry flavour.'

'What one though.'

'How do I fucking know? What do you expect, a recipe on the back and a couple of chapattis chucked in for free? It's the thought that counts.'

'It could be a jalfrezi or something. She might not like jalfrezi, all that chilli up her snatch. Or what if it's vindaloo? She's not going to want a chicken vindaloo tickling her clit is she?'

'It's not going to be a jalfrezi or vindaloo,' Harry said. 'It's not like they dip it in a cauldron. It's more likely a korma. It's all fake anyway. Like crisps. I mean, you bite into a bacon crisp and all you're getting is a load of Es.'

'Can't be bad, can it? Fried MDMA for less than a quid. What do you mean fake?'

'It's chemicals mixed up to taste like bacon. It's cheaper.'

'Fuck off. You telling me there's no pork in a bacon crisp?'

'That's right.'

'You're winding me up. No pork in a bacon crisp?'

'God's truth.'

'Fuck off.'

'Swear on the old girl's life.'

'Really?'

'Straight up.'

'Bunch of cunts. They should do them for that. Trade's Description Act.'

'Fucking hell lads,' Carter was getting wound up, with Denise on his mind and Slaughter coming towards the table, and the boys going into one about a packet of fucking crisps. 'These rubbers aren't going to burn a hole in her. It's just a laugh. That's all. A bit of fun. And what's the matter with you, Will? You look like you've just had your bollocks coated in pharl sauce and found that Mango's been at the pickle tray again. Smile, for fuck's sake.'

Slaughter nodded on his way to the bogs and Carter felt the tightness in his gut ease. His balls were lighter as well. No additives there. Hundred per cent quality. They'd been given room to expand now the danger had passed. It was like he was in the ocean with a shark circling not sure whether he was there or not, knowing that once its brain made the connection he was going to be dragged down and would have to be ready to go the distance. But he was getting to the best part and needed the distraction of story-telling to help him forgot about nutters and their psycho birds. And what was Slaughter doing walking around in his leather coat in the middle of summer? It was a hot night and he had his coat on. Mental that bloke. Fucking mental. Should be locked up where he couldn't do any harm.

'The best bit was when we'd got off the night bus going round her place, coming out of this kebab house with a bit of pre-sex nourishment. There's this big bastard standing there eyeballing us and I ask him what the fuck he's looking at. There was another geezer with him who I didn't see I was so pissed and he hits me and I was so fucking surprised I went straight down like I was Arsenal. Right embarrassment it was, though the cunt was dead once I got up.'

Eileen came to the table, picked up the dead glasses and emptied the ashtray. Carter stopped talking and asked her how she was. Even Will took a bit of notice, because Eileen was looking good, full of herself off on holiday to Ibiza the next day. Then for some reason he thought of her flat on her back with the rest of the girls who trooped over to Spain and Greece, and he was hacked off by women in general and Karen in particular, and all that respect and everything seemed like just more bollocks.

'So there's this freeze-frame moment,' Carter continued, after Eileen had moved on to the next table, 'when I'm on my arse and there's kebab meat and chillies in the air and some wanker coming through to shove his trainers down my throat . . . and then it happens.'

He paused for silence and Will raised his eyes into his head. Carter was so fucking dramatic. He belonged on a stage as he prepared to deliver the punchline. He got right up Will's nose at times like this. Why didn't he get on with the story?

'I'm on my arse and this bird just piles in. Doesn't say a word. A couple of kicks and the first bloke is crouched over, then finished off. Another one and the other bloke's down. Fucking magic. She wasn't screaming or carrying on, just did the business. Hauled me up and there's these two cowboys moaning on the pavement. Never seen anything like it. Cold and calculated and at that moment she was the most beautiful woman in London. No grannying around. Everything in one: good-looking, interesting conversation and a minder as well.'

The rest of the lads took their time digesting the story. Even Will was impressed. They tried to imagine the possibilities such a woman offered. It was like something from an old black-and-white sci-fi film, where space travellers land on a distant planet and find it populated by brainy Scandinavian beauty queens ready to treat the new arrivals as though they're kings. Fighting off the dinosaur population and then feeding them with cold bottled lager and the finest burgers.

'A single point was a bonus,' Carter admitted. 'Thing was, I woke up next morning and she was still beautiful. Seeing her in action like that, fucking deadly so you wouldn't get on the wrong side of her, but somehow it didn't make her any less a woman. It wasn't like she was cocky and going on about how fucking hard she was. She did it because it had to be done and maybe that's what a strong bird is all about. A strong bloke as well when you stop and think about it. Did what was necessary.'

The Sex Division sat in respectful silence for a while sipping their drinks and contemplating the wonders of the world. All of them were running the scene through their minds, a mild dose of confusion easily swamped by honest admiration. Will thought harder than most, shifting images through his head and matching them with the argument he'd had with Karen, her words and tears, and Karen off to see her dad leaving him to go down the pub alone and think about the news that she was pregnant and planning an abortion.

The thing that got him was that she didn't even ask what he thought. She announced she was pregnant and then hardly stopped for breath before telling him she was going to get rid of it. All that bollocks about talking to each other was just that—bollocks. It was her body, her life, her decision. Will was expected to do the decent thing and behave himself, say nothing and nod his head in time to the music, a eunuch without an opinion, a toy dog in the back of a Ford Cortina, head banging up and down. He didn't have a chance to think about the thing before she was telling him what she was going to do. He knew all the logic—women suppressed for thousands of years, the right to choose, bodies turned into intensive factory farms, the pill the great liberator giving women a stake in their own destiny, that men thought with their pricks and were incapable of emotion and feeling, that men were monsters and rapists and the scum of creation.

Thing was, he agreed with the bit about women being treated like shit, but where did that leave him? He didn't see why he had to pay the penalty for long-dead politicians who refused to let women vote and the sick bastards who raped women. It wasn't his fault. Sitting in the pub with his mates Will had time to go over it all, and the more he drank the more angry he became. He was being treated like shit. All that stuff about seeing the other person's point of view. Karen didn't give a toss what he thought. She was one more con-artist. When it came down to it, a bloke was supposed to behave according to a certain agenda and listen to a woman's problems and worries, but when it came to a bit of give they didn't want to know.

He started imagining himself as a dad and how it would mean giving up things, freedom and that, but he knew you got something in return. It would be a laugh. There wasn't one bloke he knew with a kid who didn't love it and put it up there on a pedestal and think the world of the little snot machine. They said it was hard work but worth the effort. Something to focus on and love without the complications that came along after a while with a woman. All that history and posturing. The endless need to justify and assert independence. It would be something pure and new, and while he would never be able to plan something like a kid, if it came along then maybe it was meant to be. Like fate or chance. He didn't know all the answers. Didn't pretend he did.

'What would you do if that bird with the black belt turned out to be a two-pointer, and then she got you in a neck lock a few weeks later and told you she was in the club?' Will asked.

Carter almost choked on his lager and everyone turned to the silent one in the corner. Birds you picked up in Blues didn't get pregnant. They were pumped full of chemicals and knew the score, and anyway, it wasn't their role in life. Women you pulled in Blues and shagged an hour or two later were different to mothers. After all, nobody wanted a kid off some old slapper who'd been servicing three or four different blokes a week for the last ten years. If you were planting a seed you wanted to know that the soil was in topnotch condition. It was nature's way.

'You're still with us then?' Carter replied. 'I thought you'd died over there and your right hand was on remote control, lifting the glass to your mouth every twenty seconds. What made you think of that one?'

'I was just wondering. What would you do?'

'It would just be a bit of sex. Nothing serious. Anyway, she'd be on the pill so there's no need to worry, and I'd have a condom massala on the end of my knob.'

'Suppose the spices burnt a hole in the rubber and she'd forgotten to take her pill. Or gone to pop it in her mouth and seen the face of Mango winking up at her. What then?'

Will was getting all serious on them and it made the rest of the Sex Division nervous. They came down the pub for a laugh, not a serious discussion on the state of the universe. The miserable cunt was in one of those moods. Every now and then all that common sense came crashing down.

'She'd have to get rid of it, wouldn't she,' Carter laughed. 'Give it the old coat hanger treatment. Either that or I'd have to take a loan and get it seen to so the NHS don't mess up.'

As Carter made his joke, Will understood why fundamentalists were able to get away with labelling blokes like him, why your ordinary herbert ended up tarred and feathered by the thought police. Thing was, it was a knee-jerk reaction, and Carter wasn't getting off so easy. It was the same kind of approach that Karen had used. It wasn't good enough. No fucking way. The lager was going to his head, exaggerating his thoughts, just like pills with Buddha, Mango and every other takeaway king decorating the surface, but bollocks anyway. He was narked.

'Seriously though,' Will said, keeping his voice level. 'You go out and shag a bird, any one of us, not just you, and what's it all about? What's the reason? I mean, I know we don't waste as much time talking about them as they do about us, because we have more important things in life like football, drink, curries, music and all that. But why do we go after them at all? What's it all about?'

'What do you mean?' Balti asked, confused.

'Stop and think about it,' Will continued. 'Look at the mechanics of the situation. It's like those toys you have when you're a kid. Plastic shapes and holes to put them in. Something's empty and then it's filled, but what makes you do it? I mean, sex is all about having kids, isn't it? That's the real function when you turn on the lights and switch off the music. It's just about kids.'

'Course it fucking isn't,' Carter laughed. 'Sex is about getting your end away. That's all sex is. A bit of fun.'

'But why? What's the point.'

'What do you mean what's the point? You going queer on us or something,' Carter asked, puzzled, looking to the others for support. 'Birds are there for blokes like me to service. I'm here for their enjoyment. It feels good. They're happy and I'm happy. A simple business transaction. A bit of give and take. That's what it's about you dozy cunt. Fuck me, Will, you should give the blow a rest. What do you reckon Harry, has he been touching your leg under the table?'

The rest of the Sex Division laughed and Will knew he wasn't getting his ideas across. They were coming out wrong. That's what too much spliff, too much lager, too much anything did to you. Made you talk gibberish like some sad case wandering the streets. Everyone was laughing except Harry, who'd clicked back to last night's dream.

Harry had been minding his own business on the seafront in Blackpool—watching the waves crash in as a storm built up, jagged lightning far away on the horizon, eating chips from a polystyrene plate—when he'd found half a pill in his ketchup. There was enough of the embossed image left to tell him what was coming next, the face of Michael Portillo leering up at him. It was too late to do anything about it, though, and he was hungry, so he finished the chips and went back to the hotel where he'd arranged to meet that scouse bird. He was looking forward to seeing her again and went to his room, waving to Terry McDermott behind the bar. He noticed Kevin Keegan sitting at the counter with his head in his hands mourning a lost championship. Harry opened the door and was hit by a bright light, suddenly finding himself in an operating theatre. He was in the wrong room and tried to turn back, but a steel door had slammed tight behind him.

He went to a sink and washed his hands, then put on surgical gloves and a mask. He was on automatic and watching his actions as though they belonged to someone else. The Portillo had flooded his brain and for a few seconds he wanted to stand on a stage and point a finger at the sponging single mothers who were single-handedly responsible for the decline of the British Empire. Thankfully he'd only had half the stated dose and was able to fight against the righteous indignation threatening to destroy his soul. It was a battle against superior odds. An expensive education had given the politician the vocabulary and arrogance to effectively deliver his message, hope anaesthetised as the light turned and focused on a scrawny teenage girl strapped down to an operating table. Her accent was pure St-Mary-le-Bow cockney and she was clearly terrified, the skin on her face broken by acne and an Income Support diet. Harry fought against the influence and understood the sickness of such a bitter pill. He knew what was coming. He recognised the wickedness of the Portillo.

He heard the whispered mantra from the pulpit—ALL DRUGS ARE EVIL, ALL DRUGS ARE EVIL . . . EXCEPT THOSE THAT WE TAX—and he saw the posters in the spectator's gallery promoting family values. He wanted nothing to do with the operation that was about to take place and battled harder, relieved to find himself joining the spectators. His personal resistance was too strong for the chemicals, pride replaced by disgust when he realised that he had somehow been tricked and was strapped to a padded chair. He was surrounded by various royals and upright members of the establishment. Hooded sadists and shaven-headed child molesters were well represented, the faces of the latter rotting and leering and pointed towards the operating table with unconcealed excitement.

A deep, official voice filled the room. Single mothers were ruining the nation. They conceived so that they could claim extra benefits. Family life was being eradicated by their antics. It was disgusting. Worse than this, some were prepared to abort their children rather than bring them up in poverty and sickness. They didn't want the stigma and sense of shame the government was imposing. They understood that they were wicked and wasting finite resources. Abortion was evil. But necessary. Sorry—he shouldn't have said that, it went against the Christian ethics of the shire electorate. But it just showed how depraved these little girls were and how the Conservatives loved small children, how they wanted the best for the little ones, and Harry was shouting out that it was the poverty and fear of poor mothers that led to their kids being terminated, but his accent was strange and common like the girl on the table and nobody could understand what he was saying. The hand of a liberal baroness reached out to pat his head. He was a quirk of nature who might one day be allowed to work with the terrier men, if he behaved himself and came to her boudoir that same night. He must perform, though, and satisfy her darkest desires. She wanted him to fuck her in front of The Baron. Very hard, please, young man. Otherwise he was ignored. Like a woman. Like a lump of meat.

The grey-haired surgeon wore a plastic Portillo mask. He moved towards the girl on the table. Her legs were secured in stirrups and she had been sedated. Her hands were nailed to the table, stretched above her head. The blood running from childlike palms was thin and anaemic. Cables had been attached to her ears. A tape relayed messages and created a climate of terror in the core of her brain. The scientists knew best. They would save the girl the misery of child birth and the tax-payer many tens of thousands of pounds. Another hungry mouth to feed. And then the surgeon was plugging in an old industrial vacuum cleaner and positioning it in front of his groin, strapping it into position before moving forward to push the tube attachment into the girl's vagina. He tried several times but without success. Finally a gentleman in a Peter Lilley mask had to move forward from the shadows and place his hand over the girl's mouth to stifle the agonised screams, smiling as he administered the sacred amyl nitrate. A mysterious figure disguised as Michael Howard stepped forward, greasing the nozzle with lubricant and helping the surgeon insert the tube. The girl fainted and the crowd cheered. Harry tried to shout out, but was unable. At first he thought he was pissed, but then realised that his lips had been stapled together. He was struggling, unable to break free.

A junior civil servant plugged the vacuum in and the surgeon switched the machine on. There was a screen on the far wall and a miniature camera had been inserted in the tip of the nozzle. Harry tried to shut his eyes on what was about to happen, but his eyelids had been sewn open. His heart was pumping and he felt sick. The heartbeat of the foetus became a throbbing pain in the side of his head. He had to hold back the bile rising in his throat otherwise he would drown in his own vomit. He could see the foetus stretching and struggling to hold on to the walls of its mother's womb. It was screaming. It was fucking screaming. He couldn't believe what was happening. It was screaming that it was alive and didn't want to die, that it wanted its mother, but only Harry could understand what it was saying and then the screen turned a dark red and there was a scientist's face superimposed over the gore explaining that life only began when he and other scientists decreed, that there was no God apart from the God of science. The abortionists were nodding their heads in sad agreement and, although they swore hatred for the Tory politicians and their men of the cloth, they were in total agreement, because, after all, they were two sides of the same materialistic coin.

Harry wanted to feel what the foetus felt. He wanted to know the truth. How could a lump of meat feel pain? It didn't make sense and yet he had seen it with his own eyes. All he really understood was that the kid was dead and the girl on the table was haemorrhaging and there was some kind of debate going on as to whether such a worthless creature deserved hospital treatment. Because anyone who aborted their children like that was below sympathy and NHS resources were better spent on educating doctors for the private health sector. Harry saw the foetus floating in a corner of the room waiting for some kind of ceremony. He looked at the partially formed features and wondered what it would have become, all that potential, and then there were other spirits around it, one with a clipped accent explaining that mother was big in advertising with a sparkling career ahead of her and wasn't ready yet . . . give it another few years and then she would have a family and a nanny . . . when she was good and ready . . . on her own terms thank you very much, darling . . . and the foetus said that it understood but Harry knew it didn't, not really, and the newly dead foetus, baby, child was alone again, watching its blood and guts being popped into a jar and handed over to a paedophile who passed back a thick brown envelope in return for the chance to fulfil his fantasies.

It seemed like hours and Harry understood that it was merely seconds as the girl left her body and the machine next to the bed showed that her heartbeat was finished. He saw the spirit of the girl with the child, but there was no happy ending because he was waking up and realising it was a dream, all that emotional blackmail, fucking pile of shit, a fucking nightmare, and he pushed himself to forget. There'd been nothing lucid about that one. A fucking horror show. The last image was of the surgeons and spectators leaving by a neon-lit back exit as the nurses were allowed in to mourn the dead and clean up the mess. He watched the politicians and upright citizens vanish down an alleyway lined by private-sector abortionists who cheered and shouted and slapped their fellow businessmen on the back, applauding the promotion of cottage-industry terminations and the continued state of mental siege that drove customers into their welcoming arms. Freedom of choice. That was the crux.

Harry sat up in bed feeling sick. The sun filled the room but it didn't make any difference. He wanted to erase the dream, though this time it wouldn't fade away. He went to the bathroom and sat on the toilet. Nothing happened.

'I dreamt of this kid having an abortion last night,' Harry volunteered. 'It wasn't funny. It was the worst dream I've ever had. Or at least since I was a kid. Will's right when you think about it. That's what sex was originally invented for, to have babies. It's not just coincidence, is it? That's why you get morals and everything. I suppose if you were religious in the old days then that was the nearest you ever got to playing God. It's creation pure and simple.'

'Creating havoc more like,' Carter said. 'Forget all that. It's fun. Nothing more, nothing less. You get in there, do the business, spill your beans, notch up a few points, and that's the end of the story. You've got to be a mug to end up getting a bird up the duff these days.'

'Harry knows what I was trying to say,' Will said. 'You wouldn't ever plan to have a kid, or at least most people wouldn't in their right mind. But then whatever invented men and women saw that logically the race wasn't going to continue so they built in the pleasure side of things. Orgasms and everything. That way you forget the reality, a screaming brat shitting itself and dribbling all over the place, and just look to get your leg over. Then you end up planting your seed.'

'You sound like a gardener,' Balti said.

'Why worry about it anyway?' Carter said. 'That bird Sherry I went out with had an abortion and a fucking good job too. It's just a ball of blood and veins before it's born. It doesn't matter, does it? If she hadn't got rid of the thing then I'd still have to go round and see her and pay for it. She didn't want it either so everyone's happy. It's not alive, is it.'

'Don't you ever wonder what would've happened if it had been born?' Will asked. 'Don't you think whether it would've been a boy or a girl, or what the kid would've become?'

'No. Why should I? It's done. End of story. It's your round as well. There's only half an hour till closing so get your finger out. I'm fed up with all this. If I wanted a fucking lecture I'd have stayed home and watched the telly. Listened to the religious nutters.'

Will went to the bar and ordered. Eileen served him saying how happy she was to be getting away for a bit of fresh air and sun. It was hot in London now and the place smelt like the inside of a garage there was so much pollution. She couldn't wait to spread her towel on the sand and relax. He wished he was going with her. Carter had a point. It wasn't worth worrying about things, but Will could never escape because it was in his nature. He watched Eileen's bum moving along the bar, and the curve of her breasts when she turned around. There was no escape. It was hormones that drove you on. Chemical warfare.

It was the first time he'd really argued with Karen and it hadn't even been a proper row. Not really. She'd said her piece and left. He saw her in a different light now, but hoped it was the drink making things worse than they really were. Maybe he'd wake up tomorrow morning and everything would be alright. Perhaps it would all turn out to be a bad dream.

He looked at Slaughter at the end of the bar sitting on a stool rocking forward talking with Denise. There was a kind of glow about the bloke and he was stroking her hand. Will knew he was a nasty bit of work, but underneath it all he was a big kid. They all were. They'd started as a cell somewhere and what made someone like Slaughter turn out the way he did? A good woman could bring a bloke like that back to the starting-line. Maybe all of them wanted that deep down. Even Carter. It was just that the women they usually met were acting like blokes giving it the big one all the time. Maybe he'd been wrong acting soppy with Karen. He wondered whether Carter was right and you had to hold something back the whole time so they respected you, because if men expected things from a woman then it followed they thought the same way. Carter had it sussed. He was the happiest one out of all of them. But Will was what he was. He couldn't pretend to be anything else, however much he wanted.

'Will, you remember that game against Leicester you came to with us a few years back?' Balti asked, when his mate had brought the drinks over in two shifts. 'Well, that bloke who came up with us on the train who you were talking music with, Gary, I saw him the other day and he was asking after you. Asked if I still knocked around with that Brentford record collector. He's a DJ and wanted to have a chat about borrowing some vinyl off you. He's got a plum spot in the West End.'

'That's where the money is,' Harry said. 'Keeping the kids supplied. A lot of the old boys do that now. We should go into business, though the West End's going to be sown up, and Smiler and his mob have started doing Blues and a few places round here as a sideline. There again, it's class A if you're doing Es, and the roof'll fall in sooner or later. Always does. We're not really drug dealers are we? Pissheads more like.'

Balti had an interview the next day for something a bit more legit than flogging ecstasy, but was keeping quiet till he knew the result. It sounded alright as well, Mango coming through with a job selling insurance. It might be a doddle, following up leads and trying to persuade people to part with their hard-earnt pennies. The money sounded good as well. Mango was the only one of the Sex Division missing and had been reborn since his brother returned. He was like the old positive kid they'd known and this was reflected in him coming up with the interview.

'Give me his number and I'll give him a bell,' Will said. 'It'll be nice to see Pete again when Mango finally brings him out and play a few records. He was a good bloke. Imagine that. Farming in Norfolk. Well out of order, though, not getting in touch. Mind you, Mango said he'd been ill.'

'When do you reckon we'll get to see him?' Balti asked. 'Now that's like a rebirth. All those years and he turns up with everyone thinking he was dead. Mango's well chuffed.'

Will forgot about Karen and thought of Pete. Balti was right, it was like he was newborn, in adult form. He wondered if he'd be the same, or at least similar. Maybe they wouldn't even recognise the bloke. It was a long time. He was pleased for Mango. A minor miracle. Pleased for all the Wilsons. Most of all Mr and Mrs Wilson. Their flesh and blood. It must be the worst thing in the world losing a kid.

He thought of Pete in his Snow White T-shirt and how silly it all seemed now. Childish really. His last gig with Pete had been The Clash at the Electric Ballroom. Will remembered it so clearly. The air conditioning or whatever wasn't working, and people were sweating buckets, dropping with the heat. He thought of Strummer there with the mic. All the great lyrics and commentary that fitted in with what was going on around them at the time. Another life and yet that education was the best education. Johnny Rotten's attitude that showed you could do whatever you wanted in life never mind what the wankers and controllers told you. Poor old Pete. It would be funny seeing him again. Suddenly Will was hungry and went back to the bar for some crisps.

'You know,' Eileen said, leaning across the counter, 'everyone thinks that because you're going to Ibiza you're just going for the sex. Like that changes because you get on an airplane. It's cheap and I can't afford expensive holidays. Two weeks sitting in the sun will do me fine.'

Will thought about the time he'd gone to Magaluf with the rest of the lads. Ten thousand or so British between the ages of eighteen and thirty-five living in a town of high-rise hotels and Watneys pubs. Chicken and chips and clubs full of DJs celebrating the Leeds Service Crew and Huddersfield Soul Patrol on tour. He remembered the holiday league. There'd been books run for sex, wanks and the amount of times they'd had to shit. Carter won the Sex League, Mango the Masturbation Conference, and when Harry had come down with food-poisoning he'd cleaned up in the Shit Series. If there'd been some decent music and drink, and a few nice women around, Will wouldn't have minded so much, but after two days and nights it was boring. They stood on Psycho Street watched by the Spanish riot police out in full force after, rumour had it, a Spaniard had been glassed and killed a month before. Packed in tight, hundreds of them drinking their Chelsea Aggro cocktails, with a Union Jack hanging from Balti and Harry's balcony. Up there on the ninth floor and one night at five in the morning a girl from Barnsley forgot the acid and thought she was a bird, attempting lift-off and falling to her death. Rockets exploded in the sky and van loads of police waited tooled-up looking for trouble, mopping up the mess.

That reminded him, Carter and Harry had booked up this year. Once in Spain the league would be blown apart. The season was drifting.

'What's going to happen when you two go to Spain?' Will asked, back at the table. 'You'll get so many points over there it'll mess up the Sex Division.'

The others looked at him and laughed. Now he was with Karen, Will's ground had been shut down and the gates barricaded with barbed wire. He was right all the same.

'We'll have a league of our own over there,' Carter said.

'No more leagues,' Harry moaned. 'You're always on top. We should finish the season the night before we go away. Get it ended. Like Will said, it's going to throw the whole thing out and we'll only end up even further behind. It's the same as using prostitutes over there. There's no competition. Mind you, I might get into second position.'

'It's alright with me,' Carter said. 'Funny, isn't it, how birds go mad when they go abroad. It's like because they're outside England they think they can do whatever they want, though they could do it here as well. It's the same when England play in Europe. Everyone goes on the rampage. There's no respect. The laws don't count any more and the chains are removed. It's like nothing really exists outside England. We obey the law here, but once we're over the channel we don't give a fuck.'

The Sex Division laughed because they knew Carter was right. Nail-on-the-head job. They were an island race and the laws of the land only applied at home. It was fucking mental when you thought about it. They'd left the Amsterdam trip because they were planning to see England play away and wanted to pass through Holland. That way they could make the money stretch further. Blackpool hadn't exactly been a replacement, but it had been a good laugh. The beer tasted like shit but you got used to it, and the Buddhas made for a good night out.

When the bell went for last orders, they'd all had enough and there was no last-minute rush for refills. Slaughter sat with them for a bit slagging off some bloke who'd said something to someone that he didn't like, and Carter's heart shot into his mouth as he saw a machete handle inside the nutter's coat. So that was why he was wearing it in the heat. Carter wanted to ask why he was tooled-up on a beautiful summer's evening, but reasoned that if Slaughter knew anything he wouldn't be sitting there swapping idle chit-chat. It was better to leave well alone and get moving.

The Sex Division walked out of the pub together and Will left the others in the Caribbean takeaway. He walked slowly home, turning the key in the door to the flat and noticing that the lamp in the hall was on. That meant Karen had come back. He was relieved. He stripped off, went for a piss, and then climbed into bed. She was asleep and hadn't heard him come in.

Will watched the patterns of the street lights on the curtains. It was a game he'd played as a kid, trying to create shapes and then scenes out of the curved and ragged lines. Between the ages of nine and twelve he'd had a lot of trouble sleeping, with all the wonders of life racing through his head. He'd lie there for hours wishing he could drift off. Once he became a teenager he was fine. It was funny how those things worked. Like Harry and his dreams. The bloke was wasted.

He'd dreamt about an abortion before Will even knew what Karen was planning. Harry had a gift. He should be dealing with psychiatric cases, honing his skills. Balti, too. He had a lot to offer but instead he was wasted on the social. Mango was out on his own and that was understandable considering what had happened with Pete, while he'd never really known what Carter was thinking. He didn't worry about anything. Nothing that had happened in the past could be changed, and the future was a lottery. He was right, but somehow Will didn't think it was enough. It was incomplete. If you had no sense of the past or future, then maybe you didn't really exist.

Forget the philosophy. He had work the next day and was going to have to face Karen. He looked at her back and regretted the way he slipped into the familiar pattern. Blaming her and thinking of Eileen like that.

Will remembered Balti telling them years ago that 'the only real difference between a man and a woman is that a bird can have a baby. That's it.' Of course they'd laughed, Will as well, because women were different in a lot of other ways, physically and psychologically, but on a bigger level Balti was right. Divide and rule. The ordinary men and women in The Unity and the streets around, in the clubs and markets and the rest of London, England, Britain, the world, had more in common with each other than with the tiny band of financiers who kept them at each other's throats. Women blamed men and men blamed women, but unless you were gay you couldn't really live a proper life without the opposite sex. It wasn't about having sex either, it was something else. You needed the balance. On their own they were just men; half-human almost. A man without a woman ended up in the Sex Division.

Will got up and walked to the curtains, pulling them aside. The window was open and a breeze picking up. He pictured Bev as she'd looked the last time he saw her. Was she awake or asleep at that moment? Did she ever stop and remember him? He often wondered. What she looked like. What she thought about. Whether she had a man and kids. He tried to imagine her sitting in front of the TV watching a film, or deep asleep with the blankets pushed back struggling against the heat. Did she remember that New Year's Eve they'd gone to Trafalgar Square and got pissed in a pub in Soho, just the two of them, and she had a balloon but it was popped by someone and she was so drunk she started crying. But she was happy. He couldn't remember hearing Big Ben. They took the night bus home after a long wait that gave the drink time to wear off, stopping at every stop like night buses did, with the windows misted up and an above-average ratio of nutters aboard. What happened next? He wasn't sure, but maybe they'd had a row. A nice way to start the new year. It was a long time ago now so it didn't matter any more.

No music, no blow, no nothing but the empty street outside and the heat that sent sweat trickling down his back. He stayed there for a long time, thinking, until the breeze got stronger and cooled him down a bit. Eventually he went and laid on the bed and started running through names for their baby. First he thought of girls' names because he knew it was going to be a girl. Then boys' names, because what if it was a boy? And he wondered if Carter ever thought about the kid he could have had, just the once. He must, now and then.

Will rolled against Karen's back and looped his arms around her, moving his left hand down her body until it was over her belly, resting his open palm on the warm skin, wondering what was happening inside her womb.

NORTHERN LIGHTS

Balti was well into his second day with West London Decoration. He was top of the world. Running with Jimmy Cagney as he moved the extension-fitted roller up and down the wall. Cagney on a black-and-white time bomb going mental with bullets popping off all round him, calling for his old girl, counting down till the whole place went up. Top of the world? Top of the slide more like. Sitting in the adventure playground looking down at the sad fuckers roaming the streets pushing supermarket trolleys packed with tin cans and their heads stuffed full of green politics. Sad fuckers like Balti hanging around with spaced-out care-in-the-community gents. Sweating with Lottery fever. Playing the numbers game loading his basket with cheap tins of butter beans. Standing in line handing over saved pounds, juggling balls, a clown in the circus. Helping to build West End opera houses and art galleries. Not that Balti was giving up the Lottery. There was no chance of that because he'd put a fair bit in already and had to keep going till he won. It would be easier now. He was a winner. Knew it deep down. With a wage coming in he could afford a flutter and it wouldn't mean going without. It was goodbye to the butter beans and welcome back BSE. He'd been working two days and it was great how everything raced away. It had been the worst time of his life with nothing to do during the day—bored out of his skull and fuck all in his pocket.

He kept thinking about all those blokes who had families. He didn't know how they survived. Thing was, a lot of them didn't, and then you got some Parliament cunt on the box saying how the government was paying out too much in welfare. That they were going to crack down on benefits fraud while their mates in industry pocketed hundreds of thousands in privatisation deals. It made you feel like shit.

Like there was going to be a knock on the door and then a sledgehammer following through. It was the lowest trick in the politician's book. Pinpointing the weakest people in society and redirecting the rest of the nation's bitterness their way. MPs with outside interests sitting on advisory boards earning more in a week than most people did in a year. It made Balti sick. At least he was on his own. No small kids to explain things to when all they saw in the shops and on the telly was the endless stream of consumer goods. Made to look bad in front of their mates. There was no union of the unemployed to state the case. No sense of comradeship. You were on your own. The opposition had been either crushed or paid off. Taking the shilling. The gloss applied insisted there was nothing wrong. They were all in it together and you were isolated, and Balti knew he would move on now he was working and look after number one. He didn't have the guts to do anything else. Wouldn't have known where to start.

'Come on lads, tea up,' Paul shouted from downstairs.

Balti stopped work, propped his brush in the paint tray and went into the bathroom to wash his hands. There was a massive glass mirror that reflected the size of the room. Everything was oversized. The bath, shower, sink, even the drugs cabinet. The taps were ornate brass and there was one of those French things for cleaning your arse. They were going to put in a cork floor once it had been painted.

'It's too nice to be working,' Harry said as Balti sat down next to him in the garden.

'Should be on a beach somewhere watching the girls,' Paul replied, passing Balti's tea over. 'Sitting by the pool with a bottle of lager in my hand.'

'You expect me to drink it out of this?' the Balti man laughed, holding the West Ham mug up in front of him and staring at the crest. 'You cheeky cunt. What's the matter with Mickey Mouse?'

'I want Mickey,' Harry said. 'I'm not drinking out of a West Ham mug.'

'Well what about yours, Paul? What's wrong with Goofy?'

'I've already put three sugars in. I like the Goofy one.'

Paul was West Ham, even though he came from Acton. He shrugged his shoulders and passed the biscuits. Balti took four custard creams and put them on the iron garden table they were sitting around. The chairs were uncomfortable if you sat on them too long, but the garden was smart—long and wide with old brick walls decorated with flowering clematis and Russian vine. There were ceramic pots and several small trees. It was great, having a tea break in the garden, feeling the sun. Better than some scabby common smothered in dog shit.

Balti dunked a biscuit and looked back at the house. It was amazing the money some people had. It must've cost four-hundred grand minimum and hadn't been in bad nick to start with. Even so, the family wanted the whole place redecorated and were having an extension added to the back. The builders had finished most of the work and now it was West London's job to give the house a going over. Turn it into a palace. Balti would have thought that a six-bedroom house was big enough for a couple with two children, but figured they must be used to bigger and better things. They could use the extension as a greenhouse. There was enough glass and it faced south. Grow some of the old herb. Something like that. But Balti wasn't complaining. No chance. He was glad of the work. If the owners didn't want the place done up they'd all be signing on. It was an eye-opener, that's all. The house prices in Barnes were right up with the best of them, though he didn't know if he'd fancy living there. Too far from home and there didn't seem much in the way of decent pubs and curry houses. He wouldn't mind the garden though.

The house was detached with a garage to the side and there was a taller wall at the bottom of the garden with a thick layer of ivy eating into the bricks. It was high enough to shut out the house behind, though you'd need binoculars to see in, it was so far away. A retired colonel scanning the windows for action. The lawn nearest the house was feeling the strain of the extension work. Sand, bricks and concrete slabs had destroyed the grass, a cement mixer standing idle, its work done. It was hard work building and he was glad to be out of it. Painting and decorating was better. You really felt like you achieved something. You were putting the finishing touches to the final picture. Get stuck in listening to the radio and watch the room come back to life. Balti was well into his new job and the money was alright as well. Things were looking up.

He'd lasted two days selling insurance before one of the blokes at Harry's firm left and he was straight in the door. He didn't have to think twice. Talking shit was no way to make a living. He'd hated the insurance game from the beginning, talking out of his arse trying to con people who weren't much better off than himself. The interview had been a doddle because most of his earnings were based on commission and the firm wasn't taking a risk. The rest of the blokes were wide boys who didn't give a toss about anyone, while the few women there tried to out-male the males. Not that Balti was a social worker, but he still felt like a cunt trying to worm his way into someone's wallet, a working man or woman struggling to make ends meet worried enough by the crumbling welfare state to want to buy some kind of private protection. They were trying to think ahead and he was expected to prey on their fears, the same fears he'd had signing on.

Like there was nothing to look forward to, just the skip in the street stacked with broken concrete and rotting rubbish, because everyone knew the country was being stripped bare. It was like Karen said, the more the rich got the more they wanted. They ground you into the gutter and then pissed on you as you laid there drunk on supermarket lager. It was dog-eat-dog philosophy and it set people fighting each other. Kicking and punching, trying to get something for themselves so they could switch off and pretend there was nothing wrong. Balti wanted an easy life. He was like everyone else. Cash in his pocket and a job. He wanted to be left alone. Didn't want to think about the unfairness of it all. Karen was a diamond though. She knew what it was all about, but the way he saw it things were never going to change. It was human nature to be selfish, but with time on your hands it made you feel worse knowing the truth. He didn't want to be a victim that everyone felt sorry for. He wanted respect. A job gave you that. Without money you were fuck all. You couldn't do anything and you walked with your head down. You felt different. Birds weren't interested if you were hard up. It didn't fit in with the power trip. If you acted hard then it filled in some of the gap. That was the pecking order for you.

'Remember that time in Magaluf?' Harry asked. 'We walk in the room and Carter's doing the business with those two birds taking turns sucking his knob.'

'Should have got in there as well,' Paul said. 'Me and this mate of mine did a two-ender with some bird over in Hornchurch. I unloaded down her throat and he gave her one from behind. Right filthy old slapper she was. Fucking slag.'

'These birds in Magaluf were alright,' Harry said. 'I'm not into that kind of thing myself. I mean, you don't want to see your mate on the job do you.'

'Suppose not,' said the Happy Hammer. 'But it was dark and this bird fucking loved it, the dirty cow. Back of a fucking transit van as well.'

Balti remembered the holiday snapshot. Opening the door and finding the sex machine on the job. One of the girls turned and gave them the once over, then told them it was a private party and they weren't invited. Obviously didn't think they were up to scratch. They'd gone down the bar. Five in the morning and they were knackered, forced to sit around with the whizz kids waiting for that greedy cunt upstairs to finish. They hung around patiently sipping their bottles of piss water moaning about Carter lying back with a blonde between his legs and a redhead sitting on his face. Pure heaven. That was Magaluf for you.

'It's a bit out of order, isn't it?' Balti said. 'I mean, the girl looks after you both and then you slag her off. Like if they do the business right off then they're tarts, and if they keep their legs closed they're fucking lesbians. Least she was game for a laugh.'

He was mimicking Karen on double standards, trying to get a rise out of Paul for lumbering him with the West Ham mug. Balti told him it was a divide-and-rule plan pushed by the government and promoted through the media. Something to keep the people in line. Keep them fighting among themselves so they wouldn't get organised and have a pop at the scum in charge. They had fuck all in common with some bloke who drove a Roller and lived in Hampstead, or some bistro trendy in Kensington. It was right what Karen said. She made you think about things like that, but it was hard working it all out. It wound you up something chronic when you realised you were being shafted the whole time. It was the same with blacks and that. Another way to break you down and keep you fighting each other.

It was funny, because even though the months signing on had been hard and driven him round the bend, he'd slowed down and not been so knackered all the time. Sitting on the common wasn't how he wanted to spend his life, but it made him think about things. True, it only made him more hacked off, but it was good to know he could reason things a bit. Usually he was just working and going home to sit in front of the telly, or going out and getting pissed, but without the hard graft his mind was all over the shop. He didn't like thinking too much. That's what did you in. There was no way out that he could see, whatever Karen said. Life was a struggle. You were born, grew up, fought for everything, and then you lived on a shitty pension and became a burden on the economy. Then you died. That was it for people like him. Pure and simple. He wasn't complaining. The facts of life.

'Suppose it's a bit unfair, but so what?' said Paul. 'It's just a laugh. You wouldn't want to end up with that transit van bird though. Walking down the aisle knowing she was into threesomes. No bloke would. I mean, your trendies and that, they say they wouldn't care, that they'd fall in love with gangbangers, but they don't. They say it doesn't matter what colour you are, or where you work, but you don't see the knobs marrying black girls from Woolies do you? They still stick with their own kind.'

'I wouldn't be that bothered,' Balti said. 'Doesn't worry me at all. Means she's a goer and that's only going to be good for me, isn't it?'

'You'd mind,' Harry said. 'Even though you say you wouldn't, you would. It's only natural. I'm not saying it's right, but that's the way we are. Birds are the same.'

Being out of work might have got Balti's brain going, but it had also started him thinking about sex more than normal. Specially in the summer when anything between twenty and fifty started to look good, in their short skirts and tight tops. All the gear coming out of the wardrobe. Fucking heaven, and if you weren't wearing yourself out you had time to start thinking about how you weren't getting the business. He'd spent a good few afternoons in front of the telly plugging into the old porn videos. Watching the Germans and Dutch doing their O and A levels. Jeans round his ankles with a hard-on as Wanda with the thirty-eight-inch bust took everything her three admirers could shove into her. She was getting every hole filled and when the grunting and groaning reached its climax the camera zoomed in for a close-up of the blokes withdrawing and shooting over her face, belly, arse—and there Balti was sitting with spunk over his T-shirt and the video rolling on to another scene in another house with another blonde bird getting another length off another headless junky with a sagging knob. He always felt let down after he'd come and wondered how he got so worked up, turning the video off and going to wash away the mess. He still went back for more, though, because London was hot and steaming and he wasn't getting the real thing.

That's how it went, unless you were Carter who didn't need magazines and films. Running through the contact mags he'd got his bottle together and written off to three women whose masked photos showed them in all the regulation gear. Flicking through pages of glossy pictures and lines of ads he knew they weren't going to be stunners, but so what. Balti didn't care. They must be desperate to advertise. Either that or nymphos. Nutters even, but he wouldn't know till he tried. The phone-lines cracked him up, beautiful models with big tits plastered with slogans—BORED HOUSEWIVES TALK DIRTY . . . CLIMB ABOARD AND I'LL BRING YOU OFF . . . SHOOT ALL OVER MY HOT TITS—with the tiny type giving the phone rates. He wasn't a mug. And some of the videos they sold. Fair enough, everyone liked watching a bit of oral and anal and double pleasure, but it was stretching things selling videos of freaks and all that dominatrix stuff. Mango had some of those videos, but Balti wasn't interested in spanking birds or sitting in a fucking cage. That was comedy stuff. Balti didn't mind a bit of rubber, but birds with whips was a right turn-off. He'd leave that to the Tory MPs. It made you wonder when they sold freak videos of twenty-five stone women shagging blokes half their weight. The pictures made him feel sick, the rippling flesh and collapsed bodies. That really was taking the piss. Then there'd been the midget getting it off a couple of nice-looking birds who should've known better. Fucking horrible. You had to have standards.

Then last week this bird from Archway phones. Suzie says she's got his letter in her hand and that she loves the content and the handwriting. A couple of words spelt wrong and it looks like it's been written by an artist, all spikes and tatty edges. At first Balti thought she was taking the piss, and he didn't remember spelling anything wrong, but she said she meant it in the nicest way because she'd been dyslexic at school and had a bad time of things till she finally got some proper help. Most of the time it had been teachers telling her she was stupid and wasting their time. They started talking and it seemed easy enough so they lined it up and tonight was the night. She sounded alright and he'd been up front saying he was no oil-painting, but she wasn't bothered because as far as she was concerned it was the imagination that counted and she liked solid men. Hated skinny runts with their ribs sticking through hollow skin, pale hairless bodies and a serious lack of blood flow. As long as he remembered that a woman had a clitoris then they'd get on fine. It was a right turn-on that and her voice went husky asking him how he wanted her to dress. For a couple of seconds he'd been tongue-tied knowing this was a test of imagination and that Suzie liked men with imagination. He had to come up with something fast so went for a red basque and high heels. It wasn't very original and he held his breath because he thought he must've fucked it up, but it seemed to do the trick.

Best of all Suzie could accommodate. That was important. He didn't want Harry on the scene. He'd take the tube up after work. It was all a bit sad, but exciting as well. She could be okay or a fucking headcase. Either way he was in for an interesting night. North London on tour.

'Look at this sick cunt,' Paul said, flicking through the paper. 'They should take the bastard out and hang him. Every other day there's a fucking nonce in the paper.'

There was the blown-up face of a child-killer, his brow heavy and face unshaven. He looked like a nonce. Maybe it was the way the picture had been taken looking up. The headline condemned the monster who had dragged off a six-year-old girl during a hot summer's night, sodomised her and then set fire to the body. The report said that the police believed the maniac had planned the attack, stashing a can of petrol in a blackberry bush. Hard eyes stared straight ahead. The previous day Babs had smiled and pouted and pushed her full breasts forward, nipples ice-cubed erect. Babs liked watersports in the Caribbean (especially jet skiing) as well as quiet Italian meals for two and dancing the night away in Stringfellows. She had a big future ahead of her. The paper had been in no doubt of that. But today the message had changed. The fun was on hold with outrage filling the gap. Paul finished the report and turned to the editorial with its subhead SCUM.

'What's the point letting people like that waste our money in the nick?' Paul asked when he'd finished the editorial. 'Nonces should be strung up. Them and terrorists who put bombs in shopping centres and murder innocent women and children.'

Balti nodded. There was no point arguing. He didn't believe in the death penalty simply because he knew what the old bill were like. They'd fit you up for stupid little things, so what would they do when they were faced with a crime that had to be solved fast because the media was breathing down their necks demanding instant retribution?'

He finished his tea and took three more biscuits to keep him going. He wanted to get back to work. It was too hot and he needed some shade. It was cool indoors and he didn't mind getting back into the painting. There was a steady motion working the roller and his brain got into the rhythm. He ran his hand along the polished banister leading upstairs. Right the way up and no chance of a splinter. Into the room he was painting with the radio playing Oasis quietly in the background.

The rest of the afternoon passed quickly and they were soon knocking off. Balti stayed behind and ran a bath. He had a bag with him and clean clothes. He stripped off and got in, spread out. Bubble bath hit the rim of the tub. Fucking lovely. It was amazing what a bit of luxury could do. He dried off and put on a clean pair of jeans and a new-breed Ben Sherman. He let himself out the back and walked to the BR station. It didn't feel like London in Barnes. He could've been at the seaside or in some market town. He felt relaxed. He didn't have to wait long for a train and he was on-board cruising through South-West

London and up to Clapham Junction, past Asda, New Covent Garden
and Sainsbury's. The sun lit up the MI6 building opposite Vauxhall
BR, with its flash design and glass panelling. The carriage was nearly
empty, a kid with some kind of drum n bass playing in his earphones
and an upright elderly woman reading a gardening book. Everyone
was going in the opposite direction. The train pulled into Waterloo, the
international terminal to his left.

He pushed through the crowds watching the departure board
and went underground, buying his ticket and checking the adverts
lining the escalator, West End tourist shows and dodgy soul albums.
Fucking typical—the board on the northbound Northern Line platform said the next train was in seven minutes and the cunt was going
the wrong way. The one after went through Archway, but it was twelve
minutes. He'd go up to Camden and change. The platform started to
fill up and he wasted the time watching mice play under the lines.
The Northern Line had to be the worst line in London. Nothing but
hassle. The waiting made him think about where he was going, the
woman at the end of the trip. He had to phone Suzie when he got to
Archway as she wasn't that keen on giving out her address. Fair dues.
A girl couldn't be too careful. For all she knew he might be some serial
killer. When the tube finally arrived he was pressed against the door
between the carriages, where at least there was air rushing in when
the train was moving.

Balti didn't like being packed in tight. He'd heard the horror
stories of the tube going down because the wiring was so out of date.
Thousands stuck underground and he didn't fancy it in a packed carriage. He didn't fancy being pressed up against the office girls in front
of him either. Felt like a right perv trying to think of something apart
from Suzie. He tried counting sheep but he wasn't a farm hand like Pete
Wilson. Mango hadn't brought his brother out yet and wanted to go
up to Norfolk to stay on the farm. He'd miss the luxury of his flat and
wouldn't like getting the Jag covered in cow shit. But he was pleased
for the bloke. Mango got on his wick at times, but he'd been through a
lot and now maybe he'd ease up.

Balti relaxed when a good chunk of the passengers got off at

Leicester Square. Camden came up soon enough and a short wait later he was passing through Kentish Town and Tufnell Park, walking up the out-of-order escalator at Archway past the puffing old-timers. When he reached the top he was out of breath himself. Torrential rain pounded the concrete outside. He was sweating from the train, straight out of the sauna so he shouldn't have bothered about the bath. He hoped he didn't smell too bad. He found a phone and made the call.

'Hello.' A man's voice.

Balti hesitated. Must be the wrong number.

'Is Suzie there?'

'Hold on.'

He didn't expect this. She said she could accommodate.

'Hello.' A woman's voice.

'Suzie?'

'You made it. You're a bit late. I'll come down and get you. We can go for a drink.'

Balti walked outside and waited by the railings. The rain had stopped. Short and to the point, steam rising from the pavement. A man answering the phone, meeting at tube stations, off down the pub. It wasn't what he expected. Wasn't like the films. He had the script in his head. The easy run up to Archway, round to a nice little flat where the sex goddess opened the door in some silky gear, ushered into a nicely laid-out living room. Sitting on the designer couch. The pouring of drinks. A couple of sips. Suzie downing hers in one. Rushing towards him. Off her head with lust. Sex mad. Balti carried out on a stretcher, with an intravenous drip in his arm and a big smile on his face. Something like that anyway.

'Hello.'

He turned round. The surprise must've shown. He'd never realised eyes were so important to a person's face. The photo in the magazine showed her in stockings and suspenders, with the main part of her face covered in one of those digital masks they used on the telly when they were showing police video footage of a crime. Hiding the identity of the man in custody so as not to prejudice the case. All fair and square.

'The train took ages. Sorry I'm late.'

Suzie had big blue eyes. They were massive. She was a cracker. What the fuck was she doing in magazines with the losers? He was a bit stuck for words. He hadn't expected much, just a good shag with a clapped-out nutter who had enough passion to make up for a wrecked body. Bit like him really. But Suzie could've been a model.

'It's alright. My brother was round so I had someone to talk to. He's gone now. Bet you wondered who it was answering the phone. Thought I had someone else there. Lining them up on a conveyor belt. I'm not that bad you know.'

Suzie started to talk as she took Balti by the arm and led him back through the station towards a pub she knew. She was going to be upfront with him and said that she used the contacts columns to avoid complications. She was an actress, a proper actress, and she didn't want men becoming attached. But she needed sex as much as the next person. Could Balti understand that? He nodded and opened his mouth to say something. That it was fine by him. But she asked him did he really understand, because men were pretty thick when it came to working women out. They had to understand that women had the same needs as men. They had a sexuality that could be just as material and unemotional as that of a man. What really pissed her off was all that hippy earth mother propaganda that said a woman was full of intuition and creativity. Now she was an actress, and that was something creative in itself, but she was no earth mother. She liked sex. Pure and simple. Nothing wrong with that was there? And Balti said no, of course not. She was only being honest and how was the new job going that he'd been talking about, she'd been out of work a lot and one thing she would never do was appear in porno mags. That wasn't acting. It was demeaning to the women who were forced into those roles. Women posing for men to dribble over. It made her very angry. Dirty old men in their old age masturbating over pin-ups. It was exploitative. That was the difference. She could do whatever she wanted with her body and didn't have to do what men told her. She was taking what she wanted. Suzie was no prostitute. She hoped he understood and she wouldn't go on about it any more. It was better to get things out in the open. She wasn't mad. She didn't think Balti was a failure with women because he had to hunt them down in magazines.

They walked up the hill and Balti was knackered already. His head was spinning. He wanted an easy life. An easy shag.

'That's a beautiful pint,' he said, feeling a bit better as they sat in the Whittington with Dick's cat on the wall behind glass.

It looked like something squashed they'd just scraped off the road. He concentrated on the Guinness.

'It's a nice little pub,' Suzie said. 'They have diddly-daddly on Thursday nights. Session musicians with fiddles and bodhrans and pipes and banjos who just turn up and sit around playing. There's no stage and no sense of being an audience. I like it in here. It's very natural. I often thought that plays should be performed in that way with no sense of Us and Them, but it's a visual medium so it wouldn't be much good if you can't see what's happening.'

Balti looked around the pub. It was a small Irish boozer with a central bar and the atmosphere of a pub where the quality of the drink came first. It had the mark of class most London pubs used to boast before the craze to gut them and turn the inside into imitation spit-and-sawdust barns. Thing was, it was all decoration and the drink was usually overpriced and the lager flat.

The Whittington wasn't busy. Not what he'd expected at all. He was looking to get his leg over. Nothing more. But the Guinness was worth the trip and Suzie was something else. Long blonde hair and a fit body. She wore dangling earrings and tapped her short nails on the table. She'd stopped rabbiting now so he could get a word in. It was nice having a second's pause between sentences. She spoke sense he supposed, though she went on a bit. She was another strong woman. Karen was strong. His old girl was strong. They were all different though. Most of the women he knew were strong. But it was strange because he'd had the thing fixed in his head. A wham-bam-thank-you-darling session then out the door. He hadn't planned on a pint and idle conversation. He couldn't get his head round it. There had to be something else going on. There had to be a problem. Simple as that. She didn't seem like a nutter. Went on a bit, but that could be nerves, because fuck knows he was nervous enough now.

He liked Suzie straight off. The eyes and face and rest of her body. Big warm pools of colour. He lifted the glass and took a long drink. Just the one, then he'd get things moving.

Balti knew his place in the scheme of things. He wasn't in good shape and had been out of work. He didn't expect anything other than a shag and was prepared to scrape the barrel. Suzie wasn't the barrel. It had to be inside her head. He tried to picture the basque and high heels waiting at home. Started thinking of the videos under his bed. The Germans and Dutch taking it down the throat and up the arse. False groans as some wanker with a half-erect knob rubbed KY up a Filipino's arse and drove it home. Three-onto-one wasn't nice. The girl on all fours getting it rammed down her throat. A bloke underneath who she was riding and then the third bloke arrives and climbs aboard. Camera zooming in as the bloke giving it the A treatment rubs balls with the man below. Switching angles, changing cameras to show the expression on the girl's face. He could tell she was feeling the pressure even though she tried smiling for the camcorder, but with some junky's knob halfway down your throat it was difficult.

Suzie was off again telling him all about the Archway and how she'd moved there from the south coast. She'd grown up in Brighton and would return there one day, but she was waitressing in London now and things were going well for her. He smiled and nodded and wondered what made people appear in porn videos. Maybe they didn't care, but more likely needed the money. The bird doing the threesome couldn't get much out of it, so it had to be the cash. They all looked scabby. The blokes well dodgy and the girls all worn out. Maybe some of them got off on it. Difficult to say really. Not the kind of people you met down the pub. He remembered that story about Barry Walters a couple of years back. He sits down to watch a dirty video and there's his girlfriend on the screen. Two weeks before the wedding as well. Packs her in. It made the lads laugh because the hypocrisy was so obvious. What was he doing watching in the first place? You had to apply the rules to yourself as well. You couldn't judge. But you did. Strip off the personality with the clothes. Blow up dolls. You couldn't escape it and Suzie went for the public health warning straight off and it didn't do a lot of good. He couldn't work out if she was a headcase or what.

'Do you want another?' she asked.

Balti looked at his pint. It was empty. He watched her walk to the bar. She was wearing dungarees and a T-shirt. He watched her joking with the barmaid as the Guinness settled. She drank pints as well.

'I could drink this stuff all day,' she said, raising her glass to her mouth. 'Drink too much though and it sets your heart racing. It's the iron content.'

Balti noticed she wasn't wearing make-up. He couldn't smell perfume either. Suzie was obviously a natural girl.

'That letter you wrote was great,' Suzie said. 'The way the letters mash up together and all the spikes. It had character. I'm into shapes you see. Odd shapes. Outlines and angles. I love fractals, the way they expand and trail off into the distance. Do you know what I mean?'

Balti nodded his head. He didn't have a clue. He'd never thought about his writing before, but he liked fractals.

'You made a few mistakes in your spelling as well.'

'I was never very good with spelling.'

'I got left behind at school because the teachers didn't know I was dyslexic. Funny, really, but they get the chance to set you up for life and if you struggle then they get on your back. Not all of them, but too many. It's like life when you grow up. If you're no good at your job then people take it personally, as though you're lacking something in your personality. It's like you're doing it on purpose.'

'I'm not dyslexic. Never had much interest really. We were always mucking about. They don't get hold of you and make you want to learn. Just tell you you're a problem. I couldn't wait to leave and get a job.'

'It was acting that made it alright for me,' Suzie said. 'Nothing classical. I didn't have any formal training. The local youth club did something and then I joined an amateur group. I don't make very much, but it's fun, and you can always pick up bar or restaurant work. I've had a couple of bit parts on the TV as well. That helps. Acting you get to be anything you want. You can get lost in a role and then say it's someone else. Nobody knows how much is inside you. Depends on the part of course.

They only ever see the outline. It's all shapes isn't it? I mean, you look at a woman and you see her figure. Whether she's got nice breasts and legs. How much she weighs. The height and proportions. That's fair enough. The shapes and sizes. Weights and measures. What's inside though?'

Balti smiled. He didn't know. The Guinness was slipping down a treat. He pointed at the dead cat on the wall.

'Dick Whittington's cat's been knocked out of shape a bit. Looks like he was run over by a lorry.'

Suzie laughed and looked at the cat.

'There's a bridge up the hill where the suicides go. They jump off on to the road. It's a bit unlucky if you're driving along and a face bursts through the windscreen. I can't understand how someone could be so depressed they could go and kill themselves. Life shouldn't be taken so seriously. We live forever so why worry about anything. We should go out and get what we want. That's why I use the magazines. What's the point in hanging around expensive clubs trying to pick someone up when all you want is sex?'

'I don't know,' Balti said, looking towards the barmaid who was talking to an old boy on the opposite side of the bar.

Suzie moved closer and lowered her voice for his benefit.

'I got fed up with all that. Standing around waiting for some idiot to get enough drink down his throat so he has the courage to come over and chat me up. All that mating ritual and you don't have a clue what you're going to get. You could pick up a psycho who's going to come home and kill you. The amount of boring bastards I've had in the past. All the shitty one-liners. It really gets on your nerves and then they last a couple of minutes and fell asleep. Next morning they don't have anything worth saying and you want to get them out the door as fast as possible. The pretty boys are worst. All shape and no substance. So I've given all that up now. I use the adverts. There's no hassle that way. I want sex. You want sex. Straightforward and honest and I get to talk to my partners beforehand. I get a lot of wankers mind. We're all the same you know. Everyone on the planet. There's no individuals. There's no point being pinned down with one person because then it becomes boring and miserable and you end up tearing each other's hair out.

We're going to live forever even when we die, so who cares. It's a great feeling, don't you think? Now that's real freedom.'

Balti nodded. As long as Suzie was happy. He existed. He was an individual. And while it was true enough that he would be in another situation and probably quite different if the Queen was his mum, he reckoned there would still be something that was his own. There again, he didn't know what he thought about life after death. If it wasn't for his granddad telling him about that out-of-body experience then he'd say death was just an appointment with the furnace. Nothing to look forward to after the flames had burnt you to a cinder. He knew the old boy wouldn't have lied, but he didn't have the faith. He wouldn't mind believing, because like Suzie said, it would make everything a lot easier, but you couldn't make yourself believe something if you didn't really feel it. But bollocks, he'd come up to Archway for a bit of creation, not all this talk about death.

'So what are you doing now?' he asked.

'It's a play about the Wigan Casino,' Suzie said. 'It's about these four people who have been going to the Casino for years listening to northern soul and now the Casino's closing down. There's three songs the DJs always played. Long After Tonight Is All Over by Jimmy Radcliffe, Time Will Pass You By by Tobi Legend and I'm On My Way by Dean Parrish. The play centres around the songs and what the characters are going to do with the rest of their lives. Whether they'll give up on northern soul because the Casino is the best there'll ever be, or whether they'll move on to another kind of music. Where will they go next? We're still rehearsing. It's going to be good. I'm enjoying my role.'

'What do you do?'

'I'm going to settle down and get married because nothing will ever be that good again. The Wigan Casino is the ultimate and I'm going to stop dead and start leading a very mundane, everyday life and find love and happiness. It's a good part.'

'It's a bit unfair on the bloke you end up marrying. If he's just a shape to fill the gap. He's going to have feelings as well.'

'That's the kind of character she's going to be. Decisive and working to a plan.'

Balti felt sorry for the man involved, but it was only a poxy play so it didn't matter. The time passed and he forgot what he'd come up to North London for after four pints. They were having a good old chat and before he knew what was happening it was ten o'clock and Suzie was drinking up and telling him it was time to go. He carried the glasses to the bar and followed her outside. Down the hill and through a multi-coloured, piss-soaked subway. He watched the mugging mirrors and saw their bent reflections approaching. The curl of hip-hop graffiti formed a giant snake through the passage. A bottle rolled in the breeze. Reds and greens and yellows rushed past.

He walked up the ramp and felt Suzie next to him, talking a mile-a-minute. He'd had eight pints of Guinness and was feeling heavy. He was hungry as well. They cut through the flats. He needed a piss and went behind a wall. Suzie waited under a light. Having a slash in a dark corner turning his head to find she'd come over and was standing next to him watching. He felt awkward as he shook himself dry. He felt her hand drift down and work him erect. Moving back and forward slowly, then faster.

Suzie pushed Balti back into the shadows, faint light from the Archway roundabout filtering through the trees. Balti was hot and the sound of traffic died down with a red light. He could hear Irish music from the Archway Tavern, the doors wide open for fresh air. Suzie pulling his jeans wide open and reaching inside his pants for his balls, grabbing and yanking them forward. He tried to pull her into him but she shrugged him off, moving her hand back to his cock. He had a stonker right enough and tried to kiss her but she turned her head.

'When we get back.'

Suzie was reaching into her dungaree pocket and taking out some kind of gel, undoing the top with her teeth and then lining the lubricant along his knob. She replaced it and started working harder, in total silence, bringing Balti off in a machine-gun succession of spurts that disappeared into the darkness.

'Come on,' she said. 'Let's get back.'

Balti did up his jeans and tried to catch up, following her through a small estate and up a street lined with rundown but still impressive houses. His knob was sticky. He'd been looking forward to a good bit of sex, not a quick hand job in a dark corner. Fuck that for a game of soldiers. But he'd have time to recover, though Suzie had gone all quiet on him now. Just his luck. He would need a piss again soon. The Guinness felt bad in his gut. It was the wrong drink in this kind of weather. He was sweating like a pig and the gel was uncomfortable in the front of his jeans.

A door opened and Balti followed Suzie up a flight of stairs. Another door and she was having trouble with the lock, finally inside turning on the light, walls lined with posters of famous actresses. All the big names from the past were there. Marilyn Monroe, Doris Day, Bette Davis. The pictures were big and framed and leading into the living room, where smaller glossy photos took over.

Suzie led Balti to the couch, sat him down and put on a CD. A song he didn't recognise.

'Jimmy Radcliffe,' she said. 'What do you want to drink?'

'A bit of that whisky would be alright. No water thanks.'

She handed Balti the drink and leant over. She kissed him on the lips. Her mouth was warm and friendly. She walked to the door and disappeared, leaving Balti to look around the room. It was nicely decorated, full of plants and the photographs. She must be doing okay, though it wasn't an expensive set-up. A bit of imagination had obviously been applied. This was better.

He turned his head as Suzie returned. She was wearing a long seethrough number. She looked great. Her body was perfect. The light was dimmed and she walked over towards him. There had to be something wrong. It was a dream. She was a film star in the making. Wrapping those arms around his neck and pulling him in close, whispering romance in his ear. His bladder was full. He needed a piss but didn't want to break the spell.

'You'll last longer after what I did outside,' Suzie whispered. 'You won't let me down will you?'

Balti hoped not. She led him towards the bedroom and he managed to get into the bathroom for a piss. He leant over the bog and hung his head. It was a dream come true. Like the films. He flushed the toilet and washed his face in the sink, a quick wipe under his arms. So what, she'd been drinking as well. He was more Sid James than Humphrey Bogart. You had to have a laugh. He pulled the string and hurried towards the bedroom.

HAPPY HOUSE

It was a nightmare. A fucking nightmare. Worse than anything so far and Harry was taking it seriously. He was paying attention because he had the gift. He could see the future and prophesise events. It had happened so many times before that he couldn't bottle out and dismiss last night's dream as meaningless. He was walking up and down, stopping halfway, sitting in the condemned cell waiting for the hangman to arrive, handcuff his hands and slip a hood over his head, string him up from the gallows, cut him down in the nick of time. Dragged screaming to a club full of clones with Saddam tashes. He felt like topping himself. Why him? Why? Bath houses full of queers taking turns banging out the primitive four-bar beat of the swamps on his arse. No fucking way. He'd rather die. No way was he living the life of a shirt-lifter.

'You coming or what,' his best mate Balti shouted. 'What are you doing in there, having a wank?'

Like a fucking wife.

'I'm having a piss. That alright with you?'

Harry finished brushing his teeth and left the bathroom. Thing was, looking in the mirror, he didn't look like a bum bandit. Maybe you didn't. Ken Davies, now, he didn't look like an iron, but he was bent as the proverbial. A nice enough bloke who kept his interests to himself and never got any grief. Thing was, everyone knew the bloke. That was the difference. It wasn't like he was some stereotype off the telly emerging from the bushes in a G-string.

'My knob's still sore from that bird up in Archway,' Balti said, once they'd left the flat and were walking down the street. 'What a night. Don't think I'll ever be the same again.'

'Where'd you say you met her?'

'I didn't.'

'Well, where'd you meet her then?'

'On the tube.'

'On the tube? What were you doing, touching up office girls in the rush hour?'

'She asked me what platform she was on and we got talking, went for a drink, and before I know what's happening she's inviting me back to listen to her CDs.'

'Those three points you got mean I'm bottom of the league. I'm not even joint bottom now that Will's given up.'

'Relegation mate. You've still got tonight and then you're off on holiday and the season ends. You'll get your end away over there no problem. Unless you're a pillow biter. But it won't count will it? Birds don't count in Spain. You could still catch up tonight. Never know, I might get lucky and give Carter a run-in myself. I can feel the old confidence returning. Surging back more like. What a fucking night. First wage packet in my pocket and three points in the bag. Dear oh dear, she didn't just swallow, she fucking gargled first like she was on the Listerine. I'm back in the land of the living and showing some form.'

Balti was full of himself and Harry couldn't help laughing at the thought of his mate making up the massive points difference in a single night. He'd have more than a sore knob the amount of work he had to do. They'd be carting him off in an ambulance, but at least he'd die happy, which was more than Harry could say for himself. They didn't bother with calculations as they turned on to the high street and hurried towards the pub. Carter was the undisputed champion waiting to be crowned. The shag machine was pure Dutch quality and had played the game as it should be played, using the wings and knocking the ball through the midfield with a deft touch born of practice.

It was Friday night and Balti had money to burn. It was going to be a good one. His first week's wage and it was a great feeling. Welcome back to the human race and all the bother and mind games were over. He could feel the tingle in his bones, even though his knob was aching. That Suzie was a right goer. She couldn't get enough. She fucking loved it and was moaning her head off all night. It made him feel big. He'd made her happy. Things were definitely looking up. It was just a shame it was a one off. She'd made up her mind and he knew there was no going back for seconds. She'd taken what she wanted without complications. But Balti was grateful. It wasn't every day a bloke like him ended up in bed with a bird like that. Northern soul. Catchy songs, though he'd never been into that sort of music. Truth be told, he'd always found it a bit weedy. Suzie was making the effort playing the part and said northern soul was a much rawer version of the weak stuff that you usually heard. It was soul mingled with RnB. Wigan Casino hadn't served alcohol and the all-nighters had functioned on speed. It was part of a culture that had eventually progressed to acid house, techno, jungle and all the other strands of a basic theme. Suzie said she'd always preferred old platters though. Frank Sinatra, Ella Fitzgerald, Dean Martin. Silver-screen Hollywood romance and kiss-and-cuddle music, and while it was a mechanical kind of sex she enjoyed he could understand her reasoning. She was a romantic, whatever he'd first thought about her being a nutter decked out like that posing for contacts columns. The songs were sad though. Love didn't seem to exist, however much the soul singers tried to persuade you otherwise.

Balti went into the newsagent's while Harry waited outside with his head down staring at the pavement. The bloke had a far-off look that Balti couldn't work out. He bought fifteen quid's worth of Lottery tickets. His woman was waiting over the Atlantic and she didn't appear in dodgy magazines. He could feel the oil soaking into tired muscles and see the fireflies dancing near enough to grab. A coal black night on the verandah with the perfect woman skinning up. He was on his way to paradise while Carter and Harry were jetting off to The Coast Of A Thousand Slappers.

'It's a mug's game you know,' Harry said when Balti came out of the shop waving his investment in the air. 'A fiver's alright now and then, but fifteen quid's throwing it away. You think how much that adds up to if you do it every week. You're a fucking junky.'

'I'll remember that when they come knocking on the door with the cheque. I wish you'd cheer up you miserable cunt. Fuck me, you're going on holiday tomorrow.'

Harry wasn't bothered about getting rich. Last night was enough
for him. Tossing and turning unable to breathe half the time let alone
sleep, with the window wide open wishing it would rain. A nice elec-
trical storm would have done him. Thunderbolts and lightning and a
monsoon downfall to break the spell. A terrible night. The atmosphere
heavy and sky overcast blocking the moon, drifting in and out of his
dreamworld dungeon and the steaming concrete of a Turkish bath.
Sweat on his skin brushing against the sheets sitting on his own back
to the wall, dripping water running down from the ceiling following
his spine. His rucksack was in the corner and Balti sat by a pool. Five fat
Arabs in white towels were sipping mint tea. The mist was thick like
he was back on the moors and then it began thinning, swirling and
vanishing so he could see the room clearly, a thin masseur with a skull
on his neck working an old man's back and shoulders, thumping white
flesh. There was a faint hum in Harry's ears, Turkish music drifting in
from outside. From a London roundabout, mixing Irish and Turkish
strings along the echo of a spraycanned tunnel. He could see through
walls and into the street outside. It was dark, drab, depressing; full of
lepers and orphans. Beggars sat outside a tube station. There was a faint
smell of hashish in the subway.

Balti was with a beauty queen tapping his foot to the dull thud
of a rapper calling for respect, red cap pulled over his mate's blood-
shot eyes. The kebab house on the corner serving closing-time drunks.
The mosque with its blue dome and sound system broadcasting white
noise. Balti led into a doorway by the she-man actress-actor humming
sweet soul music, just a sex machine James Brown, sex machine Carter,
big blue eyes and dungarees playing a role, travelling on the Northern
Line with the pissheads and bandits heading for Hampstead Heath.
Harry shaking his head and blocking out the vision, calling for a cup
of PG Tips, making a stand for the English way of life, leaning his head
back against the wall and allowing the heat to melt his gut, sweating
out the poison, cleaning his pores and clearing his head.

The smell of shit. Ancient sewers breaking down and flooding the
tube. The radio said that tens of thousands were feared dead. Buried
alive deep underground. Quick-drying sewage clogging the system

as dancing girls danced around their handbags. Shit flowing from the telly, from the mouths of preaching hypocrites, their faces outraged and purple as they held court, theatrically running from the studio to a waiting Rolls that rushed them to Ms Party Discipline in Mayfair, a special kind of lady who would make them obey the whip. The fuzzy logic of the Turkish bath fizzing and splashing piss over tiles. Harry feeling sweat in his eyes, salt poisoning the blue pools. Travelling the planet with Balti only to find himself back in London, watching his mate drop his jeans and flash his arse, all the time the words SEX SEX SEX beating out from a red neon display above the toilet door.

'Fucking hell,' Harry said out loud, shaking his head.

'What?' Balti asked, turning as they entered The Unity. 'What's the matter now?'

'Nothing. It's alright.'

'What's wrong with you? You look like you're sick or something. Come on, have a drink. Life's not that bad. You've been miserable all day. I wish you'd cheer up.'

Carter and Will were sitting at the bar. Balti eased his way through the packed pub and ordered, flashing a twenty. Denise took one for herself and handed back the change. Balti was rolling, with money to spend and his balls well and truly emptied of the pressure that had built up over the last eight months. He'd wanked himself silly while he was signing on, but it was more than that. Porno mags and dirty videos were alright, but there wasn't a lot of variation once you'd gone through the various combinations. The tension had to come out some way. A few more days and he'd probably be sniffing again, but for now he was satisfied to get pissed out of his head. Harry and Carter were off tomorrow but he didn't care. He was back in the swing of things. London was the best city in the world. Who wanted to go to Spain? London pissed all over Paris and Rome and Berlin, even though he'd never been to any of those places. If you were happy inside your head then you'd be happy wherever you were. West London was the place to be. Centre of the universe. Hammersmith, Shepherd's Bush, Acton. Home was where the heart was. West London was top of the tree. Fucking class as the lager-lager-lager soundtrack on the jukebox belted out and the

Chelsea boys drifted further West through Hounslow and Feltham and Hayes and Harlington, out to the satellite towns burning bright on the horizon. He felt brilliant, dipping his finger in the whizz Carter offered.

Will was smiling and making the announcement that he was going to be a dad. Him and Karen were going to get married and he wanted the rest of the lads to be ushers. His brother would be best man. Nothing too flash mind, but they'd do it nice. They'd get a decent band for the reception and someone who'd play their favourite records. He wanted his daughter, or son if it was a boy, to have the best start in life. It would give the kid security. He asked whether the rest of them understood and they nodded their heads. They were pleased for Will. Karen was a fine woman. They all loved the opposite sex, Harry especially as the lager soothed his fears. His reaction to the nightmare was healthy enough. The sheer horror he'd felt was reassuring. He was happy like the rest of the Sex Division because Will would make a good father and who knows, maybe one day Harry would have kids of his own and get a place somewhere further out where the property was cheap and you could buy yourself a bit of space.

Balti looked at Will and knew he'd make his own dad look like the scum he was, but he was doing okay now and there was even room for a few seconds of understanding. Times had been hard and his old man had taken the easy way out blaming his nearest and dearest, like all cowards, picking on those who couldn't defend themselves. Balti supposed he understood why the old man had been a cunt. He understood but would never forgive. Everything around you was geared up towards competition, and there always had to be a scapegoat. Some blokes hammered their women and kids. Others kicked the shit out of strangers. He wondered how much of it rubbed off, how much you could decide things for yourself. At least he was sound, and so were his mates. The real scum, the wife batterers and child abusers were usually out of sight, round the corner. When you found one you kicked seven shades of shit out of the cunt. Them and the rapists and muggers and other perverts. That's why his old man deserved a kicking. He'd brought the headlines home with him. He didn't care. Not now. Of course he didn't care. The Sex Division drank up and Harry ordered.

Will and Karen had sat down and talked the thing through. Will said he was sorry. Karen said she was sorry. It was a tense time full of surprises. Karen told Will that she had decided to have the child. She had been scared at first, but now she was used to the idea she didn't want an abortion. It would be okay. After all, they would be together for the rest of their lives. She said it was their decision. Will didn't think this was strictly true, but the result was what he wanted so he kept quiet. Everything was sweet. The important thing was that they were going to have a baby. They would be happy after all. It showed that stories could have a happy ending, even if it was really the beginning. They hugged each other for a while and then Will asked Karen to marry him in a rush of excitement. He was surprised when she agreed. In the end, he supposed, you all ended up just like your mum and dad. So it was agreed, and they'd plan the marriage and wait for the birth. Will felt a deep sense of relief. The rest of his life was mapped out and the security erased any self-doubt or irrational fear. He knew exactly where he was going.

The Sex Division raised their glasses and toasted the father to be, and then Carter was asking Will if he wanted to sit down, or did he have any strange cravings. Maybe he wanted some coal to eat or deep friend soap because, after all, that's what happened when you were in the club, and Balti reached over and placed his hand on Will's stomach and said he could feel kicks, and Harry fell into the joke and asked Will when he'd start showing. And Will was as happy as he'd ever been, thinking for a second or two about Bev and how lucky he'd been to find Karen because it showed there really was something called love. He couldn't have had this with anyone else. He didn't care what the cynics said. Love could be personal.

There was family love, where you didn't have much choice, and then you had the kind of love you had to discover, more down to luck than anything. A lot of people never found that. Will thought about Mango last night on the phone telling him he'd taken a couple of weeks off work and was leaving at midday to stay on Pete's farm. The brothers were driving up together and the rest of the Wilsons were going up on the train the following Friday night for the weekend. Pete wasn't sure what he'd do yet, but they'd been getting on well—apart from a couple of pissed punches that didn't mean anything—and there was a good chance he'd move back to London. Pete was older, but the same person. A diamond. The bloke had suffered, like the rest of them. It wasn't his fault. Mango was amazed how the years had fallen away so quickly. Family love rarely died, whatever happened. Mango said everything had changed. His mum and dad were born again, sisters crying all the time, but he wasn't bothered as they were crying because they were happy. Mango said life couldn't be better.

Will knew he was the other extreme from Mango in many ways, but they'd both found something special. The bloke sounded good, and though Pete hadn't been seen by Mango's mates yet it was something that would come. Will thought about the amnesia. It was as though for all those years the real Pete hadn't existed, but had been left dangling. Then he returned and that time didn't matter any more because the relief and happiness outweighed the sadness, and the happiness was current and the sadness in the past, another memory. He hoped Mango and Pete would get on alright in Norfolk. Somehow he knew it would work out. He told the rest of the Sex Division what was happening with Mango and how it was a good idea getting away. They all drank thoughtfully, not exactly toasting the Wilsons, but pleased all the same.

'Wait till we get over to Spain,' Carter shouted, trying to make himself heard over the noise of the Friday night drinkers and the music which had suddenly cranked up, easing the emotion. 'Me and Harry are going on the pull big-style when we get over there. Stick with me Harry my son and you can have the leftovers, all the old heifers I don't want. The Sex Division king is off on tour and the birds are in for a treat.'

'You haven't won yet,' Balti said.

'I'm on fifty-seven points and you're my nearest challenger with five. Will's given up, Mango's down on the farm building scarecrows with his brother, and Harry there's fallen in love with his right hand. I'm the winner. All fair and square.'

'There's still tonight. It's not over until the ref blows the final whistle. Till you take off tomorrow there's still a chance for one of the outsiders to come through with a late surge. That's the problem with the big clubs, they get too cocky. It's a funny old game, shagging.'

Carter smiled indulgently, but he'd lost interest and was watching Denise at the other end of the bar serving Slaughter. He was looking forward to the two-week break. She'd come round last night and it had all got a bit serious, when after giving her a good servicing he'd told her she should make an honest man of Slaughter. She couldn't keep the bloke hanging on forever. Denise said she knew she had to tell him something. She would miss Terry when he was away and she started going into one about how she could piss all over Slaughter any time she wanted because she had him eating out of her hand, but with Terry it was different because he would go his own way and she had to understand that. She would think of him when he was on holiday with all those randy girls chasing after him and she hoped he'd behave himself. He looked at her a bit surprised and said nothing.

'We going down The Hide then?' Harry asked. 'Let's have a drink down there.'

'In a bit,' Carter said, watching Denise and Slaughter.

The perfect couple and the imperfect twosome walking down the aisle in a double marriage. Will and Karen with a bun in the oven dressed in a white wedding gown with pink flowers in her hair, followed a minute or two later by Slaughter and Denise in a short skirt and high heels. Will would be in top hat and tails, while Slaughter would be wearing his leather coat with a specially-designed secret-agent holster for his favourite machete. The two couples would stand side by side as the vicar struggled with their names and rambled about sickness, health and obedience. The reception would be a laugh and end in a punch-up between the good, bad and ugly.

Carter didn't care if Denise married Slaughter or not. He'd still be able to give her a portion whenever he wanted. But those birds at the bar were alright and he felt the familiar urge. He couldn't wait to get away. It was going to be good. He needed a holiday, though tonight he was going to rub the Sex Division's nose in it and pull something classy to round off a successful season. It had been a good campaign and he'd had a few results along the way, irrespective of the opposition. He'd had his share of pigs, but a few crackers as well. Carter reckoned he deserved a lap of honour. Maybe later. There was a party tonight and it would be stacked with crumpet. A few beers in The Unity, down The Hide, maybe Blues, then the party. It would be a good warm-up. They'd be knackered tomorrow getting down to Gatwick, but a drink in the bar and a few sherbets on the flight over and they'd be raring to go. Carter was going to shag himself silly. He always did when he went away. He was looking forward to the sand, sun and low prices. He'd come home with a dose on a couple of occasions so this time he was taking a big supply of rubbers. Not being able to drink while he took the cure fucked him right off.

'You heard about that queer march they're planning,' Balti asked. 'They should ban it. Who wants a bunch of poofs walking through the streets upsetting everyone? It's not like they even come from round here.'

'They're dirty bastards,' Carter agreed. 'Fuck anything that moves. They should line them up against the wall and shoot the lot of them. They're full of disease. Just the blokes though. I don't mind the lesbians, because you can see their point of view. There's nothing wrong with that and I like a good lesbian video like the next man. It's only natural. Queers, though. Fucking horrible.'

'I'll tell you who's full of disease,' Harry said, shifting the conversation, 'and that's Slaughter. I heard he did some bloke down the newsagent's yesterday because he leant across him to grab a paper. Went fucking mental right there in the shop, dragged the cunt outside, and gave him a right pasting. He's got a fractured skull. The old bill were down but they didn't get anywhere. I would never, ever want to get on the wrong side of that bloke. He's a fucking killer.'

Harry was looking at Carter as he said this, but the sex machine brushed the warning aside. What did he care, he was going on holiday and didn't give a toss. He watched the birds he'd been eyeing move across the pub. They weren't all that, now he thought about it, and they'd seen him and not shown any interest. The Hide would be better.

'Come on then, let's fuck off,' he said. 'It's all blokes in here tonight except for those birds over there, and just our luck they're probably lesbians. Lets go down The Hide.'

The Sex Division drank up and were soon following the familiar run from The Unity to The Hide, a golden path that led on to Blues. They were following Children's Ward painted footprints through sterile hospital corridors, straight past Pathology concentrating on those red and blue cartoon toes and heels. The only Sex Division member missing was Mango, the rest of the lads pounding the same pavements they'd been pushed through as babies and run along as kids. Balti saw them as family men treading the rutted path, grey hair sprouting and baldness spreading, finally pensioners hunched over standing on the corner watching a demolition crew rip down The Unity, a Space Age amusement arcade planned for the site. He looked at his mates and tried to picture them with kids, because it always happened that way. It was the fucking domino effect, and he wasn't talking about the spread of communism. Will was expecting and getting married. He was the first one to go. Planting a seed in Karen's belly and the rest of their heads. It only needed one person to break the pattern and those left would eventually follow. Bollocks. Now they were following the leader into The Hide.

'That's a bit better,' Carter shouted, once they'd settled in. 'I prefer drinking surrounded by beautiful women rather than a pub full of pissed-up geezers.'

Harry pointed out the birds they'd entertained earlier in the year with tales of stretched scrotums. Balti was up for another go, because after all they were the Bollock Brothers, or was it the Lager Twins, he couldn't remember because it had been a while back and they'd been well pissed. He bounced forward as someone bumped into him, turning to look the bloke in the eye. He could feel the violence rush up from nowhere and a split-second temptation to glass the cunt was cut short as a fist connected with the man's face. It was kicking off behind them between two headbangers and Balti could afford to smile and take a step sideways, watching the cabaret. It was only half-nine and already the muppets were performing as three bouncers steamed through from the door and separated the two men, kicking them back through the pub and bouncing their heads off the brickwork in the doorway, sending them on their way. Glass and lager covered the floor and there was a pool of blood that looked worse than it was because blood had mixed in with the drink, but the show went on and the jukebox kept playing as it moved through the tunes of the moment, the incident quickly forgotten, Balti laughing and turning his head to find that Carter had moved over to the women with pierced tits and lips. The flash cunt didn't waste any time, he'd give him that, and Harry was telling the boys old Carter's on the pull tonight, and Balti knew what he meant because he was back in the groove himself.

A bit of respect. He'd come through in one piece. And after all these months he knew what was going to make it a perfect night. He was going down Balti Heaven, because it was in the name and he'd been a regular there until the beginning of the year when he made a resolution to lose weight and that was followed by a lack of cash, so tonight he was going down there even if the rest of the lads fucked off down Blues. He wasn't bothered because there was that party round Julie Jones' later and she had some nice mates. It would be heaving. Funny what the drink and a bit of whizz could do for you because when he'd come out he wasn't thinking about getting his leg over after his night with Suzie in Archway, but now he was plugged in again. It was more about the Sex Division really, because Carter was such a cocky bastard thinking it was all over just because he was fifty-two points ahead. It was the arrogance that got him. You had to believe in miracles, even if the Virgin Birth was impossible. You had to think things like that could happen. The Sex Division was supposed to be a laugh, but Carter was taking it seriously like it mattered or something and Balti was moving up the social scale. He had self-respect. Julie Jones really did have some tasty mates, and Julie herself wasn't bad and had a bit of a reputation. It would be a rave up, Harry shouting in his ear that it was time for the Nutcracking Nephews to get into top gear because Carter was bringing those posers over, the ones in the trendy clobber, the fucking lesbians who'd blown them out last time.

'Alright girls?' Harry asked, back in the swing of things, forgetting all about dodgy dreams.

The girls smiled but didn't say much, and if they had it would've been hard to hear them because the music was thumping out, tapping eardrums. Harry had to hold back from giving it the old stretched bollocks routine, while Balti was thinking how it didn't matter that all those months had passed because here they were in The Hide again with the music drowning the conversation, with the same birds.

He fancied a curry. He couldn't be bothered shouting to make himself heard over the drums, though Will was leaning into one of them going on about something. Probably telling them he was going to be a dad, and though he wouldn't be thinking anything, birds liked that, because women were soft and sentimental and Balti loved them, and he'd like to fuck the arse off every female on the planet he was feeling so good. They all loved women. Certainly Harry did, and he was keeping away from the speed because otherwise he wouldn't be able to sleep and he had to pack tomorrow. More than his rest, he didn't want his dreams scrambled. He was beginning to feel better about last night and was ignoring the possible interpretation of the Turkish bath and all the rest of the gibberish. That's what happened when you got into all that psychic stuff. How could you know what was going on in your head? They could put men on the moon and genetically manipulate life, but the scientists never worked out what was going on inside the brain of your everyday herbert. Harry wouldn't have minded a bit of help now and then, some kind of explanation.

It was all shit really, and just because he'd had a few dreams that came true, maybe it didn't mean he had a special gift. It had to be down to chance. Maybe it was a bottle job, because if you took the glory then you had to take the stick as well, but there were no rules and without rules you drifted. One thing was certain, he was no queer, because he wouldn't have minded these birds and he was looking forward to going to Spain and getting stuck in. Women made the world go round and your head spin. So fucking what anyway. If he was a bum bandit, he'd come out and say so. He wouldn't hide away. No matter what the lads said, it wouldn't make any difference. Not really. He just wanted things straight in his head and put in their proper place. He was alright.

'I was talking to this bloke I do business with,' Will said, standing next to Harry now. 'He's had three kids and been there when each of them was born. Can you imagine that, seeing your child being born. He says there's nothing like it. Says it's a bit messy and the woman suffers, but it really is a miracle. I still can't get my head round it, that

I'm going to be a father. Can't believe me and Karen have created a life out of nothing. When you really think about it, it's unbelievable.'

Harry smiled and nodded. Something like that must take you back to the beginning. It was where they'd all come from. The lust of their mothers and fathers. None of them wanted to think of their parents doing the business. It was a disgusting thought and the old folk had to remain sexless, beyond frantic mating sessions. The mask had to stay in place because it gave you a foundation. Kids made you think. Took you back to the meaning behind the action. Men and women creating life. Something from the Bible or a mushy film. Sperm and eggs working to a hidden plan. Harry felt very unimportant. He dreamt all kinds of things and it was beyond his control. Every time one of them took a shine to a bird, there was another pattern working under the surface. It was one big mating ritual really, the use of language to show you didn't care, the pisstake and humour, the pubs and clubs and clothes and music, and the need for drink and drugs to loosen the restraints. Behind it all, the eggs and sperm were waging war, demanding action, eating into you the whole time, pushing you forward. A drunken shag and the glands were sober and efficient and working fast. You were nothing more than a messenger, a slave to the almighty DNA. But you had the last laugh because the birds were all on the pill, and it was that forward planning that kept you in charge.

'This bloke even videoed one of his kids being born,' Will said. 'When that kid grows up it'll be able to see its first second of life. Think of that.'

Harry thought about it, but wouldn't have fancied sitting down in front of the VCR watching his head emerge from between his old girl's legs. He didn't like the idea at all. He thought about Chelsea's first game in Europe after more than twenty years when they played Viktoria Zizkov in the Cup Winners Cup. It was a big match for the Blues and at half-time the announcements were made over the tannoy and three Chelsea boys were informed that their wives had given birth, while another was told his girlfriend was in labour. That showed dedication. Respect was definitely due, putting Chelsea first. Talking to Will, he wondered about the ways of the world.

'Karen's got a video of her mum,' Will said, going on a bit now, enjoying the drink and the course his life was taking. 'I watched it once. I saw the past frozen and when I think of it now I reckon I've seen the future as well. A bit like you and your dreams, though this was just a machine. It was towards the end of her life. Cradle to grave and you can catch it all on video.'

'What's the point though?' Harry asked. 'If you get a rerun when you snuff it then the video's in your head already so why waste money on VCRs? It's all a bit sad. There's no point thinking about the past too much.'

'If you don't think about the past, then you don't learn, do you? If that happens then you keep on making the same old mistakes.'

Harry wasn't bothered. The more he thought about things, the more it seemed his dreams were starting to bleed in with reality. Until recently he'd have insisted the two things were separate, but since his lucid dream, and the recent blurred lines, he saw the two worlds merging. He didn't know if this was a good or bad thing, though of course generally speaking he liked everything in its proper place. Without order you ended up in the nut house. That lucid dream had been a one-off. He'd like to dream like that again and take control. Before that dream he'd been at the mercy of the controller sitting deep in his skull directing operations. It was like a computer with one of those viruses loaded for fun, to cause disruption, fucking up the circuits. It was all this digital music that was making him think about machinery, because the nightmare was up in the air and he needed order. He also needed another pint. A couple more and he was going to fuck off home. No curry, no Blues, no pierced birds, no Julie Jones. He was going home to bed. Tomorrow he was off on holiday and starting fresh. Early swims and orange juice for breakfast. Civilised living asleep by the pool. Last time hadn't been all that civilised, but that was then. He'd get himself some nice slow sex with a half-decent bird. He wished Will would shut up for a while. He was doing his head in going on about placentas and afterbirth and umbilical cords. It was making him feel sick. Will said it was amazing, and he was right, but Harry still felt ill.

Standing outside The Hide at closing, Will said he was off and left Carter, Harry and Balti with the three posers. In the lit-up street and with a few lagers and a bit of whizz they were alright. They started walking towards Julie Jones' place, Balti forgetting about his curry with the three women showing a lot of interest, while Harry reckoned he'd go along and see what happened. It was a ten-minute walk and they were soon hammering on the door to make themselves heard, a three-bedroom house that Julie shared with a couple of other women. Slaughter opened the door, and going inside they found a lot of regulars from the pub, as well as Denise and Eileen. As promised the place was stacked out, and the three remaining Sex Division members rubbed their hands and found some cans. Carter and Balti were at the whizz again and Harry knew that some unfortunate was going to get their ear bent. He looked for the three birds who'd come with them, and for a moment reckoned they'd blown the Sex Division out, but there they were coming through from the kitchen, helping themselves when Carter offered the speed.

Harry soon found himself cornered by one of the girls. He was sipping from a can of supermarket lager. It tasted like shit. It wasn't cold enough, and it was going to be one of those nights because the woman chatting him up was racing to keep up with her thoughts and it was doing his head in, but then he felt her brushing against him and the whole thing was changing because he knew he was in. He adjusted his hearing and forgot about the music, because whoever had chosen the CDs had done a good job, and the bird was only going on about blokes stretching their bollocks, and did he remember that time when him and his mate had been going on about being the Bollock Brothers? Harry smiled and was trying to think of a smart one-liner not knowing whether to play the game or take the piss, part of him wanting to feed her another line, but the sensible voice inside telling him not to be a mug because she was dying for it, fucking gagging, couldn't he see that? So he kept quiet and the girl, whose name he found out was Jo, was saying that his mate Terry had told them it was just a wind up. She was laughing because it hadn't been much of a turn-on imagining a bloke with balls round his knees, and it was her mate who had the pierced lip, she couldn't do that to herself, what did Harry think about it all?

Harry didn't know really, and fuck it anyway, it didn't matter what he thought because he was drunk enough and before long he was going upstairs for a piss, standing in line with a couple of boneheads and several birds in white leather mini skirts, taking his time, finally giving up and going downstairs and outside, pissing round the back of the house. He was a cunt sometimes, because everyone was using the garden, and when he went inside Jo was sitting at the top of the stairs calling him back up. He worked his way through the people talking in an orange glow and he was sitting next to her, feeling her mouth against his, the taste of fags and drink, a fine mixture, the best kind of perfume, and then he was walking with her along the landing to one of the bedrooms.

Harry was back in the saddle. Jo was game and wasn't bothered by the couple in the next bed grunting and groaning in the blackness. They were soon stripped off and she was tugging his bollocks, laughing quietly, moving now to his cock. Harry brought her off and she was telling him to come inside her, which he was only too pleased to do. She was digging her fingernails into his hips spreading her legs as wide as they'd go, and before long he collapsed and pulled the sheets over them. He laid his head back against the pillow and the next bed was quiet and the music far off in the distance, a gentle thud through the bricks and plaster. There were no words now, just the soundtrack, and he felt himself drifting a bit because he was knackered, and the drink was wearing off leaving a dull ache between the eyes. He felt sad, post-sex reality coming through fast and chilling. He thought about the Sex Division and realised he'd picked up two valuable points in the relegation battle. If Balti missed out tonight then he was equal bottom. Harry was well pleased. No he wasn't, Balti had picked up three points in Archway. He looked at the body next to him and wondered if she was up for giving him a blow job? Probably not. He'd leave it a while. That was the difference between someone like him and Carter. He wasn't planning ahead. He hoped he hadn't missed out. If he was Carter he'd try and slip her one up the jacksie and send Balti down, but Harry was no bum bandit. Still, he'd made a last ditch effort, but the way Balti was getting on with her mate the fat cunt would be doing himself some good as well. Harry didn't care. He could hear Jo's breathing. He wondered what she was like sober. He started drifting.

Harry was walking across a moor following the sun. He saw a farmhouse in the distance. He was tired and the weather was turning. He saw smoke from the chimney of the house and knew somebody must be at home. The inhabitants could be friends or enemies, he had no way of really knowing. He hurried towards the house prepared to take a chance. It wasn't as far as he'd thought and when he knocked on the heavy oak door he was surprised to find it answered by Mango. They shook hands and Harry was invited inside. Pete sat in a big chair in front of a roaring fire. Mango told Harry to sit down. He'd bring some brandy to warm him up. Harry sat down and looked at Pete. The missing brother smiled. He said he'd heard the news about Will. Things were working out. Carter was top of the league, Balti was working and Harry was safe from the elements. Everyone was happy.

Harry jolted awake. He was on the floor and pulling himself upright. There was a sack on his back. He was covered in soot from head to toe, and there was a fire in the next bed. He could see charcoal figures in the flames. There was no sound. It was a terrible sight, but Harry was in charge. He was inside the dream. He was lucid. He knew it was only a dream.

Harry jolted awake. Jo had disappeared. The house was silent. He needed a piss. He fumbled around on the floor looking for his pants and jeans. Where had Jo gone? Obviously not impressed by his fine love-making skills. A shame really. He felt movement under the sheets. He'd missed her somehow. He pulled his pants on and stepped into his jeans, moving slowly through the room. The landing was lit by a street light. He went into the bathroom and stood over the bowl. The room stunk. Someone had thrown up in the sink. You expected that when you were a teenager. Some people never grew up. He flushed the toilet and headed back towards the bedroom. His throat was dry and he stopped. He went downstairs looking for a drink. There were sleeping bodies in the living room. He trod quietly. He didn't want to wake anyone. In the kitchen Harry went to the fridge and found some orange juice. He washed a glass and poured the juice. It tasted alright, a bit sharp.

The kitchen opened on to a small room, which in turn led to the garden. Harry could hear something or someone moving around. He went to look. Balti was hitching up his jeans. Six open handbags were lined up on the floor. It took Harry a moment to understand the deeper significance.

The dirty bastard. He couldn't believe what his old mate had done. Harry was filled with disgust. Shit splattered the handbags. Despite himself, Harry was totting up the points. Six times ten points. Fuck, that was an extra sixty points and with the five he already had Balti was on a grand total of sixty-five. He'd roared past Carter. The sick fucking cunt. Balti was put of order, and Harry was just about to give him a bit of stick when the reality kicked in. It was a result for Harry as well as for Balti. The old magic hadn't let him down. Harry was in the clear. The dream of last night fell into place. He was a one-hundred-per-cent Anglo-Saxon heterosexual. He was also a Protestant, but he wasn't bothered about that right now. He was holding his head up high, part of the majority. There would be no bushy tashes and greased fists, no amyl nitrate and Vaseline standing orders. He was saved. Tomorrow he'd be on his way.

Harry was happy. Everything was in its place. Everything was as it should be. There were no corners in need of lighting, no hidden secrets. There was logic and understanding. He was a simple man with simple needs. And Jo was still upstairs.

Balti turned and saw his best mate standing in the doorway. His thoughts were racing and he couldn't slow down. Carter had pissed off with one of the posers and he'd been blown out, the unstoppable shag machine giving it the big one as he hurried outside to a taxi. Balti wasn't taking it laying down, even though he'd found a place on the floor and a smelly old blanket. It was a laugh, collecting the handbags, lining them up, and letting nature take its course, coming from behind to clinch the championship. Now with Harry standing there like a plum Balti felt a twinge of embarrassment, even regret, but fuck all that.

Balti told Harry that he was the witness. The Sex Division champion was going home and he'd see him later, Harry nodding and going back upstairs. He stopped by the window at the end of the landing and saw Balti walking down the street. A chill passed through him. He thought he should call out, but didn't know why. Everything had been sorted out. There were no loose ends. The sun was coming up and a warm orange glow dusted the rooftops. Harry saw his best mate getting smaller, turning the corner, out of sight now as he walked through the empty streets, Balti's head racing knowing it was going to be hard sleeping once he was back at the flat. But bollocks, he'd put a video on or something, and he had a bit of blow left. Everything came rushing towards him in one big wave, all those days and weeks and months signing on, rotting away, getting older and heading for the grave, it was all there in your genes, everything you said and did was programmed from an early age, and if you had a helping hand maybe you'd go another way, but the thing was, the people supposed to give you a hand hadn't grown up themselves.

Balti wanted to go round and see Will and Karen and have a bit of a smoke, enjoy their company, but he was together enough to know they'd be asleep. He thought of his fortune and a four-poster bed packed with Lottery supermodels. He turned into his street and slowed down. He was almost home. Safe and sound. Maybe he shouldn't have done the handbags, but it was a laugh. It didn't matter. Not really. He hoped Denise's handbag hadn't been in there though. Slaughter wouldn't like that. No, he remembered them leaving. His legs were aching. Maybe he'd have a bath with some salts and wash it all away. Scrub away his sins and start all over again. It was a new beginning and everyone was happy. Balti was back. He'd learnt his lessons. You came out of the hard times stronger. Sex Division champion and a job painting houses with his best mate. Life was there to be lived and experienced. He was the happiest he'd been for years.

Balti heard the car door and turned his head. McDonald stood behind him with a shotgun wedged into his shoulder. Pulled the trigger.

ABOUT THE AUTHOR

John King is the author of eight novels to date. His first, *The Football Factory*, was an immediate word-of-mouth success and was subsequently turned into a high-profile film. *Headhunters, England Away, Human Punk, White Trash, Skinheads, The Prison House*, and *The Liberal Politics of Adolf Hitler* followed. His stories reflect his cultural interests—particularly music, pubs and youth cultures—while challenging a range of stereotypes that are often accepted by the established political factions. Common themes are powerlessness and enemy-creation, the contradictions found in every walk of life. Before becoming an author King worked at a variety of jobs and spent two years travelling around the world in the late 1980s. He has long been associated with fanzines, writing for various titles over the years and running *Two Sevens* in the early 1990s. He publishes and edits *Verbal*, a fiction-based publication. He is working on an animal-rights story, *Slaughterhouse Prayer*. He lives in London.

ABOUT PM PRESS

PM Press was founded at the end of 2007 by a small collection of folks with decades of publishing, media, and organizing experience. PM Press co-conspirators have published and distributed hundreds of books, pamphlets, CDs, and DVDs. Members of PM have founded enduring book fairs, spearheaded victorious tenant organizing campaigns, and worked closely with bookstores, academic conferences, and even rock bands to deliver political and challenging ideas to all walks of life. We're old enough to know what we're doing and young enough to know what's at stake.

We seek to create radical and stimulating fiction and non-fiction books, pamphlets, T-shirts, visual and audio materials to entertain, educate, and inspire you. We aim to distribute these through every available channel with every available technology—whether that means you are seeing anarchist classics at our bookfair stalls, reading our latest vegan cookbook at the café, downloading geeky fiction e-books, or digging new music and timely videos from our website.

PM Press is always on the lookout for talented and skilled volunteers, artists, activists, and writers to work with. If you have a great idea for a project or can contribute in some way, please get in touch.

PM Press
PO Box 23912
Oakland, CA 94623
www.pmpress.org

FRIENDS OF PM PRESS

These are indisputably momentous times—the financial system is melting down globally and the Empire is stumbling. Now more than ever there is a vital need for radical ideas.

In the years since its founding—and on a mere shoestring—PM Press has risen to the formidable challenge of publishing and distributing knowledge and entertainment for the struggles ahead. With over 300 releases to date, we have published an impressive and stimulating array of literature, art, music, politics, and culture. Using every available medium, we've succeeded in connecting those hungry for ideas and information to those putting them into practice.

Friends of PM allows you to directly help impact, amplify, and revitalize the discourse and actions of radical writers, filmmakers, and artists. It provides us with a stable foundation from which we can build upon our early successes and provides a much-needed subsidy for the materials that can't necessarily pay their own way. You can help make that happen—and receive every new title automatically delivered to your door once a month—by joining as a Friend of PM Press. And, we'll throw in a free T-shirt when you sign up.

Here are your options:

- **$30 a month** Get all books and pamphlets plus 50% discount on all webstore purchases

- **$40 a month** Get all PM Press releases (including CDs and DVDs) plus 50% discount on all webstore purchases

- **$100 a month** Superstar—Everything plus PM merchandise, free downloads, and 50% discount on all webstore purchases

For those who can't afford $30 or more a month, we have **Sustainer Rates** at $15, $10 and $5. Sustainers get a free PM Press T-shirt and a 50% discount on all purchases from our website.

Your Visa or Mastercard will be billed once a month, until you tell us to stop. Or until our efforts succeed in bringing the revolution around. Or the financial meltdown of Capital makes plastic redundant. Whichever comes first.

The Football Factory

John King

ISBN: 978-1-62963-116-5
$16.95   296 pages

The Football Factory is driven by its two main
characters—late-twenties warehouseman
Tommy Johnson and retired ex-soldier Bill
Farrell. Tommy is angry at his situation in life
and those running the country. Outside of
work, he is a lively, outspoken character, living
for his time with a gang of football hooligans,
the excitement of their fights and the comradeship he finds with his
friends. He is a violent man, at the same time moral and intelligent.

Bill, meanwhile, is a former Second World War hero who helped liberate
a concentration camp and married a survivor. He is a strong, principled
character who sees the self-serving political and media classes for what
they are. Tommy and Bill have shared feelings, but express their views in
different ways. Born at another time, they could have been the other. As
the book unfolds both come to their own crossroads and have important
decisions to make.

The Football Factory is a book about modern-day pariahs, people reduced
to the level of statistics by years of hypocritical, self-serving party politics.
It is about the insulted, marginalised, unseen. Graphic and disturbing, at
times very funny, *The Football Factory* is a rush of literary adrenalin.

*"Only a phenomenally talented and empathetic writer working from within
his own culture can achieve the power and authenticity this book pulses with.
Buy, steal or borrow a copy now, because in a short time anyone who hasn't
read it won't be worth talking to."*
—Irvine Welsh, author of *Trainspotting*

*"King's novel is not only an outstanding read, but also an important social
document.... This book should be compulsory reading for all those who
believe in the existence, or even the attainability, of a classless society."*
—Paul Howard, *Sunday Tribune*

"Bleak, thought-provoking and brutal, The Football Factory *has all the
hallmarks of a cult novel."*
—Dominic Bradbury, *The Literary Review*

Human Punk

John King

ISBN: 978-1-62963-115-8
$17.95   368 pages

For fifteen-year-old Joe Martin, growing up
on the outskirts of West London, the summer
of 1977 means punk rock, busy pubs, disco
girls, stolen cars, social-club lager, cutthroat
Teddy Boys and a job picking cherries with the
gypsies. Life is sweet—until he is attacked by
a gang of youths and thrown into the Grand
Union Canal with his best friend Smiles.

Fast forward to 1988, and Joe is travelling home on the Trans-Siberian
Express after three years away, remembering the highs and lows of the
intervening years as he comes to terms with tragedy. Fast forward to
2000, and life is sweet once more. Joe is earning a living selling records
and fight tickets, playing his favourite 45s as a punk DJ, but when a face
from the past steps out of the mist he is forced to relive that night in 1977
and deal with the fallout.

Human Punk is the story of punk, a story of friendship, a story of common
bonds and a shared cultured—sticking the boot in, sticking together.

"In its ambition and exuberance, Human Punk *is a league ahead of much
contemporary English fiction."*
—*New Statesman*

*"The long sentences and paragraphs build up cumulatively, with the
sequences describing an end-of-term punch-up and the final canal visit
just two virtuoso examples. These passages come close to matching the
coiled energy of Hubert Selby's prose, one of King's keynote influences .....
In the resolution of the novel's central, devastating act, there is an almost
Shakespearean sense of a brief restoration of balance after the necessary
bloodletting."*
—Gareth Evans, *The Independent*

*"King's eye for detail is as sharp as his characters' tongues, and his creations
are eminently three-dimensional: insightful and funny one minute, bigoted
and fucked up the next. Like real people, then."*
—*The Face*

White Trash

John King

ISBN: 978-1-62963-227-8
$17.95   304 pages

Ruby James lives life to the full, the state-run hospital where she works as a nurse a microcosm of the community in which she was born and bred. While some outsiders might label the people of this town "white trash," she knows different, reveling in a vibrant society that values people over money, actions above words.

For Ruby, every person is unique and has a story to tell, whether it is skinhead taxi driver Steve, retired teacher and rocker Pearl, magic-mushroom expert Danny Wax Cap, or former merchant seaman Ron Dawes. She encourages people to tell their tales, thrilled by the images created. Outside of work she drinks, dances, and has fun with her friends, at the same time dealing with her mother's Alzheimer's and a vision from the past, aware that physical and mental health are precious and easily lost. The epitome of positive thinking, Ruby sees the best in everyone—until the day true evil comes to call.

A mystery figure roams the corridors of Ruby's state-run hospital. He carries special medicine and a very different set of values. He tells himself that he wants to help, increase efficiency, but cost-cutting leads to social cleansing as humans are judged according to that white-trash agenda. Excuses and justifications flow as notions of heaven and hell are distorted. Set against a background of pirate radio stations, pink Cadillacs, and freeway dreams, *White Trash* insists there is no such thing as white trash.

"Complete and unique, all stitched up and marvellous, the two sides of the equation brought together, realistic yet philosophical."
—Alan Sillitoe, author of *Saturday Night and Sunday Morning*

"King is a writer who adeptly avoids cliche and caricature and is one of the most accomplished chroniclers of contemporary life. White Trash *is very much a state of the nation book."*
—*Big Issue North*

The Colonel Pyat Quartet

Michael Moorcock
with introductions by Alan Wall

Byzantium Endures
ISBN: 978-1-60486-491-5
$22.00   400 pages

The Laughter of Carthage
ISBN: 978-1-60486-492-2
$23.00   552 pages

Jerusalem Commands
ISBN: 978-1-60486-493-9
$23.00   496 pages

The Vengeance of Rome
ISBN: 978-1-60486-494-6
$24.00   608 pages

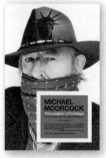

Moorcock's Pyat Quartet has been described as
an authentic masterpiece of the 20th and 21st
centuries. It's the story of Maxim Arturovitch
Pyatnitski, a cocaine addict, sexual adventurer, and
obsessive anti-Semite whose epic journey from
Leningrad to London connects him with scoundrels
and heroes from Trotsky to Makhno, and whose
career echoes that of the 20th century's descent
into Fascism and total war.

It is Michael Moorcock's extraordinary achievement
to convert the life of Maxim Pyatnitski into epic and
often hilariously comic adventure. Sustained by his
dreams and profligate inventions, his determination
to turn his back on the realities of his own origins,
Pyat runs from crisis to crisis, every ruse a
further link in a vast chain of deceit, suppression,
betrayal. Yet, in his deranged self-deception, his
monumentally distorted vision, this thoroughly
unreliable narrator becomes a lens for focusing,
through the dimensions of wild farce and chilling
terror, on an uneasy brand of truth.

Damnificados

JJ Amaworo Wilson

ISBN: 978-1-62963-117-2
$15.95   288 pages

Damnificados is loosely based on the real-life occupation of a half-completed skyscraper in Caracas, Venezuela, the Tower of David. In this fictional version, six hundred "damnificados"—vagabonds and misfits— take over an abandoned urban tower and set up a community complete with schools, stores, beauty salons, bakeries, and a rag-tag defensive militia. Their always heroic (and often hilarious) struggle for survival and dignity pits them against corrupt police, the brutal military, and the tyrannical "owners."

Taking place in an unnamed country at an unspecified time, the novel has elements of magical realism: avenging wolves, biblical floods, massacres involving multilingual ghosts, arrow showers falling to the tune of Beethoven's Ninth, and a trash truck acting as a Trojan horse. The ghosts and miracles woven into the narrative are part of a richly imagined world in which the laws of nature are constantly stretched and the past is always present.

"Should be read by every politician and rich bastard and then force-fed to them—literally, page by page."
—Jimmy Santiago Baca, author of *A Place to Stand*

"Two-headed beasts, biblical floods, dragonflies to the rescue—magical realism threads through this authentic and compelling struggle of men and women—the damnificados—to make a home for themselves against all odds. Into this modern, urban, politically familiar landscape of the 'have-nots' versus the 'haves,' Amaworo Wilson introduces archetypes of hope and redemption that are also deeply familiar—true love, vision quests, the hero's journey, even the remote possibility of a happy ending. These characters, this place, this dream will stay with you long after you've put this book down."
—Sharman Apt Russell, author of *Hunger*